Vanderheyden

The History of the Troy Orphan Asylum

1833-2018

Don Rittner
New Netherland Press

ISBN-13: 978-0-9624263-9-1

Book design by Don Rittner

New Netherland Press
Schenectady, New York

First Edition

Dedication

To all those at Vanderheyden past, present, and future who dedicate their lives to make those unfortunate in circumstances to have a brighter and more productive life.

The Troy Orphan Asylum Hymn

(Tune—"Juanita")

I.

Raise we our voices
In a song whose words shall tell
To thee, School Mother,
That we love thee well,
As thy care protects us
And thy love guards all our days
May our hearts' thanksgiving
Fill this song of praise.

CHORUS

This be our off'ring
Love and loyalty each day,
Striving to honor
Our own T. O. A.

II.

Into our child-life
Hast thou brought glad days of cheer,
Here too we cherish
Friends who love us dear.
For the lessons holy,
And the training thou hast given,
Gratitude and praises
Render we to heaven.

III.

May all our future
Be so ordered that thy name
By our dishonor
Ne'er be touched by shame.
Let us each, resolving
In our hearts to do our best,
Forward press, believing
God will do the rest.

—*Julia D. Nickerson*

Acknowledgements

Many people and institutions deserve credit for helping in a myriad of ways from providing material, photos, access to research materials and overall support.

Special thanks to Cathy Yudzevich, Director of Development & Marketing and Karen Carpenter Palumbo, President and CEO of Vanderheyden for seeing the value of documenting the history of Vanderheyden. Speical thanks to Mary Valek who's excellent research contributed to this book, especially her compilation of orphan deaths.

Special thanks to the many former residents of Vanderheyden who contributed their personal stories while at the orphanage: Pat Maloney, Nancy Davis, Marion Manchester, Steve Thomas, Marijayne Van Vost, Charles Van Vost, Barbara J. Cottrell, Marjorie (Marge) Brown (Cottrell), Don Cottrell, Elizabeth "Betty" (Sedgewick) Long and Lisa and David Villeneuve.

Gratitude is expressed to Kathy Knothe Sheehan/ Rensselaer County Historical Society, Douglas Flint, Darrell Landrum, NYS Archives, Carol Favreau and Pamela Welch from Samaritan Hospital, Lola Lodie Denise Brown for her material on Barbara Brown, and Charlene Robinson.

Photos were supplied by Vanderheyden's archives or are acknowledged in the book, as well as those in the public domain.

Don Rittner
December, 2019

From the CEO of Vanderheyden

In commemoration of the 185th anniversary of the formation of the Troy Orphan Asylum, which is now Vanderheyden, I am honored to be the President and CEO and to have had the opportunity to bring this legacy book to completion. I want to thank everyone who shared their photos and their stories for this book. There are no words to describe the gratitude we have today for the fifty-two women in the early 1800s that had a high purpose to make a difference for the unfortunate children called orphans. They led us to where we are today in the 3rd Century of providing services to change lives to save lives in the capital region through family focused, trauma informed and community based care.

Karen Carpenter Palumbo, CEO

Table of Contents

Chapters

Memories

Appendix

Special Supplement

Front and back of Troy Orphan Asylum on Spring Avenue, early 20th Century. Source: Harvard Art Libraries.

Introduction

There are few institutions in America that can claim that they have been servicing the needs of indigent children for over 185 years. Yet, *Vanderheyden*, formerly known as *Vanderheyden Hall* and before that the *Troy Orphan Asylum*, has been doing just that. *Vanderheyden's* rich history of serving the needs of young children goes unmatched in the Capital District of New York.

The United States was only twenty-four years old when several leading members from the Ladies Society of Troy banded together in 1800 to form *The Benevolent Society of Troy*. It was only two years after Troy became incorporated as a village in 1798 and it was felt an organization was needed to alleviate the hardships of indigent women and children in this new rapidly growing village. Incorporating as the Troy Orphan Asylum in 1833, it grew over the years into one of the most important institutions in Troy and has served as a home for thousands of young people and adults around the Capital District, not just Troy.

To celebrate the many years of service as an incorporated institution this book gives a history and overview on the history of orphans in New York, and in particular, the origins and growth of *Vanderheyden* and its many services it provides even to this day.

This book is divided into six chapters that explore the early Dutch and colonial history of orphanages in New York, the origins and history of Vanderheyden and its various locations within the city, and finally its move to Wynantskill and current mission. There are many photographs throughout the book that illustrate this history.

Included in the book is several testimonials from former residents of *Vanderheyden* telling their first hand experiences while living there.

In the appendix you will find the early documents that formed this long serving institution.

Don Rittner
2019

Chapter 1

Taking Care of Orphans in New York State during the Colonial Period

Seeing to the needs of orphans began in New York from the earliest Dutch period in the early seventeenth century and continues today. This chapter will review what steps were used to take care of New York's orphans until the founding of *Troy Orphan Asylum*, now known as *Vanderheyden Hall*, or simply *Vanderheyden*, in the early nineteenth century.

The Capital District region of New York State is one of the oldest continually settled regions in the United States. The first European structure built in America was Fort Nassau, a small Dutch trading fort constructed on Castle Island in 1614, now the Port of Albany. Upon moving over to the mainland in 1624 as Fort Orange, the Dutch were

Illustration of a Dutch orphan in 1598. Weesmeisje uit Venetië, Christoph Krieger, after Cesare Vecellio, 1598

here to stay and eventually formed New Netherland, the first Dutch colony in North America.

New Netherland extended from Albany, New York, in the North to Delaware in the South and encompassed parts of what are now the states of New York, New Jersey, Pennsylvania, Maryland, Connecticut, and Delaware.

New Netherland was sandwiched between the two English colonies of New England to the north and the Virginia Colonies to the South. Populating the region was slow and a series of land grants called patroonships were allowed by the Dutch government in order to beef up the population. It is estimated that by 1655, thirty-one years after the founding of Fort Orange (present Albany), the population of New Netherland was only between 2000-3500. Even by the time the English took over the region in 1664 it was estimated to be only around 9,000 people.

Kiliaen Van Rensselaer, the patron of Rensselaerswijck (all of present Rensselaer County) hoped that his colony would be an ideal place to send poor people to work his land.

Along with patroonships, the Dutch government felt that it could help the new colony by importing orphans from the Netherlands for indentured work and would also help increase the population (the same was felt for slaves).

Het Burgerweeshuis te Amsterdam, anonymous, 1843 - 1887 (The Civil Orphanage in Amsterdam).

In the 1640s the Dutch West India Company presented a plan *"to take from the alms-houses or orphan asylums 300 to 400 boys and girls of 10,12 to 15 years of age, with their consent"*[1] and to send them to New Netherland as bound servants with terms of six or seven years. Girls were to be given special incentives to marry.[2]

The Dutch West India Company at Amsterdam announced in April 1652 that orphans were to be sent to New Netherland.[3]

---

1 Neill, Chas P. 1910. Report on condition of Woman and Child Wage-Earners in the United States. Vol. V. Wage Earning women in stores in factories. Washington Government Printing Office; Page 13. Doc. No. 645.

2 O'Callaghan, 1856, p. 364

3 ibid 1865, p. 275

A ship with orphans arrived at New Amsterdam in 1654, and Governor Peter Stuyvesant accordingly rented a house *"in order to lodge therein the children sent over by the poormasters."*[4]

At the same time, Governor Stuyvesant established a new village to be laid out a short distance north of Fort Orange, to be called Beverwijck (later Albany). One of the lots in the new town was assigned to the deacons of the Reformed Church *"for the needs of the poor."* An almshouse was constructed on the Albany lot between 1652 and 1655.[5] A "poor farm" was added in 1657. A bleach field was laid out for bleaching cloth in 1658, and in 1660 there was a new addition to the almshouse.

The Dutch were already well familiar with dealing and taking care of orphans. In seventeenth century Amsterdam, the city founded the "Burgerweeshuis" or Citizen Orphanage and the "Aalmoezeniersweeshuis," (Aalmoes means alms) where the needs of children of the non-citizens and the abandoned children were addressed. The food was very simple since meat was too expensive. The daily meal was bread with butter or cheese and dried peas and beans. Hygiene was very poor. Five children had to sleep in one small bed. Boys and girls were strictly separated and both were educated in the orphanage school. The boys had to learn a trade at

---

[4] Gehring, 1983, p. 202; O'Callaghan, 1856, p. 556; Scott, 1974, p. 5).

[5] Venema, 1991, p. 1; 1993, pp. 28-29)

1641

Bond of Isaac Allerton and… [unknown] as guardians of Eva, the minor

daughter of Nanna Beets (Beeche)

This day, date underwritten, before me, Cornells van Tlenhoven, secretary in New Netherland for the General Chartered West India Company, appeared Isaac Allerton [and .], who being requested by Nanne Beets, mother of Eva Beets, that he, Isaac Allerton, and [] would act as guardians of said Eva Beets, both consented and promised to act towards Eva Beets, the aforesaid child, as upright, faithful and honest guardians of orphans ought to act. Having this day received one cow and one bull calf, which constitute her portion of the paternal estate, we shall take care of said cattle and have them kept to the best advantage of said minor little girl Eva Beets, for which we bind our persons and property, movable and immovable, present and future, without any exception, subject to the Jurisdiction of the Provincial Court of Holland and all other courts and Judges. Done this 29th of May A° 1641, in Fort Amsterdam in New Netherland.

Isaac Allerton

1643

On Thursday, the 9th of July 1643 Abraham Jaoobsz from Steenwyck, plaintiff, vs. Anna Gerrits, defendant. Demands payment of what remains due to his wife from her father's estate, as entered on the books of the orphan chamber.

Vol IV council minute 1638-49

age fifteen from a craftsman in town and the girls had to work within the orphanage in the knitting- and spinning factory. When they were nineteen years old, they were forced to leave the orphanage. On

1648

Power of attorney from Paulus Leendersen van der Grift to Hans Bartelsen and Simon Evertsen van der Grift to receive a legacy left in Holland to Gysbert Gerritsen

Eefore me, Cornells van Tienhoven, secretary of New Netherland, residing in Port Amsterdam, appeared Paulus Leendersen vender Grift, naval storekeeper here, chosen guardian, with Hans Bartelsz, of Gysbert Gerritsz, minor son of Gerrlt Gysbertsz, in his lifetime residing at Amsterdam, who before and in the presence of the undersigned witnesses appoints and empowers, as he does hereby, the above named Hans Bartelsz, residing at Naerden, his co-guardian, and Symon Eversz van [der] Grift, in the place of the principal, to demand, collect and receive in the principal's name, in their capacities aforesaid, from Willem Martensz Vlym the sum of twelve hundred Carolus guilders, willed and bequeathed to the said Gysbert Gerritsz by his aunt, Tryn Gerrits, in her lifetime wife of the aforesaid Willem Martensz Vlym, in order to place the said money, consisting of two bonds issued by the general government, for greater security in a safer and more secure place than they now are, for the greater benefit and profit of the said minor Gysbert Gerritsz. And in case the above named Willem Martensz be unwilling or refuse to deliver the said sum of twelve hundred guilders or the bonds to the attorneys, the same shall by virtue of this power of attorney and as co-guardians of the aforesaid orphan have authority to sue the above mentioned Willem Martensz at law and to prosecute the case to final determination; to observe all terms of court, whether as plaintiff or defendant, to hear Judgment pronounced and to appeal therefrom; also to substitute one or more persons and doing furthermore whatever the case may require, even though fuller and more specific authority were necessary, with power, moreover, to do whatever the principal, were he present, might or could do; he, the principal, promising to hold and to cause to be held valid all that the aforesaid attorneys or their substitutes shall do and transact in the matter above mentioned, of all of which he requests an authentic Instrument.

Thus done and the original hereof In the record signed by Paulus Leendersz and by Jacob Kip and Johannes Boodenborch, the first of September A. 1648, In Port Amsterdam, New Netherland.

Pouwells Lendersz van die Grift

Johannes Bodenborch, witness Jacob Kip, witness

Vol 3 Registers of the Provincial Secretary 1648-1660

May 1, they received a necessary outfit and some money.

In Amsterdam, much of orphan administration was done by a *weeskamer*, the orphan chamber, a government body responsible for overseeing the administration of the estates of (half) orphans. A half-orphan is a person, usually a child, with only one living parent.

Weeskamers were not orphanages and developed in the fifteenth century in numerous Dutch towns. They did not take care of the orphans, only the administration of the estates and they existed in most parts of the Netherlands until 1810. After 1810, their tasks were taken over by the court. They also existed in Dutch colonies, like New Amsterdam (present-day New York).

Tasks of the Orphan Chamber

After a parent died, the Weeskamer oversaw that a guardian was appointed for the orphan(s). The first duty of the guardian was to create an inventory of the estate that was left behind to determine the inheritance that the orphan was entitled to. The surviving spouse could pay the orphans their share and settle the inheritance, or could administer the estate until the children became of age (usually at age 25 for boys and 20 for girls). Concurrently, the guardian would submit a final settlement that showed how the estate had been divided.

When a widow or widower remarried he or she needed to submit a statement from the Weeskamer that the children of the previous marriage had received their share, or arrangements had been made to safeguard their inheritance. Occasionally, one could see a statement that they were so poor that the children did not receive an inheritance. There is an abundance of documents that show these situations between the orphan master in Amsterdam and inhabitants in New Netherland.

Since many of the Netherland orphanages were crowded and taking care of the orphans was costly, orphans were also seen as good work sources and were used not only in New Netherland by the Dutch West India Company but the Dutch East India Company used them on ships as laborers. Since life was harsh, a good majority of them died or disappeared. It appears they were expendable.

Here is a list of four children listed in the book of orphans in Amsterdam that were indentured to the Dutch East India Company[6]:

- Pieter Claasz Boter from Amsterdam, to the East Indies on the ship *de Ridderschap* in 1686 as cooper. Died on 29 August 1689 at Zouraubaija [now Surabaya, Indonesia], being owed 144 guilders, 4 "stuivers" [5 cent

[6] https://www.dutchgenealogy.nl/the-sinister-amsterdam-orphan-trade/

pieces], 5 pennies, brought into the orphanage's account on 23 July 1692.

- Pieter Mathijsz Sparmont from Amsterdam went to the East Indies on *de Ridderschap* in 1686 as a ship's boy. Missing since the end of August 1692 in Batavia [now Jakarta, Indonesia]. 1701 still missing. In January 1705 still missing, but his estate worth 131 guilders 4 stuiver and 15 pennies brought into the orphanage's account.
- Willem Pieterz from Amsterdam as young carpenter to East Indies on the *Waterlant* in 1687. Extended his employment at Onrust

1648

Indenture of apprenticeship of Jan Jansen from Rotterdam to Albert **Cornellssen**

Albert Cornellsz engages Jan Jansz from Rotterdam, a boy about ten years of age, as an apprentice for the term of six consecutive yeers, commencing the first of May A°. 164-9 and ending the first of May 1655 during which years the above mentioned Albert Cornellsz shall be obliged to bring up the said Jan Jansz and provide him with food and drink, the necessary clothing, lodging, washing, etc.; also, to teach him such trade or work as he, A. Cornellsz, himself knows and can do, and to have paternal supervision over him and to do as one ought to do and it Is proper that one should do toward orphans. During the aforesaid time the boy above mentioned shall be at the service of Albert Cornelisz and show him proper respect, as an apprentice is bound to exhibit toward his master. Thus done and signed the 6th of October 1648, in New Amsterdam.*

Vol 3 Registers of the Provincial Secretary 1648-'660 pg. 65-66.

1648

The nineteenth of October anno 1648 The guardians of the surviving orphan children of Claes Jansen from Emden, baker, are authorized and ordered by the honorable director general to sell to the highest bidder for the best advantage and profit of the minor children the goods left by their aforesaid father, deceased.

1651

Andries de Vos, having been requested to act as assistant to the guardians of the orphans of the late Cornelis Maessen, accepts the appointment before the court.

Court proceedings, February 16 Anno 1651. Page 154.

[island near Batavia and name of the first Dutch ship built in what was to become New York State in 1614] in August 1692. Is dead and done with 1695 16 August.

- Christiaen Lievenzfrom Amsterdam as young carpenter to the East Indies on the *Waterlant* in 1687. Died 28 March 1692 at Onrust. 21 July 1694: Brought into the orphanage's account 185 guilders, 7 stuivers and 10 pennies.

Three of the four children who went to the East Indies died while in the employ of the Dutch East India Company, and one turned up missing.

The Dutch founding of New Netherland (which includes all of present New York State) dealt with the issue or orphans in several ways. On March 21, 1651, the Directors at Amsterdam wrote to Director General Petrus Stuyvesant dealing with complaints and other issues Stuyvesant wrote earlier. It appears the year before there was a plan to import 300 to 400 boys and girls from several orphanages to New Netherland but it was ruled out due to too many inconveniences and they stated *"No more correspondence is therefore required on this subject."* Page 112.

"We should above, all things consider it necessary to provide ways and means; we are of opinion that permission should be obtained from the magistrates of some provinces and cities, to take from the alms houses or orphan asylums 300 to 400 boys and girls of 10,12 to 15 years of age, with their consent, however, and that their passage and board could be procured for /50 or /60 per head. With that recognition a large ship might be chartered, suitable for the conveyance of horses and salt from Curacao and afterwards return hither with a cargo of logwood. It must be, further, declared that said children shall not remain bound to their masters for alonger term than 6 or 7 years, unless being girls, they come, meanwhile to marry, in which event they should have the option of hiring again with their masters or mistresses, or of remaining wholly at liberty and of settling there, on condition that they be allowed so much land as the director shall consider it proper each should have for the support of her family, free from all rents and exemptions for the term of 10 years after entering on such land; but the inhabitants shall have, after the lapse of the aforesaid term of years, the tenth of their incomes." Page 172-73

"First, we were summoned by the burgomasters, who offered us 150 boys and girls from the asylums, w h o were willing to be brought to this place for passage money amounting to 30 per head or to pay the board at 8 stivers per day; the aforesaid lords had already made a provisional order that aU private freighters should transport all needy persons at this rate, which is a reason so many people are coming over in these ships. We had made provisional arrangements with some skippers for the passage of the aforesaid youngsters; also at the same time worked out with the burgomasters under what conditions these children were to be placed with good masters. Namely, they were to be obligated for a period of 4 years, and would receive, besides the proper subsistence of food and drink, 50 to 60 annually for clothing or as much more as your honor would be able to arrange, of which those girls wh o were to marry, with your honor's consent, within the aforesaid term would be relieved, and when the obligated term, as prescribed, would be expired, they m ay accept further service with their masters,

on such conditions to which they might agree with one another; and to those who would remain free, 25 morgens of land each were to be allotted, or as much as they were willing to cultivate. These conditions were approved by the burgomasters and pleased many of the young people and we believed that the community there would have gained their point by these means, but when we thought we were quite sure of it, it happened that the ships of the English parliament, commissioned with letters of reprisal against the inhabitants of this country, captured about 60 of our merchant ships, among others, also the small ship named Keyser Carel, coming from your place, then subsequently plundered to an extent and released."

FROM THE DIRECTORS IN AMSTERDAM

TO PETRUS STUYVESANT Page 144-45
4th of April 1652
David van Baerle and Jacob Pergens

The orphanage in which the orphans stayed received the back wages of the dead or missing orphans, which ran in the hundreds of guilders.

At least one in three, possibly as many as half the orphans who went to work for the Dutch East India Company died within a few years, often resulting in hundreds of guilders ending up in the coffers of the orphanage making the arrangement profitable for the company and the orphanage. It was a profitable arrangement for all considering that the orphanage had more children than they could care for.

Amsterdam attracted many seeking their fortune, many of whom were poor. Housing conditions were deplorable and death rates were high, so orphans and abandoned children far exceeded the orphanages capacities.

The Dutch East India Company had a big demand for labor, however the bad conditions on board and tropical conditions at the trade posts certainly insured that most employees did not last long.

The orphanage needed money to take care of all the children. If the orphan died, the Dutch East India Company would pay the orphanage the wages that these children earned. Ledgers demonstrated a sophisticated administration and effective process,

1653

"Upon the written request of the mayors and schepens of the city of New Amsterdam; provident care of the mayors and schepens is praiseworthy and the director-general and council highly approve of it, it is to be considered that there is more required to place the orphan asylum upon the same footing as that of Amsterdam than the weakness and youth of this only budding city can at present afford.

In the meantime it is necessary to take care, according to God's words, of the widows and orphans; and therefore, the director-general and council resolve that the deacons, as orphanmasters, shall keep an eye on the widows and orphans in order to report to the mayors and schepens, and through them, if necessary, to the director general and council when special curators should be appointed for widows and orphans or their property. Then the mayors and schepens, or if necessary the director-general and council, shall give such orders and appoint such curators, as the case may require; the curators are to be responsible to the mayors and schepens, and when they learn that good care is not being taken of the widows, orphans or their property, they shall summon the curators and call them to account for their negligence"

Vol V. Council Minutes 1652-54, page 63.

where even the back pay of orphans who died at the other end of the world would find its way back to the Amsterdam orphanage. It didn't end there. There

On May 18th, 1654 a letter
To the Director General and Council in N. N. stated:

As the growth and prosperity of yonder state depends principally upon the population and the cultivation of the soil, w e are constantly busy to invent measures, which might serve for their promotion. We intend for this purpose, (which has also the favorable endorsement of the Burgomasters of this city), to send you in the aforesaid two ships now ready for sea a party of boys and girls from the orphan asylum here, making first a trial with 50 persons. You may expect with them also a quantity of provisions that they shall not immediately burden the storehouse.

While you see our zeal in increasing the population, you must constantly think of promoting the cultivation of the soil that on all occasions you need not rely on others, but may have recourse to your own resources.

How much depends on this and how much you can rely in such cases on your English neighbors, you have sufficiently learned this last time. As we further understand that our inhabitants, engaged there in farming, apply themselves mostly to the planting of tobacco, thereby neglecting the cultivation of grain, we have considered it highly necessary, not only to remind you, but also to recommend to you to keep such farmers to their duty and obligations and make arrangements with them that a certain part of their land, either already under cultivation or to be cultivated hereafter, is sown in grain. When this is done, our province there will by and by become stronger and its population will increase.

Herewith go for the present five casks of meat for the soldiers now coming, also some clothing for them according to invoice, which you will distribute with such advance on their pay as has been heretofore given them. Dated as above.

By order of the directors,

Ab. de Decker de Jonge.

Vol V council minutes 1652-54 Page 15-16

are also records that orphans were used for military and war from 1784-85.

"Comforters of the sick" were some of the earliest arrivals at Fort Orange (Albany) and New Amsterdam (New York City).

The 1640 Dutch Reformed Church charter in New Amsterdam recognized the obligation to assist *"minor children, widows, orphans, and other unfortunate persons."* [7]

There was some conflict between the church and the Dutch West India Company that controlled New Netherland. A factor contributing to the need for poor relief was the colony's exposed frontiers. The Indian war created by Governor Willem Kieft from 1640 to 1645 was a disaster for the Dutch, leaving

[APPOINTMENT OF ORPHANMASTERS FOR NEW AMSTERDAM]

[Response] Request granted.

The director general and councilors have appointed and confirmed from the above [list] as supervisors of the orphans: Pieter Wolphertsen van Couwenhoven and Pieter Comelisse van der Veen to fill the same office for the benefit of the widows and orphans, in association with and on the instructions of the burgomasters. Done at the session of the director general and councilors of New Netherland, ady ut supra.

[7] O'Callaghan, E. B. (ed.). (1856). Documents Relative to the Colonial History of the State of New-York,Vol. 1, Weed, Parsons & Co., Albany.. Page 405.

houses and land charred and crops rotting in the fields.[8] A memorial listing popular grievances in 1649 claimed that the West India Company had taken and kept money collected for the poor. Furthermore it claimed, *"there is, occasionally, a flying report of an hospital and of asylums for orphans and for old men, &c, but as yet no sign of an attempt, order or regulation has been made about them" (O'Callaghan, 1856, p. 300). The Company in response said that the deacons of the church bore all responsibility for the poor fund and for how it was invested, that if the people of New Netherland needed asylums or almshouses, "they must contribute towards them as is the custom in this country." Furthermore, "if they are such patriots as they appear to be, let them be leaders in generous*

Ordinary Session Held in Fort Orange
January 9, 1657

Rutger Jacobsen, plaintiff, against Claes Teunissen, defendant.

*The plaintiff demands delivery of the defendant's house, sold to him by the defendant, in payment of a certain sum due to him by Jacob Luyersen, deceased.**

The defendant acknowledges that he is ready to do so.

The officer of the court, as protector of the rights of orphans, objects to the delivery and requests that curators be appointed to preserve the rights of the surviving children of Jacob Luyersen, deceased.

The court appoints Jan Verbeeck and Evert Wendel curators to the aforesaid children.

[8] McEntegart, 1927, p. 593; O'Callaghan, 1856, pp. 210, 213.

Fort Orange Court Minutes

Appeared before the court Jan Verbeeck and Evert Wendel, orphan masters of the court, who declared that seeing the bad management of Christoffel Davids in administering the estate left undivided between himself and his children, the heirs of Cornelia de Vos, his deceased wife, they had thought fit for the preservation of the said property and the protection of the children to nominate and propose [47] the persons of

Andries de Vos, the father of the said Cornelia de Vos, and Arent Anderiessen, uncle on his wife's part of the said children, (Arent Andriessen's wife, Catalijntje de Vos, was a sister of Cornelia de Vos.) as curators thereof, as far as the rights of the minor children are concerned; who, appearing before the court, have voluntarily agreed and promised upon oath to acquit themselves therein to the best of their knowledge and to the best advantage of the estate and the children. Wherefore the court has granted them authority as lawful curators of the said estate and guardians of the aforesaid children, with power to do therein and in all hat is connected therewith as they jointly shall see fit for the benefit of the aforesaid estate and children, binding themselves to render an accounting whenever time or necessity shall demand it. Done in court at Fort Orange, the 27th of February Anno 1657.*

The 7th of February there appeared by order of the court Jan Verbeecke and Evert Wendels, chosen curators of the estate of the surviving children of Jacob Luyersen, deceased, who accepted the said office and promised to acquit themselves of their duties to the best of their knowledge and ability.

The court, having considered the need of orphan masters in this place and experienced the faithfulness of Jan Verbeecke and Evert Wendels, have for the service and best interest of the country appointed them orphan masters, to take charge of all estates which [otherwise] would remain uncared for through the death of the husband or wife. Actum in Fort Orange, the 7th of February 1657.

Was signed: La Montagne,
vice director and commissary of Fort Orange,
Rutger Jacobsen
Anderies Herbertsen
Jacob Schermerhom
Philip Pietersen
Page 273

contributions for such laudable objects."[9]

The Orphan Chamber of New Amsterdam (New York City) was established in 1656 to guard the welfare and estates of children who lost their parents. While New Netherland was multinational

and Orphan Master (Weesmeester) was distinctly Dutch and made the colony's residents here have the connection to the mother country. Care of orphans was not only a concern to the Dutch but in English Maryland the development of the Orphan's Court in 1654 also dealt with the issue.

The Dutch Orphan Chamber dealt with more than just economic care of orphans. It was involved in familial and philanthropic concerns, played a role in politics and commerce and in a region that had no banks or stock exchange it provided money to the city government, the Reformed Church, and individuals who asked for it. This gave the chamber much influence over civic and personal affairs. Orphan Masters had judicial, administrative and financial control over minors and orphans. The office, the Weeskamer, was a chamber in city hall. The earliest orphan register in the Municipal Archive of Amsterdam dates to 1468, and the oldest orphan law was recorded in 1466.

The West India Company, while headquartered in Amsterdam, made it clear in 1626 that in New

[9] O'Callaghan, 1856, pp. 423,424,431.

Netherland *"in matters concerning marriage, the settlement of estates, and contracts, the ordinances and customs of Holland and Zeeland and the common written law"*[10] were to be followed. This included interstate estates and *"take cognizance…of the cases of minor children, widows, orphans and other unfortunate persons"* and to bring any complaints to the attention of the council which held jurisdiction. In essence, what happened in the old world happened in the new one.

Since the population was small in the early days of New Netherland the care of orphans usually fell to the surviving parent or relative. If both died or there were no relatives the deacons of the Reformed Church took over. As New Netherland increased in size a formal system of new municipal government was created by the West India Company on February 2, 1653, creating a court system according to the customs of the old country. It was composed of two burgomasters (mayors), five schepens (= aldermen or magistrates), and a schout (Sheriff, public prosecutor like a DA). The burgomasters could appoint orphan masters. Eight days after the new government was formed, two orphan masters were requested but were not filled and on February 24 Director General Petrus Stuyvesant found it premature.

---

10 Catterall, D nd Campbell, J. 2012. Woman in Port. Gendering Communities, Economies, and Social Networks in Atlantic Port Cities, 1500-1800. Brill. Pg. 184.

By September 1655 the population was large enough, partly because of the Peach War with the native population in which forty colonists died with one hundred taken captive. There now were orphans and widows. Stuyvesant appointed two oversees of orphans, Pieter Wolfertsen van Couwenhoven and Pieter Cornelissen van der Veen, to take charge. It was the only one of its kind in the North American colonies, in effect, a smaller version of the Amsterdam Orphan Chamber. In Beverwijck (Albany) two orphan masters were appointed in 1657 but they reported directly to the Court of Fort Orange and Beverwjick.

In defining their office and conducting their business, the orphan masters used the model of the Amsterdam Orphan Chamber. There, under the ordinance of 1563, orphan masters had *"general power and authority over orphans and minor children"* who resided in the city and its liberties and were charged, *"to the best advantage [to] administer, or cause to be administered, look after and supervise their property."*[11]

Orphans were defined as children under age twenty-five (age of majority) or older than twenty-five with mental or physical disabilities, and were considered incompetent to manage their own affairs and therefore in need of a guardian upon the death of either parent or both parents.

---

[11] van Zwieten, Adriana E. The Orphan Chamber of New Amsterdam. The William and Mary Quarterly, Vol. 53, No. 2 s(Apr., 1996), pp. 319-340.

By Dutch custom, all marital property was held in common, unless otherwise stipulated by a prenuptial contract. Children therefore inherited from either parent, and, upon the death of either, the estate was usually divided in half: one half for the surviving spouse and the other half split equally among all the children. As senior guardians, orphan masters administered the estates of the city's orphans or appointed and supervised guardians and administrators in their place.

When orphan masters heard of intended deaths and new marriages they directed widows and widowers among the prospective partners to appear before them, for *"by order of the Orphans Chamber nobody is allowed to marry, before having agreed with the guardians about the settlement on the children of their inheritance."*[12] By law, an estate had to be settled and divided before the remarriage of a surviving spouse. Orphan masters therefore intervened to ensure that an orphan's estate and welfare would not be jeopardized with the formation of the new household. However Dutch parents could put in their will that the orphan masters stay out of matter, but this exclusionary clause did not always prevent the chamber from taking action on behalf of the children. The absence of a will or an exclusionary clause gave orphan masters a unlimited authority to appoint guardians.

[12] Fernow, Berthold, 1902. The Minutes of the Orphanmasters of New Amsterdam, 1655-1663. New York Francis P. Harper. pg. 245.

Through their businesses in the city and extensive networks of friends and family, the masters of New Amsterdam were closely bound to the trading centers of the United Provinces. These connections and their authority as orphan masters helped them to clear estates on both sides of the ocean. The ability to resolve transatlantic matters of inheritance demonstrates their far-reaching influence and authority. Correspondence showed that they identified closely with their counterparts in Amsterdam, ensuring that the policies of the two institutions would bring similar results. The orphan masters used all the means in their power to secure the hereditary rights of New Amsterdam's orphans.

The procedures of the chambers of the homeland and the colony were so similar that inhabitants of the homeland could readily secure inheritances from the colonial chamber, and New Netherlanders as easily called for their portions from the chambers of Amsterdam and other cities in the United Provinces. Powers of attorney preserved in the colonial records reveal that it was not out of the ordinary to appoint someone who was traveling across the ocean a specific amount due from a deceased relative.

Chapter 2

The Capital District in the 17th Century

A clearer picture of how orphans were cared for in the Capital District can be seen in nearby Beverwijck (Albany). Troy was not established until after the Revolutionary War, although there were Dutch settlers in what is now Troy as early as 1646 when Thomas Chambers signed a five year contract with the officers of Rensselaerwyck. He left in 1654 and moved south, founding Kingston.

Charitable activities in this New World village of Beverwijck were a positive feature. The deacons of the Dutch Reformed Church, as caretaker of the poor, contributed, directly or indirectly, to the well being of everyone in Beverwijck. The inhabitants of this small village reflected much of the old world society: poor at the bottom with a small well to do aristocracy at the top. In between consisted of a middle class of tradesmen. It was part of the Dutch religion to give alms to the poor and the fact that large amounts of voluntary donations for charity here showed that tradition continued in the new world.

Trying to make a living in Beverwijck was expensive as many documents show. Even the commissary of the fort complained he didn't make enough for

[PRENUPTIAL AGREEMENT BETWEEN JACOB GEVICK AND GEERTRUIJ BARENTS]

[359] In the name of the Lord Amen. Be it known by the contents of this present instrument, that in the year of our Lord Jesu Christy 1662, on the 23rd day of September, there appeared before me Johannes La Montagne, in the service of the general chartered West India Company, admitted by the lord director general and councilors of New Netherland vice director and commissary at Fort Orange and the village of Beverwijck, Jacob Gevick, born at Meckelenborgh, on the one side, and Geertruij Barents from Dwingeloo, widow of Henderick Hendericksz van Harstenhorst, deceased, on the other side, who, in the presence of the afternamed witnesses, declare that, for the honor of God, they have resolved upon a future marriage, and before the bands of the same, they have consented to the following conditions: First. That the aforesaid married people for the support of this marriage mutually shall bestow and bring together all present and such goods and effects, of whatever nature, in whatever place, and with whatever persons the same may lie outstanding and remaining; none of those effects excepted, which they each at present possess, or to which they each are entitled, and which is equitable to be possessed by them in common, according to the law of our fatherland; except that from the bride's goods, [360] to wit, of the estate left [by her late husband], half shall be reserved for the two children left by the late Henderick Hendericksz van Harstenhorst; the one named Lysbet Hendericksе, about six years old, and the other, Judick Hendericksе, three years old; which, with the agreement of the bride, by the orphan masters and said witnesses was assessed to be worth about one hundred good whole merchantable beaver skins at /8 apiece. Furthermore, that, in case the bridegroom comes to die before the bride without children procreated by the two of them, the bride will remain in full possession of the entire estate, as his only heir, without recognizing any other heirs. And if the bride comes to die before the bridegroom, also without children procreated by the two of them, the bridegroom shall be obliged to pay to her children half of the remaining estate, and, in addition, to pay to he same one hundred beavers, as before. Therefore he shall remain in full possession of the entire estate, on condition that also after the decease of the aforesaid bride the children will be entitled to inherit all of their mother's clothes, including gold rings and silverware, belonging to her person. Likewise, that the aforesaid married couple will bring up the aforesaid children in the fear of the Lord, and provide for them with food and clothing until their majority and married state, without diminishing their patrimonial and inherited estate. Which marriage conditions

the said bridegroom and bride promise [361] to keep without craft or guile, pledging their persons and estates, moveable and immoveable, present and future without any exception, submitting themselves to all laws and judges. Thus done in the presence of the honorable Frans Barentsen Pastoor and Adries de Vos, as witnesses requested hereto on date as above. Done in Beverwijck.
This is the mark of Jacob Gevick,
placed with his own hand.
This is the mark of Geertruij Barents van Dwingeloo, placed with her own hand.
Frans Barentsen Pastoor
By me Andrys de Vos
Evert Jansz Wendel as orphan master.
Acknowledged by me,
La Montagne, commissary at Fort Orange.

Fort Orange Minutes
1662, Page 278

bread and firewood. Building a house was four times as expensive than in the old world. Even with the hardships there were only seventeen people in 1659 receiving aid.

A poor house was established in Albany (Beverwijck) in 1652 and financed by the wealthier inhabitants of the village. The deacons of the Dutch Reformed Church were give a patent for a lot of 11 rods length and 5 rods width to *"enter upon, cultivate and employ and use the same for the need of the poor."*[1] A rod is a linear measure: Amsterdam measure equal

[1] Venema, J. (1993) Beverwijck: A Dutch Village on the American Frontier, 1652-1664. State of New York University Press, Albany, NY. pg. 327.

On July 7th, 1674 the directors of the West India Company further wrote:

From the accompanying lists your honors shall also be able to see what provisions have been sent for the boys and girls coming over from the godtshuysen (Literally "houses of God," which were charitable institutions where the elderly, orphaned, and infirm were taken care of.) *here, of which your honors can now take on as a trial; and your honors are hereby earnestly recommended to help take good care of the same, and to place them there with good masters; or otherwise to employ them, and in such a manner as is best for them and also however it m a y be judged to be most appropriate in general, which w e most highly commend to your honors' awareness and attention.*

chamber at Amsterdam,

Ab. Wilmerdonx

David van Baerle. Page 24

to 13 voeten (12.071 feet); Rhineland 12 voeten (12.36 feet). The original deed for the poorhouse lot, signed by Petrus Stuyvesant, is on display in Albany's First Church. It was later followed by the construction of a poor farm in 1657, a bleach field in 1658, and a new addition to the poorhouse in 1660. In 1669 a garden plot was added.

On February 6, 1657, Jan Verbeeck and Evert Jansen Wendel were appointed orphan masters in Beverwijck and Rensselaerswijck. They reported directly to the court of Fort Orange and Beverwijck. On February 27, for example, they reported *"the bad management of Christoffel Davids in administering the estate left undivided between him and his children, the heirs of*

Cornelia Vos, his deceased wife."[2] Verbeeck and Wendel proposed two persons (the father and an uncle of the said wife) as curators of the estate *"for the preservation of the property and the protection of the children,"* which the court granted to them *"as lawful curators of the estate to do all that was fit for the benefit of the estate and the children."*

In the Albany area the number of poor was few since the population was small and inhabitants had access to land to grow their own food. Education was considered important and the deacons paid for the schooling of some poor children. For example, they paid for "schoolgoing" of Daniel, who was boarded with the needy Marietje Claes. Education was included in some apprenticeships for children of needy parents. The contract of the above-mentioned Arnout, Poulijn's son, for example, noted that the boy would attend evening school during two winters.

In twenty-two cases, people incapable of running household or of maintaining themselves were boarded people. Most of them were orphans, elderly, or needed to be looked after.

Albany's charity system was different from other areas in the New World, such as New England, where taxes were imposed for the needy in the community. Money collected through voluntary donations in church, in poor boxes, and through

---

[2] Van Laer, A. J. F. (trans. and ed.). (1923). Minutes of the Court of Albany, Rensselaerswyck and Schenectady: 1668–1673, Vol. 2, University of the State of New York, Albany. Pg. 19.

gifts, was almost always enough to pay for the individual needs of the poor. Volunteerism, rather than compulsion, was the norm of New Netherland's social policy.

In 1664, the English seized New Netherland. Under the new regime, the orphan chamber would soon disappear. However, upon turning over the land to the English, one of the stipulations was that the organization concerning the poor would not change hands. The responsibility of caring for orphans passed to the English courts after the second surrender of New Netherland in 1674 when the Duke's Laws extended to the whole colony. English poor relief was introduced in New York in 1683. In Albany, poor relief remained mostly in the hands of the church deaconry in 1700.

The English Problem

Governor Edmund Andros in 1678 informed the Trade in London that there were no beggars and that all in the province were cared for. Eight years later the Governor reported to the same body that *"Every Town & County to maintain their own poor, which makes them noe Vagabonds, Beggars, nor Idle Persons are suffered to live here."*[3] Replying to a suggestion made by the Board of Trade and Plantations that a workhouse be erected in New York City, Governor Bellomont in

[3] Mencher, Samual. 1967. oor Law to Poetry Program. Economic Security Policy in Britain and the United States. University of Pittsburgh Press, pg. 45.

1699 expressed amusement at the idea, assuring the Board that *"there is no such thing as a beggar in this town or country."*[4]

These statements were false but expected from administrations that were trying to paint the best picture of the province as possible to those overseas.

In Provincial New York, the time between 1664-1776, the apprenticeship system formed the cornerstone welfare in provincial times. Poor-relief in New York can be traced back to both the English 1601 Poor Law (1601:43 Elizabeth 1c2: Act for the relief of the poor) that was an Act of the Parliment of England and the Dutch practice which prevailed up to 1664. An example of binding out children in groups can be seen in a document in Southampton dated 1694:

"At a meeting of ye Trustees ye 14 of June did then order that according directions of ye Justices to take care of the poore and orphans within and the children of Thomas Reeves and Ben Davis deceased being both fatherless and motherless, that Isaac William and Aaron Burnatt do bound out said orphans, according on ye 15th day were five of the said orphans bound out..."[5]

---

[4] Annual Report of the State Board of Charities for the Year 1904. 1904. Vol. 1. Albany Brandow Printing Company. Pg. 12.

[5] Post, William J. The Fifth Volume of Records of the Town of Southampton. 1910. https://archive.org/details/recordsoftownofs00sout/page/n7

If a misfortune arose in which support of children was temporarily prevented by their parents, authorities might relieve the family in its home, or they might place the children in other hands until the parents were again able to care for them.

An example can be found in New York City where a prisoner petitioned the Common Council for relief for his family, and they ordered *"that the Overseers of the Poor doe put out the Children of the Said Petitioner in Some Good Reputable Families for their Subsistence dureing his Imprisonment."* [6]

In January, 1719, the Mayor's Court directed that: *"The Church Wardens Inspect in what Condition the Widow Thomas Grisson are in at The Bowry and if they find Their Children Objects of Charity that they Relieve them at Their Discretions or putt them out apprentice for a Term of Years."* [7]

Children could be indentured at any age in New York up to the age of twenty-one. One order for apprenticeship in 1725 designated as an alternative apprentice for Joseph Byng an infant *"aged Eighteen Month of thereabouts."* who as the son of a feltmaker

---

[6] (February 27, 1694; N.Y.C., M.C.C., 1675-1776, I, 348).

[7] (N.Y.C., M.M.C., January).

serving time was in jail[8]. In an order for apprenticeship in 1726 it named George Williams who was only four years old.

It was also a practice to offer a group of dependent children for apprenticeship at one time, such as seen in an advertisement in the June 11, 1750 edition of the *New York Weekly Post-Boy* stating that several children of age ten or less, were available for apprenticeship, and were at the almshouse for selection.

The act of apprenticeship and indentured servitude was common throughout the provincial period for dependent and neglected children. The "master" was obligated to teach a boy how to read, write and cipher (a certain way of writing in code).

On May 24, 1720, eight-year-old Justus Whitfield was apprenticed by order of the Common Council, *"to Learn the Art of a Marriner."* Jasper Busk, the master was ordered *"to Provide him with Meat Drink & Apparell to learn him to Read & to give him two good New Suites of Apparell at the Term."*[9] The term was 13 years.

In Amenia, Dutchess County, boys were apprenticed and at the end were given a beaver hat, two good new suits, a new Bible, and *"twenty pounds York money in neat cattle or sheep to be appraised by Indifferent men."*

---

[8] N.Y.C., M.M.C., December 13, 1726; July 20

[9] 46 N.Y.C., M.M.C., May 24, 1720).

Girl apprentices were given two suits of clothes, a new cloak and bonnet, a Bible, and *"30 pounds of good live Geese feathers."*[10] Goose feathers could be made into quill pens, insulation trim for women's clothes, and material for powder puffs, and stuffing for mattresses, bolsters, and pillows for example.

Abuses did occur and apprenticeships were harsh while many of the laws regulating them were often ignored. There are records of masters being fined or losing their apprentices because of it. There were also cases where a government would take preventative measures such as the case when Jonathan Haight of Rye in 1716 notified the Westchester Court of Sessions that:

"Thomas Wright, an orphan in that town, hath no certain Place of Aboide there, but lives like a Vagabond and at a loose end, and will undoubtedly come to Ruine unless this Court take some speedy and effectual care for ye prevention thereof."[11]

There were also times when dependent children were relieved in kind. The Mayor's Court of New York City, on November I, 1726, ordered the church-wardens to *"Supply Phillip Cordus a sickly boy at the House of Anantie Delamontagne with a pair of Schoes A pair of Stockings A Blankett and some Course Linnen to*

---

[10] Amenia Precinct Book for the Poor, A.D., 1760-1820 (MS), pp. 3-6.

[11] (52 Charles W. Baird, History of Rye: Chronicle of a Border Town, 1660-1870 (New York, 1871), pp. 163-64.)

make a Straw Bed, he being poor and an Object of Charity."[12]

Those children who were born out of wedlock, and mentally or physically handicapped were all included in an attempt to deal with their needs. Providing medical aid to the sick poor was usually to contract with a private physician. As early as 1687 a doctor for the needy, Dr. Jonannes Kerfyle, took office in New York City and served for two years. Epidemics occurring during this period also took their toll on the poor as well as those that were not. In 1746, Albany had a yellow fever epidemic and lost 45 inhabitants. In 1756, Albany authorities passed a law that all smallpox patients should be sent from the city to a convenient place for their reception.

Educating poor children was also a concern to many during this period. Free public school systems did not appear until later in the 19th century. There were some free schools during the provincial period but they were open mostly to the children of taxpayers in the state. Poor children did not have the opportunity. In 1691, the New York Assembly introduced a bill for popular education that would include *"a school master for the educating and instructing of youth, to read and write English, in every town in the province."*[13] The bill was intended to replace the

---

[12] Alexander C. Flick (ed.), History of the State of New York (New York, 1932-35), III, 76.

[13] Journal of New York Assembly. 1691-1743, pg.7. William Bradford Printer.

prevailing Dutch culture at the time but it failed to pass. A few years later in 1702, Governor Cornbury stressed the need for *"the erecting of Public Schools in proper places."* And the assembly passed *"An Act for Encouragement of a Grammar Free School in the City of New York."* In November 1704, the school opened and closed five years later. It wasn't until twenty-six years later in 1732 when the provincial government passed a statue to *"encourage a Public School in the City of New York for teaching Latin, Greek and Mathematics."* Free tuition was offered for twenty students from among several counties but like the other this school was closed after six years.

Several "charity" schools were established by the "Society for the Propagation of the Gospel in Foreign Parts," an Anglican organization that had obvious ties to the Crown and faith. Several schools were open in southeastern counties and the very poor were allowed tuition free.[14] It even opened a school in New York City for Negro and Indian Slaves in 1704 claiming *"many were raised from their miserable condition and became steadfast Christians."*[15] In 1710 they also opened a charity school in New York City for white children with 40 boys attending.

---

[14] Documents of the Assembly of the State of New York. Ninety-Third Session. 1870. Vol 6, Now 101-132.. Pg. 673.

[15] Pascoe, C.F. (1901). Two hundred years of the S. P. G.: an historical account of the Society for the propagation of the gospel in foreign parts, 1701-1900 (Based on a digest of the Society's records.) Published by the Society's office. Pg 769

While taken over by the Trinity Church later, the custom of preaching charity sermons in order to obtain clothing and other necessities for the poor kids was started in 1754 and continued for many years.[16] The present day Salvation Army that makes attendees pray before they are offered a meal has a similar approach.

New York City authorities tried in 1714 to raise funds to maintain a public schoolmaster for teaching and were again unsuccessful. In 1731 the city's common council paid eight pounds from public funds to the widow of Sarah Huddleston *"as a Gratification for the trouble and Care she and her late Son Thomas Huddleston deceased have taken in teaching several Poor Children of this Corporation to Read and Write and Instructing them in the Principles of Religion over and above the Number allowed by the Venerable society for propagation of the Gospel in Forregin parts."*[17]

Town schools were established in places like Eastchester, Rye and White Plains for people of English descent, and French clergy had a school in New Rochelle in the mid 18th century. Johnstown had a free school in 1769.

In summary, administering public welfare in provincial New York was haphazard with a lack of uniformity throughout the province. At first relief

---

16 New York Mercury, October 24, 1764.

17 56 N.Y.C., M.C.C., 1675-1776, IV, 74-75).

came mostly from the churches and was eventually taken over by secular authorities. Few institutions existed while dependent children were usually put in the system of apprenticeship or indentured servitude. Free education for children was less than it was under the Dutch.

Chapter 3

The Nineteenth Century

The opening of the 19th century found the English poor-law system well established in most of the sixteen states then comprising the Union. The poor, children and adults, were cared for by the local administrative units, towns (or townships) or counties and cities. There was little or no oversight or control by the States, and none by the federal authorities.

There was little distinction made between adults and children, both being cared for in one of five ways:[1]

1. Outdoor relief, given to families at their own homes.
2. Farming out to various families, usually to the lowest bidder.
3. Contracting with some individual, usually the lowest bidder, to care for all the poor of a given locality.
4. Supporting them in an almshouse directly under the control of public authorities.
5. Indenture.

---

[1] The Charities Review. Vol. IX- March-February, 1899-1900. New York. The Charities Review 105 East 22nd Street. Pg 393.

The farming-out and contract systems had comparatively little application to children. The indenture system, although especially applicable to children was also used as a means of caring for adults. At the opening of the century, the statutes of several states provided that idle or vagrant persons might be indentured to respectable citizens for a period of a year.

Outdoor relief was the method used for the larger number of pauper children, as well as adults at the opening of the century. It had already passed (in 1784 in New York) from the control of the church authorities to that of the overseers of the poor, who were strictly public officials. The later reports upon public relief made by competent authorities in Boston and New York, revealed that outdoor relief exerted the same evil influences upon children.

Almshouses were first built mostly by the large cities. Philadelphia, the largest city in the United States at the opening of the century (population, 70,287), was then occupying its second public almshouse, that opened in 1767 and was located on the area bounded by Tenth and Eleventh and Spruce and Pine streets. Both adults and children were cared for in this institution.

In New York, the second city in the Union (population, 60,489), had, in 1796, just abandoned its original almshouse, and had removed its paupers to a much larger building, located in the area of present City Hall park, and on the site of the present county courthouse.

There were numbers of children, together with the many other elements of the almshouse population that in large cities have since been segregated into special classes.

The almshouse, under the management of a superintendent, was largely controlled by the common council, that held its meetings at the almshouse once in three months and inspected the institution. On October 6, 1800, a committee of the common council appointed to create a new set of rules for the management of the almshouse, reported as among the objects to be realized was the following:

*"The children of the house should be under the government of capable matrons. * * * They should be uniformed, housed and lodged in separate departments, according to their different sexes; they should be kept as much as possible from the other paupers, habituated to decency, cleanliness and order, and carefully instructed in reading, writing and arithmetic. The girls should also be taught to sew and knit.*

When the children arrive at proper ages, great care should be taken to furnish them with suitable places, that they may be instructed in some useful trade or occupation."[2]

---

[2] Folks, Homer. The Care of Destitute, Neglected, and Delinquent Children. 1900. Monographs on American Social Economics. Department of Social Economy for the US Commission to the Paris Exposition of 1900. Pg. 7. The Charities Review.

The exact number of children in the New York City almshouse in 1801 is not available, but on August 14, 1809, they numbered 226: 125 boys and 101 girls. It is likely that the city also boarded a number of infants with families at this time. The rules established by the common council in 1800 provided that, *"care shall be taken to provide healthy and proper nurses for such of the children as may require them; and where this can be done out of the house, it shall be preferred."*[3]

Somewhat later, on April 1, 1823, there were 129 infants placed out " at nurse," and paid for by the city at the rate of $1 per week.

Baltimore, the third city in the Union (population, 26,614), most likely cared for its destitute children in the Baltimore County almshouse. The city did not have a charitable institution under its immediate direction at that time. Boston, the fourth city (population, 24,027), erected its second almshouse, for both children and adults, in 1800.

Outdoor relief was also given freely, as was the case throughout New England. The proportion of "unsettled," or state paupers was increasing, but they were cared for by the cities and towns, and were reimbursed by the state.

---

[3] Care of children in New York City Almshouses, 1800. Rules for the Government of the Almshouse, Oct 6, 1800 in N.Y.C. Council Minutes, 1784-1831, II, Pg. 671.

There were no other cities in the United States having a population above 10,000. In most of Pennsylvania, and generally in the Southern States, the county system of poor relief prevailed, and many counties erected almshouses. In Maryland, the county almshouse system was established by law in 1768. In Delaware, each county had an almshouse by 1823. It appears that the only public institution for children, not forming part of an almshouse, existing in 1801, was the Charleston Orphan House in South Carolina created in 1790 to receive 115 orphans.

The first orphan asylum in the country was that attached to the Ursuline convent in New

The Charleston Orphan House in Charleston, South Carolina is credited with being the first municipal orphan house in America. Credit: Library of Congress. c. 1900.

Orleans, Louisiana, now a museum. This convent was established by several nuns in 1727, under the auspices of Louis XV of France. It maintained a day school and a hospital and also during the first year received an orphan rescued by a missionary from a dissolute family. The massacre by the Natchez Indians in 1729 left many orphans in and near New Orleans, and the convent established an asylum for their care.

In 1824, the convent was removed to a country site, to the Faubourg Treme, and

The first orphan asylum in the country was that attached to the Ursuline convent in New Orleans, Louisiana, and was established in 1727. Credit: Library of Congress.

owing to the growth of other asylums, provision was made for the care of 30 orphans.

The Bethesda orphan house was established in Savannah, Georgia in 1738, five years after the colony was settled, by the celebrated preacher, George Whitefield. The plan was suggested by Reverend Charles Wesley and Governor Oglethorpe. This was founded by funds collected by Whitefield in England.

In 1797, the "Society for the Relief of Poor Widows with Small Children" was organized in New York City. This society did not establish an institution, but visited and gave relief to the widows and children in their homes.

In 1798, an association was organized by a Roman Catholic priest in Philadelphia to care for the orphans of Catholics who died of yellow fever during that year. Subsequently this institution became St. Joseph's Female Orphan Asylum.

In 1799, an asylum for the care and education of destitute girls was established by St. Paul's church in Baltimore, and in 1800, the Boston Female Asylum for Indigent Orphan Girls was incorporated.

For destitute children, the situation at the opening of the century may be summed up in that children who were public charges were, as a rule, cared for with adult paupers by the contract system, or in almshouses, or by outdoor relief, or were bound out as apprentices (which ended by 1875).

Troy, New York and the Caring of Orphans

The area that is now Troy started out as three Dutch Farms that eventually became divided into building lots with those from Grand Division (now Division Street) to the PiscawenKill (Middleburgh Street) laid out first in 1787. With the "Yankee Invasion" of the 1790s, post Revolutionary War, Vanderheyden as it was called then quickly became populated. Those to the north in the village of Lansingburgh also realized that the location of Vanderheyden was the best location to utilize the Hudson River for trade. Yale president Timothy Dwight said in 1820 that New York was becoming *"a colony from New England."* He estimated that 60-67% were from the *"land of steady habits."* After 1783, Yankees from New England started to swarm into Hudson Valley towns like bees looking for a hive. Albany for example tripled its population between 1790 and 1820, and by 1803 the Yankees outnumbered the original inhabitants. Their numbers also influenced the culture and they enraged the Dutch citizens of Albany when they pushed through an ordinance to cut off the long rain spouts on their houses.

In Vanderheyden (Troy) the population was estimated to be between 400 and 500 citizens by Judge John Woodworth in his *Recollections of Troy* in 1853. Woodworth had come to Troy in 1791. In 1798, Troy was incorporated as a village, and in 1816 incorporated as a city. By 1820 the population reached 5,264 and ten years later in 1830 it had 11,556 a whopping 119.5% increase in population.

Some of the early settlers of Troy included Dr. Samuel Gale who came to Troy in 1789 from Killingworth, Connecticut, with his wife, daughter, and four sons Benjamin, John, Samuel and William. He built a house and store on the Upper Ferry. He practiced medicine until his death in 1797. His son Sam was Postmaster from 1804-1828. Benjamin, John and William became merchants. Son Samuel was a physician working as a druggist in a storehouse he built on the West side of River Street. He also became postmaster around 1812. Sarah lived at 119 First Street and had frequent visitors in the form of Native Americans who would eat and drink and fall asleep on the kitchen floor, snoring all day.

John Woodworth was the first postmaster from 1793-1799. David Buel succeeded him, son of a Supreme Court judge in Troy. A store on the west side of River Street was run by Abraham Ten Eyck, Albert Pawling and Conrad J. Emendorf. Another store on the west side of River was run by Daniel and Isaac Merrit. Daniel was a Quaker. Albert Pawling moved up from Ulster County. He was responsible for the building of the courthouse, the first Presbyterian Church, and the settlement of a pastor. He also was the first mayor of Troy. A man named Stephenson from Newport, Rhode Island moved to Troy with his wife and four children. He operated a store on the west side of River Street. The eldest daughter became the wife of Hugh Peebles, a cashier of the Farmer's Bank. When she died, he married one of her sisters. The Warren family moved to Troy from Connecticut. Esaias, Nathan and Stephen also ran a produce store on River Street and carried on trade to New York City. Esaias was the first president of the Troy Bank. Stephen followed. The McCoun family moved to Troy around 1793 and the sons had a store adjoining the River opposite the Mansion House. Townsend McCoun was a director of the Farmer's Bank and built a house on Second Street. Philip Heartt was in business with Benjamin Smith and Joseph Russell. Heartt was one of the founders of the Presbyterian Church. His son Jonas C. Heartt became a judge. The firm of Morgan, Boardman and Coit were merchants in 1790. Boardman built a house on the West side of Second Street. Stephen Ashley opened the first tavern opposite the Ferry (off Ferry Street). Jeremiah Pierce came to Troy in 1793 from Massachusetts and opened a tavern on River Street near the Ferry. Benjamin Smith was treasurer of the county, a judge of the court, and an elector and clerk of the county. Benjamin Gorton was a merchant in Troy who came from Hudson and operated a store on River Street. Gen. Peter B. Porter was a law student but became a religious zealot. Old Uncle Derick Vanderheyden, the founder of Troy was still alive. Major General John Wool had a store on River Street. He served in the Revolutionary War and the Civil War. Ebenezer Jones and his son in law, Captain Skelding, lived in the upper part of the village. Dr. John Loudon and Mahlon Taylor owned the mills on the Poesentkill. Jonathan and Alsop Hunt built a store near the Ferry. Howard Mouton had a tavern near the courthouse. Emma Willard started her Troy Female Seminary near the courthouse. Rev. Jonas Coe was invited to preach in the house of Stephen Ashley in 1791 and soon a church was built on First Street. Father Beeman followed him. Moses Vail moved to Troy in 1799 from Nassau. He was a Senator in the legislature for four years and became Sheriff in Troy. He also ran a stagecoach service. Henry Vail from Troy was also a representative in Congress. Jacob D. Vanderheyden, one of the original owners of the land upon which Troy was founded, lived near 8th Street. Hon. John Bird of Litchfield, Connecticut came to Troy in 1794 and practiced law.

These people made up the founding of Troy and many of them or members of their family, especially their wives, were responsible for the beginnings of the Troy Orphan Asylum, now simply known as *Vanderheyden.*

[From the Troy Daily Whig.]

Donation to the Orphan Asylum.

TROY, August 13th, 1857.

MR. EDITOR: I acknowledge, with great satisfaction the generous donation of Messrs. Fuller, Warren and Morrisson, of one hundred and thirty-four loaves of well baked bread, weighing two hundred and sixty-eight pounds, to the Troy Orphan Asylum. And I do it with the more pleasure because, while it is an honorable evidence of their benevolence, it affords me opportunity of making known to the public an achievement in bread-baking, by a small stove, which I regard as altogether unexampled. The construction of this stove is the invention of my friend Mr. P. P. Stewart, of Troy, one of the most benevolent of men. The experiment which has resulted so successfully in illustrating the superior qualities of the

STEWART STOVE,

Originated, I learn, in a question made between the patentee, Mr. Stewart, and Messrs. Fuller, Warren & Morrison, in regard to its capabilities. Mr. S. felt confident that he could make the entire contents of a barrel of flour into bread, in one of his small stoves, having an oven of 20 inches square only, by a single fire; and offered to try the experiment on the condition that, if he succeeded, they should pay for the flour, and give the bread to the Troy Orphan Asylum. He accomplished it triumphantly, by a single fire of twenty-five and a half pounds of coal, costing only seven cents! And when he had accomplished it, the fire was still as glowing as during any part of the process. Such a result is, I think, without example; and it proves that, in economy of fuel as well as for general utility,

The Stewart Stove

Stands unrivalled. I am respectfully your obedient servant,

S. K. STOW, Treasurer.

Sole agency for the above stove, at

HADLEY & HUSTED'S,
No 119 Main street.

s-15

The Buffalo Daily Republic. Septemeber 21, 1857.

Chapter 4

The Origins of the Troy Orphan Asylum

Alexis de Tocqueville when visiting America in the 1830s remarked about the "principle of association" as he termed it that drove Americans to establish voluntary organizations. He said:

"The Americans make associations to give entertainments, to found seminaries, to build inns, to construct churches, to diffuse books, to send missionaries to the antipodes; in this manner they found hospitals, prisons, and schools. If it is proposed to inculcate some truth or to foster some feeling by the encouragement of a great example, they form a society."[1]

Richard P. Hart was one of the founders of the Troy Orphan Asylum. He was one of the directors of the Troy & Schenectady Railroad.

[1] de Tocqueville, Alexis. Democracy in America, 1862. Volume 2. Pg 129. Translated by Francis Bowen. Cambridge: Sever and Francis.

On August 28, 1803, a number of the women met in the Friends Schoolhouse on the corner of State Street and Fourth to design a plan of action to help orphans.

While most organizations were founded by men, the movement for women's organizations appeared as a religious impulse around 1800. They were dedicated to pious and charitable ends and often had consequences beyond the original aims of their founders. This movement is traced to the eighteenth century evangelical revival in England and in particular with the work of England's Hannah More. During the early 19th century many women's groups were being formed in New England based on religious reasons for *"reforming the religion and morals of the inhabitants."*

The first permanent women's societies were organized as early as 1800 in New York City such as the "Society for the Relief of Poor Widows and

Mayor George Tibbits donated $10,000 to the Troy Orphan Asylum.

Small Children" and the "Boston Female Asylum" in Boston, Massachusetts. In 1806, the "Orphan Asylum Society in the City of New York" was formed to care for the children of widows aided by the Society for the Relief of Poor Widows with Small Children. Later they took orphans from the city almshouse and indentured them. During the 1810s and 1820s, under the influence of the Second Great Awakening, there were formed new women's organizations whose members *"sought first to alleviate spiritual want, then to deal with temporal deprivation."*

Between 1810 and 1815 female "cent a week" societies became common in New Hampshire and other states and urged *"that if people would retrench a little of their expenses, a revenue might easily be saved, which do considerable toward extending the means of salvation."*[2]

Thousands of women joined and the movement spread quickly into New York State where the Female Missionary Society of the Western District, organized in 1816, and by 1818, had presence in 46 towns and villages in ten counties. Other female organizations flourished and Troy was not immune to finding women organizing for worthy causes, particularly because most of the population of the newly found city were "yankees" from New England where the movement began. This movement spurred the interest of the needs of orphans and the development of institutions to care

Hon. David Buell Jr., a founding trustee of the Troy Orphan Asylum. Buell was a director of the Farmers' Bank of Troy and Manager of the Troy Savings Bank.

---

[2] Melder, Keith. "Ladies Bountiful: Organized Women's Benevolence In Early 19th-Century America." New York History, Vol. 48, No. 3 (July 1967), pp. 231-254

for them. This was the background setting for the origins of the Troy Orphan Asylum.

The Ladies of Troy

During the closing weeks of the 18th century a number of Troy woman met together to form an organization that would help indigent women and children in *"alleviating the distresses of their bodies and cultivating their minds with the rudiments of science and the principles of morality and religion."* On February 24, 1800, the "Ladies's Society" formed "The Benevolent Society of Troy." It was the genesis of the Troy Orphan Asylum. Some newspapers in later years give the date as February 27, 1803, as the "Ladies Benevolent Society of Troy." This may have been the renaming of the society.

The site of the first location for the Troy Orphan Asylum at 124 Fourth Street.

The list of founding women is mostly the wives of many of the

The orphanage rented a building north of St. Paul's Church (white building to the left) at 52 Third Street near State Street for an annual rent of $200.

"Who's Who" of Troy's early leaders: Alleda Bassing, Betsey S. Wilson (married to "Uncle Sam" Wilson on Ferry Street), Charlotte Bliss (married to lawyer William M. Bliss at 140 Third Street), Diadama Heartt (married to farmer Philip Heartt on Mount Ida), Eliza Hunting Coe (married to Rev. Jonas Coe, pastor of the United Congregations of Lansingburgh and Troy), Eliza Kinicut, Eliza Thomas, Eliza (Harriman) Wickes (married to Van Wyck), Elizabeth Colties, Elizabeth Hubbard(probably married to Charles F. Hubbard, clerk, at 122 Second Street),

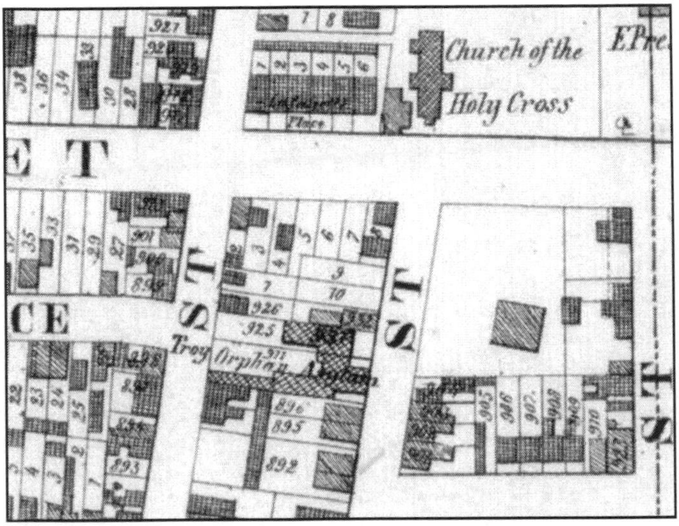

The Orphan Asylum was located on Grand Division (now Grand Street) for 27 years until the great fire of 1862 burned it to the ground. This section no longer exists.

Elizabeth Morgan (married to Ephraim Morgan), Elizabeth Warren, Frances Sim, Gitty Tibbits (married to Union College President Eliphalet Nott), Grace Davis, Hannah Forman, Hannah Lord (she married Orlando Montague and invented the detachable collar. then living at 50

State Street), Harriet Hutton (probably the wife of Walter Hutton, carpenter at 45 Sixth Ave), Harriet Hillhouse (wife of Thomas Hillhouse), Lucy Osborn, Lucy Pierce (married to Benjamin Pierce, spelled Peirce in city directory, merchant at 104 First Street), Lucy (Tillman) Vail (married to Senator Moses Vail), Lydia Chandler (was married to Stephen Chandler), Lydia Peoples, Lydia Pierce, Lydia Warren (lived at 30 Third Street), Mabel Barret, Mariah Miller, Mary Bears (married to Moses Jarvis), Mary Lane (married to Aaron Lane from Lansingburgh), Mary Parker, Mary Porter (married to Moses Hale, physician at 67 Third Street), Mary Russel, Mary Wright, Mrs. Buel (probably Mrs. David Buell at 23 First Street), Mrs. N. Wilson, Patty Yvonet (probably married to Francis V, bookkeeper at the Farmer's Bank, 47 First Street), Phebe Ordiance, Phebe Warren (married to

Hon. Isaac McConihe was a trustee of the Troy Orphan Asylum. At the time of his death in 1867, he was the oldest member of the Bar Association. He served as president of the Troy Lyceum of Natural History, one of the first scientific bodies in the United States.

TOP: The great Troy fire of May 10,1862 began here from smoking embers on the old Rensselaer & Troy Railroad Bridge. BOTTOM: The bridge burning.

TOP: The collapsed burned bridge. BOTTOM: Aftermath of the fire. Grand Division Street is to the extreme right of the photo.

Troy University (now site of RPI Library) provided a refuge for a night after the fire for the orphans.

Eliakim Warren lived at 35 Third Street), Rebeccah Kilborn, Rheua Sheldon, Ruby Pierce, Sally Bird, Ms. Sally Gale (lived at 119 First Street), Sally Nicol, Sally

Harmony Hall still exits in downtown Troy.

Tibbits (married Matthew Perkins), Sally White, Sarah Jones (widow at 341 River Street), Sarah Ten Eyck, Sarah Tibitts (married to Mayor George Tibbits, Mayor of Troy, lived in the mansion at 7th and Congress Streets), Shinah Schuyler (married to Nicholas Schuyler), and Widow Vanderheyden.

Three years later, it was decided to expand the mission, and on August 28 a number of the women met in the Friends Schoolhouse on the corner of State and Fourth Streets to design a plan of action. The meeting was presided over by Mrs. Albert Pawling, wife of the city's first mayor and Ms. Blandina Vanderheyden. The results of the meeting were *"That we deem it expedient to adopt measures to further the founding of an asylum in this city for orphan and destitute children, and that so far as our good wishes and exertions can go to accomplish it they shall most cordially given."* Eleven woman were selected in a special committee to look further into the idea. These woman were Mrs. M. Babbett, Miss C. Owen, Mrs. Ebenezer Prescott (husband was painter at 43 Fifth Ave), Mrs. Albert Pawling (husband was a mayor of Troy), Mrs. George R. Davis (husband was a lawyer and bank commissioner, 42 King St), Mrs. David Buel (husband was a lawyer), Mrs. Thomas Clowes (husband was a lawyer, 42 Congress Street), Mrs. Gurdon Grant (husband was a merchant, 45 Fourth Street), Mrs. Robert McKee, Mrs. John Goodell (husband was a baker, 118 Fourth Street) and Mademoiselle de Coulvelle. A public meeting was called to be held in the courthouse on September 11,

1833, to get citizen involvement, and on September 10 the Troy Budget, a semiweekly newspaper announced the following:

"For the sake of humanity we invoke the attendance of all who know anything of human want to human misery. The ladies of our city, inspired, as they are, with the active spirit of benevolence, have laid the foundation for the asylum in which the orphan and destitute child may receive that attention and that moral food which his nature and his necessities require. Who is there among us that cannot approve the design? Who that will not wish it Godspeed? Who that will not lend it has good wishes and his influence? Many generous hearts are enlisted in it, and they ask the countenance and the substantial aid of the community. Surely, they will not ask in vain."

A committee was formed after the meeting to draft a constitution and on October 22, 1833, in the evening, a meeting was held in the court room of Mayor George Tibbits. The constitution was presented and adopted. Townsend McCoun, former supervisor of the Village of Troy acted as chairman and John Paine was secretary. This reorganized group called themselves the "Association for the Relief of Destitute Children." The following year the name was changed to the "Troy Orphan Asylum."

A board of trustees was formed to manage the organization and included 21 trustees. It was agreed that destitute children other than orphans were not to be helped unless a vote was taken of three quarters of the trustees. It was also agreed that "*no exclusive tenets of any religious sect*" making it non religious in purpose. By-Laws of the organization were drafted by David Buel, Jr., John Paine, and John Kimble. During the meeting of October 22, 1833, the following trustees were elected to be the first of the organization and met at the Mayor's court room:

Townsend McCoun (director of the Farmer' Bank), David Buel, Jr., (lawyer, 23 First Street), Thomas L. Ostrom, Gurdeon Grant (merchant, 45 Fourth Street), Thaddeus B. Bigelow (merchant, 31 First Street), Griffith P. Griffith (forwarding merchant, 60 Second Street), Asahel Gilbert (merchant, 5 Hutton Street), William W. Whipple (lumber dealer, 80 River Street), Richard P. Hart (merchant 59 Second Street), Calvin Warner (mason and grocer, 119 Fourth Street) , John Thomas (judge and city chamberlain, 252 River Street), Nathan Warren (builder, 31 Third Street), Joshua Harpham (poormaster, 71 Third Street), Jacob Lansing (livery stable, 89 Congress Street), Gardner Landon (carpenter, 48 State Street), Jacob Bishop (merchant, 49 Fourth Street), George Vail (merchant, 46 First Street), Jacob Merritt (merchant, 53 Second Street), John T. McCoun, John Paine (lawyer, 19 First Street) and John C. Kimble.

The new board met for the first time on October 23, 1833, in the new asylum quarters at 124 Fourth Street. Richard P. Hart was elected chair, Jacob D. Lansing was secretary and the following people were elected for the coming year:

Jacob Merritt, President, David Buell, Jr, Vice President. John T. McCoun, Treasurer. Day Otis Kellogg, Secretary (merchant, lived at the Mansion House).

Griffith P. Griffith (1789–1854)

Griffith was the owner of G. P. Griffith & Co and founder of the Troy & Erie Transportation Line in 1827 that had a number of steamboats that went between New York City and Lake Erie. He owned the *Robert Fulton, Dewitt Clinton, New York*, and the *G. P. Griffith*. He was a trustee of the Troy Orphan Asylum. In 1849, he had at 191 River Street, the New York and Troy Tow Boat Line with 48 boats and barges on the Hudson. The steamboat *G. P. Griffith* took part in one of the greatest lake disasters in history when a fire onboard proved disastrous on June 17, 1850. Its captain, Charles Roby turned to the boat into port side running to the shore in darkness that fanned the flames. He didn't give order to abandon the rapidly moving ship. People dove into the waters some getting caught in the paddle-wheels, others drowned from the weight of clothes and money sacks and some swam the wrong way in the dark. The crew abandoned their posts, and the ship hit a sandbar in 8-foot water. The captain and his family drowned, others burned to death on board. In all, 241 people died, only 37 survived. It was the worse Great Lakes disaster at the time. The loss of the *Griffith* was instrumental in bringing about the first public safety laws to govern vessels on America's waterways.

The executive committee consisted of Jacob Merritt, John Thomas, and Joshua Harpham. The women were asked to appoint a committee to cooperate with them. The executive committee was authorized to hire a matron, a teacher when necessary and anything else the Asylum needed to carry on its missions. Monthly meetings were set up for the first Tuesday of each month at 7 PM in the evening. The bylaws were adopted at the first meeting on November 5, 1833. One of the priorities at the meeting was to find a suitable location for the asylum. They rented a building north of St. Paul's Church at 52 Third Street near State Street for an annual rent of $200. On April 10, 1835, the New York State Legislature approved the incorporation as the "Troy Orphan Asylum." A committee was also formed to find a location to build their own home. They located a house that was partially finished at 65 Grand Division Street (now Grand Street), on the north side of Grand Division west of Eighth, near the church of the Holy Cross, with an attached small building that could be used as a classroom. The price was $3,500. Funds were raised from the public and donors. The early days of the asylum showed promise and met its mission, which was to be based on Christian charity and with the idea that no exclusive religious doctrines be promoted and neither distinction nor discriminations as to nationality or religion was to be made in the admission of children.

TO FARMERS AND MECHANICS.—The Troy Orphan Asylum has a number of Boys of suitable age to put out. Good places in the country would be preferred. Apply to *JOHN THOMAS, ELIAS LASELL,* or *JACOB MERRITT.* ap10

An advertisement in a Troy newspaper in 1838 announcing the availability of orphans as indentured workers.

After fifteen years of operation it was clear they needed more room and improvements were made to the buildings. While at Grand Division for 27 years the medical care and welfare of the residents were served gratis by several of the city doctors. In 1834, free medical services were given by Doctors Thomas C. Brinsmade (who was the sixth president of Rensselaer Polytechnic Institute), Zenas Cary (29 Grand Division near the

Charles W. Tillinghast was president of the board of trustees for many years. He was a successful business man in hardware and as director of several Troy banks.

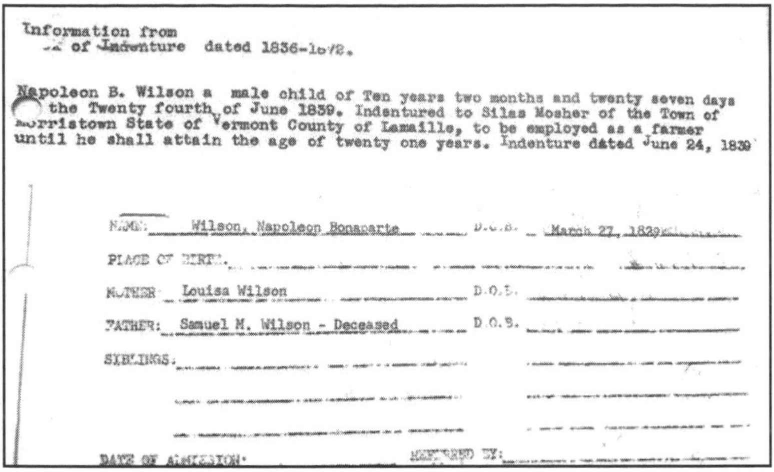

Information from
of Indenture dated 1836-1872.

Napoleon B. Wilson a male child of Ten years two months and twenty seven days the Twenty fourth of June 1839. Indentured to Silas Mosher of the Town of Morristown State of Vermont County of Lamaille, to be employed as a farmer until he shall attain the age of twenty one years. Indenture dated June 24, 1839

NAME: Wilson, Napoleon Bonaparte D.O.B. March 27, 1829

PLACE OF BIRTH:

MOTHER: Louisa Wilson D.O.B.

FATHER: Samuel M. Wilson - Deceased D.O.B.

SIBLINGS:

DATE OF ADMISSION: REFERRED BY:

Orphan Napoleon Wilson was Indentured to Silas Mosher in Vermont as a farm hand in 1829.

orphanage), Joseph W. Freiot (106 Fourth St.), Moses Hale (67 Third St.) or partner Richard H. Hale (67 Third St.), John Wheeler (86 Second St.), and Alfred or Hiram Wotkyns (73 Third St.). By 1858, it was decided they needed more room and looked for new quarters. In March 1859 greater authority and responsibility was granted by the New York State legislature.

Disaster struck the Asylum on May 10, 1862, when fire, started by loose embers from a train engine on the railroad bridge just yards from the asylum, began to move towards Grand Division Street. In the annual report of the trustees in 1862 it states:

"On Saturday, the 10th day of May, the cry was raised in the asylum, that the bridge was on fire. The cry excited no alarm in the Superintendent, for it was supposed that a good

The Reverend Samuel Blatchford, D.D. was the first president of what is now Rensselaer Polytechnic Institute (RPI) in Troy. His home served as a temporary orphanage for a year.

In 1886, Lewis E. Gurley was Vice President of the asylum. He and his brother William owned W. & L. E. Gurley, which manufactured precision scientific instruments which still exists today.

brick building, at a distance of a quarter of a mile from the

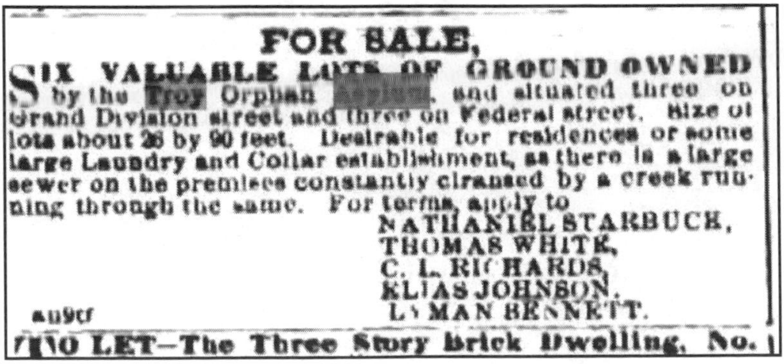

FOR SALE,

SIX VALUABLE LOTS OF GROUND OWNED by the Troy Orphan Asylum, and situated three on Grand Division street and three on Federal street. Size of lots about 25 by 90 feet. Desirable for residences or some large Laundry and Collar establishment, as there is a large sewer on the premises constantly cleansed by a creek running through the same. For terms, apply to

NATHANIEL STARBUCK,
THOMAS WHITE,
C. L. RICHARDS,
ELIAS JOHNSON,
LYMAN BENNETT.

au9tf

TO LET—The Three Story Brick Dwelling, No.

The orphans moved into the old Samuel Blatchford Mansion at the corner of 113th Street and 2nd Avenue in Lansingburgh for a year. Blatchford lived here from 1804 to 1828 and entertained the Marquis de Lafayette.

The Blatchford Mansion at the corner of 113th Street and 2nd Avenue in Lansingburgh today is now an apartment house.

fire, could be in no possible danger. But scarcely five minutes elapsed before the burning shingles from the bridge, borne by the strong west wind, had set fire to the Asylum both in front and rear; and the outbuildings, and the neighboring houses were also in a blaze. It was evident that the inmates of the Asylum must flee for their lives."

William Kemp was a trustee of the Troy Orphan Asylum during the nineteenth century. He was Mayor of Troy from 1873 to 1875.

The Troy Daily Times, special edition on Sunday, May 11, 1862, wrote:

"The Troy Orphan Asylum Building situated on Grand Division Street was among the first to which the fire communicated. The matron and assistants were enabled to remove all the children without injury. The building which belong to an incorporated group was valued at about $6,000. The furniture was probably worth about $2,500, and it is an entire loss."

There were one hundred and ten orphans in the building when it caught fire. Most were bathing at the time of the alarm and they were ordered to get dressed. The superintendent, Miss Sophia Eastman,

The lithograph drawing of the Eight Street orphanage shows a cupola tower as depicted in Arthur Weise's book, City of Troy and its Vicinity (1886).

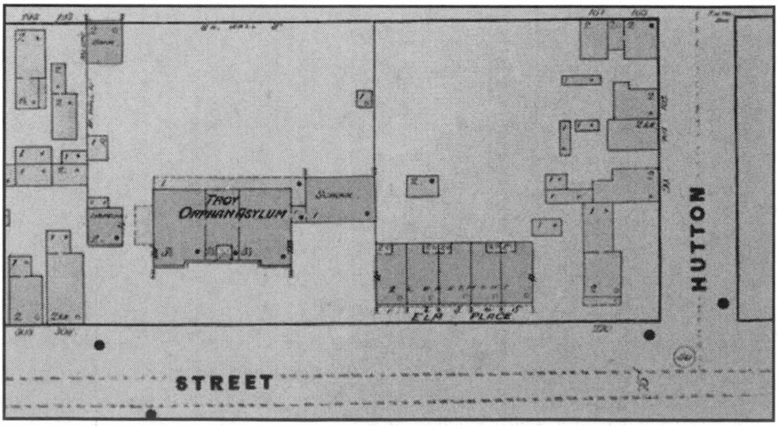

From 1864 to 1893 the orphanage was located on the east side of 8th Street between Hutton and Hoosick Streets. The site is now vacant.

TOP: From 1864 to 1893 the orphanage was located on the east side of 8th Street between Hutton and Hoosick Streets. Collection Rensselaer County Historical Society, Troy, NY.

BOTTOM: The site on the east side of 8th Street between Hutton and Hoosick Streets is now vacant.

the teacher Miss Elizabeth Morrison, along with the help gathered all the orphans outside the building while Ms. Eastman went inside to make sure no one was left behind. Reports of the day were scary. The group walked their way east while the air was filling with smoke and suffocating heat. The clothes on the children repeatedly caught fire. They made it to a house of Mr. Prescott at the end of Fulton Street and thinking since it was detached and surrounded by trees they would be safe, but it soon caught fire. They then retreated to a ravine east of the city under the trees. A roll call showed everyone made it. They stayed in the ravine until evening when it was

The old orphanage became the new Samaritan Hospital from 1894 to 1914. Courtesy Samaritan Hospital.

apparent that the children were hungry since they only had breakfast hours earlier. They spent the night in Troy University (where the RPI library now stands) and the next day was moved to Harmony Hall owned by the Dauchy family. Now homeless, the trustees met and rented the old Blatchford Mansion in Lansingburgh for a year. Samuel Blatchford lived here from 1804 to 1828. General Marquis de Lafayette entertained here during the day on July 1, 1825. Later in the day he went to Troy and visited with Emma Willard.

The orphanage had lost all its belongings and the benevolence of the citizens as well as officers of the organization came to the aid. Offers to give temporary housing were given by The Albany Orphan Asylum, Five Points House of Industry of New York and St. Mary's Hall in Troy. At a special meeting of the board on May 20, 1862, Mrs. Betsey Amelia Hart proposed to give $10,000 towards the

Doughty was a trustee of the orphanage and was one of the first incorporators and first president of Samaritan Hospital.

On July 1, 1889, the Trustees received notice that they would receive as a gift a beautiful farm of 109 acres within the city of Troy along Hollow Road (now called Spring Avenue) by Mrs. Charles B. Russell, Mrs. Mary E. Hart, Mrs Margaret E. Proudfit and Mrs Mary B. Tillinghast. Beck & Pauli 1881 Map Panorama of Troy, NY.

erection of a new building provided a suitable site can found and purchased and an additional matching sum be raised.

The Trustees appeared to have sold the former site on Division Street in August after the fire. An advertisement in the Troy Daily Whig lists three lots on Grand Division and three on Federal Street which would be in back of the Division Street lots. This pinpoints the location of the Asylum not far

In 1865 Harvey J. King was elected as a trustee of the Troy Orphan Asylum. He was an anti-slavery Northern Whig and well known Troy lawyer.

from the burning bridge.

A committee purchased a site at 294 Eighth Street from George Henry Warren for $11,200 with Warren donating $1,900 so the total cost was $9,300. A total of $10,450 was raised from the public (New York State appropriated $5,000) and the total cost of construction was $4,000 less than it was originally proposed for a total of $17,750. Henry Dudley, architect of New York City was given the contract. The laying of the cornerstone was held on May 18, 1863, and an iron box was placed in it with thirty items ranging from annual reports, charters of various organizations, local newspapers, a song written for the occasion and other items including a letter from Capt. Thomas G. Morrison of the NYS Volunteers, 66th Regiment to his sister Elizabeth, dated April 27, 1863. Morrison was a resident of the asylum and died of wounds in the Battle of Spotsylvania during the Civil War on May

8, 1864. He became a captain on August 7, 1862. A newspaper clipping revealed the following:

"DEATH OF AN ORPHAN SOLDIER.—We are sorry to learn of the death, in the recent battles, of Capt. T. G. Morrison, of the Sixty-first regiment, whose name has before been mentioned in these columns. He was brought up and educated at the Troy Orphan Asylum, and reflected honor upon that institution. A letter from Lieut. Wren, an officer of the regiment, alludes to him in the following affectionate terms: "

" I cannot speak at length of my dear comrade, Thomas. He was my friend, faithful and kind to me. The years of close companionship and intimacy in toil and peril, had endeared

NAME: Clark, Thomas D.O.B. ______

PLACE OF BIRTH: ______

MOTHER: ______ D.O.B. ______

FATHER: ______ D.O.B. ______

SIBLINGS: ______ ______

DATE OF ADMISSION: Before fire 1862 REFERRED BY: ______

REASON FOR ADMISSION ______

DATE OF DISCHARGE: ______ DISCHARGED TO: ______

REASON FOR DISCHARGE: ______

SIGNIFICENT DOCUMENTS: Died 1894 - age 62

Was a surgeon at Bellvue Hospital. Practiced in Troy in Summer.

Not much is known about the children before the 1862 fire but records do indicate that Thomas Clark grew up to become a surgeon at Bellevue Hospital in NYC and practiced in Troy during the summer.

him to my heart—knowing him as I do for the patriot and man. I trust that the few words of feeling expressed by me without premeditation, will not prove intrusive on our great grief."

Hollister was a trustee of the orphanage elected in 1875 and served as secretary for 19 years. In 1878 he was the Troy School Commissioner.

One of the Trustees of the Asylum thus records the appreciation of the deceased by himself and his associates:

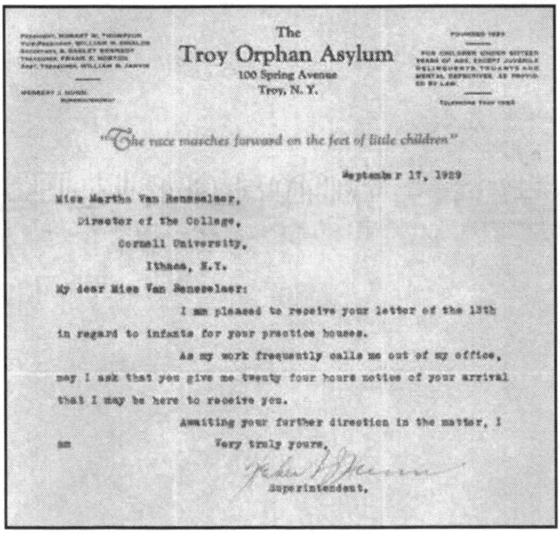

The
Troy Orphan Asylum
100 Spring Avenue
Troy, N. Y.

"The race marches forward on the feet of little children"

September 17, 1929

Miss Martha Van Rensselaer,
Director of the College,
Cornell University,
Ithaca, N.Y.

My dear Miss Van Rensselaer:

I am pleased to receive your letter of the 13th in regard to infants for your practice houses.

As my work frequently calls me out of my office, may I ask that you give me twenty four hours notice of your arrival that I may be here to receive you.

Awaiting your further direction in the matter, I am

Very truly yours,

Superintendent,

" The above letter conveys the sad intelligence to the sister of Capt. Morrison, who is now in the Troy Orphan Asylum. Sad, indeed, will be the news to her, as also to Miss

Eastman and the inmates of the Institution, as well as to many of the Trustees with whom he was personally acquainted. He had become much endeared to them all by his occasional visits and his many kind acts, deeming the Asylum his home, as he was reared in the Institution. Immediate steps will be taken to have his remains returned to the Asylum." There are efforts to locate his gravesite today.

On October 29, 1862, in the middle of the Civil War the minutes of the trustees reflected on the fact that they needed to expand further, building on their already successes. They needed additional land for larger and better living quarters, playgrounds, proper sanitary facilities and so looked for an area to expand.

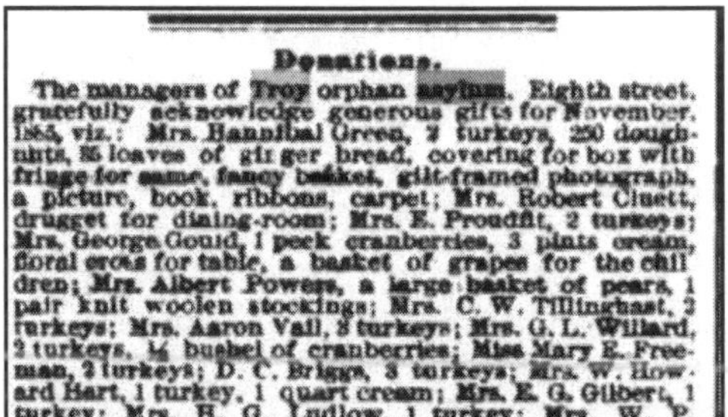

Donations.

The managers of Troy orphan asylum, Eighth street, gratefully acknowledge generous gifts for November, 1885, viz.: Mrs. Hannibal Green, 7 turkeys, 250 doughnuts, 85 loaves of ginger bread, covering for box with fringe for same, fancy basket, gilt-framed photograph, a picture, book, ribbons, carpet; Mrs. Robert Cluett, drugget for dining-room; Mrs. E. Proudfit, 2 turkeys; Mrs. George Gould, 1 peck cranberries, 3 pints cream, floral cross for table, a basket of grapes for the children; Mrs. Albert Powers, a large basket of pears, 1 pair knit woolen stockings; Mrs. C. W. Tillinghast, 3 turkeys; Mrs. Aaron Vail, 3 turkeys; Mrs. G. L. Willard, 2 turkeys, ½ bushel of cranberries; Miss Mary E. Freeman, 2 turkeys; D. C. Briggs, 3 turkeys; Mrs. W. Howard Hart, 1 turkey, 1 quart cream; Mrs. E. G. Gilbert, 1 turkey; Mrs. H. G. Ludlow, 1 turkey; Mrs. W. P. Tillman, 1 barrel apples; Mrs. Frederic A. Sabbaton, 1 turkey; Mrs. William H. Doughty, camp chair, sled, velocipede; Mrs. F. W. Farnam, 1 turkey; Mrs. Wm. E. Gilbert, 1 turkey; T. H. Shield, Pawling avenue, $5; Mrs. S. A. Peterson, 1 turkey, 1 bushel pound sweet apples; Mrs. Charles Cleminshaw, 2 chickens, 5 bunches celery, 5 pounds candy; Mrs. John B. Gale, 1 turkey; Mrs. W. P. Warren, 2 turkeys, 6 pairs woolen stockings; V. A. DeFreest, 1 turkey, 2 quarts cranberries; Mrs. Wm. O. Cunningham, a quantity of illustrated papers, picture cord, 6 pairs woolen stockings, 3 packages of drawing cards, colored crayons, game of authors, 3 strings of beads, handsome bow and arrow; Miss Sarah T. Moore, knitting 2 pairs mittens; Miss L. B. Laselle, a box of wings for girls' hats; the Apollo commandery, a handsomely framed photographed group of the sir knights for the new schoolroom; Mrs. Dr. Cutler, lemonade from Harmony hall; Master Griswold Green, 3 handsome books, 40 illustrated; J. H. Kellogg, 400 copies of the Centennial temperance service; Wm. Platt, repairing clock; Mrs. Wm. H. Doughty, 5 books, 4 boxes of puzzles, 1 box blocks, 1 box tenpins, 1 box letters, tin closet, 2 boxes of animals, 3 dustpans, harmonicon, hoops, etc.; Mrs. E. B. Cox, 10 lbs. crackers; Mrs. Wm. H. Young, 5 quires paper, 8 packages of envelopes, 12 passbooks; Park Presbyterian church, an invitation to Thanksgiving service, every child presented with an orange and apple; Saxe, the confectioner, 11 lbs. candy; the United national bank, a quantity of the Grant mourning drapery; E. & A. A. Bunce, 120 qts. of milk during the year; Vale bakery, ½ bu. cranberries; Troy Times and Press, for publishing the list.

A list of donations and donors to the orphanage on December 2, 1885.

On an optimistic note, the annual report of 1863 wrote:

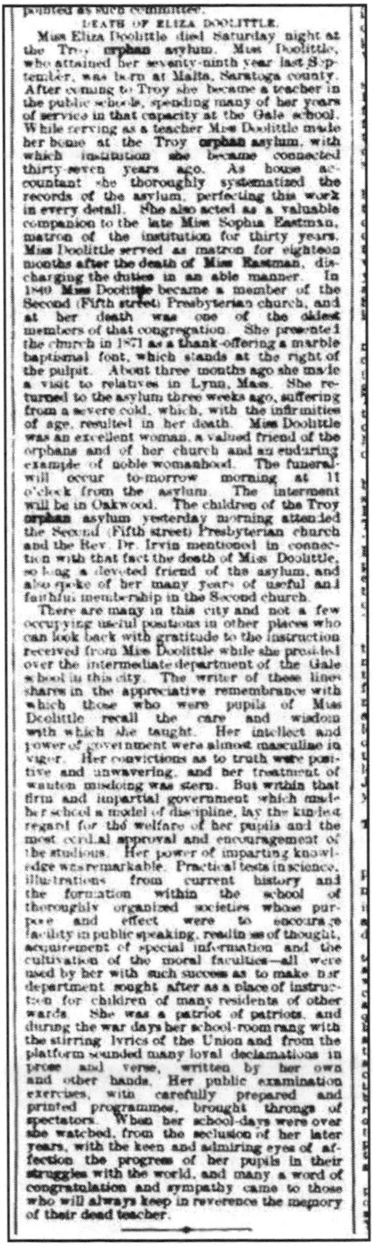

pointed as such committee.

DEATH OF ELIZA DOOLITTLE.

Miss Eliza Doolittle died Saturday night at the Troy orphan asylum. Miss Doolittle, who attained her seventy-ninth year last September, was born at Malta, Saratoga county. After coming to Troy she became a teacher in the public schools, spending many of her years of service in that capacity at the Gale school. While serving as a teacher Miss Doolittle made her home at the Troy orphan asylum, with which institution she became connected thirty-seven years ago. As house accountant she thoroughly systematized the records of the asylum, perfecting this work in every detail. She also acted as a valuable companion to the late Miss Sophia Eastman, matron of the institution for thirty years. Miss Doolittle served as matron for eighteen months after the death of Miss Eastman, discharging the duties in an able manner. In 1840 Miss Doolittle became a member of the Second (Fifth street) Presbyterian church, and at her death was one of the oldest members of that congregation. She presented the church in 1871 as a thank-offering a marble baptismal font, which stands at the right of the pulpit. About three months ago she made a visit to relatives in Lynn, Mass. She returned to the asylum three weeks ago, suffering from a severe cold, which, with the infirmities of age, resulted in her death. Miss Doolittle was an excellent woman, a valued friend of the orphans and of her church and an enduring example of noble womanhood. The funeral will occur to-morrow morning at 11 o'clock from the asylum. The interment will be in Oakwood. The children of the Troy orphan asylum yesterday morning attended the Second (Fifth street) Presbyterian church and the Rev. Dr. Irvin mentioned in connection with that fact the death of Miss Doolittle, so long a devoted friend of the asylum, and also spoke of her many years of useful and faithful membership in the Second church.

There are many in this city and not a few occupying useful positions in other places who can look back with gratitude to the instruction received from Miss Doolittle while she presided over the intermediate department of the Gale school in this city. The writer of these lines shares in the appreciative remembrance with which those who were pupils of Miss Doolittle recall the care and wisdom with which she taught. Her intellect and power of government were almost masculine in vigor. Her convictions as to truth were positive and unwavering, and her treatment of wanton misdoing was stern. But within that firm and impartial government which made her school a model of discipline, lay the kindest regard for the welfare of her pupils and the most cordial approval and encouragement of the studious. Her power of imparting knowledge was remarkable. Practical tests in science, illustrations from current history and the formation within the school of thoroughly organized societies whose purpose and effect were to encourage facility in public speaking, readiness of thought, acquirement of special information and the cultivation of the moral faculties—all were used by her with such success as to make her department sought after as a place of instruction for children of many residents of other wards. She was a patriot of patriots, and during the war days her school-room rang with the stirring lyrics of the Union and from the platform sounded many loyal declamations in prose and verse, written by her own and other hands. Her public examination exercises, with carefully prepared and printed programmes, brought throngs of spectators. When her school-days were over she watched, from the seclusion of her later years, with the keen and admiring eyes of affection the progress of her pupils in their struggles with the world, and many a word of congratulation and sympathy came to those who will always keep in reverence the memory of their dead teacher.

Obit for Eliza Doolittle, one of the Asylum's school teachers, January 4, 1886.

"In 1862 our Asylum was buried in ashes — furniture, clothing, every possession laid waste — and yet, today, we feel that our permanency as one of the leading charities of the city was never established on so firm a basis."

In April 1864, the new building was ready to occupy and about 100 children were moved from the Lansingburgh site (on April 21 or 26, both dates are published), where they had stayed for nearly two years. The new building was 100 by 50 feet rectangular in shape, made of brick, three stories high, and was on the east side of Eighth Street, at number 804 (in 1884 listed as number 804, the numbers changed the next year to the 300s and in 1886 listed as 294 Eighth Street), a short distance south of Hoosick Street (the site is now vacant) and adjacent or south of Elm Place, a five building block, still there. For 29 years the orphanage looked over the north central part of Troy. In the 39th annual report in 1871 it listed a total of 129 orphans living there that year. Some 51 were dismissed or placed in homes, one removed by death, and the current population at the end of the year was 77 children, 42 boys and 35 girls. They also noted the death of one of their long time trustees, George Vail, then president of the board and a member of almost thirty years.

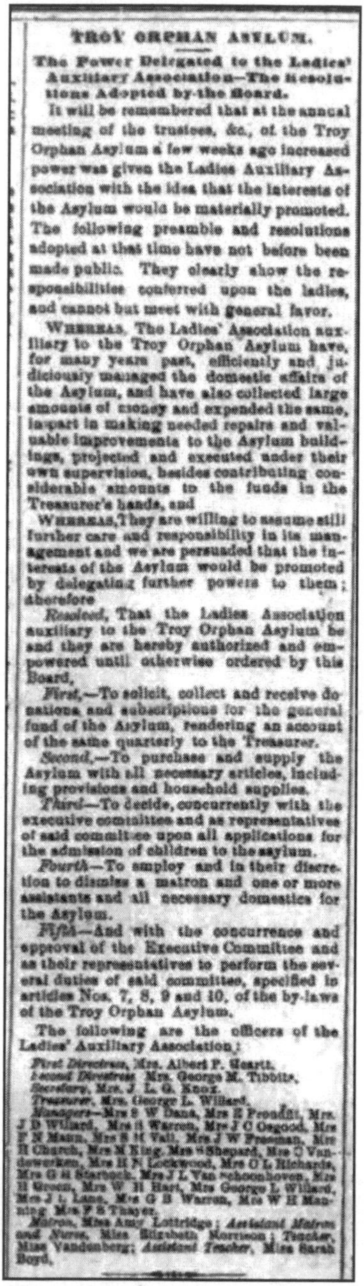

TROY ORPHAN ASYLUM.

The Power Delegated to the Ladies' Auxiliary Association—The Resolutions Adopted by the Board.

It will be remembered that at the annual meeting of the trustees, &c., of the Troy Orphan Asylum a few weeks ago increased power was given the Ladies Auxiliary Association with the idea that the interests of the Asylum would be materially promoted. The following preamble and resolutions adopted at that time have not before been made public. They clearly show the responsibilities conferred upon the ladies, and cannot but meet with general favor.

WHEREAS, The Ladies' Association auxiliary to the Troy Orphan Asylum have, for many years past, efficiently and judiciously managed the domestic affairs of the Asylum, and have also collected large amounts of money and expended the same, in part in making needed repairs and valuable improvements to the Asylum buildings, projected and executed under their own supervision, besides contributing considerable amounts to the funds in the Treasurer's hands, and

WHEREAS, They are willing to assume still further care and responsibility in its management and we are persuaded that the interests of the Asylum would be promoted by delegating further powers to them; therefore

Resolved, That the Ladies Association auxiliary to the Troy Orphan Asylum be and they are hereby authorized and empowered until otherwise ordered by this Board,

First,—To solicit, collect and receive donations and subscriptions for the general fund of the Asylum, rendering an account of the same quarterly to the Treasurer.

Second,—To purchase and supply the Asylum with all necessary articles, including provisions and household supplies.

Third—To decide, concurrently with the executive committee and as representatives of said committee upon all applications for the admission of children to the asylum.

Fourth—To employ and in their discretion to dismiss a matron and one or more assistants and all necessary domestics for the Asylum.

Fifth—And with the concurrence and approval of the Executive Committee and as their representatives to perform the several duties of said committee, specified in articles Nos. 7, 8, 9 and 10, of the by-laws of the Troy Orphan Asylum.

The following are the officers of the Ladies' Auxiliary Association:

First Directress, Mrs. Albert P. Heartt.
Second Directress, Mrs. George M. Tibbits.
Secretary, Mrs. J. L. G. Knox.
Treasurer, Mrs. George L. Willard.
Managers—Mrs [illegible] W Dana, Mrs [illegible], Mrs J D Willard, Mrs [illegible] Warren, Mrs J C Osgood, Mrs F N Mann, Mrs [illegible] Vail, Mrs J W Freeman, Mrs H Church, Mrs M King, Mrs [illegible] Shepard, Mrs [illegible] Vandewerken, Mrs H P Lockwood, Mrs O L Richards, Mrs G H Starbuck, Mrs J L Van Schoonhoven, Mrs H Green, Mrs W H Hart, Mrs George L Willard, Mrs J L Lane, Mrs G B Warren, Mrs W H Manning, Mrs F S Thayer.
Matron, Miss Amy Lottridge; *Assistant Matron and Nurse*, Miss Elizabeth Morrison; *Teacher*, Miss Vandenberg; *Assistant Teacher*, Miss Sarah Boyd.

Power to fire was given to the ladies in 1873.

"Yesterday morning, the children of the Orphan Asylum on Eighth Street were provided with a treat that was hardly less pleasant than that of their more fortunate brothers and sisters who are blessed with parents and

Headstone for Eliza Doolittle, one of the Asylum's school teachers, at Oakwood Cemetery. January 4, 1886. Photo from Find A Grave uploaded by Danielle Machynski Calhoun.

happy homes. The tree, presented by Thomas McManus, was an unusually fine one and was decorated and loaded with presents with a taste and generosity that speak well for the ladies who prepared it."

-Troy Daily Times, December 29, 1871

During much of 1871, slanderous letters appeared in local newspapers and printed brochures were passed around the city accusing the institution particularly accusing the Ladies' Association Auxiliary of nefarious deeds but no specific charges were ever made and a thorough investigation turned up nothing.

This likely was over the dismissal of the matron Miss Amy Davis Lottridge in 1871 for severely whipping two of the children. In the Ladies' Auxiliary minutes they write:

"Corporal punishment of the children by and of the officers of the house, and resolved to be decidedly wrong and to be prohibited – such dissatisfaction expressed at the course of the present matron in this respect and a change decided upon – the secretary was requested to

write a note to Miss Lottridge expressing the feelings and a decision of the managers."

"Sept 20 Wed 1871

The matter of the matron still exciting a great deal of feeling and discussion of the note sent by the secretary to Miss Lottridge had not been noticed and it was resolved unanimously that "the extension of the present matron was not desirable" and the secretary was requested to send a note to the Trustees to that effect - Mrs. Heartt stated that she retained the note to Miss Lottridge until the month of August hoping it might not be necessary to send it and sent it then only after another child had been severely whipped."

Amy Lottridge, the center of the whipping controversy in 1871, moved on and married Robert Coffin and is buried in Oakwood Cemetery in Bedford County Virginia. Photo by Darrell Landrum.

Lottridge was fired but the men on the Board of Trustees apparently were not pleased the women went over their heads.

"A great deal of discussion and feeling regarding the trouble occasioned by the dismissal of Miss Lottridge. Resolution passed that there should be a monthly meeting of the managers at the asylum and general

vigilance of house committee. "

Finally the men called for a special meeting.

"A special meeting of the ladies asked to take into consideration the vote of the trustees approving a committee of investigation into the causes of the dismissal of matron etc., the committee of three trustees were invited to meet with the ladies and Judge Mann and Mr. G.W. Tibbits were there. Mr. Burdett sent a note regretting his absence from town that day the gentlemen were requested to ask the managers any questions that they desire to ask and a special discussion of the matter ensued. Three ladies were invited to be present at the asylum at the meeting of the investigation committee and the ladies executive committee was requested by the ladies to be present, Mrs. Heartt, Proudfit and Knox."

As a result the bylaws were rewritten so that the ladies did have the power to make these kind of decisions. In 1873, *The Troy Whig* printed the changes.

In 1872 there were 129 children at the orphanage. Some 51 were dismissed or placed in homes, one removed by death, leaving at the end of the year 77 in total, 42 boys and 35 girls.

On February. 1, 1884, the funeral of Mrs Mary A. Greenman, matron at the Troy Orphan Asylum occurred from the Church of the Holy Cross. The children of the asylum with the officers and teachers attended as a body. It was also the year that the Apollo Commandery, Knights Templars, finished an unfinished part of the third story for a dormitory.

By 1886, the orphanage had taken in 1,743 children. On September 7, 1886, the Trustees discussed the possibility of purchasing the Saxton Farm on Pawling Avenue. However after three years on July 1, 1889, they received notice that they would receive as a gift a beautiful farm of 109 acres within the city of Troy along Hollow Road (now called Spring Avenue) by Mrs. Charles B. Russell, Mrs. Mary E. Hart, Mrs. Margaret E. Proudfit and Mrs Mary B. Tillinghast. The only stipulation is that new buildings would have to be erected within five years. By December 1890, one half of the necessary funds were raised. In the spring of 1890 (or 1891) the design by H. Langford Warren, head of the architecture department at Harvard and practicing architect from Boston was accepted and work began. In 1886 Miss Grace L. White was the matron. Charles W. Tillinghast was president of the board: Lewis E. Gurley, Vice President; William H. Hollister, Jr., Secretary; and Aaron Vail, treasurer. Other board members included Otis G. Clark, John S. Perry, Harvey J. King, Joseph W. Fuller, George H. Starbuck, Dudley Tibbits, P. M. Converse, Francis N. Mann, Jr., John Wool Griswold, Uri Gilbert, Charles N. Lockwood, William Kemp, William Howard Doughty, Liberty Gilbert, Walter P. Warren, G. Ludlow, and George B. Cluett - a virtual who's who of Troy's business and civic leaders of the time.

The former three story Asylum on Eighth Street from 1864-1893 was used by Samaritan Hospital until 1914. In February of 1921 and again in June of

1922 the building suffered fires. In 1924, then unoccupied, it was considered for a new Masonic Temple. When it was torn down is unknown.

Ironically, the corner stone of the Spring Avenue home was on the same day, thirty years to the day after the great fire destroyed their Division Street home, May 10, 1892. The Troy Daily Times, May 10, 1892, recorded the ceremonies:

"The corner stone of the new Troy Orphan Asylum was laid this afternoon. The children of the Asylum were present and an interesting program was given. The exercises opened at four o'clock, with the singing of "America." Rev. Dr. Eben Halley, of the Second Street Presbyterian Church offered prayer. The address of welcome was delivered by D. W. Tillinghast. The stone is in the front wall of the trustees' room, west of the main entrance. An address was given by Rev. Dr. J. W. Thompson, pastor of the State Street Methodist Church and Rev. L. M. S. Haynes, of the Third Street Baptist Church. "

The corner stone box contained a number of items from a history of the asylum by A. J. Weise, a local historian and writer, the 58th annual report of the Trustees, newspapers, money of the day, and other mementos. This was the beginning of a long tenure at this location as they neared the beginning of the 20th century. The cornerstone contents resides at the Rennselaer County Historical Society today.

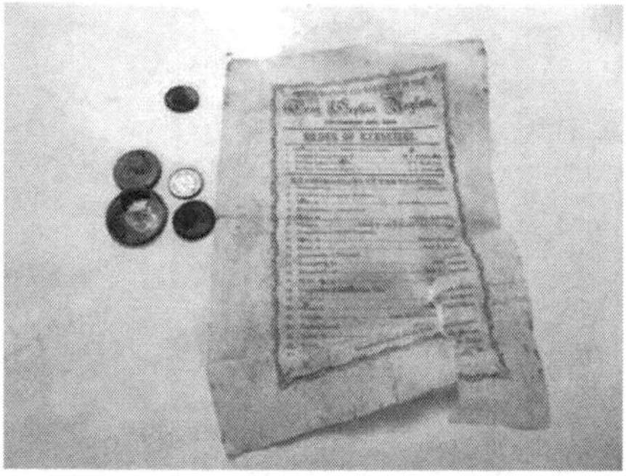

Part of the items recovered in the TOA Time Capsule. 1893. Photos by Mary Valek.

Chapter 5

The Spring Avenue Years, 1893-1980

When the orphan administration decided to build a new asylum on Spring Avenue, they put out a competition for designs. Boston architect Herbert Langford Warren[1] was successful and he was one of the outstanding architects of the time. Warren had worked for H. H. Richardson in the Romanesque style, later working in his own firm of Warren, Smith

LAYING THE CORNER STONE OF THE NEW TROY ORPHAN ASSYLUM.

[1] Coolidge, Charles A. Charles A. Coolidge Proceedings of the American Academy of Arts and Sciences, Vol. 68, No. 13 (Dec., 1933),pp. 689-691.

HERBERT LANGFORD WARREN
1857-1917

and Biscoe, and in 1888 became a professor and head of the department at Harvard. He is well known for many architectural projects including gothic revival churches in Cliftondale and Winchester, Massachusetts, a

Children in the classroom. Notice they are all wearing their uniforms.

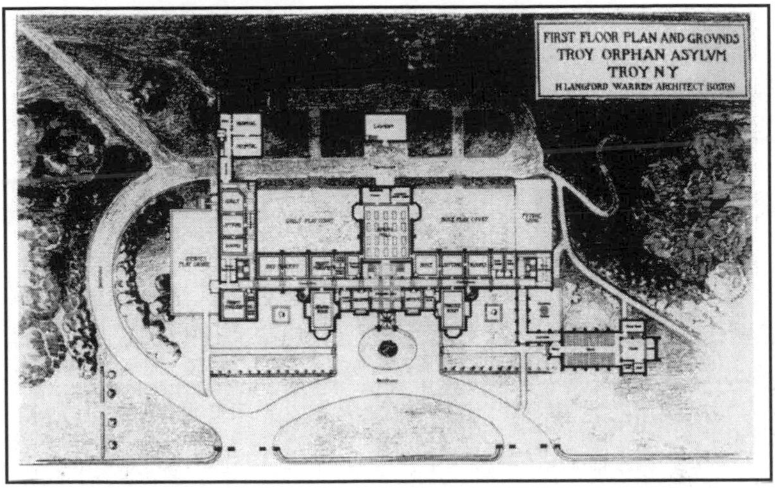

The original map drawing by H. L. Warren for the new asylum on Spring Avenue.

chapel for the New Church Theological School in Cambridge, Massachusetts, the National Church of the Holy City in Washington D.C, and campus plan and main building for the Women's Methodist College (now Huntingdon College) in Montgomery Alabama, to name a few. He was no stranger to Troy. He set up an office in the city and designed a residence for A. Alexander Orr in 1889, reconstruction of buildings for C. E. Patterson in 1890, and a study for residences and apartment house for W. H. Doughty in 1890. All of these projects were before receiving the contract for the Troy Orphan Asylum. He also designed the Saratoga Racing Association grandstand, clubhouse and betting ring in 1891-92.

Troy Orphan Asylum in 1900. The orphan asylum was close to the Emma Willard School at the intersection of Spring and Pawling Avenues. Harvard Collection.

Views of the Asylum in 1900. Harvard Collection. Dutch elements were added perhaps to pay tribute to Troy's Dutch heritage.

Carriage entrance, 1900. Below a postcard from 1947 showing the grounds and buildings.

In 1891, Warren received the commission to build the asylum. Warren preferred Gothic over Romanesque architecture at the time, so he designed

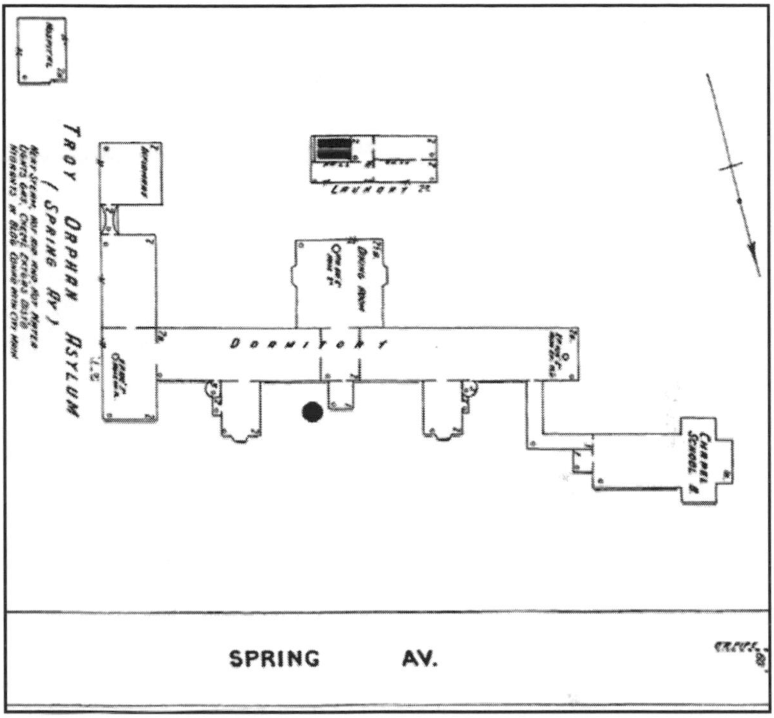

Grounds and building layout of the Asylum on the 1904 Sanborn Insurance map.

The Tillinghast Chapel.

Shep, Vanderheyden's pet dog that followed the 6th graders to school each day.

Albany's Vanderheyden Palace, the home of Jacob Vanderheyden from around 1790 to 1823, may have been the inspiration for the design of Troy's orphan buildings.

Troy Orphan Asylum boys picking currants for the Red Cross on the Clapp Farm, Kinderhook, NY, in July 1917.

Children having breakfast. Unknown date.

the asylum to instill an English Tudor style and this project was considered one of his major works. The complex featured steeply pitched slate roofs with dormers and two stair towers. According to author Maureen Meister in her book "Architecture and the Arts and Crafts Movement in Boston (2003):

"He incorporated a stepped gale ends and a brown and red patterned brickwork and gives the building its Gothic cast with a sparing use of tracery in a few of the windows. The tracery was thin as Warren abandoned the heavier forms of the 1880s and so the building was treated with a restraint. It also allowed Warren to get involved with landscape design. This was in response of his working with Frederick Law Olmsted and Richardson when the three worked on Oakes Ames Memorial Hall in North Easton. Warren developed an integrated building and landscape plan that connected the interior spaces with outdoor play spaces for the children. At the far end of the building, the night an day nurseries

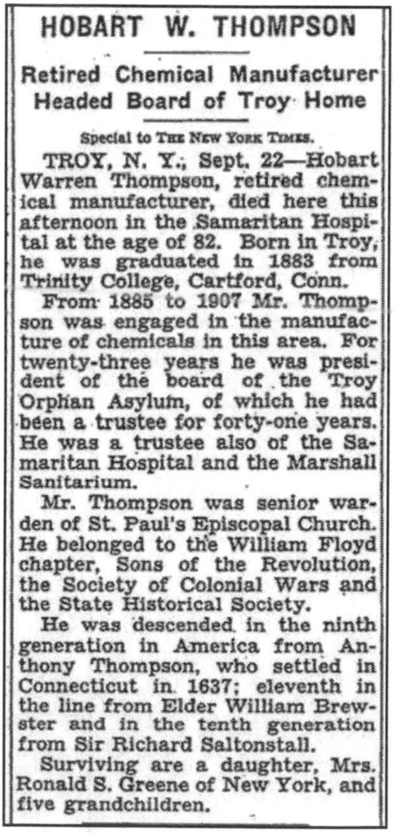

HOBART W. THOMPSON

Retired Chemical Manufacturer Headed Board of Troy Home

Special to THE NEW YORK TIMES.

TROY, N. Y., Sept. 22—Hobart Warren Thompson, retired chemical manufacturer, died here this afternoon in the Samaritan Hospital at the age of 82. Born in Troy, he was graduated in 1883 from Trinity College, Cartford, Conn.

From 1885 to 1907 Mr. Thompson was engaged in the manufacture of chemicals in this area. For twenty-three years he was president of the board of the Troy Orphan Asylum, of which he had been a trustee for forty-one years. He was a trustee also of the Samaritan Hospital and the Marshall Sanitarium.

Mr. Thompson was senior warden of St. Paul's Episcopal Church. He belonged to the William Floyd chapter, Sons of the Revolution, the Society of Colonial Wars and the State Historical Society.

He was descended in the ninth generation in America from Anthony Thompson, who settled in Connecticut in 1637; eleventh in the line from Elder William Brewster and in the tenth generation from Sir Richard Saltonstall.

Surviving are a daughter, Mrs. Ronald S. Greene of New York, and five grandchildren.

Obituary of longtime TOA board president who died in May, 1944.

Troy Orphan Asylum Basketball Team.

opened onto a large infants' playground, enclosed by a brick wall. Elsewhere, two large terraces provided play areas for boys and girls. The main building led through a cloister to a chapel, built a few years later. The intermediate space of the covered passage, connecting indoors and outdoors, exposed the children to fresh air, yet it would have sheltered them on days when the weather was inhospitable. Warren would continue to design walled gardens and terraces, especially in his residential projects, including some on a

TROY

	F.B.	F.G.	T.P.
Hansen, rf.	3	2	8
Lawton, lf.	1	0	2
L. Elden, c.	5	0	10
Fletcher, rg.	4	0	8
Coonradt, lg.	1	2	4
Pettit, rf.	0	0	0
D. Elden, lg.	0	0	0
Totals	14	4	32

HUDSON.

	F.B.	F.G.	T.P.
Staats, rf.	0	1	1
Bowush, lf.	3	3	9
Tanzillo, c.	1	0	2
Mitchinson, rg.	7	1	15
Polock, lg.	1	0	2
Moe, rf.	0	0	0
Hollran, c.	0	0	0
Brenner, c.	0	0	0
Totals	12	5	29

Referee — Huddleston. Score at half time—12-11, Troy. Team fouls called—11-8, Troy.

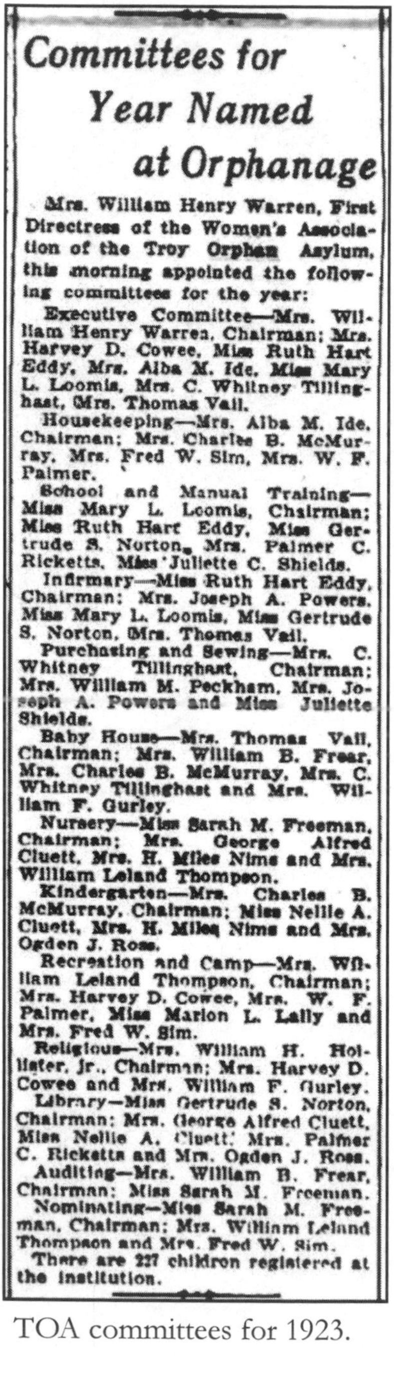

Committees for Year Named at Orphanage

Mrs. William Henry Warren, First Directress of the Women's Association of the Troy Orphan Asylum, this morning appointed the following committees for the year:

Executive Committee—Mrs. William Henry Warren, Chairman; Mrs. Harvey D. Cowee, Miss Ruth Hart Eddy, Mrs. Alba M. Ide, Miss Mary L. Loomis, Mrs. C. Whitney Tillinghast, Mrs. Thomas Vail.

Housekeeping—Mrs. Alba M. Ide, Chairman; Mrs. Charles B. McMurray, Mrs. Fred W. Sim, Mrs. W. F. Palmer.

School and Manual Training—Miss Mary L. Loomis, Chairman; Miss Ruth Hart Eddy, Miss Gertrude S. Norton, Mrs. Palmer C. Ricketts, Miss Juliette C. Shields.

Infirmary—Miss Ruth Hart Eddy, Chairman; Mrs. Joseph A. Powers, Miss Mary L. Loomis, Miss Gertrude S. Norton, Mrs. Thomas Vail.

Purchasing and Sewing—Mrs. C. Whitney Tillinghast, Chairman; Mrs. William M. Peckham, Mrs. Joseph A. Powers and Miss Juliette Shields.

Baby House—Mrs. Thomas Vail, Chairman; Mrs. William B. Frear, Mrs. Charles B. McMurray, Mrs. C. Whitney Tillinghast and Mrs. William F. Gurley.

Nursery—Miss Sarah M. Freeman, Chairman; Mrs. George Alfred Cluett, Mrs. H. Miles Nims and Mrs. William Leland Thompson.

Kindergarten—Mrs. Charles B. McMurray, Chairman; Miss Nellie A. Cluett, Mrs. H. Miles Nims and Mrs. Ogden J. Ross.

Recreation and Camp—Mrs. William Leland Thompson, Chairman; Mrs. Harvey D. Cowee, Mrs. W. F. Palmer, Miss Marion L. Lally and Mrs. Fred W. Sim.

Religious—Mrs. William H. Hollister, Jr., Chairman; Mrs. Harvey D. Cowee and Mrs. William F. Gurley.

Library—Miss Gertrude S. Norton, Chairman; Mrs. George Alfred Cluett, Miss Nellie A. Cluett; Mrs. Palmer C. Ricketts and Mrs. Ogden J. Ross.

Auditing—Mrs. William B. Frear, Chairman; Miss Sarah M. Freeman.

Nominating—Miss Sarah M. Freeman, Chairman; Mrs. William Leland Thompson and Mrs. Fred W. Sim.

There are 227 children registered at the institution.

TOA committees for 1923.

relatively small scale. These features interested other architects of the era, but they appeared with special frequency in Warren's work."

The new Asylum building was completed and on August 17, 1893 two trolleys from the Troy City Railways carried the children for free to their new home. Upon entering the grounds, Clinton H. Meneely, bell maker from Troy presented the home with a brand new bell and was rung to mark the occasion. The Reverend James Caird, Rector at the Church of Ascension on Pawling Avenue, made remarks and prayer and the children sang "Praise God from Whom all Blessing Flow." A dining room was decorated with flowers and the children

The main hall at Vanderheyden.

Boys working in the wood shop in 1914.

Nursing program graduates in 1911 Troy Orphan Asylum Training School for Children's Nurses.

and staff enjoyed a big supper.

For the next few decades more buildings were added. In 1893, Mrs. William Howard Hart (who was

Sliding down the slide in 1911.

a trustee for 40 years) donated funds to build a hospital and infirmary (annex) to take care of children who were sick and had to be isolated especially if they had a contagious disease. It proved inadequate to separate contagious children so in 1899 with the funding by Mrs. William Howard Hart

Christmas Time at the orphanage.

again, a separate hospital building was built. This was recommended by Dr. H. C. Gardinier who was on the medical staff of the asylum. The Hart Memorial Hospital opened on June 5, 1899, to care for a case of diphtheria under tight quarantine.

Dinner time during Christmas time.

Additional land was purchased for farm purposes and the trustees took over control of the farm which had previously been rented to a local farmer. There was an increase from the original 109 acres to almost 200 acres. The farm had a dairy herd of about 30 milkable Holstein cows, some pigs, and growing vegetable and fruits rounded out providing enough food for the home. Electricity was added, new machinery and a water supply was added. To save money, a separate heating and lighting power plant was built in 1911 serving the entire institution.

In 1901 a new chapel and school room was built with funds from Mr and Mrs Charles W. Tillinghast. He was president of the board of trustees for 39 years and when the chapel was dedicated stated: *"It*

gives me great pleasure, on behalf of Mrs Tillinghast and myself, to present the Trustees of the Troy Orphan Asylum this chapel complete, for devotional and school purses." Further: *"I beg to acknowledge the gift of 300 books for the use of the chapel, from the Mann endowment fund of St. John's Church, by the late Judge Francis N. Mann."*

Since Langford Warren was the original architect for the asylum he was chosen as the architect so the new chapel blended well into the main buildings. The Troy Daily Press describes the chapel on September 12, 1901:

The girls making garments in 1913.

"The chapel is a handsome structure of the Gothic style of architecture. It is of red brick, with brownstone trimmings, connected with the mail structure by a cloister. A large room for day school has accommodations for 150 children. The school room is provided with all the modern capacity of about 300. Stained glass windows and a series of arches beautify the interior. The furniture is of the best quartered oak, the floors are polished hardwood. The organ is in keeping with the rest of the building."

The chapel provided room for religious services but also the rules included that in the afternoon of the Sabbath a house would be set aside for:

"undenominational religious services" and *"instruction in the Scriptures, and such song and prayer service or religious instruction shall be had daily as my be directed."*

A few years later accommodations were provided to create a Training School for Nursing Maids.

However, by 1903 the new orphanage was crowded with 248 children and new land was needed to expand. On March 10, 1904, lighting struck the stable at the orphanage. While the building did not burn the bolt left a large hole in the roof.

In 1905 a training school for girls was opened to help girls to train for self support and to meet the constant appeal of housewives for "mother's helpers." It was called the "Training School for Nursery Maids." In 1907 land to the east of the site, known as the McChesney property, was acquired and during this year a piece of land at the junction of Pawling and Spring Avenues, known as the Point, was donated by the Harrison family. That portion was expanded

Presentation of Flag.

A large United States flag was presented to the Troy Orphana Asylum yesterday afternoon by the Gen. J. B. Carr Circle, G. A. R. Many were present at the presentation, including the children and the members of the circle. Mrs. Carrie Miller, patriotic instructor, presented the flag, and Superintendent Herbert J. Hunn made the speech of acceptance. The following program was carried out: Song, "America;" devotional service, Rev. E. A. Loux; address, Ezra Stillman, Post Griswold, G. A. R.; recitation, "Makers of the Flag," Avides Demerjian and Cecil Kline ,of Troy Orphan Asylum; address, Frederick E. Draper; address, Rev. E. A. Loux; catechism of flag, Mrs. Helen Brooks, President of Gen. J. B. Carr Circle; response, Miss Grace DeLong of Troy Orphan Asylum; salute to flag, under supervision of Mrs. Elisabeth Fowler Hilton; song, "The Star Spangled Banner;" beudiction by Rev. E. A. Loux.

April 19, 1917

Election at Troy Orphan Asylum.

The Women's Auxiliary of the Troy Orphan Asylum this morning elected these officers: First Directress, Mrs. William H. Hollister, jr.; Second Directress, Mrs. Edward M. Green; Third Directress, Mrs. Charles Cleminshaw; Fourth Directress, Mrs. S. A. Peterson; Fifth Directress, Mrs. William H. Warren; Secretary, Miss Marion Lally; Treasurer, Mrs. George B. Cluett. Two new managers were named, Mrs. Charles B. McMurray and Miss Stella Stow. Under present conditions it was thought best not to solicit donations for the Thanksgiving dinner owing to the stress of the times. However, Mrs. Charles Cleminshaw did not wish the children to be deprived of their customary dinner and she offered to give twenty-five turkeys.

November 3, 1914 elections.

when the Asylum and nearby Emma Willard School jointly purchased a larger portion that was adjacent to the donated parcel for the purpose to *"prevent the erection of buildings on the site that might mar the landscape between the new seminary buildings and the asylum. The strip of land will be improved and made into a private park."*

To insure that the children were given proper and adequate physical fitness training, the wife of Samuel A. Peterson, a patron of the asylum and prominent coal dealer, (Peterson & Packer Coal Company) donated $50,000 to build a suitable building. It was completed in 1911 and dedicated as the Peterson Memorial Building for Manual Arts on October 18. An additional $35,000 was made in 1921 in the will of his wife who died and was used to repair and equip the building. In 1912 a modern power plant was built to provide steam and electric light to the entire location. This also included a power laundry and the creation of a farm of 110 acres supplying milk, pork, and vegetables.

It was clear that the size of the institution warranted a full time administrator and in 1913, Herbert J. Hunn became the superintendent of the Troy Orphan Asylum. The August 30, 1913, edition of *The Troy Times* published a feature on the new administrator titled "Supervised Activity:" *New Superintendent of the Troy Orphan Asylum, who believes in the Baseball and the Bat and the Needle and the Cook*

Orphan Asylum Notes.

Graduating exercises of the school for training children's nurses at the Troy Orphan Asylum will be held Thursday afternoon, June 3, at the asylum building, followed by the annual dinner of the alumnae and graduates.

Superintendent H. J. Hunn of the Troy Orphan Asylum will speak before the Church Federation at the Young Men's Christian Association building Monday evening at 8 o'clock. He will discuss asylum work.

Flag Day will be appropriately observed at the Troy Orphan Asylum, when the ladies of the G. A. R. propose to present a flag to the asylum.

The girls' chorus of the asylum and some others of the children will attend Children's Day exercises at the Ninth Presbyterian Church Sunday morning, June 13, and at the First Baptist Church Sunday afternoon, June 20, at 5 o'clock.

Sessions of school will be resumed at the Troy Orphan Asylum Monday to continue until June 25. The sessions had been interrupted for three months during the period of quarantine, which was recently lifted. Parents may visit the asylum Saturday, May 29, but no children visitors will be allowed yet.

May 30, 1915.

TOA girls showing off their pickling skills at the Eastern States Expo in September 1921. The previous year three boys from TOA won second prize.

Playtime.

Stove as a Means of Obtaining Better Citizenship."

"There is a man in this town who believes in great activity as a means of interesting, and, thereby, improving the young children in his charge. This man in Henry J. Hunn, who was formerly connected with the work at the young Men's Christian Association and later with the State Charity Department. Mr. Hunn was recently put in charge of the Troy Orphan Asylum. He immediately inaugurated his schemes and they have been most successful. He got the boys in his charge out in the lot with baseball and bats and had them playing baseball. He had them taken down to Smart's Pond for swimming — that is the boys who earned the privilege by good behavior. Then he interested other institutions and inter-institutional baseball games were organized that created rivalry, healthful rivalry, and put a premium on good behavior at the institution."

The Girls Work.
Now he is taking up the girls' side of the work and, beginning September 1, a number of changes will be made to the empaled force of the asylum, so that institution will be able to go more extensively into industrial work. Miss R. Matilda Smyth of Lansingburgh has been engaged as the domestic science teacher. Miss Smyth graduated last June from the department of household economics of the Albany Normal College. She will teach cooking, cutting and sewing clothing and fine laundering. A girls' class in physical culture will also be introduced. Mart, T. Dahon, a graduate of Oberlin College, will become manual trainer. He will also have ninety-four older boys in charge and will conduct regular

gymnasium exercises. Gardening may replace the gym work next spring and summer. Miss Florence Shelley, for some time instructor in needlework at the Young Women's Association, becomes girls' caretaker. She will teach the girls to darn stockings and to perform other household duties. Miss Anna Grant, the nurse at the infirmary, who has been absent three months on a trip to Scotland, and Miss Bertha M. Rothermel, RN, Director of the Training School for Infant's Nurses at the Troy Oprhan Asylum, who has been in Montreal, will return Monday. Miss Rothermel brings with her an applicant for training, which makes the fourth probationer within a week. Miss Elizabeth Geold, in charge of the kindergarten department of the Troy Orphan Asylum returns to this city Monday. On September 8, the dreaded school of the Troy Orphan Asylum opens its season with Miss Edith Foster, Principal, and her assistants who have been re-engaged for the coming season."

Instead of treating the residents of the asylum as one large body, the administrators and staff gave more attention to individual needs and gave the children more freedom in expressing themselves, deciding their future, deciding their own dress for the day (no more uniforms), when to play and other factors that allowed them to develop their personality and not just be "good" but to be *"good for something."* The administration however made it a priority when it came to health and made sure each child had proper examinations, inoculations, and overall good health. This attitude had obvious results that can be seen by the many success stories from

TOP: Staff taking care of the little ones.

BOTTOM. Staff and young woman who may be going through the baby nurse training program.

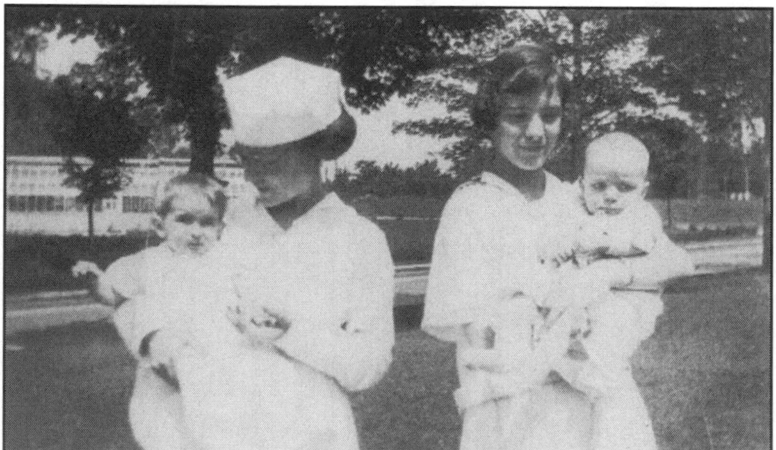

Baseball legend Johnny Evers gave a pep talk to the Orphan boys in 1915.

those who were residents. The practice of binding out children at an early age for employment was not continued and by fourteen years of age the child could choose his or her own guardian. Many became doctors, judges, teachers, clergy, bankers, nurses and served with honor in the military.

The daily task of watching the children.

Children posing in front of the buildings, circa 1930s.

In January 1915, Ms. A. Frances Chambers became the new principal of the grade school at the Asylum. She replaced the late Edith J. Foster. Chambers had

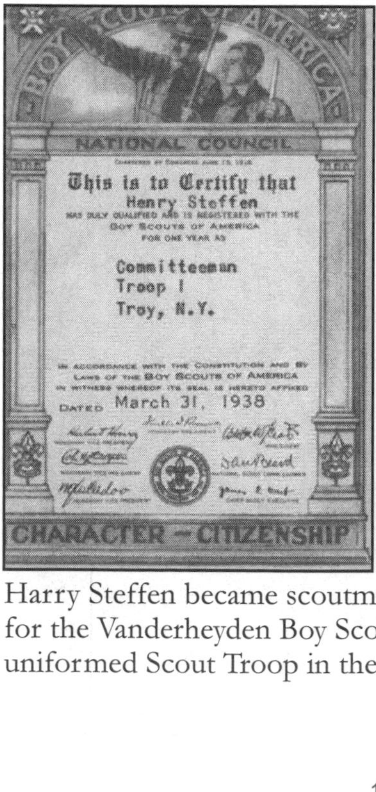

BOY SCOUTS OF AMERICA

NATIONAL COUNCIL

This is to Certify that
Henry Steffen
HAS DULY QUALIFIED AND IS REGISTERED WITH THE
BOY SCOUTS OF AMERICA
FOR ONE YEAR AS

Committeeman
Troop 1
Troy, N.Y.

IN ACCORDANCE WITH THE CONSTITUTION AND BY LAWS OF THE BOY SCOUTS OF AMERICA
IN WITNESS WHEREOF ITS SEAL IS HERETO AFFIXED

DATED March 31, 1938

CHARACTER — CITIZENSHIP

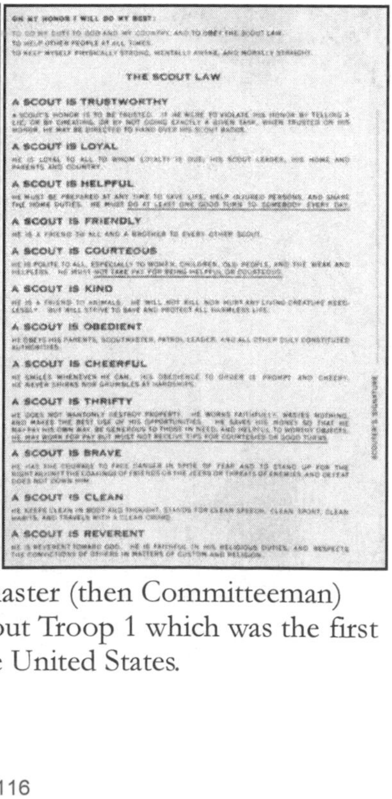

ON MY HONOR I WILL DO MY BEST:

THE SCOUT LAW

A SCOUT IS TRUSTWORTHY

A SCOUT IS LOYAL

A SCOUT IS HELPFUL

A SCOUT IS FRIENDLY

A SCOUT IS COURTEOUS

A SCOUT IS KIND

A SCOUT IS OBEDIENT

A SCOUT IS CHEERFUL

A SCOUT IS THRIFTY

A SCOUT IS BRAVE

A SCOUT IS CLEAN

A SCOUT IS REVERENT

Harry Steffen became scoutmaster (then Committeeman) for the Vanderheyden Boy Scout Troop 1 which was the first uniformed Scout Troop in the United States.

Toddlers in their uniforms.

The annual outing for the Troy Orphan Asylum by the Bethlehem Star Chapter of the O.E.S. (Order of the Eastern Star). This annual event originally was sponsored each summer by funeral director Marvin H. Clark and his wife Maria beginning in 1893 until his death in 1898. The O.E.S. chapter took it over and continued it for years. Unknown date.

already been in charge of the third grade. Ms. Ethel M. Ten Broeck took her place there. Two days later the Troy Orphan Asylum basketball team played the Troy Boys' Club team and a surprise guest in the form of baseball's John J. Evers of the Boston Braves National League team visited and gave the orphan boys *"some advice to them as to what they should do to be successful in life."* Evers was born in Troy on July 21, 1881. He was a second baseman and manager later in life. He played in the majors from 1902 through 1917 for the Chicago Cubs, Boston Braves and Philadelphia Phillies. He also appeared in one

Halloween Party. On November 1, 1923, department employees acted as judges and gave out prizes. After a grand march through the building, they went to Peterson Hall where they had refreshments.

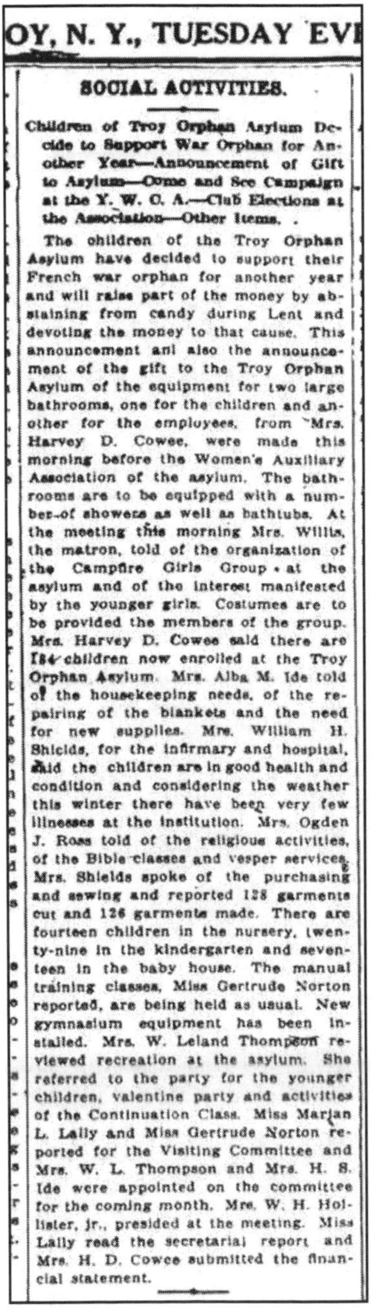

OY, N. Y., TUESDAY EV

SOCIAL ACTIVITIES.

Children of Troy Orphan Asylum Decide to Support War Orphan for Another Year—Announcement of Gift to Asylum—Come and See Campaign at the Y. W. C. A.—Club Elections at the Association—Other Items.

The children of the Troy Orphan Asylum have decided to support their French war orphan for another year and will raise part of the money by abstaining from candy during Lent and devoting the money to that cause. This announcement ani also the announcement of the gift to the Troy Orphan Asylum of the equipment for two large bathrooms, one for the children and another for the employees, from Mrs. Harvey D. Cowee, were made this morning before the Women's Auxiliary Association of the asylum. The bathrooms are to be equipped with a number of showers as well as bathtubs. At the meeting this morning Mrs. Willis, the matron, told of the organization of the Campfire Girls Group at the asylum and of the interest manifested by the younger girls. Costumes are to be provided the members of the group. Mrs. Harvey D. Cowee said there are 184 children now enrolled at the Troy Orphan Asylum. Mrs. Alba M. Ide told of the housekeeping needs, of the repairing of the blankets and the need for new supplies. Mrs. William H. Shields, for the infirmary and hospital, said the children are in good health and condition and considering the weather this winter there have been very few illnesses at the institution. Mrs. Ogden J. Ross told of the religious activities, of the Bible classes and vesper services. Mrs. Shields spoke of the purchasing and sewing and reported 128 garments cut and 126 garments made. There are fourteen children in the nursery, twenty-nine in the kindergarten and seventeen in the baby house. The manual training classes, Miss Gertrude Norton reported, are being held as usual. New gymnasium equipment has been installed. Mrs. W. Leland Thompson reviewed recreation at the asylum. She referred to the party for the younger children, valentine party and activities of the Continuation Class. Miss Marjan L. Lally and Miss Gertrude Norton reported for the Visiting Committee and Mrs. W. L. Thompson and Mrs. H. S. Ide were appointed on the committee for the coming month. Mrs. W. H. Hollister, jr., presided at the meeting. Miss Lally read the secretarial report and Mrs. H. D. Cowee submitted the financial statement.

March 2, 1920

game a piece for the Chicago White Sox and Braves while coaching them in 1922 and 1929, respectively. Evers helped lead the Cubs to four National League pennants, including two World Series championships. He spent his last days operating a sporting goods store in Albany, New York in 1923.

The year 1923 was the 90th anniversary of the founding of the orphanage and the history of the institution was read by Hobart W. Thompson, president of the board of directors. The celebration was held at Peterson Hall in Troy and all attending listened to the girls' chorus under the leadership of Will H. Wade and accompanied by Jane Ferguson, one of the matrons at the institution. A moving film of activities of the children at the orphanage was shown and it was also shown later at several of the local Troy theaters. Guided tours of all the buildings were given to the public. Up to 10,000 children had gone through the orphanage up to that date.

In 1925, the institution had 205 children at this time. In their annual appeal they needed less thanks to contributions. The Asylum Farm supplied 93,566 quarts of milk, an average of 256 quarts per day of Grade A milk from tuberlin-tested cows all complying with the State health laws. The cost of production was 6.8 cents per quart. The sewing committee announced that the girls had made 268

Prior to 1936 uniforms were abandoned for regular clothes to give the children more freedom of choice.

garments from the sewing club. The year 1925 also saw the employment of a registered nurse as a health nurse so that complete physical and medical tests of each child would be taken upon admission; varied and balanced menus and prompt and adequate dental care. Also included on staff was Dr. W. T. Shields, Jr., as an orthopedic surgeon particularly for tonsils and adenoid operations when necessary. This allowed the closing of the Asylum infirmary for more or less frequent and extended periods during the year. Also added was a new matron, Miss Katherine L. Foster. Frank H. Coffeen added a Sunday school with Bible studies. An additional teacher was added to the grade school. A man was hired to repair and improve the buildings and

The annual outing for 1914 of the Troy Orphan Asylum by the Bethlehem Star Chapter of the O.E.S. (Order of the Eastern Star).

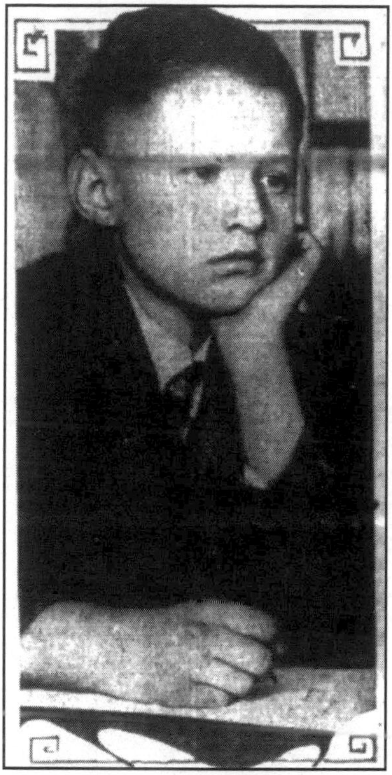

Orphan poet William Krough made the news with his poetry in the 1920s.

grounds. It was estimated that the cost of caring for a child at the asylum was $8.01 per week. Of that amount 92 cents per week was for clothing, $1.54 for food, and $2.50 for supervision. The balance between care of their health, education, religious training, shelter, etc.

In 1927, Superintendent Herbert Hunn was held up and robbed in his automobile by John Mahoney, a Troy man, who was sentenced in January 1928 to 20 years in the Clinton Correctional Facility, a prison in upstate Dannemora, New York.

In 1929 a young 11 year old boy at the Troy Orphan Asylum was featured in the Times Union newspaper titled "Boy Poet in Orphan Asylum." William Krough was called "A Buddin Genius," in a writeup about the young poet. Krough had stated that he liked being at the asylum and did not want to be adopted. Here he had his privacy to write his poems.

Two of his poems were published with the article, one about getting a bloody nose during fun time with another mate.

Over To Peterson's one night
I got a hard punch in the nose,
As a red rose
I ran to the basin,
But someone else was there
With a small comb
A-combing his hair,

I said "Get-out",
But he did not take heed,
Then I yelled "Get out!,
"I'm here in need."

The blood was all over me,
I was a sight,
But I'll never forget
That dark, dark night.

Now it's over,
And I am glad,
But I'll never like another
Like I just had.

He also wrote an ode to Charles Lindbergh proclaiming himself a pronounced prohibitionist:

One day I lay awake,
I'll tell you that it is no fake,
It came upon the twentieth day,
Right in the middle of May.

Everybody was in a commotion,
About the Atlantic ocean.
Lindbergh had a funny notion
To fly across the Atlantic ocean.

He started on a rainy day,
A lot of people bid him stay.
He had a lot of courage and pluck
And a lot of people wished him luck.

He flew to a city across the ocean,
For that was his funny notion,
They offered him some wine,
When he was going to dine.

Did he take it? No. No. No.
Not Charles A. Lindbergh, Oh no,
For the great Charles A. Lindbergh
His heart his country's laws had heard.

In May 1929 The Troy Orphan Asylum baseball team played Watervliet's Fairview Home, the winning team to be dined by the loosing team. This year the orphanage won the interscholastic pennant for the first time in 20 years.

On May 6, 1931, the Asylum lost through death their longtime trustee and secretary Frank E. Norton. Norton was a trustee for thirty-one years and treasurer for thirty-five years.

Many local civil organizations affiliated with the orphanage over the years. In December 1935, the East Side Community Association invited the whole

Boys working the farm in 1938.

The 1938 Camporee at Frear Park. Troop 1 was the first uniformed Boy Scout Troop in America. Bottom left, same.

East Side neighborhood to a night of Christmas carols and more than 400 people attended. A total of 240 children from various organizations

Swinging in the 1930s.

The 1939 Boy Scout troop. Below at Camp Rotary. The orphanage troop was the first uniformed in the country.

Contest Radio Goes to Troy Orphan Asylum

The Troy Orphan Asylum was awarded the Brunswick radio in the recent vote contest at the Warner theatres. It is valued at $160 and of very attractive design. It has been installed in the library of the Troy Orphan Asylum, where the kiddies of the home may assemble and enjoy the programs.

This set is of such a range that the officials at the home can tune in many stations.

The Little Sisters of the Poor received the greatest number of votes in the contest, but rules of the Order of the Little Sisters of the Poor would not permit its acceptance.

The vote contests created much interest on the part of the patrons of the theatres and the result has met with general satisfaction. Frank Farley, manager of the Troy Theatre, presented the radio to Herbert J. Hunn, Superintendent of the Troy Orphan Asylum.

The radio donors included Gordon L. Hayes, Union Furniture Co. Cluett & Sons, Inc., H. T. Miller, H. E. Eckert Sons of Watervliet and Harry H. Henry.

December, 1930

participated including the Troy Orphan Asylum's boys and girls choir. The boys choir opened the festivities with "The First Noel and "Silent Night." The girls choir sang "Away in the Manger," and "Deck the Hall." First place went to the Asylum girls and second prize went to the boys group. Prizes were awarded to the two groups.

By 1938 the Troy Orphan Asylum had served more than 10,000 children and there were 249 children at

Girls posing in their uniforms.

the institution that year.

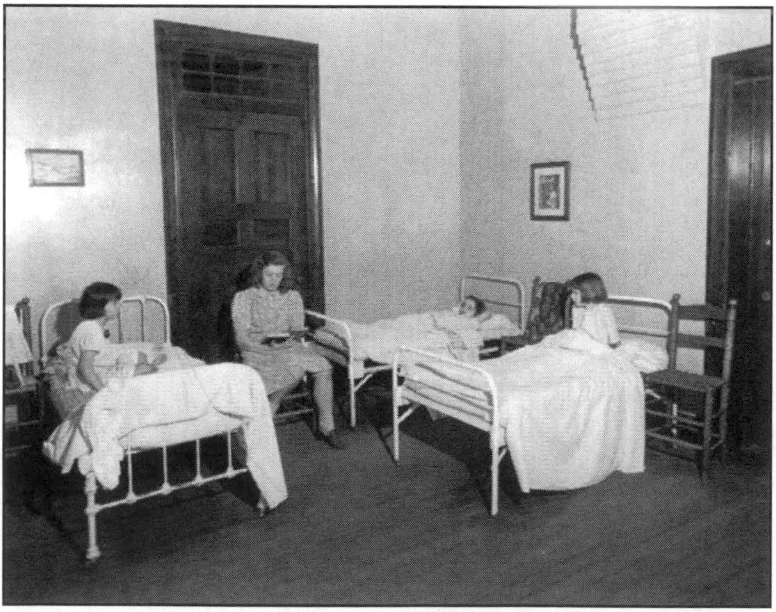

Older girl reading bedtime stories to the younger girls.

The 4-H girls in 1941.

On March 19, 1940, the Troy Children's Center Quintet, the Troy Orphan Asylum's basketball team, went undefeated with 15 wins. The team consisted

The girl's garden group in 1941.

The Woodshop in 1942.

of Howard Fullington, Walter Fletcher, Robert Coonradt, Capt. Frank Hanson, Leo Elden, Donald Elden and Bernard Pettit. Coach Ronald Huddleston, Naomi Green, Manager Leonard Sharpies, George Swarthout, Arthur Herald and Lyle Lawton, assistant coach. It was the first time in the history of the institution that it went undefeated. Troy defeated the Hudson Boys Club 32 to 29.

The 1939 Boy Scout troop at Camp Rotary.

On September 3, 1940, a sewing project was started at the Troy Orphan Asylum. This project employed 15 girls during the first month or two of operation. After the project had been operating for two months other youth were added, bringing the total to 20. The orphanage girls made dresses, underclothing, night wear, shirts and blouses. The girls received training

Boys working the farm in 1939.

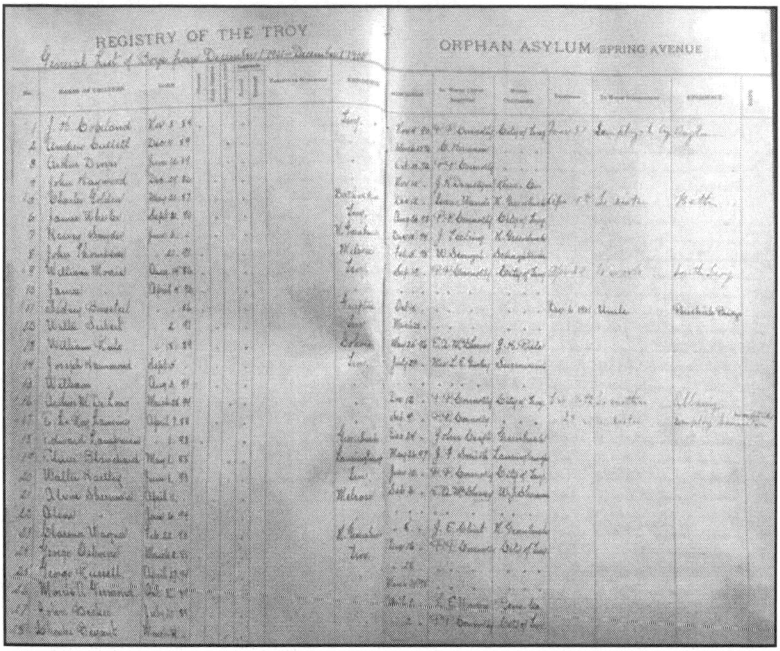
REGISTRY OF THE TROY ORPHAN ASYLUM SPRING AVENUE

Pages from the registry of orphans at the Spring Avenue location in 1900.

in operation of power machines, pattern cutting, altering and remodeling of clothes. Full time supervision was provided by the Troy Orphan Asylum. There were 209 children in the orphanage in 1940. Of that total 59 boys and girls, nearly one-third, were placed in foster homes. Some of them at the asylum's expense and all the children were regularly visited by staff members of the asylum.

For those in the asylum, as the children grew older those that were academically included were kept in school while the others were taught a trade or vocation not based on book learning. One of the

TOA Children parading down Pawling Avenue.

asylum boys was studying for a degree at the State Agricultural College at Cornell with the help of the asylum. A total of 18 boys and girls were in high school and some were completing courses in beauty culture and horticulture. During summer months the

Vocational class in 1934.

A Nursery picnic in 1941.

boys were taught gardening in the institution's own farm in the back of Spring Avenue and some were given specialized training in chicken and hog raising while boys handy with their hands were taught manual arts. The older girls were given specialized courses in domestic arts to help them find jobs as domestics in private homes.

Between 1913 and 1941, Herbert J. Hunn was the first superintendent of the Troy Orphan Asylum. In an interview in a local newspaper in 1936 where local institutions in Troy were featured and their leaders interviewed, the TOA was the eighth institution written up in the newspaper and Hunn described his theories about the orphan issue and how the Troy Orphan Asylum operated: "*Ninety percent of all children brought up in the proper environment become good citizens,*" he said. "*Don't quote the silk purse and the sow's ear to me, children aren't born good or bad. The*

Children playing outside in 1942.

results achieved by the Troy Orphan Asylum during its 102 years of existence have made me confident that environment is the most important part of the game."

"Recently a young woman who had been brought up in the home wrote to us, 'I learned to work there, to be clean and to know right from wrong.' To me that epitomizes what the Troy Orphan Asylum always has stood for. We try to fit our children to take their places in the world and to be lifters, not leaners. The Troy Orphan Asylum is a great big home conducted as much like a normal household as possible but with scientific supervised diet, recreative programs, educational programs and expert mental, medical and dental care."

At the time of the interview there were 184 children in the home, 105 boys and 79 girls. Three of the boys and 13 girls who did not progress in group-life were cared for in boarding homes. Some twenty boys and 16 girls were in free homes some awaiting adoption. Further, the Troy Orphan Asylum at the time was the only institution between New York City and Utica that admitted children from birth to 16 years old. Hunn also stated that the: "*youngest child we ever*

Herman Gajeway, Jr., four years at TOA. He went missing when his ship the USS Kearny was sunk by a German submarine in 1941, before the US was in the war. The ship survived.

NAME: Gajeway, Jr, Herman D.O.B. Dec 18, 1914

PLACE OF BIRTH: Troy NY

MOTHER: Ella Sage D.O.B. N.Y.

FATHER: Herman Gajeway D.O.B. N.Y.

SIBLINGS: Charles

DATE OF ADMISSION: March 4, 1921 REFERRED BY: Troy Comm. Charities

REASON FOR ADMISSION: Death of Father

DATE OF DISCHARGE: Sept 8, 1928 DISCHARGED TO: Mt. Herman School, Mt Herman, Mass.

REASON FOR DISCHARGE: Reported missing aboard USS Kearny when torpedoed by German submarine, Oct. 1941, WWII

SIGNIFICANT DOCUMENTS:

Ray Cottrell (standing) and Lewis Butler. March 1945. The new laboratory.

Using the horse to plow the fields in 1942.

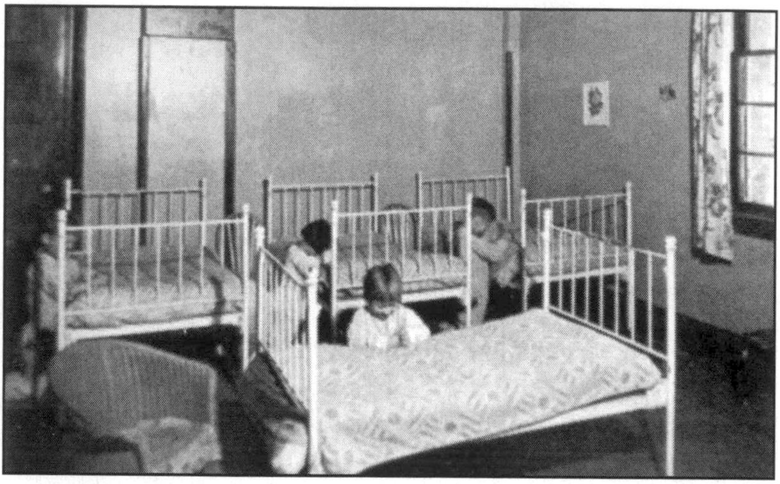

Saying prayers before bedtime.

received was three hours old and arrived in a market basket. Another baby traveled 100 miles to us on the day of birth."

Boys playing baseball game behind the orphanage in the fields.

Boys working in the shop in 1941.

He stated that they received children from Glens Falls down to Newburgh and west to Johnstown and Gloversville.

According to Hunn, institution life had changed remarkably during the previous 50 years. Bright, pretty dresses and suits, chosen by the children themselves, had replaced uniforms. *"All unnatural constrainment was been done away with as the merry laughter*

Farming during the 1940s-50s.

of the children echoing through the halls of the home, testifies. "Much of the life has to be routine," Hunn said. *"The children arise and have breakfast at 7 a. m. After breakfast the older ones make their beds and help in the work until school time. In the afternoon there are hours for play, hours for naps for the little ones and then supper at 5 p. m. Study hours*

4-H'ers working their cabbage patch in 1948. Look at the size of those heads.

Boys hoeing the fields in 1956.

are from 6:45 to 7:45 p. m., followed by recreational and educational classes. We have meetings of the Fife and Drum Corps, the Girl Reserves, Troop I, Boy Scouts, classes in wood work and sewing, directed games, moving pictures three Saturdays a month during the winter and meetings of the Boys and Girls Choruses. Chapel exercises are conducted each morning and the children attend service each Sunday."

"Once a month we have birthday parties, for all the children whose birthdays occur during that month and at Christmas time everything is done to give the children a jolly time. Parents are allowed to visit the children every month."

"The asylum is a never ending source of surprise and pleasure to the visitor viewing it for the first time. The children's faces reflect good health and happiness. During play hours they romp and shout with supervision but not restraint. The play rooms, one side of which is glass, let in good sunlight and have concrete floors for roller skating, mechanical games and toys, marble games and sports of all kinds. Out of doors the children slide, ski, play ball and heartily enjoy themselves. Their living and sleeping quarters are not "institutional" but home-like. This week the home was filled with Christmas remembrances and greetings from former wards and gifts from kind friends of the children."

The Orphan Asylum at the end of Hunn's tenure consisted of a campus of buildings in Tudor Gothic architectural style of the 11th and 12th centuries consisting of the main building, the Baby House, Tinllinghast Memorial Chapel, Peterson Memorial

Group portrait. Unknown date.

Building, and the reception building, a laundry and power house. There was also a farm with out-buildings. The gable ends of the buildings had a

The TOA Drum Corps.

Vanderheyden boy scouts getting their picture with Governor Nelson Rockefeller in the 1960s.

distinctive Dutch appearance probably giving a nod to the Dutch founders of Troy. One writer noticed the similarities with the old Vanderheyden Palace, a Dutch house in Albany that also had a double stepped gable roof and was torn down in 1833.

The stately "Palace" building was located on the western side of North Pearl Street just north of the Elm Tree Corner (North Pearl and State Street, northwest corner). A double gable-faced and connected edifice, this elegant looking residence was a unique community landmark. The structure is believed to have been built about 1725 by Johannes J. Beekman. Following his death in 1756, his

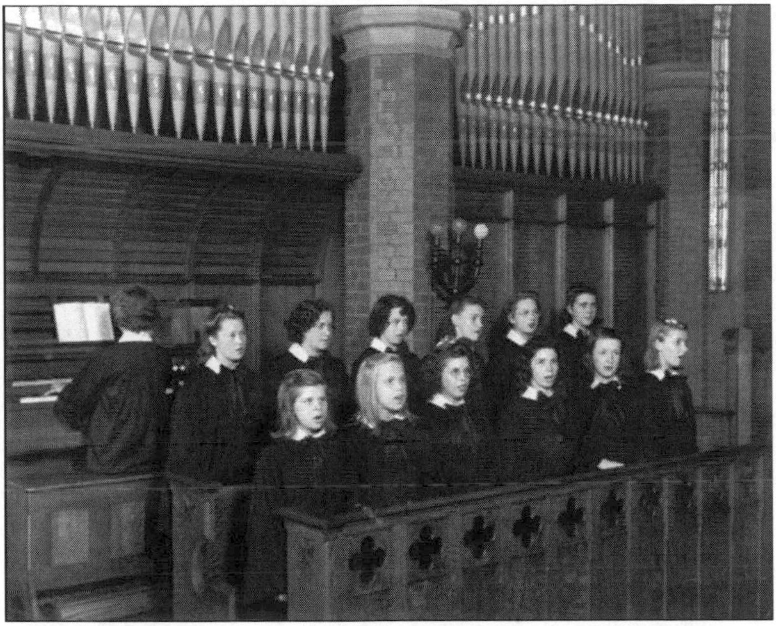

The girl's choir performed often and won prizes for their performances.

daughters continued to live in thc home until it was purchased by merchant Jacob Vanderheyden during the era of the American Revolution. By 1800, Vanderheyden was living there and remained at 85 North Pearl Street until his death in 1820. After the death of his widow in 1823, the building deteriorated and then was demolished in 1833. A Baptist church was then built on the site.

One of the gabled ends and a running horse weathervane of the palace were taken by Washington Irving and now are part of his home known as Sunnyside in Tarrytown, New York.

A board of 21 trustees and the Women's Association Auxiliary of 25 members were responsible for the welfare and conduit of the institution. Hobart W. Thompson was president of the board and Mrs. William Henry Warren of the Women's Association.

When Hunn retired in May, 1941, a testimonial dinner was given in his honor at the Hendrick Hudson Hotel. R. Oakley Kennedy who was president of the board at the time reviews his accomplishments since July 1, 1913. The Times Record published the testimonial:

"You have the knowledge of work well done in helping so many boys and girls prepare themselves for life. During your administration great changes have been brought about so that no longer is there just a house of shelter but a very real home to which so many look back with deep affection."

As a token of affection of both the trustees and the Women's Board, he presented Mr. Hunn a purse "which carries with it the ardent hope that the happiest times of your whole life will be found In the days and months and the years to come."

A gift of flowers was presented Mrs. Hunn on behalf of the Women's Board of which Mrs. Alan S. Cobden is president.

Mr. Hunn responded in appreciation for the gifts and for the repeated expressions of greetings. Sounding a call for a continuing high standard of social work in Troy which already has placed the city among the leaders in social welfare, he asserted that a nation's most important asset and greatest liability is its youth. "If you and I and all of us continue to fight our best to put into youth today the love of home and of things true and clean and kind we needn't worry about the future of the country."

Words of tribute were expressed by Miss Grace E. Allison, president of the Social Work Executives' Seminar and superintendent of the Samaritan Hospital, in recognition of the "noteworthy and helpful contribution" of the guest of honor to social work and of his "sympathetic and human understanding" of children brought to the hospital; Miss Mary C. Coughlin, president of the Troy Social Workers Club, who said that Mr. Hunn's success in social work can be measured in one way by "the acceptance by the community of the things he has been trying to do" and by his individual service in the "job of being a substitute parent to the children themselves."

Ellis H. Robison, president of the Troy Rotary Club, recalled that Rotary had paid Mr. Hunn its highest honor, the presidency. Mrs. Mary Murray McArdle, president of the Troy Council of Social Agencies, of which Mr. Hunn has been a member since its inception in 1931; and Eric W. Gibberd, executive secretary of the council and of the Community Chest, also voiced their praises.

Telegrams of congratulations to the guest of honor were also read. Raymond J. Hannon, president of the Troy Community Chest, was toastmaster. The Invocation was delivered by

Rabbi Alan S. Green, D.D., of the Third Street Temple and Rev. Elmer J. Donnelly, director of Catholic Charities Troy Office, gave the benediction.

The principal address was given by Rev. Arthur Johnston, pastor of Mr. Hunn's church, Mount Ida Memorial Presbyterian. Translating a Latin Inscription on the base of a high shaft in the town where he began his ministry, Mr. Johnston quoted, "We give the palm to him who merits it." "That," he declared, "is the purpose of our meeting this evening."

No Farewell. "There is no sadness of farewell about it, for it is neither a funeral nor a baptism, not even a wedding. It is the body social honoring itself by meeting to rejoice in the achievement and attainment of one of its members. To reverse Shakespeare, we come not to consign our friend to oblivion, but praise and pledge our affection for a new lease of service and effective endeavor. To do that is no mean thing, indeed one of the fine arts of the world is the indispensable duty of praising people. In praising people we lift and ennoble ourselves.

"I have read of 'minus' and 'plus' people. The minus people are those who never add anything to your happiness, your hopes, or your faith in yourself or anybody else. They leave you poorer in your own esteem and in your belief in others. But life is made rich by men and women other than that and you and I know that one of them is in our midst this evening.

"They are people who draw the best out of us. Who believe in us and make us even surprise ourselves. These are benefactors. They teach us to radiate courage, faith and hope.

"One of the things that our friend has taught some of us is to do what we do well. That is to say he has shown us the genius of wholeheartedness. Did he ever forget your birthday? Not if he knew it.

"This wholeheartedness is always the condition of the only kind of success that is worth having. It is the secret of happiness. For every man who has gone to the wall through want of Intellect a hundred have reached that pathetic condition through want of heart. Herbert Hunn's heart has been in his work.

Father of Big Family.

"More than that his heart has been given to little children. For 17 years I have seen him not as a Superintendent of a well-greased, smoothly going institution, but as the father of a big family, who has never lost the human touch in the maelstrom of social science.

"If you seek a monument, look around. He may pass from one residence to a new one but the good he has done is not dependent on any sphere. That good cannot pass. His work has been edifying for generations of boys and girls whose influence will touch untold and unpredictable bounds. I have used that word 'edify" advisedly. Do you know what edification means? It means, 'to make a building or to build a house.' The edifier is both an architect and a builder. But the

word "edification' has even a more original meaning than that. It means to make a fireplace. To set a place of warmth in the midst of things.

"Lord Gray said of his father. Governor General of Canada, this lovely word, "He lighted many fires in cold rooms.' That is edification, sheltering and warm. It is not cramming puzzled minds with dry rot things. It Is building well whatever you do. Building high and straight and broad. Building for the eve of God."

Musical Program.

Music for the program was arranged by Lester C. Higbee, president of the Troy Vocal Society, and included selections by a quartet composed of John Dandurand, first tenor; Walter Snyder, jr., second tenor; Theron L. Reynolds, barytone, and Hadley Rasmuson, bass, with H. Townsend Heister as director and accompanist.

The testimonial was arranged by a committee composed of Miss Allison, Frank H. Ames, Mrs. Cobden, Frank H. Coffeen, Norman F. Coons, Mrs. Coughlin, Mr. Gibberd, Harold M. Grout, Mr. Hannon, Mr. Johnson, Mr. Kennedy, Mrs. McArdle, Mr. Robison and William Henry Warren.

Among the organizations identified with the occasion were the Troy Community Chest, Troy Rotary Club, Troy Council of Social Agencies, Troy Orphan Asylum, Apollo Commandery, K. T., Mount Ida Memorial Presbyterian Church. Troy Social Workers' Club and the Social Work

Executives' Seminary. Mr. Hunn, engaged in welfare work since 1899, was associated with Y. M. C. A work until Feb. 1, 1911, when he became state inspector of children's institutions.

On July 1, 1913, he became superintendent of the Troy Orphan Asylum. Making his home now at 23 Lansing Avenue, he has announced his future plans only as "to take it easy this summer."

His successor at the orphanage, Richard L. Thomas, and Mrs. Thomas were introduced to the social workers at the dinner.

On March 24, 1941, *The Troy Record* wrote a piece about some of the successes of the institution. One such example had to do with two hot tempered brothers:

"The flying brick would have killed him, had it not missed its mark. Brothers James and John were at it again. Hot tempered, they were always fighting with somebody. If uncontrolled as they grew older, they would undoubtedly end up in Jail on a charge of assault or murder. Their tempers were as violent as the red of their hair.

James and John, the Sons of Thunder. Their mother was dead. Their father placed them at the Troy Orphan Asylum. For six years they lived there under the influence of a good home and school. Repeatedly they were counseled about leashing their tempera. You've got the pep to amount to something, they were told. Be impudent like that once in the Navy and you'll hit the deck.

James eventually was placed with an uncle. John got mad and ran away.

But Here We Are

A few years later, two strapping fellows came to the home. "You told us we'd be in jail but here we are," was their greeting as they walked into the office. James was a motorman on a subway in New York. John had served a term in the Navy. Their hair was just as red as it ever had been, but they both had learned the lesson in self discipline begun at the home."

The newspaper continued for more examples:

"Two girls, their mother dead and their father unable to provide for their care, were placed at the home. Not delinquent in any way, they were greatly in need of the home care which their father wanted them to have. The sisters went on through the grades and up through high school. One married and now has a home of her own. The other took a course at business college, obtained a confidential position in a state hospital, has married a doctor. She returns to her former home for a visit every summer.

Children of a not up-and-coming family in the country were placed at the home when their parents died. One, more ambitious than the rest, was found a home with a farmer in another county. He was graduated from high school and wanted college training in agriculture. His foster father was willing to help but could not finance the college course alone. The boy is a sophomore this year, his marks very high, at an agricultural college — his education made possible in part by help from the orphanage.

The "home," as alumni literally scattered all over the world affectionately refer to the Troy Orphan Asylum, allows the child's individuality to assert itself through an elastic program designed to meet the needs of each child. Don't be a leaner, be a lifter, he is taught."

There were 194 children at the "home" that year.

In May 1941 the new superintendent of Vanderheyden 33 year old Richard L. Thomas moved in with his family. Only a few months later he heard the news of the attack on Pearl Harbor that Sunday morning while he sat in the office reading the paper. According to his son, he went downtown to enlist. They looked at him and said, "Dick, go home. The children need you." He became a neighborhood black-out warden.

During World War II, TOA did its duty. The Troy Boys 4-H Club, the Troy 4-Hers, created a Victory Garden to grow vegetables for Vanderheyden. The club was formed in 1940 but started tiling an acre of land in back of the main building. Because of the war effort and the Victory Garden Campaign

Girls preparing the meal. Date unknown.

Richard Thomas became the head of Vanderheyden in 1941 and retired in 1973, after 32 years. Photo courtesy Steve Thomas.

instituted by the government, the garden was expanded to three acres in 1942 and boys ages 12 to 14 grew vegetables that could be used at the orphanage. There was enough so that the girls of the Hall could can many of them for the winter. Vanderheyden in using it as a teaching moment purchased the vegetables from the boys and

The Thomas family moved into 232 Spring Avenue, next to the Bessey House (then Baby House) in 1941. Left to right: Richard Thomas (1907-1977), Allen (b. 1939), Joel (1936-2011), Dorothy (1908-1950), and Stephen (b. 1943). Photo courtesy Steve Thomas.

Boys working on their projects. No date.

The Thomas household moved next door to the Baby house (now Bessey House) at 232 Spring Avenue when Richard Thomas took over as the head of Vanderheyden in 1941.

deducted what they would normally get in money such as the cost of fertilizers, seeds. The boys kept accounting records and each of the 18 boys that worked their own piece of the garden made $18 each from his produce. They worked in the morning during spring and then one hour each evening during growing season. Henry G. Steffen who was the vocational training instructor at the time was the leader of the club. During that same year the Modern Misses 4-H Club of Vanderheyden Hall held a square dance in the Hart Memorial Building and invited boys and girls of other 4-H clubs in Rensselaer County. The girls club was formed the previous year and they decided they wanted to meet other 4-H members. Visiting clubs included East Greenbush, Brunswick, Eagle Mills, East Poestenskill, North Greenbush and West Sand Lake. Total attendance were twenty young people, five girls and 15 boys. Also included at the event was Richard L. Thomas, superintendent of Vanderheyden and staff members.

During the war many of the children at Vanderheyden were using their allowances to buy up 10 cent Defense Savings Stamps to help Uncle Sam. Some 30 of the residents at Vanderheyden had joined the armed services over the previous few years to fight for the country. The infirmary at Vanderheyden was designated an emergency first aid station in case of air raid attacks. Windows were blacked out and there was a nurse and doctor at all times on duty nearby. Vanderheyden also stored extra cots and mattresses and plenty of room for extra children in case of attack. During blackouts the children were distributed throughout the grounds instead of having them grouped all together in case of an attack and the older children all had duties assigned to them.

When the Board of Trustees decided to change the name of Troy Orphan Asylum to Vanderheyden Hall, an editorial in The Times Record newspaper praised the change in its January 9, 1942, edition:

Vanderheyden Hall

The decision of the governing board of the Troy Orphan Asylum to change the name of the institution to Vanderheyden Hall should win the applause of all interested Trojans. Rightly or wrongly the word "asylum" has gained, in modern parlance, a connotation which is unpleasant. It is used more often in speaking of hospitals, for mental disorders and for hide-outs used by criminals than in the old manner which ruled in the days when the Troy institution was founded.

Vanderheyden Hall established in the mind of every boy or girl who enters and is graduated a historical connection which ought to tend to build a better Trojan. The Vanderheyden family found Troy. For generations they were outstanding citizens. They had high ideas and faith in the area where they had settled. They deserve the honoring memory of those who have come after them.

So Vanderheyden Hall! May it always perform the services for which it was founded in the spirit of its precursor, the original Trojan!

When the trustees decided to change the name of the orphanage several names were suggested but as board member attorney Edward H. Pattison explained to a journalist:

"The name of Vanderheyden was favored for at least two reasons. It was an old Dutch name prominent in the history of the region; in fact, Vanderheyden was an early name for the

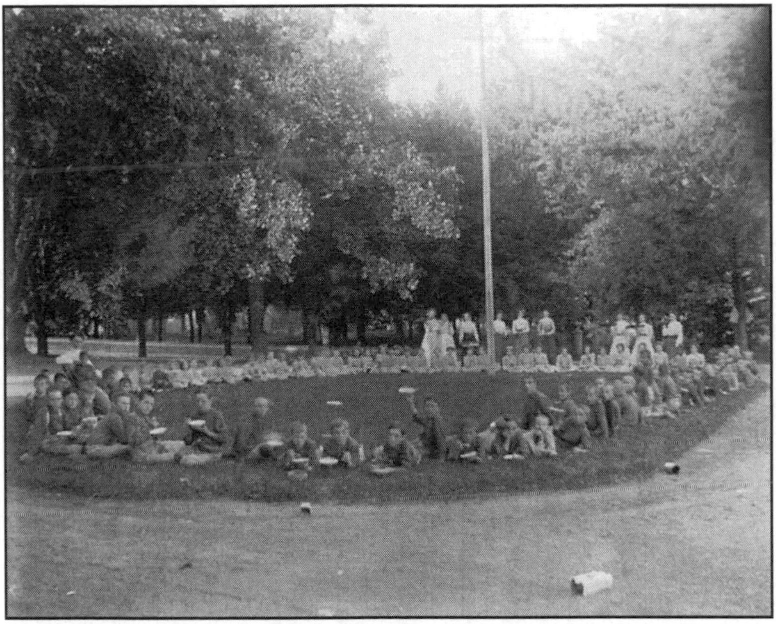

Orphans sitting on the front lawn of Fairview Home later absorbed by Vanderheyden Hall.

site of Troy. Secondly, the board was looking for a name which would counteract the stigma of "orphanage" and sound more like a school."

Tragedy struck the institution on August 6, 1942. Two year old Joseph Primeau, Jr., who went missing two days prior was found drowned in Smart's Upper Pond. He was the son of Joseph Primeau the farm superintendent at Vanderheyden. He was present when he, Nicholas T. West and John Wetsel, an employee of Vanderheyden, found the little boy.

In November 1945, Mrs. Ogden J. Ross resigned as president of the Women's Association of

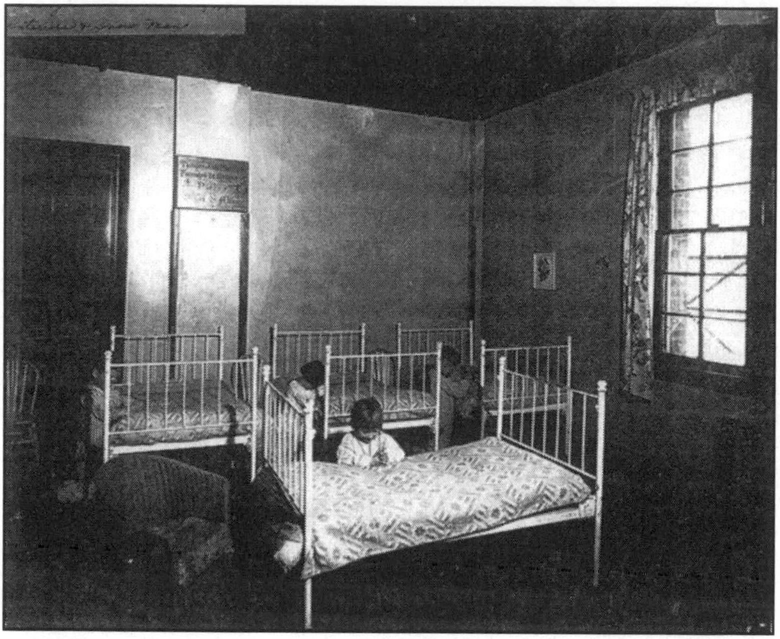

Children saying their prayers in the nursery in the 1940s.

Vanderheyden Hall. It was also reported that a small living room was being furnished in the baby house for use of guests when visiting the children. One of the boys had been appointed as an alternate for judging at a 4-H Club contest in Syracuse. In June, the children from Vanderheyden were invited to participate during Children's Day services at First Baptist Church. The Vanderheyden Girls Choir sang as well as Superintendent Richard Thomas who opened with "A Garden of Praise." The girl's choir sang "This is MY Father's World."

One of the strengths that Vanderheyden began early was training their children in community

OBITUARY

Dion Petteys. TROY Dion Petteys, 66, of Clark Avenue died suddenly Monday, September 13, 2010, at Albany Medical Center Hospital, New Scotland Avenue. Born in Babylon, N.Y., he was the son of Agnes Cox Cassidy and step-son of Ken Cassidy and husband for 40 years of Barbara Vidmar Petteys. He lived in Babylon for 10 years and later resided in St. Coleman's Home for Boys and most of his early years at Vanderheyden Hall in Troy. He was a 1965 graduate of Hudson Valley Community College. In 1963, Dion became an employee of Vanderheyden Hall, over the years, holding the positions of counselor, program director, recreation director and retiring after 34 years as the staff development coordinator. He enjoyed spending time with family and friends, especially his two year old granddaughter, Ava; gardening, photography, travel, fishing, kayaking, hiking, biking and walking his dogs. In his early years, he was a member of the Salvation Army Troy Corp Band. He was an Army veteran of the Vietnam War serving in Vietnam. He was an avid reader and music lover and enjoyed learning new technology. Survivors in addition to his wife, include his daughter, Danielle (Pat Miranda) Petteys of Atlanta, Ga.; a granddaughter, Ava Dionne Miranda of Atlanta; and a brother, Warren Petteys of Saratoga Springs. He was predeceased by two brothers, Cornel and Clifton Petteys.

relationships in their nursery school. Children three to four years of age learned to share their toys and take turns in the play yard while older children were

4-H'rs on October 24, 1958.

taught to use some of their allowances for gift giving and dues in such organization such as Camp Fire Girls, Boys Scouts, or 4-H. Character building was an important goal of the Hall.

In 1948 Vanderheyden made press when it was revealed that for the last three years, Shep a large shepherd dog had been living at Vanderheyden and accompanying the 6th grade to school each day. He walked the class to school and left with them as they walked back from School 16. If the children marched, the dog marched. If the children played in the playground so did Shep. Why Shep picked the 6th grade no one knew but he welcomed each new class.

Vanderheyden came to the rescue in 1949 when School 16 was destroyed by fire in January. Vanderheyden made space available to the students of School 16 until 1953 when a new building was constructed.

In 1951, the Troy YMCA presented a Christmas Present to Vanderheyden allowing them to join opening their juniors, intermediates and seniors for a weekly club, swim and gym program. The board of directors of the Y raised $240 to provide this free membership to Vanderheyden boys from eight years up. There were 200 children at the institution with a 50% turnover yearly as the children went to foster homes or their own homes after being rehabilitated. When children left Vanderheyden they often wrote letters back to staff letting them know how they were doing. In June 1951, Vanderheyden received a package to everyone at the Hall from Cpt. Robert Oathout who entered Vanderheyden as a child and was stationed in Germany. The gift was two sets of encyclopedias, one was specifically for children with pictures and stories.

In 1954, one of Vanderheyden's pigs named "That Darn Old Sow" gave birth to 28 little piggies! She gave birth to fifteen piggies on July 29, ten more July 30 and three more on the 31st. She also weighed 500 pounds. All in all, the children were well fed for many months to come.

THE TIMES RECORD

Published daily except Sunday by Troy Publishing Co., Inc., 501 Broadway, Troy, New York 12181. Telephone 272-2000.

H. R. HORVITZ
President-Publisher

WILLIAM J. RUSH
Vice President-General Manager

WALTER J. BENEDETT
Vice President

JOSEPH R. SNYDER
Editor

SUBSCRIPTION TERMS—The Times Record, Delivered by carrier: One year $40.56; one week, 78 cents, single copy, 15 cents. By mail in Albany, Rensselaer, Saratoga and Washington Counties in New-York State and Bennington County in Vermont payable in advance: One year, $25.00; six months, $13.00; three months, $7.00; one month, $2.50; one week, 90 cents. By mail outside of above counties payable in advance: One year, $30.00; six months, $16.00; three months, $8.50; one month, $3.00; one week, 90 cents. Extra charge on Troy City and Mounted Postal Routes and to foreign countries. Mail rates apply only where there is no carrier service available

MEMBER OF THE ASSOCIATED PRESS—The Associated Press is entitled exclusively to the use of publication of all local news printed in this newspaper as well as all AP news dispatches.

Member of Audit Bureau of Circulation

Helped The Young

Trojans who daily pass the impressive brick buildings of Vanderheyden Hall on Spring Avenue may often give thought to their graceful architecture without giving much thought to the drama within.

Here for 32 years until his retirement this week Richard L. Thomas ministered to children who needed help and he did thte job well.

His job as director was all the more effective because he realized the usual limitations of institutional care as opposed to home care and he strove mightily to lessen those limitations

Warmth and love for children is a prime requisite for such a position. Mr. Thomas was well supplied.

But in seeing that good care was given he never lost sight of his principal goal of getting the child back to his home whenever that became possible.

He presided over the institution in an era of changing social concepts, all of which made his work the more challenging. But he met all the challenges.

We feel that even though he may have had difficult charges among the hundreds of young people there will be those among them who will remember and be thankful for him in the later years of their life.

March 3, 1973, Editorial.

In 1955, Vanderheyden received another unusual donation of $11,407 from the estate of Daniel Pitts of Troy. He left his estate to his son when he died in 1897. The son was found dead in Cossayuna Lake in 1954 but because the son was partially on welfare he could only receive $600 a year. In Pitts' will he bequeathed Vanderheyden if there were no other relatives.

In 1956, it was announced that two of the oldest institutions for the care of children decided to merge. Vanderheyden Hall and the Fairview Home for Friendless Children in Watervliet which formed in 1880. Fairview was founded by James Barclay Jermain a lawyer who built the home and endowed it. Jermain also founded the Home for Aged Men in Menands and the Jermain Memorial Church in Watervliet. Fairview had received negative publicity when a national magazine published an article in 1952 that said the home was a "crumbling old institution." A year before, the home was inspected by Colonie officials and found many violations of the state multiple residence law including the need for a sprinkler system. However Richard Thomas, superintendent of Vanderheyden explained that the real reason for the consolidation was the increase cost of child guidance and the *"lessening of the sizes of institutional populations."* Both homes felt it would be better serviced under one roof. On July 31, 1956, the merger was signed by Supreme Court Justice Kenneth S. MacAffer whose uncle, the late Angus D. MacAffer of Cohoes was once president of Fairview Home. The combined population of Vanderheyden Hall with the addition of Fairview children at the time was 177 children. The new organization, Vanderheyden Hall, Inc., combined boards with all the male members of the former board at Fairview with the present board of Vanderheyden at the time. The first set of officers for the new board were John S. Mabin, president, Robert W. Tomlinson, vice president, Edward H.

Vanderheyden Boys Scout Troop, circa 1960s with NYS Governor Nelson Rockefeller. Team leader Fred Bowen, back right.

Pattison, secretary, and Chester Wood, assistant secretary.

In 1959, there were 170 children at Vanderheyden from 12 eastern New York counties. There were 15 buildings in total that comprised Vanderheyden. The average stay was two years. Most of the children at this time were sent by public welfare departments and children courts, so that much of the cost of operations was defrayed by those public agencies.

Raising money to keep Vanderheyden in business was always an annual affair but more than once the

Interior of the Tillinghast Chapel.

institution would get a surprise gift. In 1959, Charles William Steines, a former native of Troy, who had left 50 years earlier, left $300,000 to Vanderheyden in his estate. He died in 1930 and his estate was distributed to several people. However his will stated that when the last heir died the resulting money would go to Vanderheyden as the "Steines Endowment Fund." Anna Steines, from Saratoga Springs died the previous year and the estate was finally settled. Steines was born in Troy in 1869 and was a tailor who lived on 5th Avenue near Broadway. He had no relation to Vanderheyden other than he approved of their work.

Christmas time was always a tough time for the children. In 1961, the Eastern Star, Palestine Chapter received Christmas letters from the children with their wishes and members of the Palestine group filled them. This was an annual event and the chapter had been fulfilling these wishes for many years. The Women's Association of Vanderheyden along with the Emma Willard School also took up donations to provide to the children. Besides getting gifts, entertainment and food was often supplied. In 1962 for example, the Women's Association purchased at least three presents per person for the 130 children staying at the institution, a total of over 400 wrapped items. Other agencies often got involved in helping the Vanderheyden children. For example the Willard Day School had its school children make tree ornaments for each of the Vanderheyden children.

In 1965, Vanderheyden created a Counselor Clinic. This was an effort to make life for the 133 children in residence more home-like. The new director of Social Service, Edmund E. McCann and director Richard L. Thomas emphasized that they were looking *"to meet the needs of the children placed in our care."* McCann hired 10 part time case workers all with Master degree's in social work to consult with the boys and girls at Vanderheyden. Six hours one evening per week were scheduled by each therapist with the exception of two for afternoon hours for individual talks. The goal was to establish a working one-on-one relationship with each resident an effort not common in many similar institutions. The goal was to help develop the child's latent talents for community relationships, realistic goals for entry to the world and workplace, whether it was technical training, college, military service, homemaker or good employment. Half of the youngsters at the time were assigned by Rensselaer County Family Court while the others came from over a dozen northeast New York counties. The therapist also worked with the parents of the child in hopes that someday they were be united. During school breaks the parents were encouraged to have their children at the institution stay with them during that break. This new clinic was in addition to the already practice of testing and interviewing by Dr. Thomas J. Qualtere, a clinical psychologist and consultant, to each new arrival at Vanderheyden. Another change at Vanderheyden was the omission of babies and preschool youngsters. Most of these younger children we sent to foster homes where the cost was less. Vanderheyden closed its infant department in 1959, and since 1962, only admitted two or three below second grade. As a result the population in 1965 shrunk from 175 to 133 with a staff of 40. Those still at Vanderheyden attended Schools 15 and 16, Sacred Heart, or Troy High. They continued to eat at the hall's dining room, though Troy High schoolers ate lunch at the school. Residents at Vanderheyden continued to enjoy benefits such as television and game facilities, and woodworking and craft shops, basketball court, baseball diamond, and outdoor pool. The boys and girls continued to compete with other teams in CYO leagues. The three 4-H clubs were popular and Vanderheyden could boast that their Boy Scout Troop 1 was the first in America to have been outfitted with uniforms and was the longest in continuous existence.

On August 3, 1971, 25 children escaped a major fire at Vanderheyden which gutted the West wing of the institution. The two alarm blaze started in the boys dormitory and fortunately only two youngsters of the 125 house in the wing were only slightly injured. The alarm was called in at 7:16 AM by Stella Speanburg who was the child care supervisor who saw smoke coming out of the back of the West wing from her bedroom window in another wing. The fire was caused by one of the boys who had stolen gasoline he had hidden in a pan under his bed and a lighted candle.

On February 23, 1973, Richard Thomas retired as director of Vanderheyden for 32 years. According to his son Steve, Richard had been a busy director. *"I mean running the place when it was vastly understaffed. He preached on Sunday (until the local preachers complained), he ran the movie projector, he umpired baseball and basketball games, he was disc jockey at dances, and every evening after our supper, he went back up the street to say good night to the little kids and helped the older kids with their homework."* Even Richard's wife was involved. She helped sometimes in the administrative office when things were busy, especially at Christmas. She also regularly worked closely with the "Women's Board/ Association" of volunteers (formerly the Visitors). Later, around 1957, his second wife Carol worked full time as a social services administrator and helped a number of people get into educational programs at the high school. One example is Dion Petteys, who eventually worked at Vanderheyden (see obituary).

Thomas, who was born and raised in Montana and schooled there, and in Oregon, had prior knowledge of institutional learning as his father was a college professor and social worker. He later headed a similar institution. Thomas came to Vanderheyden before World War II when the trend was when most children who needed care outside their immediate homes were placed in institutions. His philosophy was simple. *"Even though you and I might not think much of the home, it is most important for a child to be home. And it is our primary aim to get him back there if he has to be taken from it for a while. We are not looking for permanent residents."* He further stated in an interview that, *"A person who conducts his life in such as way that his children are taken from the home should realized that he is dealing those children the worst blow they could receive."* Richard also felt that most children who need only care fare best in substitute homes because all they needed was parent substitutes and need to feel a part of the neighborhood. As Steve Thomas pointed out, most of the residents at Vanderheyden at the time were

Boys and girls preparing the "We Help One, We Help All" brochures in 1959.

placed there though family court and it was only three years prior that Vanderheyden changed its policy to allow admission of court-referred children rather than those that just needed care. It was a big change for Vanderheyden as Thomas pointed out: *"These young people are considered persons in need of supervision as distinguish from delinquents. We could not take delinquents because we have an open program here. We keep it as unstructured as we can, having our children go out to school, to church, and to the store."*

However, Vanderheyden did provide some classes for those that had school-based problems that made it difficult for them to go outside the institution. In order to provide tutorial services, Vanderheyden was able to take advantage of federal funded work study programs so that college students could act as tutors. Richard Thomas also stressed the difference between the children who were there because of tragedy and those there solely because of broken home environments. The former he said were hurt but did not become bitter and could understand better why there were placed there. At the time most of the residents were there less than two years. During his tenure the biggest institutional change was trying to substitute small groups from large groups of children.

Two Vanderheyden boys receiving trophies which appear to be for basketball.

In 1973, there were 75 residents where in years past there were upwards to over 200. That year a group home opened on Pawling Avenue, now called the Crandall Home.

By having 12 to 14 children in a single department where they once had 40 made it easier to give children more individual attention. For example, uniforms were discarded and children could pick out their own clothes. Other institutional changes during his tenure was making Vanderheyden more public. Before his time, the institution had its own school rooms, chapel, and was shut away from the greater

Boys visiting the offices Colonel E. S. Mathers, Commanding Officer of the Watervliet Arsenal in 1956.

Troy community. As they developed a more unstructured program and allowing residents to go out into the community it became more known to the outside and allowed the residents to intermingle. Richard's last wish as director was that Vanderheyden someday would move to a group of smaller buildings, less institutional and more home-like where young people can be afforded the much needed individuality and privacy.

Richard's wish did come true in 1975 when Vanderheyden purchased eighty acres in Wyantskill on March 17, the former Pawling Sanitarium and New York State Training School for Girls.

Two young girls getting their height and weight measured.

NINTH ANNUAL REPORT

OF THE

BOARD OF TRUSTEES

AND THE

Board of Female Managers

OF THE

TROY ORPHAN ASYLUM,

DECEMBER, 1842.

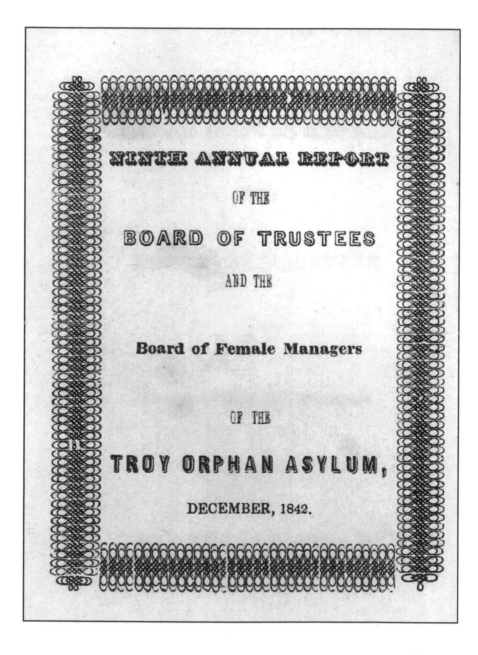

Chapter 6

The Wynantskill Campus 1980 and Beyond!

Vanderheyden Hall moved out of Troy in 1980 where it had lived for over 140 years.

Vanderheyden moved into facilities in Wynantskill, New York, that was the former Pawling Sanitarium in 1919 and later the New York State Training School for Girls, a reformatory school that closed in 1971. The former school had 80 beds.

In 1971, then Governor Nelson Rockefeller requested that all state agencies take financial cuts and the training schools were targeted. Along with the Wynantskill Center for Girls, a 330 bed New Hampton School for boys (New Hampton, NY) was also closed.

Vanderheyden acquired the former training school on March 17, 1975, and began ground breaking and construction for family style cottages in 1978. Two years prior, in 1976, a group home for girls was established called the Rubin Home in Troy.

In addition to the opening of the main Wynantskill campus in 1980, a community residence was opened

TROY ORPHAN ASYLUM.

LAYING OF THE CORNER STONE, MAY 10, 1892.

MARCHING SONG.

1 There 's Springtime in the air
When the happy robin sings,
And earth grows bright and fair,
Covered with the robe she brings.

CHORUS:
March, oh march, 'tis holiday,
Joy for all and cares away;
March, oh march, to our new home,
To the laying of the stone.
[*Repeat pp.*

2 There 's Springtime in the air
When the buds begin to swell,
And woodlands, brown and bare,
All the Summer joys foretell.

3 There 's Springtime in the air
When the heart so fondly pays
This tribute, sweet and rare,
To our God whom we would praise.

AMERICA.

1 My country, 'tis of thee,
Sweet land of liberty,
Of thee I sing;
Land where my fathers died,
Land of the pilgrim's pride,
From every mountain side
Let freedom ring.

2 My native country! thee,
Land of the noble free,
Thy name I love;
I love thy rocks and rills,
Thy woods and templed hills;
My heart with rapture thrills,
Like that above.

3 Let music swell the breeze,
And ring from all the trees
Sweet freedom's song:
Let mortal tongues awake,
Let all that breathe partake,
Let rocks their silence break
The sound prolong.

4 Our father's God, to thee,
Author of liberty,
To thee we sing:
Long may our land be bright
With freedom's holy light;
Protect us by thy might,
Great God, our King.

DOXOLOGY.

Praise God, from whom all blessings flow,
Praise him, all creatures here below;
Praise him above, ye heavenly host;
Praise Father, Son, and Holy Ghost.

in Averill Park for children with severe developmental disabilities. Community residences

The disastrous fire in 1981 destroyed all of the buildings at Vanderheyden except for the baby house (now called the Bessey Home).

All that is left of the Spring Avenue campus is the infant building now called the Bessey House. It escaped the major fire of 1981, which took down all the other buildings.

were also opened in East Greenbush and Schodack for children with developmental disabilities and the first independent living apartments opened in Troy in 1987.

Main building of the Wynantskill Center for Girls which became the new Vanderhevden Hall in 1975.

Vanderheyden continued to expand at its new home over the remainder of the twentieth century and into the Twenty-first century where it developed new programs, modified old ones and eliminated ones that were no longer needed.

What is Vanderheyden in 2018 and what services do they provide today?

Vanderheyden began its life as an orphanage serving the needs of Troy residents in the nineteenth century. Basic needs and a simple education were all that was needed then. The twentieth century

Early view of Pawling Sanitarium and later Center for Girls complex of buildings before it became Vanderheyden.

provided new challenges for institutions which Vanderheyden met head-on. As the world moved into the twenty-first century new challengers were posed and again Vanderheyden rose to meet them head on. Today, Vanderheyden is recognized as one of the premier youth, adult and family service agencies in the Capital Region of New York, serving over 500 individuals and families each year. For more than 185 years, it has been providing programs and services to youth and adults from over 30 counties in New York who:

•Have been abused, neglected or abandoned.

•Have emotional, academic and behavioral challenges.
•Have developmental disabilities.
•Are caring for a special needs child or individual at home.

•Are seeking to make sure their children and individuals get the care and services they need to stay healthy with managed behavioral health services and/or comprehensive care management services.

Services

Vanderheyden offers a wide range of programs and services to youth, adults and families through various residential programs at their main campus in Wynantskill, New York,

The original Meneely bell was saved from the Spring Avenue fire and sits on the grounds of the present Vanderheyden Hall in Wynantskill. On the right is a closeup of the bell with TOA on it. A second bell is at the Burden Museum in Troy.

and in the Capital Region community as well as community-based supportive services and programs that encompass a wide geographic area.

For Youth

- Campus Residential Treatment Center (RTC)

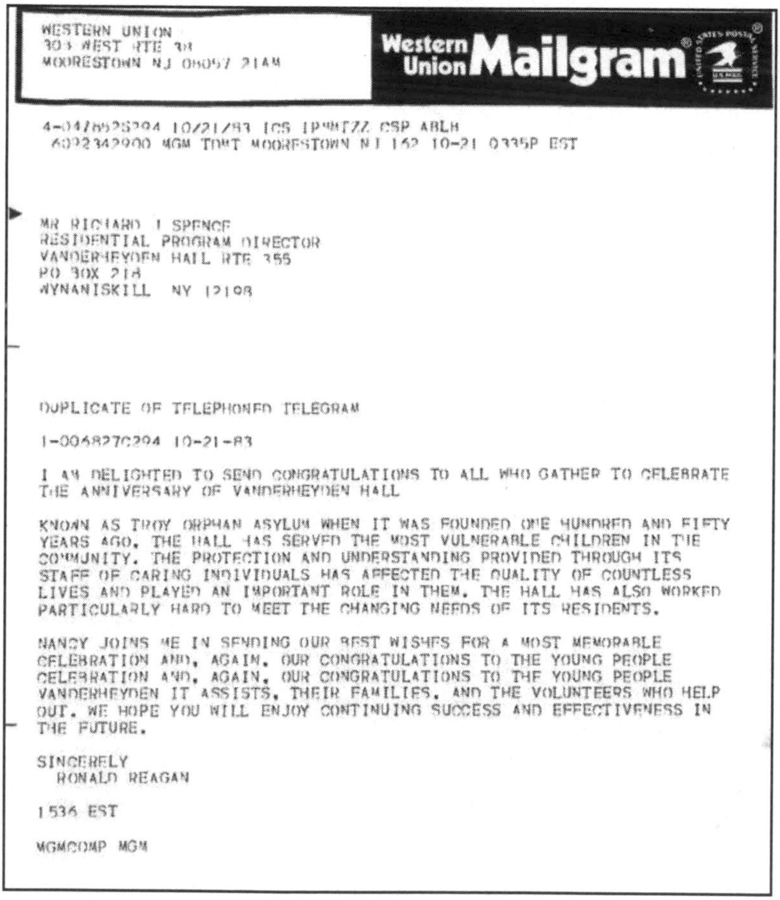

WESTERN UNION
303 WEST RTE 38
MOORESTOWN NJ 08057 21AM

Western Union Mailgram

4-047662S294 10/21/83 ICS IPMMTZZ CSP ABLH
6022342900 MGM TDMT MOORESTOWN NJ 162 10-21 0335P EST

MR RICHARD I SPENCE
RESIDENTIAL PROGRAM DIRECTOR
VANDERHEYDEN HALL RTE 355
PO BOX 218
WYNANTSKILL NY 12198

DUPLICATE OF TELEPHONED TELEGRAM

1-0068270294 10-21-83

I AM DELIGHTED TO SEND CONGRATULATIONS TO ALL WHO GATHER TO CELEBRATE THE ANNIVERSARY OF VANDERHEYDEN HALL

KNOWN AS TROY ORPHAN ASYLUM WHEN IT WAS FOUNDED ONE HUNDRED AND FIFTY YEARS AGO, THE HALL HAS SERVED THE MOST VULNERABLE CHILDREN IN THE COMMUNITY. THE PROTECTION AND UNDERSTANDING PROVIDED THROUGH ITS STAFF OF CARING INDIVIDUALS HAS AFFECTED THE QUALITY OF COUNTLESS LIVES AND PLAYED AN IMPORTANT ROLE IN THEM. THE HALL HAS ALSO WORKED PARTICULARLY HARD TO MEET THE CHANGING NEEDS OF ITS RESIDENTS.

NANCY JOINS ME IN SENDING OUR BEST WISHES FOR A MOST MEMORABLE CELEBRATION AND, AGAIN, OUR CONGRATULATIONS TO THE YOUNG PEOPLE CELEBRATION AND, AGAIN, OUR CONGRATULATIONS TO THE YOUNG PEOPLE VANDERHEYDEN IT ASSISTS, THEIR FAMILIES, AND THE VOLUNTEERS WHO HELP OUT. WE HOPE YOU WILL ENJOY CONTINUING SUCCESS AND EFFECTIVENESS IN THE FUTURE.

SINCERELY
RONALD REAGAN

1536 EST

MGMCOMP MGM

A telegram from President Ronald Reagan congratulating Vanderheyden on its 150th anniversary in 1983.

Marking the 150th anniversary of Vanderheyden in 1983.

• Seven cottages in a home-like setting for youth ages 12-21.

• Diagnostic Respite Center that provides up to a 90-day assessment for youth ages 12-21 who are in crisis.

• In 2018, there were 41 admissions into the RTC, with an average length of stay of 377 days. The RTC had 41 discharges.

• The highest referrals to the RTC came from the NYC Department of Education followed by Albany DSS, Schenectady DSS, Saratoga DSS, Ulster DSS, Rensselaer DSS, Dutchess DSS, and Kingston CSE.

Vanderheyden Fishing Derby, 2007 . TOP. Trophies lined up for the winners. BOTTOM, VH kids going for the gold! One of the many activities Vanderheyden provides for its children.

Education

Fully accredited Richard A. Desrochers Educational Center offers 7-12 grade programs for 88 students that live on our campus and in group homes, and day students that live in the surrounding community and the Hudson Valley.

• Students earn Regents, a local, or a career development and occupational studies commencement certificate (CDOS).

• Older students with multiple disabilities may earn a diploma in an intensively staffed setting, while learning vocational and job skills with an on-site job coach and transition coordinator.

• Vanderheyden's Regents passing percentage increased from 17% in 2018 to 47%. Building teacher skills and competence using professional learning communities and access to integrated technology for inquiry-based learning, along with teachers who focused on providing intensive review and preparation for Regents exams to their students were key to the upsurge.

• The addition of technology hardware and software enriched the learning environment at Vanderheyden with over 60 Chrome Books available to students.

• Career readiness and pre-vocational skills are a focus for all of our high school students.

• Student employment numbers have increased significantly. During the summer, 30 students acquired part-time jobs both on and off campus. This represents a significant and sustained increase of over 50% from the previous year.

• After school activities such as drama, the student council, dance, music and basketball continue to flourish, with clubs meeting as least weekly. Their singers, band members and dancers had multiple, successful performances and sports games outside the campus.

Supervised Living — In Our Community

Youth

• Males and females ages 12-21 live safely in two group homes in Troy under the regulation of the New York State Office of Children and Family Services.

• Vanderheyden has a hard-to-place group home where the individuals attend local schools and receive services that include life skills, building and relationship development, counseling, family counseling and crisis management services.

• In another group home, young males 16-21 years old have support to learn skills necessary to live on their own when they are discharged at age 21. The youth live at Vanderheyden and work and/or go to school and receive services that include valuable life skills development.

• Vanderheyden expanded its supervised independent living program from eight to 12 young adults to live with support. The young adults live in the supervised independent living program apartments, with support to learn skills necessary to live on their own when they are discharged from foster care at the age 21. They work and/or go to school and receive services that include valuable life skills development.

Adults

Day Services

• Day Habitation Without Walls is a five-day-a-week program that provides community-based volunteer and recreational experiences that builds skills and develop competency.

• Vanderheyden provided 1,353 full days of service and 249 half days of service to individuals in this program with an average of ten individuals.

• Volunteer sites includ Meals On Wheels, Hope 7 in Troy, Atria Communities and the Albany City Mission. Other volunteer opportunities included local churches and thrift stores.

• The Day Habilitation with Walls program combines community-based skill development activities with in-house program-based learning activities.

• The program serves individuals along with other adults eligible for this service. The activities in the program & promote building skills in the areas of appropriate behavior, relationship building, community inclusion, self-advocacy and independent travel and overall greater independence.

• On average, Vanderheyden served 13 individuals and provided them with 768 full days and 132 half days.

• The Residential Community Habilitation is for individuals living in a supervised OPWDD (Office for People with Developmental Disabilities) residence. A team member works with the individual to access resources and support to be part of the community. In 2018, over 5,526 hours of service were provided.

• The Community Support Individualized Residential Alternative (CSIRA) program provides apartments in Troy and Menands where adults and their children receive the level of support they need to continue to thrive.

Community Habilitation

• Community Habilitation services are provided at home and in the community to help individuals to learn and keep the skills they need to live safely and more independently; meet people; take part in community activities; be part of their community.

• Families/individuals with a developmental disability received over 1779.75 hours of service while in 2016 Vanderheyden provided 1,453 hours of these services.

Individualized Services and Support (ISS)

• Ensures individuals can live independently by providing funds to pay for housing costs and on a limited basis, for such things as food, transportation and clothing. These individualized services include more opportunities for self-direction and independence.

Bridges to Health (B2H)

• Provided over 254 hours of services in-home and in the community.

- Family/care giver supports and services.

- Special needs community advocacy and support.

- Planned respite and immediate crisis response services.

Home and Community Based Service Waiver

• Provided needed services to children and families to enable their family to remain intact.

• Provided 81 hours of respite services in 2018.

• Provided 102 Caregiver Family supports and service hours.

• Provided 74 hours of skill building services.

Health Services

• In October 2018, employee and residential influenza clinics were held, where 37 residents and 44 employees were vaccinated.

• In January, the Health Services Office was reconstructed, revised and additional equipment was purchased to comply with 291 requirements.

• An annual blood drive in conjunction with the American Red Cross of NENY was held in February for the past 5 years.

What is Day Habilitation With Walls?

Day Habilitation With Walls is designed for young adults and adults with developmental disabilities seeking a personalized, site-based day habilitation experience.

Day Hab with Walls is a site based day program that serves Office for People With Developmental Disabilities (OPWDD) adults, Programing is designed to ensure that small: groups and individual experiences take place to foster ski development and community involvement. Enrolled individual work with a counselor who will help develop skills, things: and integrate them into their local community through various activities. All activities are based on the interests of individuals being served, and include exercise classes, basic money management, sports participation, recreation, art volunteer work for non profit agencies and organization which allows the individuals to learn job skills while being a help to their community.

Day Habilitation Without Walls

Day Hab Without Walls is also a day program that serves OPWDD adults. Day Hab emphasizes real community experiences for adults with developmental disabilities. Programing is designed to ensure that small groups and individual experiences take place to foster skill development and community involvement.

Enrolled individuals work with a counselor who will help integrate them into their local community through various activities. All activities are based on the interests of the individuals being served, and include exercise classes, basic money management, sports participation, recreation, art classes and much more. Day Hab also participates in volunteer work for non-profit agencies and organizations, which allows the individuals to learn job skills while being a help to their community!

Who can receive services?

To become a part of Day Hab, an individual must be OPWDD eligible. The individual must also have Medicaid and a Medicaid Service coordinator. The MSC can submit can submit a referral request for services if an individual would like to enroll in Day Hab.

Family Drive-in Care Management Services

The Basics

A “Health Home” is not a place. It is a group of health care and service providers working together to make sure that a child gets the care and services they need to stay healthy—at the right time in the right amounts.

Vanderheyden will provide a care manager to eligible families, children and youth to provide access to services assuring they have everything necessary to stay healthy, out of the emergency room and out of the hospital. The Care Manager supports services that a family may already be receiving and will help families get new ones if necessary.

Who can receive services?

Children from birth to age 21 must be enrolled in Medicaid and have either two chronic health conditions such as, but not limited to:

• Asthma, diabetes, cardiac disorder, alcohol or substance abuse, obesity BMI>25.

• Mental health condition, Cardiovascular disease (Diabetes), Respiratory disease (Asthma).

Or one single qualifying diagnoses:

• HIV/AIDS, Serious Emotional Disturbance, Complex Trauma.

Vanderheyden has experts on staff that will work to determine if a child is eligible.

What are the benefits of a Health Home?

Through a Care Manager at Vanderheyden, a Children's Health Home provides:

• Assistance in making sure a child obtains appointments with doctors, dentists, mental health providers or specialists, and will remind the family about appointments.

• Inviting everyone the family considers important to keep the child healthy and safe alone with scheduling meetings to discuss how everyone can participate.

• Talking with family and those involved how to understand the child's needs.

• Having guidance available 24/7.

What does a Children's Health Home do?

• Comprehensive Care Management

• Care Coordination and Health Promotion

• Comprehensive Transitional Care

• Individual and Family Support

• Referral to Community and Social Support Services

• Use of Health Info Technology to Link Services

Why would someone want to enroll my child in a Health Home?

Vanderheyden understands that caring for a child can be a complicated and often exhausting experience.

In response to the needs of the families they serve, they joined together with the Children's Health Home of Upstate New York (CHHUNY) and the Central New York Health Home Network (CNYHHN) to provide Care Management Services that put the family first.

Key Point of Contact

Vanderheyden understands families spend countless hours being transferred from department to department trying to get critical answers and information regarding a child's services. When enrolled in a Health Home, the Care Manager becomes the key point of contact in obtaining the answers needed.

Service Coordination

Critical to a healthy child is ensuring each service provider works together and always in the best interest of the child. A family's Care Manager will have access to information on each service a child is receiving, enabling the parent to stay in constant communication and eliminating redundancy of service. The vast network also provides linkages to related services such as Adult Health Homes and many more.

Compassion and Experience

The Care Manager is an independent position that works for the parent. Following the Health Home model of care, this position strives to learn about the unique needs of each family and work with them to make the most appropriate decisions for the family.

What is the parents responsibility in this process?

• Inviting everyone the family considers important to keep the child healthy and safe, along with scheduling meetings to discuss how everyone can participate.

• Be part of and participate in the development of the plan of care, and attend team meetings.

• Discuss the strengths of the child and family, and share opinions in be part of the plan—ask questions and let the care manager know if something is not working and needs to change.

• This is a voluntary program. The parent has the right to give and withdraw consent to share information about a child's treatment.

Children and Family Treatment and Support Services

What are children and family treatment and support services (CFTSS)?

The Basics

Children and Family Treatment and Support Services (CFTSS) are free behavioral health services-covered by New York State Medicaid. CFTSS helps with mental health and substance use needs, which give children/youth (under age 21) and their families the power to improve their health, well-being and quality of life. The services strengthen families, and help them make informed decisions about their care. Services are provided at home or in the community,

Vanderheyden works with each child/youth to provide care in a way that works best for them-and their families.

Who can receive services?

• Children and youth under the age of 21.

• Medicaid eligible or those enrolled in a Medicaid Managed Care plan.

And who:

• Need help with social, emotional, or behavioral health challenges

• Need help with substance use issues

How will these services help?

CFTSS are part of Early and Periodic Screening, Diagnosis, and Treatment (EPSDT) services. EPSDT is a federal law. EPSDT services help find and treat children's health problems early so that they can have the best health and development possible.

Through the CFTSS Team at Vanderheyden, the CFTSS meet the individual needs of children and their families/caregivers by:

• Identifying mental health and/or substance use needs early.

• Providing support in the home and community.

• Preventing the need for emergency room visits, hospital stays, or out of home placements.

How are services provided?

• All children/youth-under age 21 who are eligible for Medicaid are covered.

• CFTSS works for children/youth from any background, or who speak any language.

• Put child/youth and family choices "first."

• CFTSS can be provided in the home or community, whatever works best for the family.

Why would someone want to enroll their child/youth in CFTSS?

In response to the needs of the families they serve, they offer Children and Family Treatment and Support Services that put the family first.

Therapy Services (Other Licensed Practitioner)

• Assessments for mental health and/or substance use needs.

• Identify strengths and abilities through individual and group therapies.

• Individual, group, or family therapy where you are most comfortable.

Rehabilitation Services (Psychosocial Rehabilitation and Community Psychiatric Supports and Treatment)

• Learn to incorporate therapy goals into everyday life and receive extra support Managing medication.

• Build relationships and communicate better with family, friends and others.

• Learn self-care, and use coping skills to manage emotions.

Family Peer Support Services

• Support if a person is raising a child/youth with mental health and/or substance use challenges.

• Provided by a Credentialed Family Peer Advocate/ Certified Recovery Peer Advocate who has similar experiences.

• Get support and assistance with locating information and resources available to meet the youth/family's needs, making informed decisions, building and strengthening natural supports and resources.

How to access CFTSS for a child/youth

How is determination of a CFTSS referral and recommendation needed?

• Anyone who knows a child/youth who may need CDTSS can make a referral to a CFTSS provider. A youth who thinks they need CFTSS can make their own referral to a CFTSS provider.

Recommendation

A licensed practitioner who sees the child/youth, for example a pediatrician or therapist, can make a recommendation.

• A qualified CFTSS provider may make a recommendation for CFTSS Referral.

This is a voluntary program.

Christmas at the orphanage brought presents to all children.

Dorothy Lavinia Brown
(January 7, 1914 – June 13, 2004)

Dorothy L. Brown, also known as "Dr. D." was an African-American surgeon, legislator, and teacher who had a long connection at Vanderheyden Hall.

Brown was born in Philadelphia, Pennsylvania to Edna Brown and Julius Brown, who gave her up to the Troy Orphan Asylum at the age of five months. She was at the orphanage until age 12 and while there, at age 5, had her tonsils removed sparking an interest in the medical profession. She was one of only a few African American children there at the time and never received a visitor. Herbert Hunn, Superintendent of the orphanage noticed that Dorothy had become depressed at the lack of visitors and he arranged for a local family, Frank and Cornelia Coffeens to visit Dorothy. They were members of the local Presbyterian Church and Frank was the Bursar at Emma Willard

School that was near the orphanage, and an insurance broker. The Coffeens lived at 1 East Sunnyside Street in Troy. They would visit with Dorothy and offer encouragement.

Dorothy's mother returned when she was age 13 and took her back and told her she had *"to do what other colored girls did,"* but during the year she kept running away -- five times -- to the Troy Orphan Asylum where she felt safer until her mother put her in domestic service.

While at the orphanage she worked as a mother's helper for an Albany family, Mrs. L. F. Jarrett. Louis Jarrett was vice president of Berkshire Motor

Dr. Herbert Hunn conducts the girl's choir in the Chapel. Dorothy Brown is far right by herself. No date.

Company in Albany. They had a great deal of books and Dorothy read them. After saving a few hundred dollars, she returned to Troy homeless. As a teen, she worked as a maid at the Wing Sing Chinese Laundry at 153 Fourth Street in Troy, now demolished.

Impressed with her intelligence Herbert Hunn, superintendent of the orphanage brought her to the attention of the principal of Troy High School. Hunn also introduced her to an African American couple Samuel W. and Lola Redmond who became her foster parents at 2850 5th Avenue in Troy (now demolished) at 16 years old. The Redmond's loved her and they encouraged her to stay in school.

Samuel W. and Lola Redmond took Dorothy in and cared for her.

After finishing high school in 1937, at the top of her class, Brown worked as a domestic helper while attending Bennett College in Greensboro, North Carolina, and received assistance from the Troy chapter of the Women's Division of Christian Service of a Troy Methodist church in order to receive a four-year scholarship to Bennett College in Greensboro, North Carolina. While she was urged to study to become a schoolteacher she took classes that would benefit a medical career. The college told the church that she was not "Bennett material" but she graduated second in her class in 1941 with a Bachelors of Arts degree and went back to Troy.

Brown took a job as a presser in a large commercial laundry in Troy, still famous as the Collar City, but soon after World War II began she found a job as a civilian inspector of Army ordnance in Troy and at the Rochester Army Ordnance Department in Rochester, New York for two years. In 1944 she applied to more colleges and accepted the offer to attend Meharry in Tennessee to study medicine. Each summer she returned to Troy and the church and Hunn would make sure she could get an additional $700 in support.

Dorothy completed medical school in 1948, in the top third of her class, and interned at Harlem Hospital in New York City, but when she applied for surgical resident she was turned down because she was a woman. She went back to Meharry pleading

A teen aged Dorothy was determined to become a doctor.

with Dr. Matthew Walker to let her in and she was accepted to the surgical residency program and earned the nicknamed "mule" because of her work ethic. "Dr. Matthew Walker was a brave man," she later said because he accepted her into the program despite advice from his staff that a woman couldn't *"withstand the rigors of surgery."*

Since she was the only female surgical resident when she completed her residence at Hubbard Hospital, an affiliate of Meharry in 1954, she was the first Black female surgeon in the Southeastern United States, overcoming the prejudice of white female surgeons while at Hubbard. She also became one of the few Blacks elected in the American College of Surgeons. She was appointed Chief of Surgery in 1957 at Riverside Hospital in Nashville and held it until the hospital closed in 1983.

In 1956, Brown agreed to adopt a female child from an unmarried patient at the Riverside Hospital. The patient pleaded for Dorothy to adopt her because the patient knew she couldn't support the child without a husband, and knew that Brown would be an excellent mother. As a result Brown became the first known single female in Tennessee to legally

In 1959, she became the third woman to become a Fellow of the American College of Surgeons, the first African-American woman to be elected.

adopt a child, whom she named Lola Denise Brown in honor of her foster mother, Lola Redmond.

In 1959, she became the third woman to become a Fellow of the American College of Surgeons, the first African-American woman to be elected.

She also served as Educational Director of Riverside Meharry Clinical Rotation Program and in 1983 became Professor of Surgery at Meharry all the while having her own private practice. She became members of the National Advisory Board of the National Institutes of Health, the American Medical Association's Joint Committee on Opportunities for Women in Medicine, The National Heart, Lung and Blood Advisory Council, the Board of Trustees of Bennett College, and was active in the Methodist church. She was a life long member of the National Association for the Advancement of Colored People (NAACP).

In 1966, she became the first black (male or female) elected to the Tennessee State Legislature. She became involved in the passing of the Negro History Act, which required public schools in Tennessee to *"conduct special programs during Negro History Week to recognize accomplishments made by African Americans"* and she sponsored a bill to change the state's outdated abortion laws almost succeeding in having abortions legalized in cases of rape or incest, and expanding the law when a mother's life was in danger. When the bill lost she resigned her seat. In 1968, she ran for the Tennessee Senate but lost and her support for abortion is credited partly with that defeat. She went back to being a full-time physician at Riverside Hospital until 1983 when it closed.

In 1971, the Dorothy L. Brown Women's Residence at Meharry Medical College, Nashville, was named after her. She also received honorary doctorate degrees from the Russell Sage College in Troy, New York, and also from Bennett College in Greensboro, North Carolina. She received her honorary degrees in the Humanities from Bennett College and Cumberland University in Lebanon, Tennessee.

In 1982 she was featured in a film on her life produced by the United Methodist Church called "Run to Live: A Day in the Life of Dr. 'D' Brown."

Brown wrote her autobiography, essays, and inspirational guides. She built her own office building in the inner city across from Tennessee State University. She was a member of the board of trustees at Bennett College and of the Delta Sigma Theta sorority. She participated as a speaker on panels that discussed scientific, religious, medical, and political issues. Brown was also awarded the Horatio Alger Award in 1994 and the Carnegie Foundation's humanitarian award in 1993.

She was a member of or has been honored since 1959 by more than 100 organizations and institutions. She was proclaimed "Citizen of the Year," "Woman of the Year," and honorary mayor of several cities. In addition she received keys to cities, many certificates of appreciation, awarded medallions, was given testimonials and days of recognition have been named for her.

In her later years she came back to visit Vanderheyden Hall and told the kids that they were important. She never lost touch with her roots.

Brown died in Nashville, Tennessee, in 2004 of congestive heart failure at age 90. When she died Dr. John E. Maupin, Jr., the president of Meharry Medical College said: *"Dr. Brown will forever be a role model, not as she once said, 'because I have done so much, but to say to young people that it can be done. Death always brings sadness, and her passing causes us grief and sorrow.' But how fortunate we all have been to have had Dr. Dorothy Lavinia Brown among us as a surgeon, educator, leader, friend and Meharrian."*

Dorothy Brown discusses part of her life on this YouTube video:

https://www.youtube.com/watch?v=7LMiu6BqnH8

Barbara J. Cottrell, Marjorie (Marge) Brown (Cottrell), Don Cottrell, and Elizabeth "Betty" (Sedgewick) Long Share Their Memories

Two sisters, their brother, and a best friend to this day share their memories of being at Vanderheyden. Barbara and her sister Marjorie (Marge), their brother Don, and their friend Betty are still friends today.

The Day Home on Short Seventh Avenue and Congress Street. This was the former Tibbits Mansion.

Marge graduating eighth grade. Barbara on left.

Barbara was born in Troy's St. Mary's Hospital on June 23, 1934, and her sister Marge was born in Plattsburgh on July 10, 1935. Two brothers, Raymond and Donald, also made up the rest of the family. They all were brought to Vanderheyden in 1941, a day after Barbara's 7th birthday in June. Their father Ray went off to war. It was also a special day as they were the first family admitted to the orphanage by the new superintendent Mr. Richard Thomas.

Barbara and Marge's parents had split and the mother had four children by herself to support. While living in Troy, all the children would go to the Day Home, the old Tibbits Mansion on Short Seventh Ave in Troy. The mother would go to work with all the children with her. All the children went back to the home. They now assume that this action was

Barbara (left) as a teenager and probably contemplating her future. Barbara today on the right retired from a career in nursing. Photo on right by Don Rittner. Photo on left supplied by Barbara.

Barbara's best friend Kathleen.

They stayed in the infirmary for a week, two boys and two girls. Children were not separated at the infirmary. The boys were older and were separated from the girls also by age.

The home was undergoing a big change in operations and renovations as Mr. Thomas made improvements, and Barbara considered him a wonderful man.

Barbara eventually was moved to a dorm of about 24 girls. Marge went to the kindergarten Department. Different ages were grouped into "departments." Marge turned six years old two weeks after she was there.

Barbara's brothers Don and Ray and mother's boyfriend.

Barbara worked in the laundry department and hated it. Boys wore white shirts to the chapel and she had to iron them. She also worked in baby house, hated it,

Marge and friend Ronald in October 1952.

and did not like the work.

The children were not always in the same dorms, since they were based on age. Barbara was placed in Hart Cottage for teens, high school girls, and was big enough for only 16 girls. It is here that the institution wanted them to learn how to cook and keep house. They had their own counselor. This is when Barbara worked in the infirmary.

Barbara walked to and from School 16, as did all the kids for their education. All the children walked to School 16 from grade school and took the city buses for high school.

Then and Now. Betty, Barbara and Marge. Left photos supplied by Barbara Brown. Right photo by Don Rittner.

Barbara and her friend Betty graduated in old Troy High in 1952, now the county office building. When she graduated from high school in June, Betty and Barbara, over the course of the summer worked 12-hour shifts until they went to nursing school in September. Both Barbara and Betty became nurses thanks to one of the nurses at Vanderheyden. Barbara went to Samaritan Hospital School of Nursing, and Betty entered Putnam Nursing School. A nurse, Mrs. Arp at Vanderheyden came to work, to assist Mr. Thomas; her son was at RPI in grad school. She drove Barbara to nursing school, and gave her a trunk for her belongings. Mrs. Arp also drove Betty to Bennington, Vermont and came to her graduation.

Barbara made it to nursing school by winning first prize in an essay contest sponsored by Samaritan Hospital. In 1952, it was announced on July one that Barbara won a full tuition scholarship to the school of nursing. The theme was *"A Twentieth Century Samaritan – the Nurse."* She began her studies in September 1952.

The girls were encouraged to learn trades while there, and Mrs. Amsted taught all the girls how to make skirts. Once a week they were taught how to sew by hand. Marge made skirts out of farm feed bags during World War II.

Barbara's brother Raymond, now deceased, went to college and came back and worked at Vanderheyden Hall during summers. He earned his Ph.D, and became a professor at George Washington University.

The ladies remember saying prayers every night, but when Franklin Roosevelt died they said prayers twice. They all went to chapel every Sunday. Behind the chapel was a storage area, where there were boxes and boxes of books. They read most of them. There was a big box of used shoes during World War II and the girls and boys were fitted.

While at Vanderheyden, the girls received an allowance and worked for 10 cents an hour. Barbara also was a cheerleader in high school but did not brag about being at Vanderheyden. Hardest part of living at the orphanage was having no help if you were studying. There was no help or tutors at Vanderheyden. Barbara was having trouble in algebra and even Superintendent Thomas could not help her. One of the hardest parts of being at Vanderheyden for her was not having help for her studies.

Her Grandmother would come visit Barbara, Marge, and Don and made them sit in a swing. Both Marge and Barb would take the bus to go visit her mother. No one at the orphanage stopped them from seeing siblings or parents. They were required to see each other on birthdays, up to 10 people, and had to include family, but siblings included so if you had a big family it reduced the number of friends that could be invited. Barbara walked to a bakery up Pawling Avenue to get a birthday cake.

The girls had a bit of freedom and were allowed to go places on their own. Mrs. Darby who owned a hardware store in Troy would take the four of them to church, the brothers were acolytes at the church, St. Paul's

Episcopal Church. Marge would go to Beldens Pond for ice-skating, to Prospect Park for swimming, and did that on her own, as well as taking swimming lessons. While the girls had to get permission to do things, they certainly didn't feel free, but were allowed to do things on their own. They would get tokens to go to high school on the city buses. If you missed the bus you had to walk back to Vanderheyden.

The ladies all felt they were treated like humans. The counselors were good. They received all their medical shots and medicines. In fact, Dr. Bessey took out Barbara's tonsils. He lived near Pawling and Spring Avenues. If a girl was bad she was sent to St. Anne's in Albany; the boys went to Berkshire Industrial Farm in Canaan, New York. They remember one night a boy snuck in the girls room and the next day was sent away.

Barbara's best friend, Kathleen helped the Thomas family when his first wife died of cancer. She was a great help according to Barbara. Kathleen went to SUNY Plattsburgh for a year and then married. Once Mrs. Thomas came in on Christmas and she asked what was on Barbara's Christmas list that she didn't get, and Barbara said boots. The day after she had boots. Every year they wrote

Class of 1955. Betty at the first reunion of her Nursing School in 2018. Photo by Holly Pelczynski from the Bennington Banner.

letters to Santa and usually got what they wanted. During Christmas time, someone came in and played Santa Claus and handed out presents. This was often one of the local organizations and many local businesses and non profits donated to the orphanage each year. The presents were often wrapped by the Women's Association of Vanderheyden

They all worked in the workshop, and made things, lots of things. They also worked in 4-H, placed their products in the Schaghticoke fair, and went to camp Kiwanis for a week. Barbara was a Campfire Girl. The orphanage sponsored the TamiKata Group of Vanderheyden Hall. Her brother Raymond was Boy Scout. Movies were shown in the chapel. There was Square dancing and Vanderheyden had a good Basketball team that they would root for.

Betty (Sedgewick) Long

Betty was born in Albany Medical hospital, January 27, 1935. Betty came to Vanderheyden in 1948 as a freshman in high school. She originally lived in Rensselaer and went to Van Rensselaer High. Someone came to the school and took her and her sister (Charlotte, died 25 years ago) who was 3 and half year younger and took them to Vanderheyden. Their mother could not take care of them after their father, who was the fire chief, died.

Betty was at Vanderheyden for four years, and went to high school there before going to college. Her mother visited once in a while but not often. While in high school she took biology and chemistry and was interested in the sciences. She knew she did not want to be a secretary. In 1953, she enrolled in the nursing program at Putnam Memorial Hospital School of Practical Nursing in Bennington, Vermont. She graduated in 1955.

When her youngest son went to junior high, she became an elementary school nurse for two years and then went into an orthopedic office in Bennington for 23 ½ years. While there she took lots of casts off people with broken appendixes and with a huge elbow cast cutter. One day a four year old who called her Dr. Betty had no problem with her taking the cast off in contrast to many adults who would cringe. To this day, he still calls her Dr. Betty and she went to his high school graduation and to this day exchange Christmas gifts and cards. He is now 24 years old and is teaching physical education in Vermont.

As a nursing student she lived and attended classes in a three story brick building on the hospital grounds called the Nurse's Home. It was built in 1921 to house nurses working at the Putnam Hospital, now Southwestern Vermont Medical Center. They had their first ever reunion in 2018 that Betty attended. The nursing school officially closed in 1999.

Betty and Marge reconnected through a Hoosick Falls Polish Center's senior picnic in Rensselaer County. Marge and her husband ran a convenience store in Grafton, New York

Don

Don now lives in central Georgia on a 235-foot lakefront of Lake Oconee.

His earliest recollection was living in Clyde, New York close to Rochester. His dad had a Greyhound bus route from Clyde to Rochester every day, and then to Buffalo, so he came home after the round trip. He kept the bus in Clyde. Don remembers that he and his brother Ray would take the Greyhound bus to school on its way to Syracuse.

Don's dad had five kids in seven years, the first died when very young. Don's mother was an orphan before she was 10 years old and had no sisters or brothers. She was born in Little Falls, New York, but raised in Plattsburgh by a grandmother. When she went to Russell Sage College in Troy she met Don's father. They eloped and had five kids in 6 years. Unfortunately the mother had no family and didn't know anyone. His father and mother divorced, he found another woman. Don lived with them after the divorce.

After the father left, the wife and children moved back to Troy near Hoosick Street on Seventh Street. His grandmother on his dad's side lived only three doors from high school.

Helen, the mother, took to drinking and left four kids alone. When the State found out they took them and put them in the Troy Orphan Asylum in June 1941.

At the home, the boys were separated from the girls, He remembers the main entrance of Vanderheyden where Mr. Thomas' office was on the left, VH office was on the right, and a dining room straight ahead. The boys were all kept on the right side, while the girls were on left. The nursery and kindergarten children were kept together.

There were three different classes at Vanderheyden, seven, eight, and nine. Raymond, who was Don's brother, was a year older. Don considered him not very bright but Ray went to college, George Washington University, and received his Ph.D and worked a great deal in special education. He turned 70 on Christmas Day, and only two months later he died.

Marge, Don and Barbara.
Photo by Barbara Brown.

When Don left Vanderheyden he lived with his dad and stepmom, he got married and had three children—two boys and a girl. One son died from SIDS and the other is in the military. His daughter still is in touch.

Don joined the military, married, and has been married for 64 years. He met his wife Carol Scott when he was introduced to her by

NAME: Cottrell, Jr. Raymond A. D.O.B. Dec 25, 1931
PLACE OF BIRTH: Troy, N.Y.
MOTHER: Helen Dayton D.O.B. N.Y. 9/4/11
FATHER: Raymond A. Cottrell D.O.B. N.Y. 12/31/07
SIBLINGS: Donald
Barbara
Marjorie
DATE OF ADMISSION: June 24, 1941 REFERRED BY: Renss Co Comm. of Public Welfare
REASON FOR ADMISSION: Parents separated
DATE OF DISCHARGE: Sept 11, 1950 DISCHARGED TO: Father - Rochester NY
REASON FOR DISCHARGE:
SIGNIFICANT DOCUMENTS: 1960 - Newspaper clipping mentioned Roy Cottrell as Principal of Poestenkill school

a friend Bill Zimmer who she was attracted to. He was an athlete. He joined the Navy Reserve and got drafted and told Don to keep an eye on her, so he did. Don married her on February 5, 1955.

Overall all of their experiences at the home were very good to them. They believe they have a better life because of their stay there. Betty thinks it made her work better and helped her raise a 13 yr. old alone.

Nancy Davis

It is probably one of my earliest memories. Perhaps I was three or four years old.

My older brother and I are sitting in the back seat of our family's blue Plymouth station wagon, with fins. It is getting dark, past twilight, but there is still just a hint of light in the deep, dark blue sky. There is snow on the ground and it is almost Christmas.

My brother and I are dressed up to go to a Christmas party with our parents. We have a quick stop to make before we go to the party.

We have pulled off the main road, and slowly make our way down what seems to be a long,

Christmas at the orphanage. No date.

winding or curving drive, tall trees on either side further darken the sky.

The largest house I have ever seen is in front of me and, even through the dark, I can see outlines of gabled roofs and turrets. It's magical. Yellow light glows through beautiful windows. My dad stops the car and Mom gets out carrying packages, Christmas gifts.

As she walks up to the huge house the front door opens… bright yellow light emerges... do I see a large Christmas tree in a tall hallway?

I can barely see Mom coming back through the dark and get in the car. We drive away.

One day years later, perhaps 30, my dad and I are reminiscing. We no longer live near Troy, but for some reason he mentions Vanderheyden Hall.

I ask why the name sounds so familiar. *"It's a big old place in Troy. Used to be the orphanage. It's where we got your brother."*

I knew my brother was adopted, but I'm staring at Dad for a different reason.

"Vanderheyden Hall… a big, big house, with gabled roofs?"
"Yep."

Slowly, I ask, *"Is that where we took Christmas gifts, Dad?"*

"Yes, and it's where we got your brother."

It's where we got your brother. I never knew. That beautiful, mysterious place. I never saw it in the daytime. I never went inside. But I remember at Christmas time looking forward to seeing the big house with the gables, the golden lights, and the tree in the hall.

And it turns out that this wonderful, mysterious place is where my brother came from.

My brother…the best gift I have ever received.
In my whole life. Ever.

---Nancy Davis

Mayor George Tibbits donated $10,000 to the Troy Orphan Asylum.

Recollections of the Troy Orphan Asylum - 1928-1938

Recollection of my life as a young child in an orphanage and growing up in a foster home.

By Marion Manchester

My mother died in 1928 when I was five years old. She was warned not to have any more babies after my sister Pauline was born in December of 1926 but had gotten pregnant anyway — maybe just through ignorance of birth control methods. Anyway, she started hemorrhaging and my father waited too long to take her to the doctors. By then it was too late. She spent 19 days in the hospital before dying. I turned five while she was there.

I had several aunts and uncles — my favorite being my Aunt Anna and Uncle Ben who lived in Long Island and had two small boys. They tried to take care of us but just couldn't take four extra babies. Uncle Ben was a milkman who used to get up at 2 AM every morning and go to the dairy or wherever the milk was bottled. After loading up his big milk wagon, pulled by two horses, he would travel

his milk route and deliver milk to all his customer's doorsteps. He picked up empties at each stop and returned to the plant. He would be home by 10 in the morning and sleep during the day. After trying to take care of my brother, sisters, and myself for a few months, we were finally put in the Troy Orphan Asylum. This was a large home just for children whose parents had either died or maybe one parent couldn't manage to take care of them. In the home, there were several hundred kids from babies up to 18 years of

age. All the babies were taken care of in a separate building (the Baby House) with special nurses until they were about two years

old. Then they were transferred to the big main building. They had one big room in one corner of the main building for children two to four years old and one older woman to take care of them. She had two or three of the older teenage girls to help her. This big room had about 12 to 15 cribs all around the walls and each toddler had his/her own crib with his/her name on it. Across the hall from the nursery was a bathroom with fixtures just the right size for small children. There were several small toilets, three or four tubs and about six sinks. It was the job of the teenagers to wash them in the morning, give them baths at night, and brush their teeth.

One of my several jobs as a teenager was working in the nursery with these small children. I loved playtime and on nice days take them outside in a high walled-in courtyard. I probably worked in the nursery about four or five months before being given another job.

After the babies reached the age of four, they were transferred to the Kindergarten room. This was a very large room, next to the nursery. Here they would play all day and used the same bathroom as the toddlers. At night, they had separate dorm rooms across the hall — one for boys the other for girls. When I first got to the home, I went into the Kindergarten rooms along with Annie. Pauline went to the baby house and Bill to the big boys department. I remember waking up one night having to go to the bathroom but scared to walk down the long hall and finally wet my nightgown. There was an extra nightgown on the clothes rack so I put it on and threw my wet one down the laundry chute just outside in the hall.

I never saw much of my sister Pauline when she was real small but I know she was put in several different foster homes but was such a terror she never was kept too long.

Eventually, when I got to be about seven years old I was sent downstairs to where all the older kids were — they ranged from seven to 18 and I was the smallest one there. When we lined up for meals and I do mean lined up — it was in order of height, not age, and I headed the lines. There was a long white line painted on the floor the entire length of the big playroom and five minutes before
mealtime, all the girls had to toe this line and then we marched single file into the corridor up the stairs and into the large dining room. There were several tables seating eight to 10 kids and you always sat in the same seat. We'd march up to our regular places and stand there until everyone was in place — girls on the left side of the room and boys on the
right. There was a small table at the entrance with a bell on it. The matron would ding the bell and everyone would sit down. Then she'd ding the bell and everyone said grace. Then we could eat. The meals were served family style at each table and the girl at the head filled your plates. No one was allowed to talk except to ask for bread, salt, etc. If you were caught talking, you'd lose your desert. Once a week, after supper, we filed into the office and were allowed to pick out two pieces of penny

candy. It was a great treat. But if you were caught talking at the table two times in a row, you didn't get any candy and that was a terrible punishment.

The main part of the huge building was divided into two sides. The left side was for the girls and the right side for the boys and we were never allowed to play together. The play area where we spent our daytime hours was downstairs from the lobby and was a large long room with a cement floor. There were several brick arches down through the rooms I suppose to hold the weight of the two stories above them. Along the back wall were rows of big drawers and each girl had her own drawer to keep her toys and personal belongings in. There was no way to lock them, so if you had something you treasured, it was sometimes stolen. These drawers extended about 2/3 of the way along the back wall the other third of the back wall had bout
18-20 sinks along it with a five-foot wall in front of it for privacy. Here we had to wash our faces, brush our teeth, and once a week wash our hair. Those too small to wash their own hair had one of the older girls do it for
them.

Even here in the big girls department, we were divided up into groups. Those 7-9 years old were sent to bed at 7:00 p.m. The 10-12 year olds had to go to bed at 8:00 p.m. and the rest at 9:00 p.m. Each of these age groups had their own dorms and an older girl in
charge. Each dorm had about 30 cots in it with a chair between each one. The favorite spots were the cots next to the windows as it was cooler in the summer. There were three rows of cots in the dorm, and a couple of large dressers at the end of the room. The older high school girls used these drawers for their extra clothes. The younger girls didn't have extra clothes. Lights were out at 7 to 8 or 9 o'clock according the dorm you were in and no talking was allowed. Some of the matrons were old, very strict, and mean. If the girls got to talking and giggling, they'd be right there to find out who it was. No one ever snitched, so we'd just get a warning.

A couple of times, some young matrons would be hired and they were very nice to us
girls. Treated us more like individuals and not just a lot of chattel. They would even tell us a bedtime story and give each of us a good

night kiss. Really made us feel wanted and loved. The only problem was the mean old matrons didn't like the young ones so they generally didn't stay long.

Our day started early in the morning, everyone up to the bathroom, then get dressed, and head downstairs to the playroom. The dorms were on the second floor — the first floor was the lobby, offices, dining room, nursery and kindergarten. Our playroom was on the lower level — girls on the left and boys on the right. In between on the lower level was the huge kitchen with its own dining room and storage rooms. They had a special room, just for bread and rolls.

After getting dressed and going downstairs, we washed and lined up for breakfast. Breakfast was usually cold cereal, bread and either coca or postum. I always like the postum and thought it tasted like coffee. In the winter we had hot cereal – Wheatena or gummy oatmeal. I don't believe in all the years I lived there we were had a pancake or waffle or biscuits though we might have had biscuits.

After breakfast we marched back upstairs and made our beds. After the beds were made, each girl went on to do her assigned chores. I had some easy chores and some very hard dirty ones, which I will tell you about later on in this writing. After you finished your job, it had to be inspected and passed. If it passed you were free to go play until lunchtime. If you didn't do it right, you had to do it over again.

During the school, you didn't have time to play, until late in the afternoon. Summers were nice as you could get outside in the yard. Here we had several swings, some trapeze rings, and high and low bars to swing on. If you were lucky to have skates, you could skate on the sidewalks in the yard or maybe jump rope. Almost every one had a ball so we had games to play hitting the ball on the walk. Inside we could play jacks, as the floor was smooth concrete.

In the summer, we were allowed to go swimming in an old mill pond about a mile from the home. We had to walk the back way thru a couple of fields and then a short way on the main road. Everyone had the same kind of plain suit and cap, plus a big towel. We generally stayed about an hour — part of the time we had lessons, the rest of the time we could just swim. There were three or four chaperones to watch us.

Interior courtyard of TOA on Spring Avenue. Source Harvard Art Libraries.

Richard P. Hart, a Troy businessman, was one of the original incorporators of the Troy Orphan Asylum.

Pat Mahoney

"You may not control all the events that happen to you, but you can decide not to be reduced by them."
Maya Angelou

Memories of my time at Vanderheyden are primarily captured in these photographs. And a copy of my baby footprint identification record, which I did not see until I was 67.

Since I was placed there when three weeks old, and left shortly after my second birthday, my experience at Vanderheyden is unrevealed. Never having known my father, and being the daughter of a single teenage mother who could not keep me, I can only assume that I got off to a good start. Whatever attention and care I received during those critical first few years has carried me in to a productive adulthood.

Notwithstanding the disruption of four successive foster care placements, and the ongoing feelings of worthlessness and abandonment, I found adults whom I could trust along the way. My final set of foster parents, a teacher, a neighbor, all cared about and guided me. The turbulence of my adolescence was buffered by these supporters and -- although my goal of going to college was discouraged by many -- my determination doubled; and I was able to achieve that dream with a scholarship, multiple jobs (starting at age 14), hard work and caring professors.

I moved to New York City in 1973, college degree in hand but no career plan at all. Through the kindness of countless individuals, I

was referred to every job I ever held, including those with a Judge (at the time one of very few female attorneys-at-law), Speaker of the New York State Legislature, national family planning agency, Mayor of NYC (Office of Children and Families), housing authority, and an organization similar to Vanderheyden that housed teenage girls in the foster care system who were pregnant and had no place else to go.

You see the emerging theme: a lifelong dedication to supporting and strengthening children, youth and families. It never occurred to me that this was connected to my own background and childhood. And I never spoke about either, even in to my 30's. Until I met Robert Little, brother of Malcolm X, who was head of the child services administration in NYC. He, Malcolm, and all of his siblings were separated when young and moved around between foster homes. This is true of other well-known individuals, such as Ray Charles, Eddie Murphy, Marilyn Monroe, and Ice-T. Yet, we all did succeed in life. Robert Little taught me that it is not only okay, but actually better, to talk about our past. There is no shame in being a foster child or in a facility where adults other than our parents care for us, listen to us, and truly earn our trust.

Things are far different in the world today than back in the early 1950s. What will never change, however, is that families will not always be together, and there will always be a need for places like Vanderheyden. During its 185 years, Vanderheyden has changed with the times, incorporating new knowledge about trauma-informed services and the positive development of youth. May it ever be so. And may every alumnae of Vanderheyden believe its motto: IMAGINE MORE. With encouragement, understanding, compassion and trust, every young person can beat the odds and become the caring adult who made the difference in her or his own life.

Marijayne Van Vost

In 1939, Marijayne Van Vorst (Wernett) was one of four children, (twins Jean and Joan and brother Charles [Chuckie]). Because the children were neglected by their parents they were removed from the family home with the intent of placing them in the Troy Orphan Asylum, now known as Vanderheyden Hall. Instead, the twins and brother Charles were taken into the home of two aunts (father's sisters) and Marijayne was the only one transported to the TOA. Her introduction to the institution was unlike that of many others, however. Instead of being placed in the general population, she was taken into the home

Marijane Wernett (Van Vost) today.
Photo courtesy of Marijayne.

of Richard and Dorothy Thomas, the Superintendent and his wife. They had a son, Joel, who was six months younger than Marijayne and the Thomas family thought they would be good playmates.

Marijayne and Joel became good friends and were best friends through 8th grade and into high school. They lost contact after high school, but remained in touch over the years, maintaining their friendship until his death a few years ago.

In 1940, the family was reunited and the four children returned to their home with both their mother and father. In September of that same year, a fifth child was born, Judith (Judy). In 1941, the father was drafted into the US Army Air Corps and

Marijayne and her daughter Mary Ellen.

the children were again removed from the home and placed in Vanderheyden. A sixth child, Joyce, was born in November 1941 and went from Albany Hospital directly to the

Judy Van Vost, Marijayne's little sister is seen on the far right sitting and holding her baby doll in this Christmas photograph.

Baby House at the home. Marijayne remembers being allowed to visit her baby sister, at first with her mother, then by herself, and spending many hours with her new sister.

When they went to the home in 1941, Marijayne, although only 5 years old, was placed in the Junior Girls (ages 6-10) because she had already completed kindergarten and was ready for first grade. The twins and Charles were placed in the Nursery (ages 3-5) and Judy went to the Baby House. The Kindergarten, Nursery and Baby House were unisex departments and Marijayne was allowed to visit her siblings frequently. She

Sister Judy on left facing the camera.

had access to visit them at almost any time and always had contact with them. She would go and investigate if anything happened to them.

Marijayne remembers while in the Junior Girls group, she wore red Gingham dresses. She believes the younger girls wore blue Gingham, the Intermediate Girls green, and the senior Girls (in Hart Cottage) wore yellow. Sometime between 1941 and 1946, however, the children were given "regular" clothes, and that was a welcomed change by everyone. The children always went to the local public school, PS 16, and were easily recognizable as "home" kids or "orphans," even though many were not, by their clothing. Now they blended in and looked like everyone else.

She recalls that downstairs, below the main-floor offices and lobby, was a huge clothing room with "tons" of clothes. Twice a year (usually the end of summer, late spring), the children were allowed to go in and select their school clothes for the next several months. In addition to dresses, they had jumpers, blouses, skirts, playsuits, dungarees, coveralls, coats, and snowsuits. There was also a large shoe room, where they would be fitted for at least two pairs of shoes no less than twice a year

Marilyn Monroe with Milton Greene at Billy Reed's nightclub.
Photo from Pinterest.

(more, if necessary), one for play and one for "good."

After graduating from PS-16 in 1950, Marijayne went to Troy High School, where she was part of the 1954 "Centennial" class, that was the first class to graduate from the "new" school, on Burdett Avenue in Troy. She recalls that at the home, all the children received an allowance each Saturday.

In the Junior Girls, she received 12 cents (usually a dime and two pennies). This was a time when penny candy truly was PENNY candy. She was allowed to spend the dime as she wanted, but was expected to deposit the two cents in the collection plate at the Chapel the next morning.

The younger children were expected to make their own beds and keep the space around their immediate sleeping area clean, but generally had no real duties. If they were naughty, however, they could be made to wash the windows with soap or scrub the back stairs with a toothbrush. (That same punishment also applied to the Intermediate Girls, when required.)

In the Intermediate Girls, the children had more responsibilities in keeping their dormitories clean and neat. They were also allowed to work in the dining room, before and after meals, helping to set tables. Food was delivered to the dining room from the kitchen, below, by way of dumbwaiters. The children and staff transferred food from huge pots lifted to the dining room level from the kitchen below into serving dishes, placed dipperfuls of milk into stainless steel milk pitchers, loaves of bread onto platters, and generally set the tables for children and staff. Performing these tasks entitled a willing worker to 25 cents a week, plus the two cents for Chapel. Of course, Marijayne volunteered for that job.

CHILDREN MAKE ANNUAL REQUESTS TO SANTA CLAUS

Vanderheyden Hall Youngsters Pay Visit To O.E.S. Chapter

"A whole box of candy all to myself" was the modest request made to Santa Claus by a child at Vanderheyden Hall as the annual letters to Santa were presented Palestine Chapter, O.E.S., by the children last night. For many years the chapter has received the requests of the orphanage children and has carried them out at Christmas time.

Mr. and Mrs. Richard H. Thomas and Eugene Rogers, organist, accompanied a group of children from Vanderheyden to the Lansingburg Masonic Temple. The children watched the 45th anniversary drill presented by the chapter and then sang three songs, "The Sky Can Still Remember," "I Thank Thee" and "Follow the Star." The singers were Marguerite Spotten, Marjorie Cottrell, Mary Jane Van Vorst, Catherine Verghen, Joan F---- Laura LeFavour, Vada Con-

DEAR SANTA—Children from Vanderheyden Hall gave Santa advance notice of the gifts t[...] like for Christmas last night when they appeared at Lansingburg Masonic Temple as gue[...] Palestine Chapter, O.E.S. Each child presented a letter to Santa which, just prior to Chri[...] will be answered in full. Above, with the children are, left to right, Carleton A. Newton, Madge Davis, Richard L. Thomas, Mrs. Alice I. Samuels, district deputy; Mrs. Helen E. For[...] Mrs. Jane B. Powers.

12/25/47 THE TROY RECORD, THURSDAY MORNING, DECEM

Marijayne is in the top photo (the shortest girl on the left, in the front row) and appear to be the second one in from the viewer's left in this newspaper article. Her second-to-youngest sister Judy is present, this time smack-dab in the middle in the bottom photo. She is looking straight ahead, and there is a little boy to her left.

As she got a little older and stronger, she also volunteered to wash the dishes, which were then placed into huge "racks" and run through the sterilizer by a senior boy. It seems the boys were the only ones allowed to do this because the racks were so heavy and the steamer might have been considered dangerous. She is not too sure about this. But she now earned 50 cents a week, plus two cents for Chapel, and accepted this chore gratefully.

Intermediate Girls were also allowed to work in the Laundry, generally folding sheets as they came through the giant rollers and towels. Again, they were paid 2 cents per week.

The senior girls had the responsibilities of "babysitting" the nursery and kindergarten children, mostly on weekends and during summers. This required two girls per day (7:00 a.m.—7:00 p.m.) with a two-hour break in the afternoons. For this, they received $1.10 per day. She is not sure about the Chapel contribution at this level. It may have been a nickel.

They were also allowed to work in the Infirmary, which involved greeting children/ staff who arrived with minor complaints, answering the phone, seeking medical if/when necessary. This, too, was paid at the rate two-hour break. Marijayne really loved working in the infirmary, but did not like having to be with the children for those long hours.

Generally speaking, the children were treated very well, and during wartime grew their own "Victory Garden." Marijayne recalls shelling peas, snapping beans and husking corn every summer before being allowed to go swimming in Cole's Creek, a short walk from the home. The vegetables were then frozen and available throughout the winter months, so the children never went hungry, even in wartime.
The farm, which was a short drive down the dirt road behind the institution, had horses, cows, pigs and chickens.

She recalls it being an event when the home was given six steers. This meant beef, a commodity that was scarce to children who were faring better than most during the difficult war years. Stress though being in a "home" and not allowed to be at home with her mother, Marijayne recalls she and all the other residents at Vanderheyden Hall were generally treated very well. They had food, clothing, comfortable surroundings and a safe place to live.

Left to right. Marijayne's daughter in law, son, Marijayne and her daughter celebrating Marijayne's 83rd in Mendocino, California in 2019.

She recalls while in the Intermediate Girls, about 18-20 of them lived in one huge room, that had a bay window looking out onto Spring Avenue. At that time, the bathroom was one large room, at the end of the hall, with four or five bathtubs lined up one after the other on the left as one entered the door, and perhaps 8-10 sinks liked up on the right. Behind the sinks and tubs were toilet stalls.

During this time, this entire floor was remodeled. Instead of one huge room, which was both bedroom and play/activity room, girls now had two separate bedrooms, with a bathroom between, which not only had toilets, sinks and tubs, but now had SHOWERS! The children had never had showers before this time.

The new bedrooms initially contained eight beds each with a 4-drawer dresser in between to be shared by two girls (2 drawers each), a nightstand and a chair.

The children were required to bathe and change their clothes every Tuesday night and Saturday morning. They also had to wash their hair on Saturdays. Of course, if they needed or wanted baths in between, they could ask for them. If they required clean clothes between the scheduled days, they were usually provided.

Marijayne began to see some of the advantages she and the children enjoyed when a high-school friend was granted permission to spend an overnight with her while Marijayne was a resident of Hart Cottage, a separate house intended only for high-school girls. It could house a maximum of 18 girls, but was never totally full while she was there.

The main bedroom was a large dormitory with seven bunk beds, several dressers and two large closets. There was one smaller room, which housed only one bunk bed and dresser.

When her friend spent the night with Marijayne, she asked if she could take a shower. When told "yes," the girl spent a good 10-15 minutes there. When she emerged, she was almost ecstatic. She had never had that long a shower in her entire life, certainly not one with hot water. Marijayne learned the girl came from a very poor family. They not only didn't have a shower, they didn't have running water. The girl was beautiful, smart and a cheerleader.

Marijayne always admired the fact she made her own clothes from flour sacks and scraps of cloth if she hadn't realized it before. Marijayne certainly now realized she had it "pretty good."

Every year, the dining room was transformed into a Christmas paradise, starting with the 20-foot tree. All the sideboards were decorated with snow scenes and skaters made of pipe cleaners and crepe paper, stars and angels hung above the walls separating the serving/dishwashing area from the main dining room.

Santa arrived every Christmas Eve with no less than two gifts per child, and almost always two gifts from the list of ten each child requested in his/her annual letter to Santa Claus around Thanksgiving-time.

Immediately after Christmas, but before New Year's, the Knights of Columbus arrived with a few hundred Christmas-decorated boxes filled with peanuts, all sorts of mixed nuts (in shells), tangerines, ribbon candy, popcorn balls and other delicious "goodies." Marijayne recalls her judicious sampling from her box could last until almost Easter. (Some of the boxes were emptied almost immediately.)

Mr. Thomas went around every night to every department and said goodnight to everyone. Oftentimes, he would read a story. Mr. Thomas would call out individual names, and was overall a father figure and a wonderful man according to Marijayne.

She remembers that Mrs. Thomas used to come and help her with homework and special projects and thought of her as her daughter. However, when their son Steven was born, Marijayne did not see the mother as much, but remembers seeing her pushing baby Steve down Spring Avenue almost every day.

Vanderheyden was a beautiful place, and Marijayne was proud of it. She remembers getting up in the morning meant making the beds, washing up, brushing teeth and hair, getting dressed, then sitting with hands folded and ankles crossed until the bell rang for breakfast. Intermediate girls could earn 25 cents a week by helping set the tables and serve food to the tables from the kitchen. Food was delivered to the kitchen from the "big" kitchen downstairs via dumbwaiters. The servers then transferred it to bowls and platters and delivered it to the tables. Milk was delivered, via dumbwaiter, in 10-gallon cans and was transferred, via dippers, to pitchers. The same routine was followed pretty much for all meals.

During the school year, the children walked to PS 16, walked home at midday for a hot dinner, then walked back for the afternoon session. After school, they had to change from their school clothes into "play" clothes, usually coveralls in the early years, then more modern street clothes later on. They could then play, do homework or specific chores, and have supper around 5:30 p.m. In the summer months, they could play outside until just before bedtime.

In the winter months, they returned to their respective departments where they played games, read, or visited with one another. In about 1948-49, the Intermediate girls received a television set, so they were allowed the opportunity to see some of the very early snows.

Marijayne left Vanderheyden in April 1953 when she applied for a part-time job with the New York Telephone Company and was one of eight winners selected for 8 positions as long-distance operators in Albany. Her mother had told her if she could get a job and pay rent, she could go home and live with her. So Marijayne managed a way to do it. She realized early on that was a mistake. She really should have remained at Vanderheyden where she would have continued to have room and board and, most likely, a job while she continued school at a local college. Moving home was not all she had hoped it would be and she no longer had the security she had while a resident at Vanderheyden. Although Marijayne always loved her mom, she was a difficult person to live with and really did not know what to do with a 17-year-old teenager.

On graduation from Troy High School in 1954, Marijayne continued to work for the NY Telephone Company for the next year. Then, in 1955, she moved to New York City where she enrolled in the Barbizon Modeling School and was accepted into the American Academy of Dramatic Arts to learn about the performing arts. She worked that summer as a hat-check girl at Billy Reed's Little Club (1946-1965), a swank supper club at 70 East 55 Street, where she met famous people such as Jackie Gleason, Marion Davies, Frank Sinatra and more. As a side note, the Club maintained a selection of neckties for Jackie Gleason, who selected the one he wanted to wear each time he went there. The Club had a rule...men had to wear ties.

Marijayne then took a job with American Airlines in New York City as a reservations agent and enrolled at Columbia University School of General Studies, where she remained for about 15 years before moving to Hollywood, California with the airline. (She really moved there because her beloved team, the Brooklyn Dodgers, had moved there in 1958.) She continued to work with American while simultaneously pursuing a TV acting/ modeling career. She had some success, but soon realized this was not the life for her.

Marijayne was then hired as a stewardess for the Hacienda Hotel in Las Vegas, Nevada, which had its own fleet of planes and flew passengers from the Los Angeles and San Francisco areas to Las Vegas several times a day, returning them to their homes at the end of the same day.

In addition, the hotel flew people from Dallas, Houston, Detroit, Philadelphia and New York to Las Vegas on Sundays, returning them to their homes the following Thursdays. She recalls this was a terrific job.

But the CAB (Civil Aeronautics Board), the airline governing authority at the time, ordered the hotel to "cease and desist" its operation in about 1962-63. So Marijayne jumped into her 1949 Lincoln Cosmopolitan and drove north to Oakland where a supplemental carrier, TIA (Trans International Airlines), was hiring a stewardess. She was hired on the spot and immediately began serving military personnel as they were being transported to and from domestic military bases and overseas bases such as Honolulu, Wake Island, Guam, the Philippines, Viet Nam, Korea and Okinawa.

After TIA was purchased by Kirk Kerkorian, an American-Armenian businessman, they started to fly junkets between Las Vegas and various US cities.

About 1966-67, a chief stewardess position opened up with Overseas National Airways (ONA), another supplemental carrier, in New York City. Marijayne was offered the job and drove back to accept it. This airline also transported military personnel domestically and abroad, but now the destinations were across the Atlantic, mostly in Europe. ONA also offered private "junkets," similar to those offered by TIA and World Airways on the West coast, but the most frequently served city was Miami, Florida.

While with ONA, Marijayne met the man she eventually married and left the airline. She continued to live in the New York City area until her divorce in 1973, when she relocated to Santa Rosa, California. She started her own business, where she provided bookkeeping, secretarial, transcription services to attorneys, investigators, court reporters and the general public. She continued this business for about 10 years when most of her clients retired. She continues to work daily for an attorney and drives for Doordash at night. She also drove for Uber for nearly three years.

And although Marijayne felt, early in her life with her mother, she had made a mistake, she realizes now it was no mistake at all. The paths she took and the life she has led brought her two incredible children and three beautiful granddaughters. Life has been good and continues to be so. None of this could have happened had she not taken every single step she has taken. And she regrets not one moment.

Winter scene of TOA on Spring Avenue, earlyt 20th century. Source: Harvard Art Galleries.

Charles Van Vost

Back in the 1930s, life was tough for many Americans. Charles's mother was no exception, especially with 5 children and being a single mom. It seemed clear she was not going to be able to make it, so all the children found themselves in Vanderheyden. Charles was only 2 years old and remembers the day he was brought there. He was taken down to the kindergarten section and climbed up the ledge to look out the window, not fully understanding he was not going to go home and be with his mother again.

The orphanage had different departments and regulated by age. The kindergarten was at the far left side of the orphanage where they could play in the area enclosed by a brick courtyard. The kids slept in a dormitory and with many beds. Boys and girls were together in the nursery and kindergarten departments but were separated into separate girls and boys dorms at the higher ages. Charles stayed at Vanderheyden until the age of fourteen and experienced living in most of the departments.

He admits that he was hard to handle and at one point the orphanage asked his mother to take him out.

Charles remembers walking to school 16. While at school he and his fellow orphanage mates knew they were outsiders, but they turned it around and called everyone not from the orphanage "outsiders." They knew they were different. They dressed different in school in the 1940s. He was still wearing knickerbockers and long socks, and so they stood out like a sore thumb.

Other reminders of being outsiders occurred every day in school. A milkman would come to school daily and bring a little bottle of milk for all the students except for the kids from the orphanage. The milk was 2 cents a bottle and it appears the orphanage did not want to incur the daily cost.

Moreover, it was apparent that the kids in the home were different simply by using ink pens. They had inkwells in the school. Kids from Vanderheyden were given a pen with an applied tip on it. Everyone else had a fountain pen. These examples and others obviously brought problems between the "outsiders" and the regular school kids.

For a small boy without a mother was tough. His mother would come infrequently to see all the children. The sisters were not affected as much but he was affected and it stayed with him his entire life. If she said she was coming the following week, that was chiseled in stone according to his thought process. When she did not appear he would wait all day only to be disappointed.

Even with these setbacks, Charles didn't realize the entire time he was there how fortunate he was to be at Vanderheyden. That realization came when he went home to live with his mother again. He was the first of the five children to go back home. She encountered behavioral problems with Charles. She was living in a flat with a simple potbelly stove and in the kitchen was a gas and coal stove. The flat had no hot water and no refrigerator. He didn't realize until years later when he saw his friends growing up in the 50s that the life at Vanderheyden, though a regimented life, was more of a stable environment. He had 3 square meals a day, showers, and he was always warm in winter months. There was a church (chapel) at the end of the building, protestant, he believed, and a preacher came every Sunday from Salvation Army, a Father Nelson.

Overall Charles believes he did not have a bad life at Vanderheyden compared to what other families were going through in the 50s. He was free to go where he wanted to go, since they were not locked in.

At Christmas Time, the children could go downtown to Frear's Department Store or the Five and Dime. He belonged to the local 4-H Club while at the orphanage. He also enjoyed working on the farm. Everyday that you weeded or did a chore, the person in charge of the farm, Mr. Steffen, put a mark in his book. During the fall, when the Schaghticoke Fair came around he would get 10 cents for every day a mark was in the book. He would find himself with a couple of dollars to spend. The kids didn't have a lot of possessions in the home so it was nice to get a little spending money.

Charles found himself to be somewhat a loner and would venture off. He knew when the berries would be ripe for the picking. He also knew where apples and pears were being grown, so would pick them too, even if they were on someone else's property.

His sisters were in the Hart building. It had its own kitchen facilities, etc. The counselor Mrs. Stella, had polio he believed, had braces on both legs and walked with a cane. Once Charles and a friend, around 10 or 11 years old, were in the woods adjacent to the home, called the loft because of the shape. They would go in and run around the paths pretending they were horses. His friend Philip and Charles came out of the woods and saw three peach pies cooling on the windowsill. They snuck up and dipped their hands in the pies, taking handfuls, and stuffed it in their mouths. Not leaving well enough alone they then marked up the other pies with their fingers. They did not realize Mrs. Stella saw them do it.

In the main dining room all girls were seated on one side, the boys seated on the other. If you got in trouble, the counselor would come down and whisper in your ear that someone wanted to see you. They had to go to see Mrs. Stella in the Hart building. They walked over knowing what was in store for them and friend Philip was crying all the way over. He kept saying he didn't do it, over and over, but Mrs. Stella saw them and knew the truth. She didn't blame them for eating the pies, but was angrier that they marked them up with their fingers.

Charles got a whipping with her cane while between her legs. Philip got a beating he would not forget mostly for lying about it.

Overall Charles learned good personal habits and especially cleanliness. When he gets up in the morning he still makes his bed. Habits he formed while at the home he still performs. Throughout his career as an owner of concrete company his employees would get a charge because he carried a handkerchief with him. All these funny little quarks he still has from being at Vanderheyden. To this day, his wife makes fun of him for it. He remembers clearly 7 or 8 children lined up for church with a necktie on. They would go down to the first floor where someone held a glass and comb so they could comb their hair. When Charles and his wife go out to dinner he still puts on a necktie and he tries to dress up on Sunday.

He has fond memories of Christmas time. Every department from the Nursery on up had their own Christmas tree and on one side of the dining room stood a huge Christmas tree. All the children were able to fill out a Christmas list. He believes it was the Eastern Star and Knights of Columbus that fulfilled the wish list. Each child would receive three items of the ones you picked out. In view of the timing of the 1940s and 1950s that was pretty generous.

While Charles has had a successful life even to this late date he feels like other people are outsiders. He can't get rid of the feeling, but he always looks at the positive aspects of growing up there, and he certainly learned some good habits. He often thinks that he was happy he grew up there rather than the streets of Rensselaer. He saw the way many of friends grew up and he realizes his life had it a little bit better.

On his office wall, he has a photo of his days there and often looks at it reflecting on his memories.

Like most kids his age, Charles and friends would get into mischief. They use to go up to the corner where Spring Avenue and Pawling meet where at the point there once was a soda fountain shop owned by an elderly man and his son. Charles was good at going in and taking stuff. One of the easiest things to 'borrow' was candy LifeSavers, the multicolored ones. They were small and could be grabbed quickly and put in the pocket. At Vanderheyden he only received an allowance of 5 or 7 cents. So he and friends would go up to the soda fountain and grab what they could. His friend Eugene and he would go up with a penny to buy something, and one would grab the roll of LifeSavers when the owner was not looking. When they got back to the home they shared with friends. Another kid, named Donnie, asked how they got them and Charles admitted taking them. So Donnie asked to go with him, and right in front of the owner's eyes placed a bag of potato chips in his pocket. The owner came over and slapped him in the face. Donnie didn't understand you don't steal when they are watching you. Lesson learned.

Another episode took place at Vanderheyden. In one of the buildings the front of the home it had a large stone portico. Vanderheyden's superintendent, Mr. Thomas's office was on the left, and a large basement was under the home where on the right side was the boy's playroom, and on the left side for the girls. There were rooms in between, where they kept shoes and 55-gallon drums of candy. In front of the office was a grill and window. One night when Charles and friends were coming back from shop, he got the idea of removing the grill to get into the room and grab the candy filling his shirt full. Everyone that night received candy but he got a whipping for that. Everyone tattled on him.

Overall, Charles had pleasant memories of being at Vanderheyden. He saw his sister occasionally in different departments and they would talk. Because of the situation, they grew up estranged and never were that close. He still has difficulty with that and to this day has difficulty with being affectionate.

He points out that as a kid you learn to Un-love when you don't see you mom in a happy relationship. It is a big diffidence between a kid growing up with two loving parents. When you grow up in a different situation like his you are learning not to love. Consequently, a lot of people don't realize that's why they have trouble in relationships, there are no role models growing up and is one of the downsides of growing up like that. But he also points out that it could have turned out the same way if he grew up in the city of Rensselaer.

The thing Charles remembers mostly is the beauty of the buildings inside and outside at Vanderheyden. They were all paneled inside, in the main foyer, and entry hall all had oak benches. It was a Castle like atmosphere. While you think you are missing out on a great deal not being with your mom as it turns out you weren't missing out on anything.

While he never saw his father, he was once shown an envelope that was sent to him from his dad that had some coins in an envelope. His father had a total of 43 children with other women.

Charles lived with his mother until he went into the Navy. He moved back with her when he returned and then went his own way. He did care for her in the later years and moved her close to him in Mechanicville, New York. She told him he was the only child that stood by her. Sisters had mixed feelings. Totally understandable, he says. He did too. He had trouble being affectionate with her and in later years he cared for her the best he could. He understands that his mother did not have an easy life. He also remembers that she did not abandon the kids like others did. She could have totally walked away and though she came infrequent at least she did come. After he came home in 1953, sister MaryJayne came home, and then the other kids came home. All in all, Charles has had a successful life and he gives acknowledgement to Vanderheyden for that.

Memories from the Past

Let some of the former wards of the Asylum speak for themselves.

Brooklyn, N. Y., Sept. 23, 1913.
I am glad to tell you (of) the benefits I received at the Home. The first thing I learned was that cleanliness was next to Godliness, which was one thing that I have never forgotten and I shall teach my children the same. I learned never to get discouraged but try and try again until success: finally wins out. Also I have been benefited by being taught never to be afraid of work, work, not only for oneself, but in working for others.

In 1872 my brother and I entered the Troy Orphan Asylum, where we spent three of the happiest and most helpful years of our lives. I was fortunate enough to be placed under the influence of that grand, good woman, Miss Doolittle. At the age of twelve years, a home was found for me where I enjoyed three years of farm life.

During these six years, the religious and physical training I received, fitted me for a healthy and wholesome manhood.

Some of the days at the institution stand out in my memory as the happiest of my life, and I shall always think of the Home with the tenders affection, for I owe so much to those who provided such a pleasant shelter for two unfortunate children, who even at that early age, could appreciate their good fortune. I could never do justice to my subject if I endeavored to tell of the excellent management of the institution at that time, but will say that I am confident it could not be too highly praised.

A high school language teacher: March 20, 1933.

To be very honest, I attribute most of my success to the advantages I received there. In no other way could I have received the education, which I value far above most of the possessions one can gain in this world.

Not only do I feel grateful for the educational advantages offered but also for the quickening of other sensibilities which make life worth living: such as love of beauty, the appreciation of music, and the esteem of strength of character.

Another letter from a wife and mother says: February 28, 1953.

I can state in all sincerity that whatever success has been or will be mine can be credited to the splendid, wholesome upbringing received at the T. O. A.

February 28, 1935.
A United States Marine writes:

I am aware the training of the orphanage has influenced me a great deal in life, The Home and the many facilities there have given me a sound start, which I am very proud of. I have had three years of duty on Latin American soil and have visited many ports. The good work of the Orphanage deserves the fullest admiration.

I always carry a postcard picture of the Home among my personal effects, and at times I scan every window and door to recall many happy memories of early lite.

A girl sends this undated note:
I received a very good education at the Home, and was taught to be honest and good. I obtained a very nice position, which I have had for 13 years. I want to thank you all for your kindness to me. Miss Haus has always been a great help to me. I joined the church while at the home.

March 20, 1935.
A United States soldier in the Panama Canal Zone is proud that he spent eleven years at the Troy Orphan Asylum. Continuing in a letter of the above date, he says:
Now in later years I realize that I couldn't have had a better home. I regret the day I left and went into the world to shift for myself. I should have finished my education at the Home.

I can thank the Home for the job that I now hold in the United States Army. I hope someday I can do something to repay the Home for what it has done for me.

Another undated letter says:
I can no more forget my childhood at the Home than I can forget my name. Thru the teachings of the Orphan Asylum I learned to appreciate the finer things of life and this refining influence has assisted me in securing and retaining my various positions.

It was the knowledge that her children were well cared for that helped my mother thru the dark years following my father's death. My mother knows the Home to be a true haven of refuge for children and a consolation to those who need to place them there.

My early training has always been a guide for my actions of which I have never been ashamed.

A friend remarks in a letter date March 6, 1933, that:

The Orphanage has influenced me to be loyal and true to the people and to my country. It has enabled me to save my money. It has made me become a church member, has taught me to be kind and gentle to little children and to be courteous to grown-up people.

A physician states that he attained success because of the fact that the Troy Orphan Asylum taught him that good, honest work and decent behaviour are always rewarded. He continues in a letter of April 7, 1933, by saying that the influences the Troy Orphan Asylum has had upon his success in life were many:

During my stay at the orphanage, I, with the other children, was taught daily that work, being wholesome, was something to be performed in a matter of fact way. That after our tasks were done, we were then free to enjoy ourselves. And again, the degree of that freedom depended upon our general deportment and scholastic records.

Thus we were taught that good work and decent behavior were always rewarded.

I left the Home a high school graduate, and went to work for the summer, as an assistant gardener on a Long Island estate. While working there, I decided that I should like to attend a certain college and become a physician. Accordingly my wages were well saved that summer, and in the fall the amount was sufficient to pay the tuition fee.

While going to school and during Vacations, I found work, variously, as a machinist's helper, later becoming a helper in a wire and cable manufactory, mail carrier, night man and car washer in a garage, counterman in a restaurant, furnace tender and feeder in a rolling mill, riveter's helper on electrical construction jobs, chauffeur and cabdriver. Finding time to study was the most difficult task.

During the last year at school, an aunt came to my assistance financially, which I enabled me to fully apply myself, especially during the internship. After commencement, using some money that had been left to me, I attended a midwestern university for a post-graduate year.

Returning to the East, I took the examinations of two State Boards. After practicing with an older physician in New Jersey for a few months, I came to this city to open my own office.

It is doubtful if any boy, suddenly left alone and penniless in the world, after the usual home life in a good family, could start out on his own initiative with the assured determination and energy of another boy, who has already learned the first important lessons of work in life,

These lessons were taught us in the orphanage, although we were not conscious of it at the time. Upon looking back from the viewpoint of a few years, they stand out very plainly.

A man in the business world writes in letter dated April 1, 1935.

During the formative period of my life, when other influences might so easily have been disastrous, I was protected, educated and nourished, and fitted for the life into which I was later to grow. I have nothing but pleasant recollections of the treatment received while at the Orphan Asylum, and have never been ashamed to let it be known among my friends that I received a large part of my education and life training there.

I am glad to put in a good word for the Asylum and the work they are doing among children. When I left the Asylum, it was my purpose to take my place as a man in the world, and in the Church of Christ. Whatever I may be able to accomplish is due very largely to the training that I received in the institution. It has been a pleasure for me to return to the Asylum occasionally and take part in the chapel service on Sunday afternoons. I hope I may have this pleasure tor many years to come.
Undated.

An attorney, and former City Treasurer of the state of New York, learned to be clean in body, mind and soul. He tells us that whatever success he has attained in life he owes in a very large measure, to the influence of the Troy Orphan Asylum.

During those early years when I most needed maternal care, the Orphanage was a real mother to me. Within those friendly walls I found a Christian home. There under a most wholesome environment, I grew from boyhood to young manhood and received a thorough Christian training.

That every task however small is worthy of one's best endeavor: that true success in life is commensurate with service rendered to others: and to be clean in body, mind and soul are but few of the lessons learned while there. These, others, and the Biblical admonition: Keep thy heart with all diligence, for out of it are the issues of life, so strongly and consistently emphasized by Miss Bailey and her successors, have been of immeasurable value to me.

Although many years have passed since I left the Asylum, never have I forgotten the debt of gratitude I owe to the tome and those who cared for and guided me while there.

The great good the Asylum has done for me and others cannot be measured by human standards, for God alone can now the true value of that lofty Christian service.

March 5, 1933.

I wish to pay the well-deserving tributes to my T. 0. A. friends who have helped to mold and shape and guide my life into worthwhile channels.

She pays tribute to and expresses admiration for, many of those persons who have given so freely and unsparingly of their Home and talent, in some instances of material riches so that the great work of the Asylum might go forward. Miss White, matron at the Eighth Street Orphanage.

My dear Miss Bailey, under whose sweet guidance I became a Christian. The wonderful little mother, Miss Witbeck, who taught me so many worthwhile lessons, Her little phrase, "We've got to meet it," sounds in my heart again and again and helps me over many a difficult place. The sweetest women that ever lived in a childish heart-Miss Emma McChesney, taught us all to save our pennies, and to give a tenth of our earnings to God. Mrs. George Harrison, who sent me to Northfield Seminary, and delighted my girlish heart with a beautiful white graduation dress, with a dignified, graceful train on it. Mrs. L. E. Gurley, who sent me to India as a Missionary. Mary Lane, who made my childish heart happy. Mrs. Wm. M. Peckham, one of my best friends through life. Grace L. Hammett, a staunch friend to me. Miss Emma Barnum, whose patience and love in the schoolroom called forth the best in every childish heart. Mr. Charles Allen, who for years conducted the Sunday school, and taught us the practice of scripture verses in daily life, and Miss Edith Sampson, Sunday school teacher, who made a lasting impression on my life.

This woman, striving for the highest ideals, service to mankind, has a noteworthy record of achievement. She graduated from Northfield Seminary in 1904 (and) from the Samaritan Hospital in 1907. She passed the R. N. State Board in 1908. She went to India as a Missionary, 1909-1912. She was supervisor of the Troy Orphan Asylum Baby House, from 1912 to 1917. She took a post-graduate course in Massage and Hydrotherapy at Battle Creek Sanitarium, and studied in college "How to Teach Nursing" in 1917. She was a substitute Instructor of Nurses at the Samaritan Hospital, 1917-1918, since 1918, she taught Massage and Hydrotherapy in the hospitals of Troy, Cohoes, and Lansingburgh. She volunteered service in Dr. Grenfell's Mission in Labrador from June to October 1922. She attended the Emerson College of Oratory and obtained the degree of Bachelor of Literary Interpretation, 1923-1926. And later she had full charge of the Oratory Department of Houghton College, Houghton, N. Y., 1926-1933, and attained an A. B. Degree from Houghton College.

Eager to accomplish still greater things, this noble soul attended summer sessions at New York State College tor teachers, Albany, New York; at Stanford University, Palo Alto, California; Columbia University, and Union

Theological Seminary, New York City, (the work being accredited toward an M. A. Degree). She writes further in June 1933:

I shall receive the theological diploma from Houghton College. The college is at present obliged to cut expenses, therefore discontinuing Oratory, so I find myself facing a hard situation, but I hear Miss Witbeck's words ringing in my ears, "We've got to meet it." I will. A scholarship in Colgate Divinity School for the year 1933-1934 will cover my room rent and tuition. I will have to earn my board and books. My heart is set toward the ministry. In all of my climbing, except for my tuition at Northfield, I have paid my own way by dint of effort and hard work, but J wouldn't change places with a queen. I am fifty-two years old, but still going strong.

The closing thought is:
"I ask no greater joy than to have one little part in carrying on the great work of bringing the Gospel message of Jesus Christ—whom I learned to love and serve at the T. O. A. to some hungry Americans."

A Methodist minister member of the New York Conference, after six years of college work, writes in May 1933:

After coming to New York and working for some time, in 1927 I decided to return to school and work for a degree, It took me three years at City College of

New York to graduate with a Bachelor of Arts degree. Now, I am graduating from Union Theological Seminary, where I have been studying for another three year's for a Bachelor of Divinity degree.

On April 2nd I was ordained by the Methodist Church and admitted to the New York Conference. I expect to be appointed permanently, shortly. At present I am supplying in a church here in the city.

I have, I feel, been successful in living a good, clean life and keeping to a set of ideals. This going to college and then three years to a graduate school has meant constant attention for business and keeping a goal before me every bit of the way. The ideals and principles which have found root in me while was a boy at the Home. The kindly interest of teachers in the classrooms, the family spirit which grew up among us boys and the example set by many of the caretakers in sportsmanship were strong factors in moulding my life. I was never so homesick for any place as I was for the Home when I first went away to Mount Hermon. I sincerely hope that some of us who have enjoyed the care of the Home, will some day take a hand in the carrying on of the work. All good wishes for the great work carried on.

In the annual report for 1863 of the Ladies' Association, we find:

Miss Eastman matron had received a letter from Capt. T. G. Morrison, of Co. G. Sixty-first Regiment, who was educated in this institution, and is now serving this country honorably in the field. He took part in the Battle of Chancellorsville, and is highly spoken of by Lieutenant Colonel commanding the regiment who says, I would especially recommend for bravery, excellent good conduct and soldierly qualities—Capt. T. G. Morrison.

This young man made the supreme sacrifice for his country and the Flag. The Trustees have this to say, in their report for 1865: One we have in mind, for whom there was every promise of a brilliant future, but who, alas, fills a soldier's grave. His love for the institution, which had fostered him in infancy and youth, and especially for her whom he ever addressed as "mother," knew no bounds: he let pass no opportunity to revisit it, coming with all the enthusiasm of a child to a cherished home.

Continuing the report says: *Promotion rewarded his gallantry in the field, and his duties were of an engrossing character, yet he found time to write often, and at much length, to our Superintendent, and his letters always breathed the same deep filial spirit.*

Another, who at the time was serving as a volunteer in the Union Army, writes to one of the Trustees:

I send you $30 by express, which you may keep for the benefit of the Troy Orphan Asylum. It is a small sum, I know.

Later, on acknowledging the receipt of the money, a reply was received, in which the writer says:

I am glad to think the time has come when I can give something for the Troy Orphan Asylum, even if in small donations. Give my respects to the Directors, and tell them I am doing well.

Throughout the records, frequent mention is made of the success of young men and young women who had been former wards of the Asylum. Let us note but such a few.

The report of 1859, relates that: *Recently we have been gratified by a visit from Robert Williamson, one of our orphans who does our institution, as well as himself, great credit. He has completed his course of Theological study, and already entered the work of the Gospel ministry.*

In the same year the report relates that: *Mary Fleming has won our regard by her amiable deportment, and by the manner in which she has improved advantages: and has, within a few months, been employed as a teacher in a family of wealth and refinement, at the South, and gives, we are glad to learn, good satisfaction.*

The records for 1915 of the Lady Managers state that a boy educated here (the Asylum) is assistant secretary at the YMCA

Another, a former ward of the Asylum who served in the World War, is now (1933) a successful physician in a town in western New York.

We note the tributes paid by a former ward of the Asylum to members of the management in a communication dated May 24, 1933, in which she says:

Among my tributes I would like to place on record the sweet memories that I retain of our good nurse, Margaret Sharp. We called her Aunt Margaret, and always felt free to go to her with our physical ailments and our childish heartaches; and Aunt Margaret with her beautiful Christian spirit always had a remedy for us.

Linked with the infirmary was a long list of physicians, and as children we all had our favorites — the one of whom we were not afraid. My great hero to my childish hearty, was a sainted Santa Claus with a kind, fatherly nature. I counted it a great honor when later in life it was my privilege to follow my hero about in the wards of the Samaritan Hospital, and serve him as he waited upon the patients. I refer to our great surgeon, Dr. James P. Marsh.

I want to recall one other great character that left a kindly impress upon a child's heart at the Troy Orphan Asylum. We looked forward to his regular Sunday visits. When bedtime came, and we exchanged the glad experiences of the day, it was with great glee that this one and that one would relate to the others how they had received a warm handshake and a kindly smile from the cultured gentleman, President, Charles W. Tillinghast, Sr.

Surely, with these great contacts how could we face life otherwise than with high ideals?

Source: A History of the Troy Orphan Asylum. Iriving E Fancher, 1953. Private printing.

Lisa Villeneuve (Dayton)

When Lisa Dayton's dad died the family had a difficult time and she found herself at Vanderheyden Hall on Spring Avenue for a short time from 1972-1973.

Her first impression of Vanderheyden was under awkward circumstances. Lisa was not even aware she was going to Vanderheyden until she returned home from school on that fateful day. She arrived during the evening meal which was not the most opportune time to be a new admission. The entrance to the dining room was framed by large wooden doors. Inside children sat at long tables eating their dinner curious to get a glance at the new girl. The room, the children, the stares, the whole experience was very intimidating for the new arrival.

While Lisa was only there briefly her story of how one woman, on one evening, significantly influenced her life. Lisa was assigned to the Delta Unit, and it had an unusual group mother, Betty George and her pet dog, Moo the Wonder Dog. Betty had been a famous stage and TV star in the 1940s through 1960s. She worked with Milton Berle for more than 16 years, frequently talking about those special times in her life with the girls. She was a runner up for the Donaldson Awards (pre Tony Awards) in 1955 for the play "Ankles Aweigh." Betty moved to Troy after her mother died to live with her sister. She worked at Vanderheyden for two years before she became the "Weather Girl" at Channel 13 in Albany, at the urging of the Vanderheyden girls. Betty just naturally had a spark for life that always had a way of uplifting those around her. Lisa and Betty got along well. She frequently helped out by taking Moo for walks. On Christmas Eve Lisa had gone home to spend the holidays with her family. Circumstances as they were found her returned to Vanderheyden late on Christmas Eve night. All of the other Delta Girls were on visits so she was the only child in the unit. Betty was notified at around 10:30 pm by the staff member on duty of her return. While she had absolutely no obligation to come in, she did! Betty arrived unannounced at Delta dressed in her full Santa costume with Moo dressed as an elf. Betty sat with Lisa the whole night through until dawn. While there aren't memories of what the two talked about, Lisa clearly remembers how Betty truly made her feel cared about. This one act of kindness

Lisa at her desk at Vanderheyden. Photo by Don Rittner.

and compassion made an impression on Lisa's heart and when she grew up that experience remained with her. When it came time to decide what her career choice would be those memories led her back to Vanderheyden and to college graduating with her Human Services degree.

Lisa shared some of her favorite memories. Every Sunday a minister of different faiths would say mass at the chapel. The canteen was a gathering spot for everyone during the evening. The juke box loudly played favorite tunes for dancing and of course it was the place to meet and date! Lisa attended School 16 in Albia. Back in the day Vanderheyden attended public school and she has memories of visiting friend's houses after school and on the weekends. Frequent trips to the local

Tony Award winning actress Betty George was a big influence on Lisa's life when Betty worked at the home. Photo from Wikipedia. Betty died in 2007 at age 81 in North Greenbush.

stores for candy and soda included Two Way Food Market and Fitzi's Store. When it came time the unit would head to downtown Troy for new shoes, sneakers and boots at Endicott Johnsons and Triangle Shoe Stores.

Lisa returned to Vanderheyden in 1985, this time as an employee. Thirty-four years later she remains employed and committed to Vanderheyden and the mission of working with and supporting individuals and families. She readily will tell you that her career has been fulfilling and rewarding beyond what she could have ever hoped for! Another monumental life choice also involved her connection with Vanderheyden. This is where Lisa met her future husband David in 1987. David Villeneuve worked as the Recreation Supervisor and he too was a resident at the home in the 1960s. One of the many things the two shared in common. They were married in 1991 and continue to live happily ever after.

Lisa's experience with Vanderheyden began when she was a child and has continued through adulthood. It influenced her life and led her to a career path in Human Services. This is a prime example of bringing things full circle!

David Villeneuve

David was the eldest in a family of six children. He had four brothers and one sister. He was born in Cohoes New York at the old Cohoes Hospital to Jeannette and Roland Villeneuve on August 2, 1955. His mom was a seamstress and his dad managed area restaurants and clubs. When they divorced his mom faced many challenges and significantly struggled in being a single parent. One day in March of 1968, David was told by his mom that he and his brother Richard were going to the doctor's office. To his surprise they did not go to the doctor, but rather, they were brought to Vanderheyden Hall on the top of Spring Avenue and dropped off.

While David and Richard were only one year apart by age, they were separated upon admission. The first step in the process involved orientation with Mr. Cook. His office was adjacent to the big foyer entrance. David was assigned to the Middle Boys unit and his brother Richard to the Junior Boys. Since they arrived at supper time they were accompanied to the dining hall and directed to different tables to eat their first dinner at their new placement. David clearly recalled that first meal was wing dings (now called chicken wings) something he liked and had never had before.

When it was time to head to the living unit David found the accommodations were limited. He had to sleep in the hallway. David joined a few other boys whose beds were also in the hall until bedrooms were available. After about three days he was assigned a room that he shared with three other boys. Each boy had their own small chest of drawers and a foot locker.

On his first morning routines were being established; being woken, getting ready for school, breakfast and being assigned his first job in the kitchen. David attended School 16, and he recalls walking to school with his new friends. David has fond memories of the opportunities Vanderheyden provided. There were activities every night! He liked going to the canteen; listening to music of the sixties. His first real girlfriend was one of the best dancers. He enjoyed sports and remembers playing in the field at the point adjacent to Spring Avenue and Pawling Avenue. Regardless of the sport at hand; kickball, softball, football — all were fun! Holidays were always celebrated and he particularly liked swimming in the pool especially on the Fourth of July. A watermelon would be thoroughly greased up and the challenge was being the one who was able to secure it. He did well with the task!

The counselors were very much like family and some lived on site. That meant easy accessibility and close relationships being formed. David was particularly close with Mr. Wood and his wife. Mr. Wood was in charge of the farm and the woodshop. He taught David how to drive a tractor, something that he has never forgotten. A big adventure for a young boy! Another memory was Mr. Wood taking the time to help David build a beautiful wooden doll house for his little sister Annette who had not been placed at Vanderheyden. David gave this to his sister that Christmas. This was a gift that she always treasured because it was specially made for her by her big brother. David enjoyed working with wood and credits his mentor for taking the time to teach him so much. He also learned about horses. Miss Carrie was the manager of the Junior Boys unit where his younger brother resided. She took care of the horses that were housed in the barn in the rear of the massive buildings. David loved to spending time with the horses and being able to feed them!

Relationships developed that fostered into friendships lasting for decades. This included meeting a counselor named Dion Petteys. While he had been a resident himself as a child, following his deployment to Vietnam, Dion returned to Vanderheyden as a counselor. David shared fond memories of Dion teaching him to fish at Glass Lake and Crooked Lake. After the boys were acclimated they would be dropped off in Averill Park, rent row boats, and spend the day on the quiet and serene lakes. Great activities that helped David stay on track with his behavior, and allowed him to earn the necessary level that would permit him to go on the outings. Fishing has remained a hobby throughout his lifetime and as an adult he went fishing with Dion many times. Another favorite memory and long term relationship was with a counselor named Fred Bowen. He introduced David to the Boys Scouts. Mr. Bowen was in charge of Boy Scout Troop Number 1; this being the first uniformed troop in the United States. David worked hard on earning his badges and felt a great sense of accomplishment when he did! He also loved the camping trips they took. Each year one trip involved traditional camping and the other being the annual pilgrimage to the Auriesville Shrine.

Sometimes mischievous, David recalled memorable moments when he and his friends would climb up on the rooftops of the buildings playing Spider-Man. The architecture of the buildings captivated their imagination. They would climb up to the belfry in the dorm, climb out the window, and play ball on the rooftops. Fortunately no one ever caught them and no one ever fell off!

When David was discharged from Vanderheyden he went to live with his grandparents. His siblings went into foster care and some remained with his mom. After graduating David worked for the D & H Railroad but when laid off he would return to his childhood alma mater for employment opportunities. He worked in the capacity of the Recreation Supervisor as well as a Residential Counselor for seven years before moving to the Capital District Secure Detention Facility in 1993. During his tenure he had the pleasure of working with hundreds of children. He is now retired. During one of the stints of returning to Vanderheyden David met his future wife Lisa. They remain happily married 32 years later! David has a daughter Crystal and two granddaughters Alysha and Sadora who reside in Texas.

While the Villeneuve family underwent quite the scattering during childhood, their roots remained strong and viable and continue to be into present day. Looking back at his experiences at Vanderheyden good friends were made and remain in David's life. He relates he was treated well, he was happy, and he was provided with opportunities he might not have otherwise had. The interview ended with David admitting it took some time to get adjusted but his fondest memory was that he had three square meals a day, something he never had before his stay at Vanderheyden Hall.

He was counselor for seven years and worked with 2-300 kids before he moved on to the Capital District Secure Detention Facility in Loudonville in 1993. He is retired now.

While the Villeneuve family underwent quite the scattering eventually the family did get together in later years. He made a lot of friends while at Vanderheyden and they still keep in touch. He also feels he was treated very well there. While it took a while to get adjusted his fondest memory is that he had three square meals a day, something he never had before his stay at Vanderheyden.

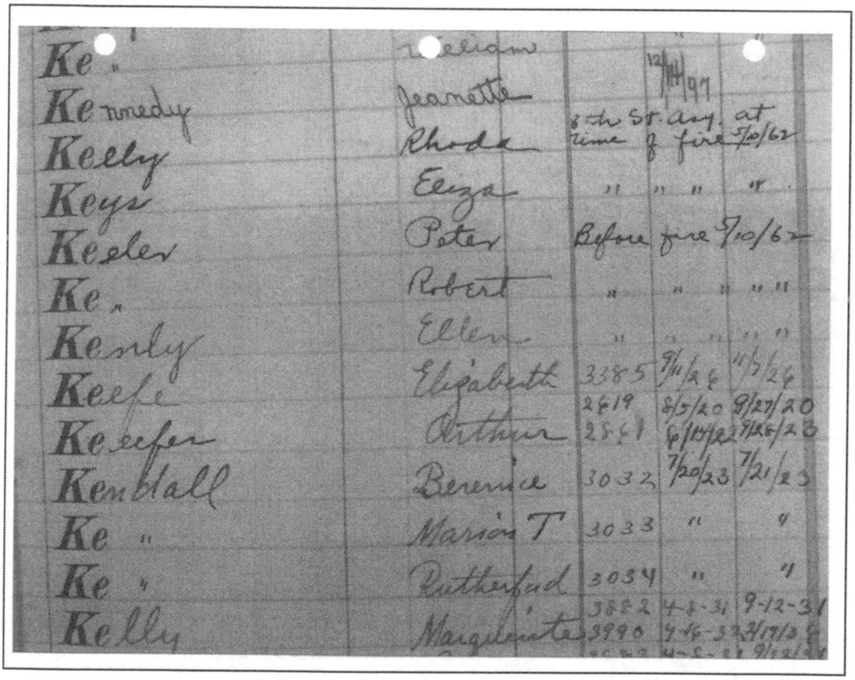

Ke "	William		12/14/97	
Kennedy	Jeanette			
Keely	Rhoda	8th St. Asy. at time of fire 5/10/62		
Keys	Eliza	"	"	"
Keeler	Peter	Before fire 5/10/62		
Ke "	Robert	"	"	"
Kenly	Ellen	"	"	"
Keefe	Elizabeth	3385	9/11/26	11/7/26
		2819	8/5/20	9/27/20
Keefer	Arthur	2861	6/10/22	9/28/23
Kendall	Berenice	3032	7/20/23	7/21/23
Ke "	Marion T	3033	"	"
Ke "	Rutherford	3034	"	"
		3882	4-8-31	9-12-31
Kelly	Marguerite	3990	4-8-32	[illegible]

Admission book showing Peter Keeler admitted before the great fire of 1862.

Marine Sergeant Bruce Allen Atwell

One of the celebrated men who stayed at Vanderheyden was Bruce Allen Atwell (1944 – 2006). Bruce was at Vanderheyden from August 27, 1959 to May 15, 1962 when he went into the service going the Marines. He became a battle photographer during the Vietnam War and served with distinction. His obituary follows:

Bruce Allen Atwell SALISBURY - Bruce Allen Atwell. Sr., 61, of Salisbury, died Friday, Sept. 1, 2006 at Carolina`s Specialty Hospital in Charlotte. He was born Sept. 26, 1944 in North Adams, Massachusetts to the late Dorothy Shephard Atwell Strange and Earl George Atwell. He was a graduate of Granville High School in Granville, NY. He was a Sgt. in the 3rd Marine Division serving from 1962-1968 as a combat photographer during the Vietnam War. While

Bruce Allen Atwell. Photo from his obituary.

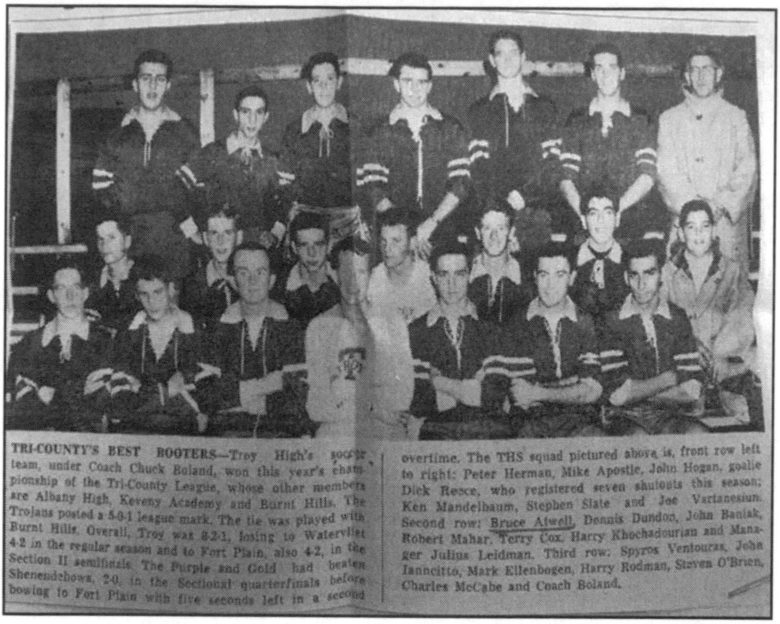

TRI-COUNTY'S BEST BOOTERS—Troy High's soccer team, under Coach Chuck Boland, won this year's championship of the Tri-County League, whose other members are Albany High, Keveny Academy and Burnt Hills. The Trojans posted a 5-0-1 league mark. The tie was played with Burnt Hills. Overall, Troy was 8-2-1, losing to Watervliet 4-2 in the regular season and to Fort Plain, also 4-2, in the Section II semifinals. The Purple and Gold had beaten Shenendehowa, 2-0, in the Sectional quarterfinals before bowing to Fort Plain with five seconds left in a second overtime. The THS squad pictured above is, front row left to right: Peter Herman, Mike Apostle, John Hogan, goalie Dick Reece, who registered seven shutouts this season; Ken Mandelbaum, Stephen Slate and Joe Vartanesian. Second row: Bruce Atwell, Dennis Dundon, John Baniak, Robert Mahar, Terry Cox, Harry Khochadourian and Manager Julius Leidman. Third row: Spyros Ventouras, John Iannicitto, Mark Ellenbogen, Harry Rodman, Steven O'Brien, Charles McCabe and Coach Boland.

Bruce was athletic and belonged to Troy High School's soccer team. N.D.

assisting the 1st Division in the capture of the city of Hue he was injured and received a Purple Heart. He photographs were published in many newspapers and magazines across the US. Mr. Atwell was an Engineer with Norfolk Southern Railway until 2000, retiring on disability. He was of the Lutheran Faith and a Member of the Spencer Moose Lodge, VFW Salisbury and Samuel C. Hart Post. In addition to his parents he is preceded in death by three brothers, Jerry, Eddie and Phillip Atwell and two sisters, Janice Atwell and Cheryl Houck. Survivors include his wife Phyllis Parker Atwell whom he married Oct. 3, 1973; sons Bruce Atwell, Jr., Darryl Atwell, both of Salisbury; daughters Cynthia Compton and husband

"North Vietnamese Rocket Attack, 1968. A 106 mm recoilless rifle team become victims of a North Vietnamese rocket attack. The photographer of this scene, Sergeant Bruce A. Atwell, was also wounded during this action and medevaced to safety (official USMC photo by Sergeant Bruce Atwell)." From the Jonathan Abel Collection (COLL/3611), Marine Corps Archives & Special Collections. Atwell received the Purple Star for his wounds. He continued to take photos even while injured.

David and Cynthia Cofer, both of Salisbury; brothers Melvin, Richard, Earl and Stevie Atwell, all of Mass.; sisters Barbara Atwell of NY and Candice Czupkiewicz of Massachesetts.; seven grandchildren and four great-grandchildren. Graveside Service: 11 a.m. Friday at Brookhill Memorial Gardens, Rockwell with Military graveside rites by the Rowan County Honor Guard.

Hue City. Marines A Company, 1st Battalion, 1st Marines [A/1/1] return fire from a house window during a search and clear mission in the battle of Hue, February 1968. (official USMC photo by Sergeant Bruce A. Atwell, Marine Corps Archives & Special Collections). Atwell received the Purple Heart for his wounds during this battle.

War Heroes Who Served in the Civil War, World Wars I and II, and the Vietnam War. Vanderheyden Hall, the Troy Orphan Asylum and the Fairview Home

John Charles Hines

Vietnam War Corporal, US Marine Corps 3rd Battalion, 7th Marines, Company M MARDIV (Rein) FMF Died in Quang Nam, Vietnam August 24, 1970. Hines was awarded the Bronze Star with Combat "V" and the Navy Commendation Medal with Combat "V." He was 23 years old.

Corporal Hines, who lived in Cohoes, re-enlisted in the US Marine Corps September 10, 1968, at MCB Quantico VA. He arrived in Vietnam on January 31, 1970, and was assigned to Company M, 3d Battalion, 7th Marines, 1st MARDIV (Rein) FMF. As the squad patrol was walking along a trail near Hill 50 north of the Ly Ly River in Que Son District Quang, one of the men decided to kick a can that had been sitting on the path. His action caused an instant explosion. The can had been rigged as a BT (Booby Trap) containing an M-26 grenade that wounded three men who required evacuation. Evacuated to the 95th Army Evacuation Hospital in DaNang, Cpl Hines died a few hours after arrival as a result of multi fragmentation wounds from the hostile explosive device. He is buried at St Agnes Cemetery in Menands, New York.

Corporal Hines' name is listed on the Vietnam Veterans Memorial on Panel W7, Line 1.

Cornell "Corky" Petteys

Vietnam War Specialist E-4, US Army, USARV D Troop, 1st Squadron, 1st Cavalry Died in Quang Ngai, South Vietnam September 1, 1969, Petteys was awarded the Purple Heart, National Defense, Vietnam Service and Vietnam Campaign. He was 22 years old. Petteys is buried at New Mount Ida Cemetery, Troy, New York His name is listed on the Vietnam Veterans Memorial on Panel W18, Line 21.

Arthur Clarence Squires, Jr

World War II Private, US Marine Corps 22nd Marines, 1st Provisional Brigade, Company C, Fire Brigade Died at Agat, Guam July 24, 1944, Squires was awarded the Purple Heart. He was 20 years old.

Capt. T. G. Morrison,

DEATH OF AN ORPHAN SOLDIER.—We are sorry to learn of the death, in the recent battles, of

Capt. T. G. Morrison, of the Sixty-first regiment, whose name has before been mentioned in these columns. He was brought up and educated at the Troy Orphan Asylum, and reflected honor upon that institution. A letter from Lieut. Wren, an officer of the regiment, alludes to him in the following affectionate terms: " I cannot speak at length of my dear comrade, Thomas. He was my friend, faithful and kind to me. The years of close companionship and intimacy in toil and peril, had endeared him to my heart—knowing him as I do for the patriot and man. I trust that the few words of feeling expressed by me without premeditation, will not prove intrusive on our great grief." One of the Trustees of the Asylum thus records the appreciation of the deceased by himself and his associates: " The above letter conveys the sad intelligence to the sister of Capt. Morrison, who is now in the Troy Orphan Asylum. Sad, indeed, will be the news to her, as also to Miss Eastman and the inmates of the Institution, as well as to many of the Trustees with whom he was personally acquainted. He had become much endeared to them all by his occasional visits and his many kind acts, deeming the Asylum his home, as he was reared in the Institution. Immediate steps will be taken to have his remains returned to the Asylum."

Records indicate Morrison's body was to be returned to New York State and to the Troy Orphan Asylum where his sister Elizabeth Morrison was a Teacher.

There is no known record of where Captain Morrison was actually buried.

US Civil War Captain, Union Army Company G, 61st Infantry Regiment Died near Todd's Tavern, Virginia Battle of Spotsylvania, May 8th, 1864 He was 37 years old

Sergeant Preston R. Smith,

PETERSBURG MAN KILLED IN ACTION Sergeant Preston R. Smith, twice decorated for valor overseas, was killed in action July 27 in the North African area, the War Department notified his mother, Mrs. Cora E. Smith of Petersburg, by telegram yesterday. Smith, an only son, was first decorated overseas with the silver star on Jan. 20, five days before he celebrated his 22nd birthday. He received the oak leaf cluster for gallantry on March 21 and shortly after was promoted from corporal to sergeant. For the silver star, the citation said that while in the vicinity of Djebel Chemal he "led small patrol deep within enemy territory and skillfully observed enemy installations." For the oak leaf cluster, Smith, in the vicinity of El Guettar, Tunisia, "Led a 60 mm mortar squad, skillfully directing the fire of his mortar, completely destroying several enemy machine gun and mortar emplacements, thereby expediting the rapid advance of the unit." Sergeant Smith left Hoosick Falls High School to enlist in June 1939, and was assigned to Company K,

26th Infantry. He had been graduated from Petersburg School No. 4 and had studied violin with the late Prof. W. T. Lawrence of Troy. He was made corporal in July 1942, shortly before sailing for England, and he was landed in Africa last October, serving through the whole African campaign. He was a member of the Petersburg Methodist Church and of the Sunday School. His last letter to his mother, written July 4, contained the text of the poem, "Be Strong," often sung as a hymn.

Russell Smith

World War II Sergeant, US Army 26th Infantry, 1st Division, Company K Died in Sicily, North Africa Campaign July 27th, 1943 Smith was awarded the Silver Star and an Oak Leaf Cluster. He was 23 years old.

Charles Floyd Mosher

Private First Class, USMC, 5 th Regiment, 2nd Battalion, 23rd Company, Mosher was 21 years old and was in the first contingent of Marines to land in France.

World War I Private First Class, US Marine Corps 5th Regiment, 2nd Battalion, 23rd Company Died near Vierzy, France July 29th, 1918 Prlvntc Charles Floyd Mosher. Private Charles Floyd Mosher, 22 years old, a marine who died of wounds on June 29, was a brother of Miss Evelyn Mosher, who lives at 408 Beverly Road in Brooklyn. The telegram received by Miss Mosher last night said: "Your brother nobly gave his life in defense of his country." Private Mosher was born in Troy, N. Y. His parents died eight years ago, within two months of each other, and the sister came to Brooklyn to live with friends. Her brother remained in Troy, where he was an automobile machinist. He enlisted in Troy and when he called on his sister the night before he started for France with the first contingent of marines it was the first time she had seen or heard from him in eight years. That night he joined St. Mark's M. E. Church. She had not received a letter from him since January 30.

John George Gunn

World War II Corporal, US Ar my 31st Infantr y Regiment Bataan Death March. Died as a Prisoner of War in a Japanese Prison Camp in the Philippine Islands August 10, 1942. Gunn was awarded the Bronze Star. He was 22 years old.

Reflections from his Great Niece, Christina Pelland of Central Massachusetts… "My Great Uncle, John Gunn, was placed for adoption at what was then the Troy Orphan Asylum when he was 9 years old along with his sister, my Grandmother, Harriet in 1929. In 1930, when she was just 3 years old, Harriet was adopted and took on the new name of Marguerite. My Great-Grandparents made sure that Johnny and

Marguerite maintained a relationship as "cousins" until his death in July of 1942. Prior to his death, my Grandmother intercepted a letter from Johnny to her Mother asking when she would be told that he is her brother. Johnny was in the Philippines on December 8th 1941, the day that the Japanese invaded the Bataan Peninsula. After 4 months of battle, exhaustion and seeing their rations being cut from 2500 calories a day to 1250 calories and then to only 600 calories a day, General McArthur ordered the Allied forces to surrender. In April of 1942, Johnny would have joined thousands of US and Filipino troops on the Bataan Death March as the last survivor of his regiment. The Death March was a 60-70 mile walk in which prisoners weren't given food or water and those who fell behind or stopped to sip water out of a mud puddle were murdered on the spot. Others were killed or beaten for no reason other than the Japanese were disgusted by the surrender. Johnny survived the walk and continued to survive for more than two brutal months of overcrowded conditions at the POW prison of Cabanatuan, before being transferred to Camp McDonnell. Food and clean water were scarce in the POW camps. Many men died of diseases related to poor nutrition and dysentery. Weakened by starvation and now without the quinine that protects from many mosquito-born diseases, Johnny succumbed to cerebral malaria on July 5th 1942. My Grandmother never got over Johnny's death or that she hadn't known he was her brother until it was too late, but she always kept his memory alive as she passed down stories of him to my mother and aunt. Our family would like to thank Vanderheyden for honoring John George Gunn for his heroism and his sacrifice during WWII and also helping us keep his memory alive." Reflections from his niece, Kelley Okolita of Florida: "I never met my Uncle Johnny, but he was the brother that my Mom knew as he would come and stay at my grandparents' house in the summer after they adopted my mother. I know she was heartbroken when he passed away during the war. My son Jonathan is named for him to honor his memory, and what he meant to my mother."

Herman August C. Gajeway, Jr

World War II Water Tender First Class US Navy. Died in the Battle of the Atlantic October 17th, 1941. Gajeway was awarded a Purple Heart. He was 26 years old Gajeway's Memory Stone At Eagle Mills Cemetery, Eagle Mills, New York.

Vanderheyden Photo Scrapbook

History through the Ages

The following pages contain many photographs that have been taken of the 185 year old Vanderheyden institution. Where dates or descriptions are known they have been included. Thousands of children have benefited from their stay at Vanderheyden. Many have gone on to make contributions to society but they all have one thing in common. Vanderheyden was their "home."

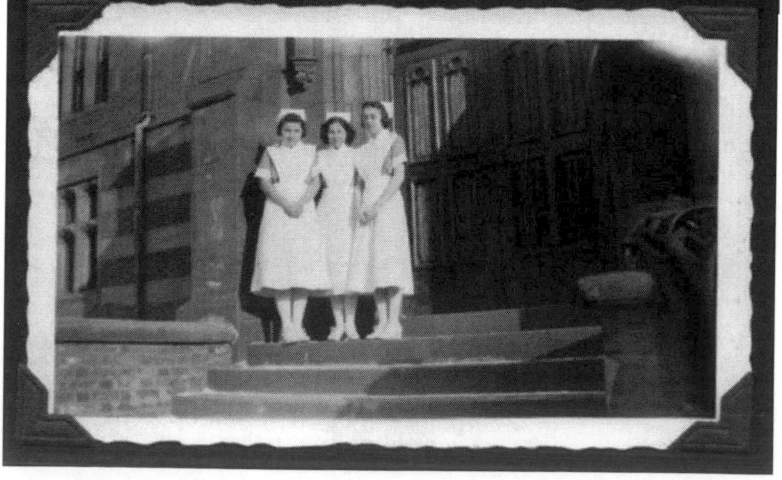

TRO
WEST S

APRIL 14, 1938

TWENTY-FOUR HOURS LATER AT THE TROY ORPHAN ASYLUM

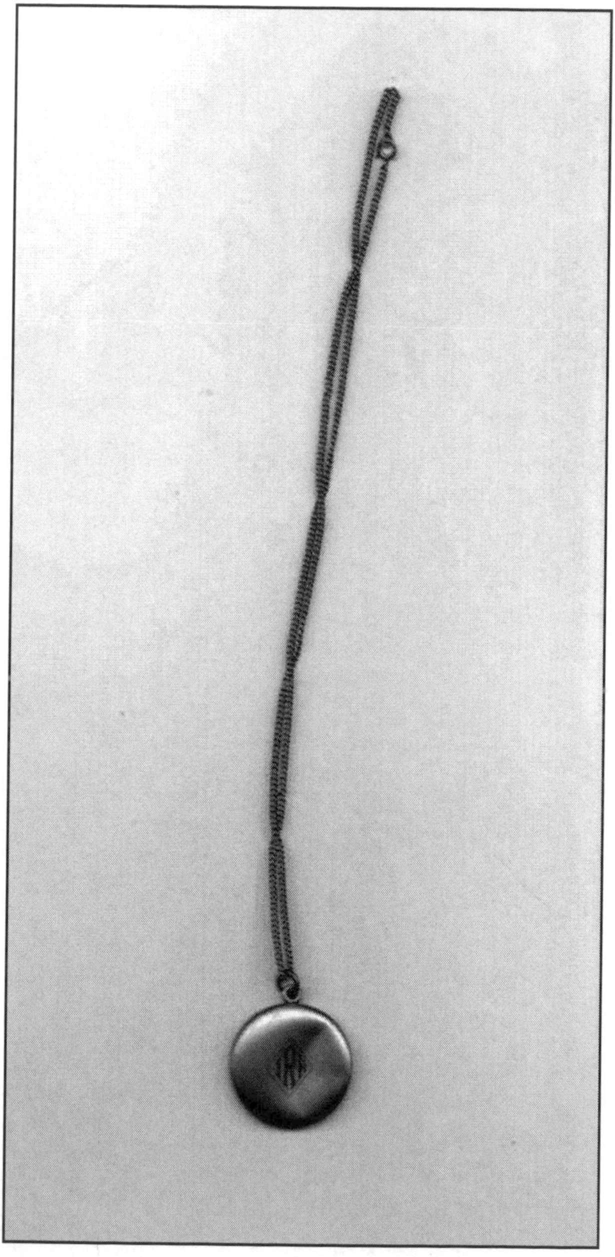

Necklace belonging to Ida Hillie, December 26, 1919.

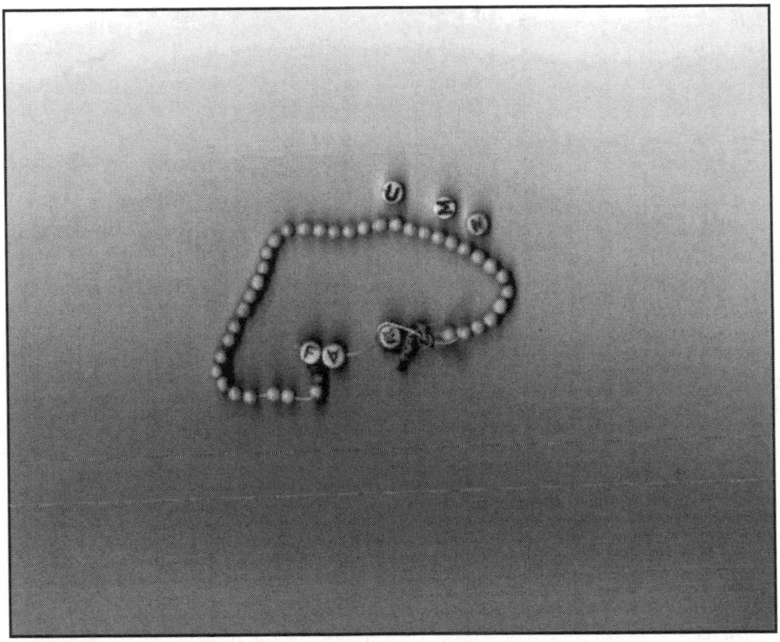

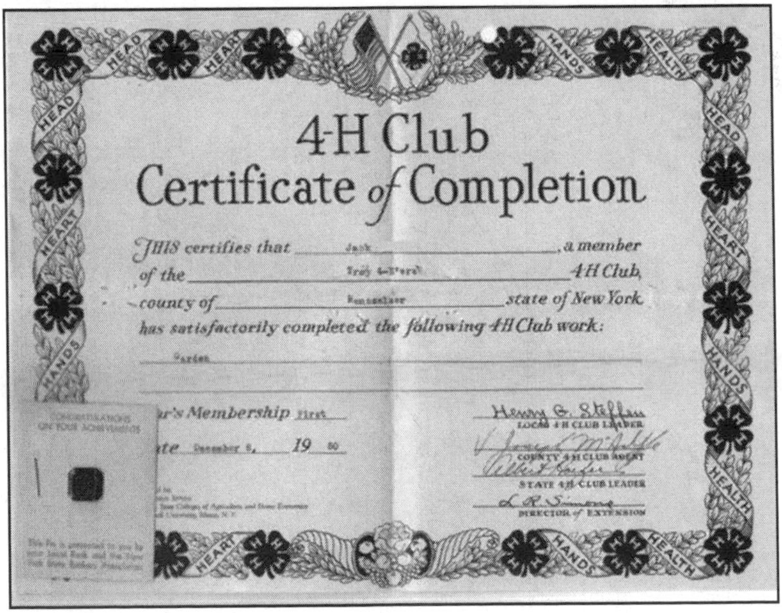

4-H award for Jack S, December 8, 1950

4-H Vegetable Garden Club work, 1941.

Nursery Picnic in 1941.

1941 Apprentice Gardeners.

1941 Kindergarden Picnic.

The cabbage garden in 1940. Two thousand cabbages were harvested.

Tractor being used on the garden in 1940.

Boy Scout Camp
Troop 1, Summer,
June 3-4, 1938.
Frear Park.

BOY SCOUTS OF AMERICA

NATIONAL COUNCIL

This is to Certify that
Henry Steffen

Boy Scouts of America

Committeeman
Troop 1
Troy, N.Y.

Dated March 31, 1938

CHARACTER – CITIZENSHIP

Winter Classes Boys. 1938. Top. Girls Winter Classes, Bottom.

1938

Kindergarten

1940

"Going to
Breakfast."

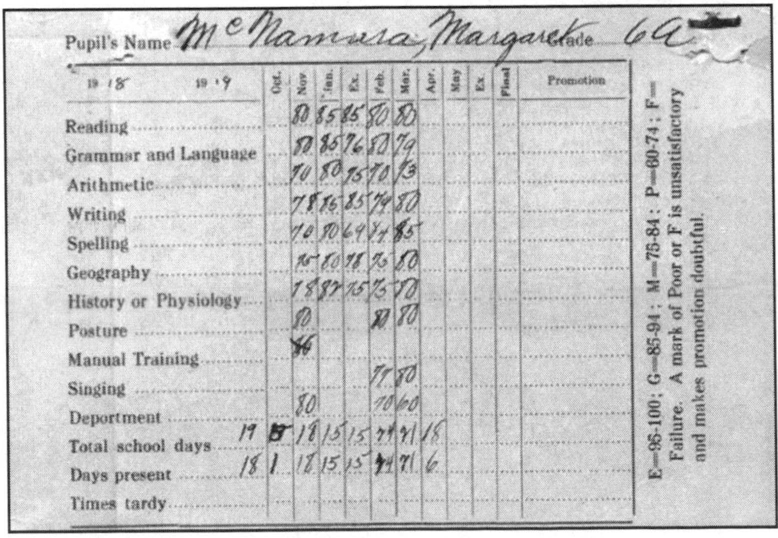

Pupil's Name McNamara, Margaret Grade 6A

1918 1919	Oct.	Nov	Jan.	Ex.	Feb.	Mar.	Apr.	May	Ex.	Final	Promotion
Reading		80	85	85	80	80					
Grammar and Language		80	85	76	80	79					
Arithmetic		70	80	75	70	73					
Writing		78	85	85	74	80					
Spelling		70	90	64	74	85					
Geography		75	80	78	75	80					
History or Physiology		78	87	75	75	70					
Posture		80			80	80					
Manual Training		86									
Singing					77	80					
Deportment		80			70	60					
Total school days 19	18	18	15	15	24	21	18				
Days present 18	1	18	15	15	24	21	6				
Times tardy											

E—95-100; G—85-94; M—75-84; P—60-74; F—Failure. A mark of Poor or F is unsatisfactory and makes promotion doubtful.

Student's report card from 1918-1919.

The following photos are Vanderheyden Hall. June 5, 1938-June 20, 1941. Counselor of Kindergarten Dept., August 18, 1941-June 30, 1942. Nursery Department.

Coach Huddleston. BasketBall Squad 1938-42. Walter H., George S., Bernie P., Bob C., Donald E., Walter F., Leo E., and Howard F.

The
Troy Orphan Asylum
100 Spring Avenue
Troy, N. Y.

HERBERT J. HUNN, SUPERINTENDENT
TELEPHONE TROY 1083
MEMBER TROY COMMUNITY CHEST
FOUNDED 1833
FOR CHILDREN
UNDER SIXTEEN YEARS OF AGE, EXCEPT JUVENILE
DELINQUENTS, TRUANTS AND
MENTAL DEFECTIVES,
AS PROVIDED
BY LAW

"The race marches forward on the feet of little children"

Don O, Charles L, Garrett D, Hazel O, Edward K, Freddie M, Arthur B, and John S. 1938-42.

John U and Raymond R.

Floyd L. "Little ChatterBoy." 1938-42.

Dorothy L, "Pigtails." 1938-42.

Gwendolyn R. "Sweet and Demure." 1938-42.

Dorothy on Jungle Jim. 1938-42.

"Donnie" on Teeter Totter. 1938-42.

Looking for that lucky clover. 1938-42.

Maudie, Rhoda, Jackie, Eddie and Bernard. 1938-42.

Demure and sweet, Rhoda Anne D. . 1938-42.

Virginia Ashley, Prob atoner in Kindergarten. Ruth H. "Cindy" in the rear. 1938-42.

"Josie" S and Carol J. Kindergarten. 1938-42.

Playing in the Grove. Eddie W., Bobbie G., Jackie B., Freddie M. and Francis R., 1938-42.

Bobbie G, Donnie M., and Don Lee O. 1938-42.

Beverly, Floyd, Bobbie and Dorothy. 1938-42.

Eating Ice Cream. Harold A., Jean W., Virginia B., Gwen R., Francis R., Vera S., Dorothy S., Miss Eleanor, Nancy J., George L., Jimmy A., Bill H., Donald M., Billy B. Picnic at Ostrander Farm, June 1942.

The Kindergarten Playroom.

The Grove.

Vanderheyden on Spring Avenue.

Hazel O.

APPENDIX A

Constitution Of The Ladies Society Established In Troy For Affording Assistance To Indigent Women And Children February 24th, 1800

NAME
The Benevolent Society of Troy.

OBJECTS

To afford assistance to indigent women and children in alleviating the distresses of their bodies and cultivating their minds with the rudiments of science and the principles of morality and religion.

MEMBERS

All ladies of fair reputation may be admitted by a majority of votes to the Society upon paying one dollar entrance and one dollar annually into its funds.

The Managers shall carry into execution the plans of the Society and be responsible to them for their conduct. Shall seek proper objects of charity and afford them necessary assistance and a report to the Society at their stated meetings the whole of their transactions with such measures as they deem proper to accomplish their benevolent designs.

They shall meet the first Monday in every month. Three shall be deemed competent to transact business, and the Secretary and Treasurer shall have a seat at their board and a vote in their decisions but not form a part of the quorum.

The Society shall meet twice annually, on the first Tuesday in April and October, the latter to be considered the anniversary, and twelve members shall be competent to transact business. They shall devise plans for increasing the members and funds oft the Society; designate the general objects of attention, examine appropriations, and combine their exertions to promote the interesting designs of their associations.

Assistance shall not be afforded to any applicants until their characters, situations and necessities are investigated, and the Board has decided they are proper objects of charity. The assistance shall usually be afforded in necessities and not in money, unless the Board deems it requisite.

The funds of the Society shall arise from the deposit and annuity of the members and from subscribers and donations of ladies and gentlemen who are not members, whose names will be enrolled with peculiar pleasure on the list of benefactors.

If deemed expedient, the whole of the funds may be annually appropriated to promote the objects of the Society, in such a manner as the Board may deem proper. Whatever supplies may at any time remain shall be rendered productive to increase the funds. And, when they shall be judged sufficiently ample, it is contemplated that a school be established for the education of the children under the care of an instructress, capable of instructing them in science, virtue, and religion.

This constitution shall remain unattestable until two-thirds of the members shall vote for its alteration or amendment.

MANAGEMENT

This shall be vested in a Directress, Secretary, Treasurer, and six Managers, who shall be annually chosen by a plurality of ballots of the members present. The Directress shall preside at all meetings, both of the Society and Managers, preserve order, state questions, have decisions, and in all equal divisions shall have the casting vote. Shall call special meetings of the Society or of the Managers at the request of two or more members, giving suitable notice of the same, and shall see that its regulations are duly observed. And, take a general superintendence of its interest. In her absence the senior Managers present shall take her place and perform her duties.

The Secretary shall notify the meetings both of the Society and Managers and regularly attend upon them. She shall record their proceedings in a book provided for that purpose, register their members and be the organ of communication to and from the Society. In her absence there shall be one chosen to take her place.

The Treasurer shall receive, collect and take charge of the funds of the Society, make disbursements by order of the Board of Managers and report the state of the funds at the stated meetings of the Society.

APPENDIX B

Constitution Of The Troy Association For The Relief Of Destitute Children: As Adopted October 22, 1833

Article I.
The Association shall be called the Troy Association for the Relief of Destitute Children.[1]

Article II.
All persons who shall annually contribute to the funds of the Association by donations in money or property to the amount of three dollars shall be members of the Association.

Article III.
The concerns of the Association shall be managed by twenty-one Trustees, to be chosen at the time of adopting this constitution. The property which may in any way be acquired for the use of the Association shall be deemed to be vested in the Board of Trustees for the time being. The

[1] Amended, December, 1834, to read the "Troy Orphan Asylum."

Trustees shall have power to choose their own presiding officers and appoint all other officers and agents necessary to conduct the concerns of the Association, to make by-laws, create and fill vacancies in their own board, and publish and annual report, including an account of the receipts and expenditures of the Association. Seven Trustees[2] shall constitute a quorum for the transaction of ordinary business. A majority of the whole number of Trustees shall be present at the adoption of any by-laws, or the choice of a presiding officer, or in filling a vacancy in the Board of Trustees; and the concurrence of three-fourths[3] of all Trustees shall be necessary to create a vacancy in the office of Trustee.

Article IV.
The females of the city are invited to take an active part in conducting the affairs of the institution subject to such regulations as shall be provided by the Trustees.

---

[2] Amended, December, 1834, to read "five Trustees shall constitute a quorum."

[3] Amended December, 1834, to read "A majority of all trustees."

Article V.
None but orphan children shall be relieved by the Association unless three-fourths of the Trustees shall agree to extend relief to other destitute children.

Article VII
The annual meeting of the members of the Association shall be held on the third Wednesday in December in each year after the present. At such annual meeting the constitution may be amended if three-fourths of all the members present shall agree to such alteration or amendment, of which proposed alteration or amendment two weeks notice shall be given in at least two of the newspapers of the City of Troy, signed by one or more members of the Association.

Unidentified nurse with TOA toddler.

APPENDIX C

Constitution Of The Ladies' Auxiliary Society For The Relief Of Orphan And Destitute Children Adopted 1833

Article I.
The Ladies of Troy do hereby form themselves into an association to the Gentlemen's Association for the Relief of Destitute Children which shall be called the Auxiliary Troy Female Association for the Relief of Orphan and Destitute Children.

Article II
The officers of the Association shall be four Directresses, to be denominated the first, second, third and fourth Directresses; a Secretary, Treasurer, and twenty-four Managers; to be elected at the annual meeting; and shall have the power to make by-laws and fill vacancies.

Article II
It shall be the duty of the first Directress to preside at all meetings of the Association; and in her absence the duty shall devolve on the second or third Directress present.

Article IV
It shall be the duty of the Secretary to record then proceedings of the meetings, and to make an annual report.

Article V.
It shall be the duty of the Treasurer to keep a strict account of all moneys received or expended.

Article VI.
It shall be the duty of two of the Managers and one of the Directresses, in succession, to meet once a week at the Asylum, to inquire into the condition of the Asylum, and to transact such business: as may-be necessary.

Article VII.
The Directress and Managers who meet weekly, shall be a Committee to decide upon all cases of application for destitute children, and present the same to the executive committee of the parent Association.

Article VIII.
Any person who contributes annually either in money or goods, shall be a member of the Association.

Article IX.
The annual meeting of the Association shall be held on the first Tuesday in November, in each year after the present.

Article X.
This constitution shall not be altered or amended, except at the annual meeting; and not then, unless two-thirds of the members present shall agree to such alteration or amendment.

Richard Thomas, Superintendent, 1941-1973.

Appendix C

The Troy Orphan Asylum Boy Scout Troop 1 was the first uniformed Scouts in America. 1938 campout.

APPENDIX D

By-Laws
Of The
Troy Association
For The Relief Of Destitute Children
As Adopted November 5, 1833

I. The stated meetings of the Trustees shall be held at the Asylum on the first Tuesday of every month, at 7 o'clock P.M. Special meetings may be held by order of the President, or when he is absent or unable to act, by order of any two Trustees; notice of which special meetings to be given by the Secretary, by causing written or printed notices to be left at the places of business or residence of the Trustees, on the day of the meeting.

II. The Trustees shall annually, at their first stated meeting after the annual meeting of the Association, choose a President and a Vice-President of their own number, and shall appoint a Treasurer and Secretary. Vacancies in either of those offices, occurring within the year, may be filled at any stated meeting after the vacancy happens.

III. All committees shall be appointed on the nominations of the presiding officer, unless when otherwise ordered.

IV. An executive committee, consisting of three Trustees, shall be appointed annually, who shall have power to decide on all applications for the admission of children into the Asylum of the Association: no child to be received unless at least two of the committee shall sign the permit, authorizing the superintendent to receive the child. It shall also be the duty of the executive committee to supply the Asylum with all necessary articles; it shall be the duty of the executive committee to meet at the Asylum on Monday afternoon of each week, to decide on applications for admission of children to inquire respecting the health and conduct of the children of the Asylum; to give advice and directions to the superintendent and other agents employed by the Association. The committee of the Ladies' Auxiliary Association are invited to meet at the same time: and cooperate with the executive committee in discharging the duties assigned to them.

V. Children over ten years of age shall not be admitted into the Asylum; nor shall any children be received, unless their parents or guardians shall relinquish all claim to their future disposal & shall be the duty of the committee to ascertain that the children admitted are free from any infectious or incurable disease.

VI. The children are to be taught reading, writing and arithmetic. They shall be instructed in the New Testament, and formed to habits of industry.

As soon as they shall be sufficiently instructed and be deemed by the Trustees capable of earning their living, they shall be bound to persons of fair character, on such terms as the Board shall approve. Children shall not remain in the Asylum after the age of ten years, if suitable places can be procured for them.

VII. The management of the children, and the care of the Asylum, shall be entrusted to a superintendent, with the assistance of a teacher and such domestics, as the executive committee shall deem it necessary to employ. The superintendent shall report at every stated meeting of the Board, the names, age and place of residence of all children received into or discharged from the Asylum during the preceding month; and it shall be the duty of the Secretary to enter the substance of such reports in a book, to be prepared for that purpose, So that a complete record may be kept of the names, ages, residence, time of admission, and discharge of the children.

VIII. On the decease, permanent removal from the city, or resignation of any Trustee, the vacancy shall be filled at the next stated meeting of the Board after such vacancy happens, at which a majority of the Trustees shall be present. The Board, by a constitutional majority, may declare the seat of any Trustee to be vacant, who shall, without assigning a reason satisfactory to the Board, omit to attend its meetings during the period of six: months, or who shall be unable, on account of disease or infirmity, to attend the meetings of the Board, for the period of one year, or who shall become an habitual drunkard, or be convicted of any infamous crime, or be notoriously guilty of acts of immorality; and thereupon the Board shall proceed to fill the vacancy so declared.

IX. It shall be the duty of the Treasurer to exhibit to the Trustees quarterly, the state of the funds of the Association.

APPENDIX E

By-Laws
Of The
Ladies' Auxiliary Society
Adopted 1833

To Regulate The Asylum For Orphans
And
Destitute Children Of Troy

1. The family shall rise, through the winter season, at daylight, and in summer at-five o'clock; the children as soon as convenient. They shall be immediately dressed, washed, combed, and together with the family, assemble in the school room — where a chapter from the Bible shall be read audibly by the superintendent or teacher; and the children may then follow in repeating the Lord's Prayer, if requested by the teacher or superintendent. After which the children shall go in perfect silence to the breakfast room; they shall be required to make a long pause before eating, and be taught to thank God tin silence for their food.

2. The hour for breakfast in winter shall be eight o'clock; but from the first of April until the first of November it shall be seven o'clock. The children shall be required to keep

silence at their meals; they shall make known their wants to their attendant by a given signal, which they may be allowed to explain if necessary. They shall retire in order from the table, either to their play room or school room.

3. They shall dine at twelve o'clock. Their supper shall be at five, or earlier in winter if deemed expedient. Immediately after supper the family shall all be assembled in the school room, where the superintendent shall close the day as she commenced it, by reading a portion of the Scriptures; after which the younger children shall be put to bed.

4. The breakfast of the children shall consist of chocolate, or some preparation of milk, in winter, boiled and poured over bread broken fine, or made into milk porridge. In summer, simply bread and milk, or rice or mush and milk.

5. Their dinner shall be simple—a plain soup twice a week. The intermediate days some simply cooked meat or fish, with plenty of potatoes, or Indian pudding, or something of that character. Pudding and soup or meat are not admissible at the same dinner. Should this diet be found to disagree with any of the children, the superintendent is allowed to

substitute more appropriate diet in the case of such child.

6. It shall be the duty of the teacher to see that the children under her particular charge are up and prepared for breakfast in season. She is also to have general care of them through the day, and to see that they retire in proper order to bed. She is under the direction of the Managers, or a committee from their numbers, as to the kind and order of instruction pursued in her school. She is to do all in her power to train the children to habits of industry and neatness, and to feel the responsibility of keeping them, and everything belonging to them, in order and in its place.

7. The superintendent will feel it her duty to instruct and employ the older children, out of school hours, in such domestic work in the family as they may be competent to do, under the directions of the Managers or a committee for that purpose, and with the more immediate care of those children too young for the school room. She is also to receive all children when first brought into the institution, and see that they are in a cleanly state before delivered over to the teacher. It will belong to her department to see that the children's clothes are kept in good repair. The

children themselves to be taught to aid in this duty as much as possible. The teacher is also expected to assist in sewing, as she may find leisure.

8, During such season of the year as the Managers shall deem it inexpedient to take the children to some place of worship on the Sabbath, they shall spend some portion of the day, both in morning and evening, in reading the Scriptures at home, under the direction of the superintendent or teacher. Their ordinary plays and occupations shall be suspended on that day.

9. No member of the family may, on any occasion, inflict punishment on a child, but the superintendent or teacher, on pain of being reported to the executive committee. All offences of magnitude must be reported to the weekly visiting committee whose duty it shall be to reprove the offenders and point out the course of treatment which their crime merits.

10. The Managers shall appoint from their own body, committees to cooperate with the executive committee appointed by, the Trustees, on the different branches of duty connected with the institution, on whom shall

rest the responsibility of that particular branch.

11. All meetings of the Managers shall be opened by reading the Scriptures.

12. The school shall be omitted Saturday morning, but not in the afternoon, it shall be the duty of the superintendent and teacher to wash and dress the children clean. Visitors are invited to call in the afternoon of Mondays, from two to five o'clock.

Unidentified toddlers and nurse at TOA.

APPENDIX F

By-Laws[1]
Of The
Troy Orphan Asylum

Article I.
The stated meetings of the Trustees shall be held on the first Tuesday of March, June, September and December, in each year, at 7 o'clock P.M., at the Asylum; or at such other hour and place as the Board by their vote, or the President may appoint. The President may call special meetings of the Board; and it shall be his duty to call such special meeting when requested in writing by three or more Trustees. In the absence of the President, special meetings may in like manner be called by the Vice President.

The Secretary shall cause written and timely notice of each meeting, (except adjourned meetings of the Board) to be given to every Trustee who is in town, either personally, or by leaving the same at his dwelling or place of business, or through the Post Office.

---

[1] These By-Laws appear in the annual report of 1860. Unchanged, they were in operation until 1870.

Article II.
The fiscal year begins on the first day of December. The Trustees shall annually, at the stated meeting in December, choose from their number by ballot a President and a Vice President; and shall also appoint by ballot a Treasurer and a Secretary. If a majority of the Trustees shall not be present at that meeting, the election may take place at the next stated meeting of the Board, or at a special meeting to be called for the purpose; and in the meantime, the officers of the preceding year shall continue to discharge the duties of their respective offices. Vacancies in either of those offices occurring within the year, may be filled at any stated meeting after the vacancy happens. In case a vacancy occurs in the office of Treasurer, the President, if in his judgment the exigency requires it, may, with the approval of the Finance Committee, appoint a Treasurer pro tem, to discharge the duties of the office until the next stated meeting of the Board.

Article III
The Trustees shall annually, in December, appoint from their number the following standing committees for the ensuing year, viz: an Executive Committee and a Finance Committee.

Article IV.
The Finance Committee shall have the care of the funds and of the corporation, subject, to the control of the Trustees. To them is entrusted the investment of the permanent fund; and also with such assistance as they may call to their aid the making of collections and soliciting donations. The Finance Committee shall consist of five members, of whom the Treasurer shall always be one.

Article V.
The Treasurer shall have the custody of the moneys and securities of the corporation; he shall keep an accurate account of all moneys received, paid out, and remaining in his hands, and of all other property belonging to the corporation and committed to its charge. He shall make an exhibit to the Trustees quarterly of the state of the funds.

He shall also, annually, at the stated meeting in December, make to the Board of Trustees a full report of the transactions in his department, for the year preceding.

The salaries fixed by the Board shall be paid by the Treasurer, as they fall due, without any order for that purpose. The other payments by the Treasurer shall be on the order of the Executive Committee, or of the Finance

Committee, acting within the scope of their respective duties, or by direction of the Board of Trustees.

Article VI.
The Executive Committee, which is to consist of three Trustees, shall have power to decide on all applications for the admission of children into the Asylum. It shall also be the duty of the Executive Committee to supply the Asylum with all necessary articles. It shall be the duty of the Executive Committee, in connection with the Superintendent, to see that careful economy is observed in all the expenses of the institution; in order that the funds furnished by the kindness of the benevolent, may procure relief to the largest possible number of destitute orphans. It shall be the duty of the Executive Committee to meet at the Asylum as often as may be necessary, and at stated times to be fixed by them, to decide on applications for admission of children; to inquire respecting the health and conduct of the children in the Asylum; and to give advice and directions to the Superintendent and other agents employed. The Committee of the Ladies' Auxiliary Association are invited to meet at the same time, and cooperate with the Executive Committee in discharging the duties assigned to them.

Article VII.
Children over ten years of age shall not be admitted into the Asylum; nor shall any children be received, to share in the relief of the institution, unless their parents or guardians shall, by an instrument in writing, surrender them to the care and custody of the Trustees, and relinquish all claim to their future disposal. It shall be the duty of the committee to ascertain that the children admitted are free from any infectious or dangerous disease.

The children are to be taught reading, writing and arithmetic, and, as opportunity shall offer, such other elementary branches as may be prescribed. They shall be instructed in the Bible, and especially in the New Testament. There shall be constant vigilance of their moral culture: but the exclusive tenets of any religious sect shall not be inculcated upon the children by the officers or agents of the institution. They shall be carefully formed to habits of industry. Their clothing shall be comfortable, but plain. Their food shall be abundant but helpful and plain. As soon as they shall be sufficiently instructed, and be deemed by the Trustees capable of earning their living, they shall be bound to persons of fair character, on such terms as the Board shall approve. Children shall not remain in the

Asylum after the age of ten years, if suitable places can be procured for them.

Article VIII.
The management of the children, and the care of the Asylum, shall be intrusted to a Superintendent, with the assistance of a teacher, and such domestics as the Executive Committee shall deem it necessary to employ. The Superintendent and teacher shall be appointed, and their compensation fixed by the Board of Trustees; and they shall hold their offices during the pleasure of the Board.

The Superintendent shall report at every stated meeting of the Board, the names, ages, and places of residence of all children received into or discharged from the Asylum during the preceding quarter; and it shall be the duty of the Secretary to enter the substance of such reports in a book to be prepared for that purpose, so that a complete record may be kept of the names, ages, residence, time of admission, and discharge of the children.

Article IX.
The Executive Committee, in connection with the President, have authority, in behalf of the Trustees, to superintend direct the binding out of children who have been received in the

Asylum, to such persons as they may think advisable, conforming in all respects to the provisions of law, and taking care, especially, to provide for their proper education.

The indentures of binding shall be signed in the name and behalf of the Trustees, by the President, and the corporate seal affixed: and the counterpart of every such indenture shall be kept under the charge of the President.

Article X.
All special committees of the Board shall be appointed on the nomination of the presiding officer, unless when otherwise ordered by the Board.

Article XI.
The Ladies' Association Auxiliary to the Troy Orphan Asylum are invited to take an active part in conducting the affairs of the institution, subject to such regulations as shall be provided by the Trustees.

Article XII.
On the decease, permanent removal from the city, or resignation of any Trustee, the vacancy shall be filled at the next stated meeting of the Board after such vacancy happens, at which a majority of the Trustees shall be present. As the office of Trustee should be held only by

those who are willing to devote, for the good of the orphan, the necessary time for the discharge of its duties, the omission of any Trustee, for six months, to attend the meetings of the Board, without assigning a reason satisfactory to the Board, shall be deemed a sufficient cause for removal.

Article XIII.

These By-Laws may be amended at any meeting of the Trustees at which the quorum required by law for that purpose, shall be present but no amendment shall be adopted except by the affirmative vote of a majority of the whole number of Trustees in office, unless it shall have first been offered, in writing, at a stated meeting of the Board, and laid over for consideration at the next stated meeting.

APPENDIX G

By-Laws[1]
Of The
Troy Orphan Asylum

Article I.
The stated meetings of the Trustees shall be held on the first Tuesday of March, June, and September, and on the third Wednesday of December, in each year, at 7 o'clock P. M., at the Asylum: or at such other hour and place as the Board, by their vote, or the president may appoint.

The president may call special meetings of the board; and it shall be his duty to call such special meeting when requested, in writing, by three or more trustees.

In the absence of the president, special meetings may in like manner be called by the vice president.

The secretary shall cause written and timely notice of each meeting except adjourned meetings of the board to be given to every trustee who is in town, either personally or by

---

[1] These By-Laws appear first in the annual report of 1870. With few changes, they remained in operation until early in the present century.

leaving the same at his dwelling or place of business, or through the Post Office.

Article II.
The fiscal year begins on the first day of December. The trustees shall annually, at the stated meeting in December, choose from their number by allot a president and vice president; and also appoint by ballot a treasurer and secretary. If a majority of the trustees shall not be present at that meeting, the election may take place at the next stated meeting of the board, or at a special meeting to be called for the purpose; and in the meantime the officers of the preceding year shall continue to discharge the duties of their respective offices. Vacancies in either of those offices occurring within the year may be filled at any stated meeting after the vacancy happens. In case a vacancy occurs in the office of treasurer, the president, if in his judgment the exigency requires it, may, with the approval of the finance committee, appoint a treasure pro tem to discharge the duties of the office until the next stated meeting of the board.

Article III.
The trustees shall annually, in December, appoint from their number the following standing committees for the ensuing year, viz:

an executive committee, a finance committee and a committee fund.

Article IV.
The finance committee shall have the care of the funds and finances of the corporation, excepting the permanent fund—subject however, to the control of the trustees. To them is entrusted the management of the general fund, and also, with such assistance as they may call to their aid, the making of collections and soliciting donations. The finance committee shall consist of five members, of whom the treasurer shall always be one.

Article V
The committee on permanent fund shall consist of three members. They shall, subject to the control of the board of trustees, have the sole charge of the investment: and reinvestment of the permanent fund; and no part of the same shall be allowed at any time to be mingled with the general fund. Whenever any part of the principal of said fund shall be paid in, it shall be deposited by the treasurer as a special deposit, and so remain until reinvested under the direction of the committee, when the same shall be drawn by him only upon a check made payable to the order of, and endorsed by, the chairman of

the committee. Only the interest received from this fund shall be subject to the control or direction of the finance committee or of the treasurer.

Article VI.
The treasurer shall have the custody of the moneys and securities of the corporation; he shall keep an accurate account of all moneys received, paid out, remaining in his hands, and of all other property belonging to the corporation and committed to his charge. He shall make an exhibit to the trustees quarterly of the state of the funds.

He shall also, annually, at the stated meeting in December, make to the board of trustees a full report of the transactions of his department for the year preceding.

The salaries fixed by the board shall be paid by the treasurer as they fall due, without any order for that purpose. The other payments by the treasurer shall be on the order of the executive committee, or of the finance committee, acting within the scope of their respective duties, or by the direction of the board of trustees; but the moneys belonging to the permanent fund shall be drawn and disposed of only in accordance with the provisions of the last preceding article.

Article VII.
The executive committee shall consist of three trustees and a committee of three from the Ladies Auxiliary Association, to be elected by that Association, who shall have the power to decide all applications for admission of children into the Asylum. It shall also be the duty of the executive committee to supply the asylum with all necessary articles. It shall be the duty of the executive committee, in connection with the superintendent, to see that careful economy is observed in all the expenses of the institution, in order that the funds furnished by the kindness of the benevolent may procure relief to the largest possible number of destitute or plans. It shall be the duty of the executive committee to meet at the asylum as often as may be necessary, and at stated times to be fixed by them, to decide on applications for admission of children, to inquire respecting the health and conduct of the children in the asylum, and to give advice and directions to the superintendent and other agents employed.

Article VIII.
Children over ten years of age shall not be admitted into the asylum; nor shall any child be received to share the relief of the institution unless the parents or guardians shall, by an instrument in writing, surrender

them to the care and custody of the trustees, and relinquish all claim to their future disposal. It shall be the duty of the committee to ascertain that the children admitted are free from infectious or dangerous diseases.

Children are to be taught reading, writing and arithmetic, and, as opportunity shall offer, such other elementary branches as may be prescribed. They shall be instructed in the Bible, and especially in the New Testament. There shall be constant vigilance for their moral culture: but the exclusive tenets of any religious sect shall not be inculcated upon the children by the officers or agents of the institution. They shall be carefully trained to habits of industry. Their clothing shall be comfortable, but plain. Their food shall be abundant and healthful, but plain. As soon as they shall be sufficiently instructed, and be deemed by the trustees capable of learning their living, they shall be bound to persons of fair character, on such terms as the board shall approve. Children shall not remain in the asylum after the age of ten years, if suitable places can be procured for them.

Article IX.
The management of the children and the care of the asylum shall be entrusted to a matron; with the assistance of a teacher, and such

domestics as the executive committee shall deem necessary to employ. The matron and teachers shall be appointed and their compensation fixed by the board of trustees, and they shall hold their office during the pleasure of the board.

The matron shall report at every stated meeting of the board, ages, and places of residence of all children received into or discharged from the asylum during the preceding quarter; it shall be the duty of the secretary to enter the substance of such reports in a book to be prepared for that purpose, so that a complete record may be kept of the names, ages, residences, time of admission, and discharge of the children.

Article X.

The executive committee, in connection with the president, shall have authority, in behalf of the trustees, to superintend and direct the binding out of the children who have been received in the asylum, to such suitable persons as they think advisable; conforming in all respects to the provisions of law, and taking care, especially, to provide for their proper education.

The indentures of binding shall be signed in the name and behalf of the trustees, by the president, and the corporate seal affixed; and the counterpart of every such indenture shall be kept under the charge of the president.

It shall be the duty of each trustee, so far as circumstances will permit, and especially of the executive committee, to continue a watchful and protecting care over those children after they are so bound out.

Article XI.
All special committees of the board shall be appointed on the nomination of the presiding officer, unless when otherwise ordered by the board.

Article XII.
The Ladies' Association, auxiliary to the Troy Orphan Asylum, are invited to take an active part in conducting the affairs of trustees.

Article XIII.
On the decease, removal from the city, or resignation of any trustee, the vacancy shall be filled at the next stated meeting of the board after such vacancy happens, at which a majority of the trustees shall be present. As the office of trustee shall be held only by those who are willing to devote, for the good of the orphan, the necessary time for the discharge of its duties, the omission of any

trustee, for six months, to attend the meetings of the board, without assigning a reason satisfactory to the board, shall be deemed a sufficient cause for his removal.

Article XIV.

These by-laws may be amended at any meeting of the trustees at which the quorum required by law for that purpose shall be present; but no amendment shall be adopted except by the affirmative vote of a majority of the whole number of trustees in office, unless it shall first have been offered in writing at a stated meeting of the board, and laid over for consideration to the next stated meeting.

TOA Headstone at Oakwood Cemetery plot.

Unidentified children's nurse at Vanderheyden.

APPENDIX H

By-Laws[1] Of The Ladies' Association Auxiliary To The Troy Orphan Asylum

Article I.
The Ladies' Association Auxiliary to the Troy Orphan Asylum shall consist of twenty-two ladies who shall constitute a Board of Managers, and be chosen from the City of Troy and vicinity. The Board of Managers shall have the general management and supervision of the internal affairs of the Asylum, and the care and conduct of the children to the extent that the same may be entrusted to them by the Board of Trustees of the Asylum.

Article II.
All vacancies in the Board shall be filled by ballot, at any regular meeting at which a majority of the entire Board shall be present.

Article III
The annual meeting of the Association shall be held on the first Tuesday in December of each year, at eleven o'clock A.M., at the Asylum building, at which time the reports of

---

[1] These By-Lws appear in the annual report of 1892. With few changes they were in operation until quite recently (1933-DR)

the work of the Association for the year shall be presented, officers for the ensuing year elected, and any other business done which may come before the meeting.

Article IV.
The officers of the Association shall be a First Directress, Second Directress, Third Directress, Secretary, and a Treasurer, all of whom shall be elected by ballot. The officers shall hold office for one year, and vacancies may be filled by ballot at any regular meeting for the remainder of the year, at which a majority of the entire Board may be present.

Article V.
The First Directress shall preside at all meetings, and perform such duties as are incident to the office of a presiding officer. In her absence one of the other directresses, in the order of rank, shall perform such duties.

Article VI.
The Secretary shall keep the records of the Association and take and record all minutes of meetings of the Board, conduct the correspondence, give proper notification of meetings, and perform such other duties as the Board may direct.

Article VII.
The Treasurer shall keep an accurate account of all receipts and disbursements of the Association, make a monthly and annual report of the same to the Board of Managers, and make an annual report of such receipts and-disbursements to the Board of Trustees.

Article VIII.
The regular meeting of the Board of Managers shall be held at the Asylum on the first Tuesday of each month, at 11 o'clock A.M., unless for reason the presiding Directress shall authorize another place of meeting. Special meetings may be called by the presiding Directress at any time, and shall be so called upon the request of three of the Managers. Five members shall constitute a quorum for all ordinary business at any meeting of the Board.

Any Manager not attending a regular meeting shall pay a fine of twenty-five cents; prolonged absence from the county only being a sufficient excuse.

The following shall be the Standing Committees of the Association, to wit:
Executive Committee.
Auditing and Finance Committee.
School Committee.

Sewing Committee.
Purchasing Committee.
Infirmary and Nursery Committee.
Repairing Committee.

Article IX.
Such committees shall consist of from three to five members, and shall be appointed by the presiding Directress at the annual meeting, or immediately thereafter. The respective duties of the several committees shall be such as shall from time to time be prescribed by the Board of Managers. Each committee, through its chairman, shall present a report of its work at each monthly meeting.

Article X.
The Matron of the Asylum shall make a report to the Board of Managers, at each monthly meeting, showing what changes have occurred in the register of the children and the internal affairs under her management, and the general condition of the Asylum; and make-such recommendations concerning the same as she may deem prudent. She shall also report on any other matters which the Board may direct. She shall receive the amount of fines collected for absences from regular meetings, and the money collected at the Asylum for board, and give an accurate

account at each monthly meeting of how the same has been expended.

Article XI.
The following order of exercises shall be observed at the meetings of the Board of Managers:

1. Reading of Scriptures.
2. Minutes of the last meeting.
3. Treasurer's Report.
4. Report of Matron.
5. Reports of Committees.
6. Miscellaneous Business.
7. Calling the Roll.
8. Adjournment.

Article XII.
All moneys collected and donations received by the Association shall be expended for the clothing of the children, and other necessaries for the house, under the direction of the Board of Managers.

Article XIII.
These by-laws may be altered, amended or repealed by an affirmative majority vote of the entire Board, provided notice of such proposed change shall have been given at the next prior regular meeting, and a copy thereof then deposited with the secretary, and

provided also the same shall be approved by the Board of Trustees.

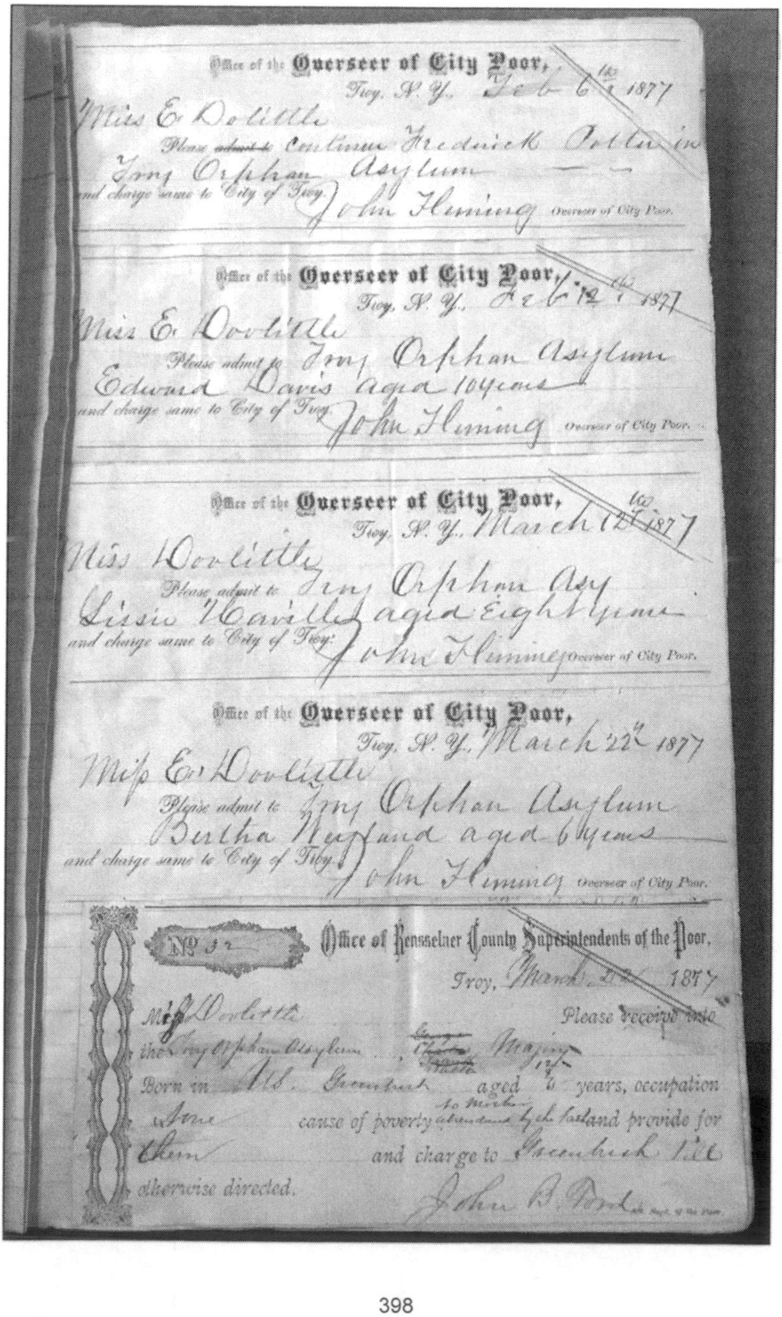

APPENDIX I

Rules[1] Of The Troy Orphan Asylum (As Given In The Annual Report Of 1893)

1st. Children shall be received into the Asylum only on the first and third Mondays of each month, (unless in exceptional cases) and shall be detained in quarantine in the infirmary at least ten days before being admitted to associate with the other children.

2nd. The Matron shall have the general charge and management of the internal affairs of the Asylum, except as is herein otherwise provided. She shall have the general supervision and care of the children, and everything that pertains to their comfort and welfare. She shall also have, under the approval of the Board of Managers, the employment and supervision of all assistance in the house, except as shall be required by the housekeeper in matters under her charge. She shalt also, so far as possible, provide instruction and practice for the girls in sewing, and each other domestic duties as they may be able to perform, and make all the necessary arrangements therefor.

---

[1] Subject to such changes and variations as are needful in order to meet the demands of differing times and conditions, the rules are, in the large, in effect at the Asylum today.

3rd. The Housekeeper shall keep the house in order, and employ and supervise such assistance as she may need for that purpose. She shall have general charge of the kitchen and laundry, and all the help employed therein. She shall also have charge of all provisions, stores and supplies, and every second Monday shall make out requisitions for such articles as may be required in her department. She shall also see that such requisitions are properly filled and certify to the same. The food for the children so supplied being subject to the approval of the Matron.

4th. The food for the children shall be furnished and served according to the approval of the Matron, and shall be simple, agreeable, and wholesome, and shall be varied as circumstances seem to require.

5th. So far as possible, each employee may be allowed a half day's absence once in two weeks. Such absence to be at such time when it least will interfere with the duties of the Asylum, the Matron and the housekeeper to designate the same.

6th. All wages and salaries of the female employees shall be fixed and adjusted by the

Board of Managers, except that all wages and salaries which are over $15.00 per month shall be fixed and paid only with the approval of the Board of Trustees.

7th. The children who are of sufficient age, shall be permitted, on the Sabbath, to attend church and Sabbath school in the morning, wherever in the city they may prefer, if practicable, under the care of such persons and under such regulations as the Matron may direct. In the afternoon of the Sabbath, an hour shall be set apart for such undenominational religious services and instruction in the Scriptures as shall be provided by the Board of Managers and such other song and prayer services or religious instruction shall be had daily, as the Board of Managers may direct.

8th. The Board of Managers shall through its purchasing committee, purchase all the clothing and wearing apparel for the children. The funds collected annually by the members of the Board, shall be devoted, so far as may be needed, to that purpose. This committee shall certify to the correctness of all bills for goods purchased by them, and only after such certification, and audit by the finance committee, shall they be paid by the Treasurer of the Board.

9th. The Board of Trustees shall appoint a purchasing committee of at least two Trustees, to serve for the term of two months, whose duty it shall be to purchase all the food and supplies for the house, upon the requisition of the Matron or housekeeper, made every two weeks upon blanks prepared for that purpose. Such purchase shall be made, so far as possible, upon competitive bids.

In cases of emergency, the committee, or the Executive Committee shall have authority to make such purchases between the regular times of requisition. All bills for such purchases shall be certified to by the housekeeper or Matron as having been received, and the same shall be audited by the purchasing committee of the Board of Trustees before they shall be paid by the Treasurer.

APPENDIX J

By-Laws[1] Of The Troy Orphan Asylum (Adopted October 9, 1924)

Article 1.
Stated meetings of the Trustees shall be held on the second Thursday of January, April, July and October in each year, at the Asylum, or at such place and at such hour as the Board by vote, or the President may appoint.

The President may call special meetings of the Board, and it shall be his duty to call such meetings, when requested by three or more Trustees.

The Secretary shall cause written and timely notice of all meetings to be given to every Trustee either personally or by mail.

Five Trustees shall constitute a quorum for the transaction of ordinary business, and a majority of the whole number of Trustees shall be present at the adoption of by-laws or amendments thereto, or in the choice of a President, or filling a vacancy in the Board of

---

[1] Subject to such changes as may have been necessary in order to meet the changing conditions, these By-Laws are now in use.

Trustees. A vacancy in any of the standing committees or a vacancy in the office of Vice-President or Secretary may be filled at any meeting duly called at which a quorum is present, provided notice to that effect has been sent to each Trustee in writing at least five days before the meeting is held.

Article II.
The fiscal year shall begin on the first day of January. The Trustees shall annually at the stated meeting in January choose from their number by ballot the following officers: a President, Vice-President, Treasurer, and Secretary. If a majority of Trustees shall not be present at that meeting, the election shall take place at any stated meeting or at a special meeting to be called for that purpose, and until such election the officers of the preceding year shall continue in office.

The Trustees may at any meeting appoint and at pleasure remove an Assistant Treasurer, and fix his compensation.

Vacancies in any of these offices occurring during the year may be filled at any stated meeting. In case a vacancy shall occur in the office of Treasurer, the President may, if in his judgment the exigency requires it, with the approval of the finance committee, appoint a

Treasurer pro tem to discharge the duties of the office until the next stated meeting of the Board.

Article III.
The duties of the President and Secretary shall be those usually incident to such offices respectively.

In the absence or inability of the President, the Vice-President shall have full power to act as President.

The Treasurer shall have the custody of the moneys and securities of the corporation; he shall keep an accurate account of all financial transactions and shall make an exhibit thereof to the Trustees at the stated quarterly meetings. He shall also at the stated meeting in January make to the Board of Trustees a full report of transactions in his department for the preceding year. He shall pay all salaries without further order. All other payments by the Treasurer shall be on the order of the executive committee or of the finance committee, acting within the scope of their respective duties, or by direction of the Board of Trustees.

The duties of the Assistant Treasurer shall be the performance of such duties of the

Treasurer, as may be delegated to him by the Treasurer.

Article IV.
The Trustees shall annually at their stated meeting in January appoint from their number the following standing committees for the ensuing year, to wit:
An Executive Committee.
A Finance Committee.
An Auditing Committee.
A Committee on Farm.
A Committee on Buildings.

Article V.
The Executive Committee shall consist of five Trustees to be elected by the Board at its annual meeting, together with the President of the Board, ex-officio, and three members of the Woman's Association to be selected by that Association. The President of the Board shall be chairman of the Committee.

The Executive Committee shall appoint from its number a Secretary who shall keep the records of all meetings and report its proceedings at each stated meeting of the Board.

The Executive Committee shall have power to control and manage all the internal affairs of the Asylum, employ all persons necessary for its management and fix their salaries, pass upon all children received and direct the binding out of all those who are thus disposed of, and generally, during the period between stated meetings of the Board, to perform all acts which they may legally do, not otherwise provided for, in the management of the Asylum, which in their judgment may become necessary and require immediate action.

Article VI.
The Finance Committee shall have the care and management of the finances, subject, however, to the control of the Trustees. The Committee shall consist of five members, of whom the Treasurer shalt be one.

It shall have the charge and management of all invested securities, the investment and re-investment of the permanent fund separate and apart from the current fund.

Al checks on account of such Fund must be countersigned by the Chairman of the Finance Committee, or in his absence or inability to act, by a member of said Committee.

The income from the permanent fund shall be used for the general expense except that the income from gifts made for special purposes shall be used solely in accordance with the conditions of said gifts.

All gifts, donations and legacies to the Asylum, other than for current expenses or for some special purposes named by the donor, shall become a part of the Permanent Fund, unless the Board of Trustees shall vote to apply the same to some permanent improvement or in payment of any indebtedness incurred for that purpose.

The Finance Committee is authorized and empowered, whenever in its judgment it is deemed advisable or necessary to sell, assign, transfer, compromise and dispose of any such investments and securities which in its judgment should be sold, compromised or disposed of, and to negotiate, compromise, adjust, foreclose and settle all such matters in any way that it may deem advisable and tor the best interests of the Asylum and to take all necessary steps and proceedings to that end, using the corporate seal if required.

Article VII.
The Auditing Committee shall consist of three members. The duties of the Auditing Committee shall be to examine quarterly the accounts of the Treasurer, and audit the same,

also to examine and audit the bills of the superintendent whenever the same shall be required or directed by the Board of Trustees.

Article VIII.

The Committee on Farm shall consist of five members. The Committee on Farm shall, subject to the approval of the Board or the Executive Committee, have charge of the farm, including its buildings; equipment, live stock and crops, and shall engage such employees for the proper maintenance of the farm as it shall deem necessary, and shall present a report of its action to the Board or to the Executive Committee.

Article IX.

The Committee on Buildings shall consist of five members, it shall, subject to the approval of the Executive Committee or the Board, have charge of the alteration, repair and maintenance of the Asylum buildings and equipment (except the farm buildings and equipment): and shall present a report of its action to the Board or to the Executive Committee.

Article X.

The Asylum receives the children committed to it by proper poor officers, by a court of competent jurisdiction or by parents or guardians as provided by law, at rates fixed by the Board of Trustees, providing such children are not known to be juvenile delinquents, truants or mental defectives.

Children are to be taught such elementary branches as may be required by law and shall further be trained, cared for and instructed in compliance with the rules of the State Board of Charities.

Article XI.
The supervision of the Asylum property and the management and care of the children shall be entrusted to a superintendent with such assistance as the Executive Committee shall deem necessary. The superintendent shall be appointed and his compensation fixed by the Board. He shall maintain such records, and prepare and present such reports and perform such other duties as the Board of Trustees or the Executive Committee shall direct.

Article XII.
The Women's Association, Auxiliary to the Troy Orphan Asylum, is empowered to take an active part in conducting the affairs of the institution, subject to such regulations as shall be provided by the Trustees.

Article XIII.
A vacancy in the Board of Trustees may be created by the decease, permanent removal from the city, or resignation of any Trustee and such vacancy may be filled at the next stated meeting of the Board. The omission of any Trustee for six months, to attend the meeting of the Board, may be deemed sufficient cause tor his removal, upon two-thirds affirmative vote of the Board.

Article XIV.
These by-laws may be amended at any meeting of the Board by an affirmative vote of the majority of the Trustees, provided, however, no amendment or change shall be adopted unless a draft thereof shall first have been deposited with the Secretary of the Board at a stated meeting, and provided further that the secretary mail a copy of said amendment to each Trustee at least five days before the final consideration thereof.

Appendix J

AN ORPHAN CHILD'S FATE

He was six feet tall and muscular,
And broad across the chest,
And he had a heart of sympathy,
That beat within his breast.

His face and arms was brown,
For he daily drove a float,
And came out as a witness,
For this little girl in court.

And as he rose before the Judge,
The truth he did explain,
Told how this poor little orphan,
Had to stand out in the rain.

Told of how her step-mother,
Would drive her off from home,
To stay all day in the meadow,
With the cow, and all alone.

Oh! what a wretched mother,
With a heart so cruel and cold,
To punish this poor little orphan,
Who is scarcely eight years old.

So often she would beat her,
And drive her out of doors,
Compell this poor little orphan,
To suffer in the cold.

Her Father he was very stupid,
He surely had no heart,
To see his poor child suffer,
And never take her part.

The need for orphan asylums can be summed up in this 19th century poem. Poems of the 19th century, J.W. Fletcher 1909.

Appendix K

By-Laws[1] Of The Women's Association Auxiliary To The Troy Orphan Asylum (Approved By The Board Of Trustees, January 8, 1925)

Article I.
The Women's Association, auxiliary to the Troy Orphan Asylum, shall consist of not more than twenty-five members who constitute a Board of Managers, shall have the management and supervision of the care and training of the children of the Asylum as the Board of Trustees may direct.

Article II.
All vacancies in the Board shall be filled by ballot, at any regular meeting at which a majority of the entire Board shall be present.

Article III.
The annual meeting of the Association shall be held on the first Tuesday in January of each year at 10 30 A.M., at which time the reports of the work of the Association for the year shall be presented and officers for the

---

[1] These By-Laws, subject to such necessary changes as may have seemed wise, are in use at the present time (1933).

ensuing year elected, and any other business which may come before the meeting.

Article IV.
The officers of the Association shall be First, Second, Third, Fourth, and Fifth Directress, Secretary, and a Treasurer, all of whom shall be elected by ballot. The officers shall hold office for one year, or until their successors are chosen, and vacancies may be filled by ballot at any regular meeting: for the remainder of the year, at which a majority of the entire Board may be present.

Article V.
The First Directress shall preside at all meetings, and perform such duties as are incident to the office of a presiding officer. In her absence one of the other Directresses, in order of rank, shall perform such duties.

Article VI.
The Secretary shall keep the records of the Association and take and record all minutes of the Board, conduct the correspondence, give proper notification of meetings, and perform such other duties as, the Board may direct.

Article VII.
The Treasurer shall keep an accurate account of all receipts and disbursements of the Association, make a monthly and annual report of the same to the Board of Managers, and make an annual report of such receipts and disbursements to the Board of Trustees.

Article VIII.
The regular meetings of the Board of Managers shall be held at the Asylum on the first Tuesday of each month at 10:30 o'clock A.M., unless for reason the presiding Directress shall authorize another place of meeting. Special meetings may be called by the presiding Directress at any time, and shall be so called upon the request of three of the Managers. Five managers shall constitute a quorum for all ordinary business at any meeting of the Board.

The following shall be the Standing Committees of the Association, to wit:
Executive.
Sewing.
Finance.
Nursery.
Housekeeper and Kitchen.
Baby House.
Religious.
Nominating.

Infirmary and Hospital.
Library.
Education.
Recreation.
Kindergarten.
Older Children.

The duties of the respective committees shall be as follows:

Executive Committee. —Shall present to the Board of Trustees such matters as need their consideration and shall report to the Managers matters of interest acted upon by the Trustees. To keep in touch with the work of other institutions for children, to suggest improved methods of administration, to decide questions, of general administration when referred by the Matron.

Finance Committee. —To have the care of the funds of the auxiliary, to prepare an annual budget for submission to the Managers, and to annually inspect and approve the accounts of the Treasurer.

Housekeeper and Kitchen Committee —To have general supervision of the care and keeping of the house and dietary.

Appendix K

Religious Services Committee—To direct the religious training of the children.

Infirmary and Hospital Committee—To supervise the care of the sick and promote methods of maintaining the health of the children.

Education Committee. —To visit the school and keep in touch with the teachers and their methods of instructing the pupils. To engage and direct the Manual Training and Domestic Science teachers.

Kindergarten Department Committee. —To direct the work of the caretaker and to provide kindergarten supplies.

Sewing Room Committee—To purchase house linen and clothing.

Nursery House Committee. —To have the oversight of the nurses in training, to see that the infants have good care, to otherwise direct the work of the baby house, and to see that it is properly equipped.

Nominating Committee. —Shall present nominations for officers and members of the Board.

Library Committee. —Shall provide and maintain a suitable library for the children.

Recreation Committee —Shall study the play life of the children and provide adequate recreation, equipment.

Committee on Older Children. —To provide for the education, personal training, and recreative life of the older children, including particularly the girls of the Continuation Class and of the Nursery Maids Training School.

Article IX.
Each committee shall consist of not less than two Managers, and shall be appointed by the Board of Managers at the meeting following the annual meeting. Each committee shall present a report of its work at each monthly meeting. The First Directress shall be ex-officio, a member of all committees.

Article X.
The following order of exercises shall be observed at the meetings of the Board of Managers:
1. Reading of Scripture.
2. Minutes of Last Meeting.
3. Treasurer's Report.
4. Reports of Committees.
5. Miscellaneous Business.
6. Calling of Roll.

7. Adjournment.

Article XI

All moneys collected and donations received by the Association shall be expended for the clothing of the children, and other necessaries of the house, under the direction of the Board of Managers.

Article XII.

These by-laws may be altered, amended, or repealed by an affirmative majority vote of the entire Board, provided notice of such proposed change shall have been given at the next prior regular meeting, and a copy, thereof then deposited with the Secretary, and provided also the same shall be approved by the Board of Trustees.

SHOOT 100 POUND DEER

TROY, March 20—A 100-pound spikehorn buck deer, which came to its grief Sunday night after being struck by an automobile on the Cherry Plain and Berlin highway, was dressed by Valentine R. Teal, game protector, who was obliged to shoot it on being notified that it was lying in the highway. Mr. Teal on arriving found all four legs broken and the deer's condition was such that he was compelled to end its suffering. After dressing it Mr. Teal sent it to the Troy Orphan asylum, where the inmates were treated with a venison dinner.

Ballston Spa Daily Journal, Wednesday, March 20, 1929.

APPENDIX L

An Act
To Incorporate The Troy Orphan Asylum
Passed April 10, 1835

The People of the State of New York, represented in Senate and Assembly, do enact as follows:

Sec. 1.
All such persons as are now members of the Troy Association for the relief of destitute children, and all persons who shall hereafter become members of said Association by subscribing to the Constitution thereof, and paying the sum of three dollars annually to the Treasurer of said Association, according to the bylaws thereof shall be, and hereby are constituted a body corporate and politic, in fact and in name, by the name of "The Troy Orphan Asylum."

Sec. 2.
The estate and concerns of the said corporation shall be managed by twenty-one trustees; and David Buel, Jr., Thomas L. Ostrom, Gurdon Grant, Griffith P. Griffith, Thaddeus B, Bigelow, Asahel Gilbert, Jr., William W. Whipple, Amos Allen, Richard P. Hart, John Thomas, Stephen Warren, P. H.

Buckley, Elias Lasell, Jacob B. Lansing, Gardner Landon, Elias Pattison, George Vail, Jacob Merritt, John T. McCoun, Day Otis Kellogg and John Paine, shall be the trustees.

Sec 3.

When a child be surrendered to the charge and custody of the trustees of the said corporation, by an instrument in writing, signed by the parents or guardians of such child, or by the superintendents of the poor of the County of Rensselaer, the said trustees may, in their discretion, receive such child, and bind out such child, being of the full age of eight years, and not under, to some suitable employment, and in the same manner as overseers of the poor are by law authorized to bind out poor and indigent children; but proper provision shall in every case be made and inserted in the indentures by which such child shall be bound to service, for securing an education fitting and proper for the condition and circumstances in life of such child.

Sec. 4.

The Board of Trustees shall, on the third Wednesday in December in each year, exhibit to the members of the said corporation, an exact account of the receipts and disbursements of the preceding year.

Sec. 5.
None but orphan children shall be relieved by this corporation, unless three-fourths of the Trustees shall agree to extend relief to other destitute children.

Sec. 6.
It shall be lawful for the superintendents of the poor of the County of Rensselaer, to contract with the trustees of the said corporation for the maintenance, education and support, within the place provided for the keeping of said children; of any poor or indigent child under their care; and such child while under the charge and within the custody of the trustees of said corporation, shall be subject to the same rules, regulations and government, as if such child had been surrendered to the charge and custody of the trustees, by the parent or guardian of such child in manner aforesaid.

Sec. 7. The real and personal estate which this corporation may hold shall not exceed at any time the yearly value or income of two thousand dollars, nor shall it take by devise, real or personal estate, of a greater amount than ten thousand dollars.

Sec. 8.
The legislature may at any time alter; modify or repeal this act.

Two Small Girls Are Saved from Drowning

TROY, Aug. 7—Two small girls and their attendant from the Troy Orphan Asylum were saved from drowning yesterday afternoon in Smart's pond, South End, by the efforts of two local men who dashed into the water fully clad and brought the struggling trio to shore.

According to witnesses, Sarah Griffith and Dorothy Wishart, 12 and 10 years old, respectively, were in bathing and went beyond their depth. Mrs. Florence Chaplin, recreational director at the asylum, rushed into the water but was unable to rescue them. She took one under each arm and cried for help. Edward Maxwell and John Gaunay heard the cries and rushed to their assistance.

Ballston Spa Daily Journal, Thursday August 7, 1930.

APPENDIX M

An Act
In Relation To The Troy Orphan Asylum
Passed March 18, 1859

The People of the State of New York, represented in Senate and Assembly do enact as follows:

Sec. 1.
The Trustees of the Troy Orphan Asylum, and all persons who shall pay the sum of three dollars or more, annually, to the treasurer, shall be members of the corporation which was created by the act entitled "An act to incorporate the Orphan Asylum," passed April 10, 1835.

Sec. 2.
The estate and concerns of said corporation shall be managed by twenty-one trustees, who shall be residents of the City of Troy; and David Buel, Jr., Lyman Bennett, John Flagg, Gurdon Grant, William Howard Hart, Elias Johnson, George Lesley, Hanford N. Lockwood, John W. Mackey, Joel Mallery, Francis N. Mann, Isaac McConihe, John S. Perry, Charles L. Richards, Nathaniel Starbuck, Silas K. Stow, George Vail, D.

Thomas Vail, Philander Wells, Thomas White, and John D. Willard, are the present trustees. The Trustees shall have power to choose their own presiding officer, and appoint all the other officers and agents necessary to conduct the concerns of the corporation, to make bylaws, and create and fill vacancies in their own board; and they shall publish an annual report, including an account of the receipts and expenditures. Five trustees shall constitute a quorum for the transaction of ordinary business. A majority of the whole number of trustees shall be present at the adoption of any bylaws, or the choice of a presiding officer, or in filling a vacancy in the board of trustees: and the affirmative vote of two-thirds of all the trustees shall be necessary to create a vacancy in the office of trustees. In case of the removal by the board of a trustee from his office, they shall set out in their report the cause of such removal.

Sec. 3.
Said corporation may take by gift, devise or bequest, real and personal estate, and hold the same for the benevolent purposes for which it was created, viz: the relief, support and education of orphan children; but the real estate which said corporation may hold, exclusive of its orphan house or asylum, and grounds thereto, shall not at any time exceed

the net yearly value or income of ten thousand dollars.

Sec. 4.
The seventh section of the act entitled "An Act to incorporate the Troy Orphan Asylum," passed April 10, 1835, is hereby repealed; and all other provisions of said act, inconsistent with the provisions of this act, are repealed.

TO EXTEND WORK

TROY, July 13—A movement whereby the Troy Orphan Asylum contemplates undertaking increased welfare work among Negro children, not only of Troy, but throughout this section of the state, was inaugurated yesterday during a meeting of the Executive Board of the Asylum in the Troy Savings Bank building. Hobart W. Thompson presided.

The Saratogian. Wednesday, July 13, 1932.

Appendix M

Killed at Coon's

Mrs. Charles Burchard and adopted son, about 14 years old, who resided about a mile and a half south of Round Lake, were instantly killed by being struck by a train at Coon's crossing, between Round Lake and Mechanicville, at 1.15 o'clock last Saturday afternoon.

Mrs. Burchard and the boy had been to this village with a one-horse wagon containing farm produce. They had disposed of their load and, having made some purchases, started for home. When they reached Coon's crossing, where the highway crosses the Delaware & Hudson tracks, the horse took fright. The animal took the bit in its teeth and could not be controlled. Instead of keeping to the road, the horse took to the railroad track, and started north dragging the wagon over the ties, every bound bringing the ill-fated occupants of the wagon nearer and nearer train No. 16, southward bound, from Saratoga to Albany.

After Engineer Eugene Richards of Whitehall, who was at the throttle of the locomotive, saw the horse and wagon with its frightened occupants on the track, he had no time to bring the train to a stop. It was going at its customary speed. There was a horrible crash. The pilot of the locomotive struck the horse, killing it instantly. With a craunch the wagon was broken into fragments and tossed to one side of the road, while Mrs. Burchard and the boy were instantly crushed to death.

The train was stopped and Conductor Cull of Whitehall, who was in charge, ordered the bodies of the victims placed in the baggage car. Tenderly the train hands took them up. The train stopped here and the bodies were removed to the emergency hospital the Railroad Y. M. C. A.

Coroner Johnson and Dr. Palmer were quickly on the scene. They could tell at a glance that both victims were beyond human aid. The coroner ordered the bodies removed to Mace's undertaking rooms. Coroner Johnson annouced that he would make an investigation. He left at once for the home of the victims to break the news to the husband, who survives, with another adopted son.

The killing of Mrs. C. W. Burchard and William Hammond is further saddened by the sudden death of the former's father, Nelson Towne, aged seventy-eight years, who was found dead by his daughter, Mrs. W. H. MacGinchey, in his back yard at Hudson an hour and a half before Mrs. Burchard's accident. The funerals of father and daughter were held Wednesday at Hudson

The body of William Hammond, the 15-year-old boy, who was in the carriage with Mrs. Burchard when the train hit it, was taken to Troy by Undertaker G. Herbert Blake. The boy was an inmate of the Troy Orphan Asylum. He is survived by his sister.

William Hammond, 15, was killed by a train in June of 1906. Hammond was an inmate at Troy Orphan Asylum.

The Story of

VANDERHEYDEN HALL

The Story Of VANDERHEYDEN HALL

Were You Ever a Child?

Can YOU REMEMBER—the things you had, the care you had, the parents you had? If you can remember how it felt to be a child, with a home, with a family to love you, then you can imagine what it would be like to be that child, without a home, without a family.

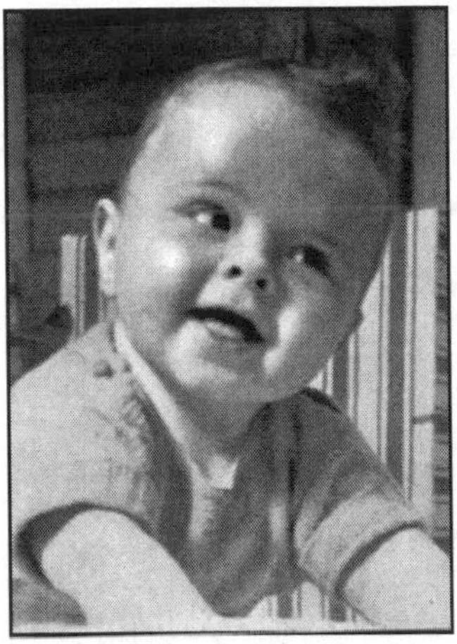

Every year, sure as death and taxes, a certain number of children are in need. Homeless. Without care. Without love.

For more than a century, Vanderheyden Hall in Troy, New York has tried to meet the bitter need of the children. To provide a place where the children could be safe, when they had no other place to go.

In the past 110 years 13,368 children have lived at the Hall.

They have gone to the city schools, studied their lessons and said their prayers at night. They have

romped over the grounds, cried over childish hurts and laughed over childish joys. They have learned how to work and how to grow into useful men and The old name was the Troy Orphan Asylum. You won't need to be told why the children prefer the new name. In the pages that follow you will see how they live at Vanderheyden Hall.

VANDERHEYDEN HALL provides a home for children of all ages, from babies a day old to boys and girls of seventeen. The children do all the normal things a child does in his own home. Strong emphasis is placed on religious education, character development and training for citizenship, but there is always time for wholesome play and reading.

Boys in Workshop

THE WORKSHOP is in the basement of the Peterson Memorial Gymnasium. Students receive elementary training in carpentry, metal work, caning chairs, etc. Best of all they gain a feeling for handling tools.They make simple repairs in furniture for the Hall. One boy is making picture frames while another is putting the finishing touches to a bird house. The top floor of the Gymnasium is the center of athletic life. Basketball is a favorite sport in winter. In the spring a rough field is converted into a baseball diamond. The Boy Scouts and the Girl Reserves also meet in the Gymnasium. The Scout troop has the longest unbroken history of any troop in the country.

Learning to be Homemakers

THE ADOLESCENT girls have their own house, where they receive the training that will help them to care for their own homes some day. In the separate building not far from the Main Hall they have their own living room, bedrooms, etc. Under the direction of a house mother they prepare all their own meals. They make play suits for the younger children and some of them help in the Baby House, receiving training as a child's nurse. The girls themselves chose to use this light pleasant room as a combination kitchen and dining room. They take turns at setting the table, cooking and washing the dishes, and doing the laundry.

Boys and a Farm

THE FARM is an important part of the life at Vanderheyden Hall. It supplies much of the food for the 160 children and the Staff. Chickens, turkeys and pigs are raised. In the spring the boys go into business as farmers. Each one is assigned his own garden plot and seeds are issued to him. From then

on through the summer he works his rows of vegetables, planting, hoeing and weeding, learning some of the essentials of agriculture. The Hall buys his crops from him, thus securing fresh vegetables for the table.

In the fall comes the accounting. He pays for the supplies he has been issued and learns what profits he has made. Boys who have not been diligent may find themselves in the red, but good workers may net as high as seventy-five dollars. They are encouraged to save part of their earnings and to spend the rest wisely, on things they need.

From the farm and garden projects the boys obtain many important vocational experiences. The live stock holds their interest even more than the gardens. This year they cared for 1,900 chickens, 400 turkeys, 50 pigs and 2 horses. Next year they hope to have a herd of beef cattle. The boys are under the supervision of an able farmer who has proved to be a good teacher not only on farming but on the repair and upkeep of farm equipment, buildings and everything used in farming.

As a good farmer has to be a Jack-of-all-trades the boy farmers acquire the fundamental skills of many occupations. When they leave Vanderheyden Hall they are well equipped to work on farms and to become first class farmers, if their interests fall in this field. What is even more valuable, they have learned how to work.

Prayers at bedtime

RELIGIOUS TRAINING is a part of the daily life of all the children at Vanderheyden Hall. They take turns in asking the blessing that precedes each meal. Religious services are held each Sunday morning in the Tillinghast Memorial Chapel. The girl choir leads the singing of hymns. Bible texts are studied and a short talk is given on religious subjects. Older children are allowed to attend services in local churches of their own choice.

At the close of day each child has a quiet period with a counselor. The little children have stories read to them and learn their Bible verses. The older children are given an opportunity to talk over the events of the day and discuss any problem that is troubling them. Each group has a prayer as the final event of the day.

A Visit to Vanderheyden Hall

By Lorine Pruette

If you go to visit Vanderheyden Hall, as I did, you will notice the sprawling brick buildings at 100 Spring Avenue, in Troy, New York. You will see the long corridors, the big dining room, the bedrooms with one small white iron bed close to the next, the

bare, utilitarian furnishings, the absence of bright colors. You may be thinking that an institution is a grim place for a little child to live.

But then you will see the children, and it will not feel like an institution, for the children are doing all the things that children like to do in their own homes. Two little girls are sitting in a corner, reading a book together. A group of adolescents about an old piano. From the ball field you hear the crack of a bat against a baseball. Down the hill at the back you see a cluster of youngsters. They are shouting at their game and one little girl in slacks, with pigtails flying, is leaping down to join them.

The children are not in uniforms, but in the helter skelter sweaters and caps and slacks and dungarees that children like to wear. There are no long lines of bored children, being drilled and ordered here and there. You do not hear any orders being given. The staff of adults is there, looking after the children, quietly and amiably, firmly and sensibly.

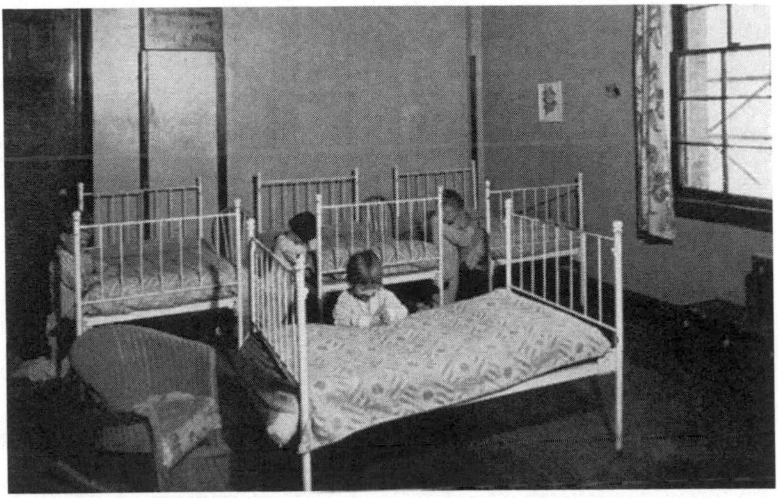

You go into one large room with the superintendent and watch several six-year-old girls rush up to him. They have been bad, they say cheerfully, they would not take their naps and now they have to stay indoors a little longer and rest. They giggle about this, and none of them complain.

You go down to the basement to see the big kitchen. You look into the freezing unit where hundreds of chickens, grown on the place, are plucked and ready for use. You see the homegrown hams in the pantry and the rows of big milk cans. Milk for a hundred and sixty children. You hear about the farm where the boys work, growing the vegetables for the Hall.

The children like to talk to you. Two little girls come bouncing into a room filled with small iron bedsteads. They are eating candy bars their father has brought them. "Want to see my bed?" asks the one with the bangs. She pats her bed proudly. It's hers, you see. And the older sister, a year older perhaps, calls you to come over to the other side of the room to see her bed, because it has a new bedspread. You can't see that it looks any different from the others, but she knows it is different.

Down a long corridor I found myself suddenly surrounded by very little boys. The black-eyed one put out a small brown paw and I took it in mine. He said his name was Don. He did not want anything except to walk along, holding to a woman hand. When I came back later he was still waiting there, and again we walked along gravely, hand in hand.

We came to the Baby House, a separate establishment where 95 infants live with their nurses. The usual contusions surrounded us, diapers being changed, a baby crying, two solemn eyed babies in a play pen. In one room we were surrounded by a swirl of two-year-olds. Three blond boys, a girl with black curls and impish eyes, another with soft brown hair. I knelt to speak to them and the little girls patted the feather on my hat and showed an intense interest in my handbag. The little boys looked on in manly detachment.

Black Curls traced the outline of the shiny initials on the purse and put out a hand to touch the gold compact I took out. On impulse I powdered her nose and she gurgled with joy. The tiny girls crowded about, each wanting her nose powdered. They were enchanted as I went from one to another, flipping each with the powder puff. Such a small thing can enchant a child.

I asked which ones were orphans and found that many were not, that the Hall is no longer an orphans' asylum, that it is simply a place where children who need protection can get it. Crises come

to families, in war and in peace. Here is a place to take up the slack, to deal with some of the problems that arise in our modern world, a place that protects the children from suffering.

In another room two very small boys flung themselves against the superintendent's legs, clinging to him until he gathered both of them up in his arms. And then a third boy, a little Jonnny-come-lately, lurched up hopefully, his arms outstretched. When he saw that there was no place for him he turned trustingly to me and I stooped down and picked him. He was so little and confiding; he knew that this is a place where children can expect affection.

It seemed to me that Johnny-come-lately had passed a verdict on Vanderheyden Hall. In coming trustingly into the arms of a stranger he was saying that here is a place where boys and girls do not need to be afraid, where children can hold out their arms and know that somebody will take them up.

We came upon two small boys building a tower with broken bricks and I thought that all the towers in the world started from something like this, because boys liked to put one thing on top of another, to see how high they could build. Men have thrust their buildings into the sky—the white shaft of the Washington Monument, the beautiful lines of the RCA Building, the topless towers of Ilium, grew out of this perpetual dream of boys, of their determination to put one thing on top of another to see how high they could go. And I wondered how best we could help them build.

Won't You Come to See Us Sometime?
Brochure prepared for Vanderheyden Hall (Troy Orphan Asylum) by Lorine Pruette, Pn.D.
Author of "The Parent and the Happy Child," etc.
Cover photograph contributed by Toni Frissell.

Who prepared this brochure?

Lorine Livingston Pruette (November 3, 1896 – December 20, 1976). The following bio of Pruette is taken from Wikipedia. This brochure created by Pruette was probably written after 1941 since it featured Richard Thomas on the cover. Thomas took over Vanderheyden in 1941. It is unknown what her connection or interest with Vanderheyden was.

Lorine Pruette was born in Millersburg, Tennessee, to college-educated parents. Her mother and her maternal grandmother were among the first generation of college-educated women in the United States. Pruette's mother's dream of a career in writing were never fulfilled; she placed enormous pressure on Pruette to fulfill the life she always wanted.

Pruette was exceedingly bright, but regarded herself

as a social outcast throughout her childhood and adolescence and did not date in high school. In college she joined a sorority, acted in plays, edited the college newspaper, and played the violin in the orchestra. Pruette graduated in 1918 from the University of Tennessee at Chattanooga with a Bachelor of Science in chemistry and went on to Massachusetts' Worcester College, where she began her Master's degree.

Mary Trigg, in her dissertation entitled Four American Feminists, 1910–1940: Inez Haynes Irwin, Mary Ritter Beard, Doris Stevens, and Lorine Pruette, explains that unlike many other twentieth century feminists, Pruette did not limit her vision to women's suffrage but worked toward a broad agenda of *"reshaping marriage, the family, and society."*

Throughout her career, Pruette addressed issues such as "the need for married women to achieve fulfilling lives in both public and private spheres, the weakness of men and the strength of women, [and] the importance of the parent-child relationship." Pruette held strong anti-men views, which were products of a childhood overshadowed by her mother's oppression and unhappiness; Pruette wrote that by the age of nine she firmly believed that *"all the evils of the world came from these intolerable males."*

Pruette was initially determined not to wed or bear children. However, her strong anti-men viewpoint changed during her graduate work under psychologist G. Stanley Hall, whom she greatly admired, and also coursework that exposed her to the work of Havelock Ellis, Sigmund Freud, and Carl Jung. She married a fellow graduate student, Douglas Henry Fryer, and moved with him to New York, where "he became an instructor in the Columbia University psychology department and she enrolled in the PhD program, receiving her degree in 1924." Pruette and Fryer's union did not last, and shortly after their divorce she had a two-year marriage to John Woodbridge Herring. Pruette cites both of her marriages in her book, Why Women Fail, and states that men do not like to see women outperforming them in academia or in the career field, and hints that this may be a key reason both of her marriages did not succeed.

Pruette lived through both world wars and associated feminism with pacifism; she believed women could make the world a more peaceful place. When Franklin D. Roosevelt proposed his New Deal cabinet, Pruette suggested he "instead inaugurate 'a real New Deal,' a cabinet made up of women, whose 'broader social viewpoint' and concept of social justice could help steer the world away from militarism." Pruette was firm in her feminist beliefs and spent much of her time traveling, lecturing, and writing about her views on feminism, yet the bulk of her work remains unpublished. She found work in various vocations such as editing, writing for newspapers or professional journals, she also taught sociology and psychology at several universities, and was a research and consulting psychologist for several institutions.

Despite the setbacks and difficulties of old age, Pruette continued to work as long as she could, and to address the social problem of aging. But despite being mentally sound, Pruette's agnostic beliefs caused her some spiritual grief as she contemplated what was to become of her soul after her death, and within her last few years of life she is recorded as waking up in a feverish sweat numerous times yelling out, *"Immortality is what I want!"* She died on December 20, 1976, less than seven weeks after her 80th birthday. She is buried in Forest Hills Cemetery in Chattanooga, Tennessee.

Lorine Pruette was childless by choice but in her later years she regretted that she had no one to "carry on her 'bit of protoplasm." Because Pruette lived through the transition from a homosocial to heterosocial society, aided in and witnessed many of the triumphs of feminism, she regarded the modern day woman as taking her rights for granted and being ignorant to the struggles of the women who came before her. Pruette dismisses the idea of a modern feminist, saying *"there is no reason why she should think of herself as a feminist; she inherited feminism."* Nearing the end of her life, Lorine

Pruette urged women not to unquestioningly accept the social stigmas of the current society and to remember to use each other's help and support to press for change. See: http://www.feministvoices.com/lorine-livingston-pruette/

Antoinette Frissell Bacon (March 10, 1907 – April 17, 1988), known as Toni Frissell, was an American photographer, known for her fashion photography, World War II photographs, and portraits of famous Americans, Europeans, children, and women from all walks of life.

Toni Frissell. From Wikipedia.

RESOLUTION OF RESPECT

C. W. TILLINGHAST BARKER.

Resolution unanimously adopted by the board of trustees of the Troy Orphan Asylum, July 14, 1938.

The trustees of the Troy Orphan Asylum record with deep regret and personal sorrow the death of C. W. Tillinghast Barker, for twenty-four years a member of the board of the institution. He was faithful in his duties, always willing to sacrifice time and energy to its interests and intelligent in addressing himself to its problems.

Mr. Barker represented a family tradition in Orphan Asylum affairs. His grandfather, Charles W. Tillinghast, served as trustee for more than four decades and as president for more than a third of a century. His grandmother, Mrs. Charles W. Tillinghast, was a member of the Women's Board from 1874 to 1913. They will always be remembered for the beautiful memorial chapel which they placed upon the grounds in 1901, one of many generous contributions they made to the asylum.

Mr. Barker's mother, their daughter, Mrs. Stephen W. Barker, was also a member of the Women's Board of Managers and served on many of its active committees. His cousin, General C. Whitney Tillinghast, was also a trustee; and General Tillinghast's wife was for a generation a member of the Women's Board.

Mr. Barker, his mother and his grandparents gave to the institution no less than 118 years of service. This remarkable record terminates with Mr. Barker's death. No family has ever been more devoted to the asylum; no member of it was more deeply interested in its welfare than Mr. Barker himself. Such services are a radiance which will bless the institution for generations to come. They can never be forgotten.

HOBART W. THOMPSON,
DAVID B. PLUM,
Committee.

HENRY S. LUDLOW.

Resolution unanimously adopted by the board of trustees of the Troy Orphan Asylum, July 14, 1938.

The death of Henry S. Ludlow removes from the circle of the friends and supporters of the Troy Orphan Asylum one who for more than thirty years had given himself freely to its interests. Mr. Ludlow became a member of the board in 1906 and remained a member until his decease.

Nor is this the whole measure of the association of the Ludlow name with the institution. His father was a trustee of the asylum from 1883 until 1904 when he died in office. He was a large contributor to the fund raised for the purchase of the present property and the erection of the plant. Upon his death he left a substantial legacy to the permanent fund. His mother was an active member of the Woman's Board of Managers from 1894 until 1901. Members of the Ludlow family therefore gave no less than 60 years of efficient service to the institution.

Men of their type are the bulwarks of any philanthropic cause; it was in such a tradition that Henry S. Ludlow was steeped; and it was with such ideals that he assumed his duties as a trustee.

It was not long before the board realized that he wore competently the mantle of those who had gone before him. He was constant in season and out of season, ready with his money and his time, constructive in his suggestions, willing to put his shoulder to the wheel whenever the need arose, invariably regular in attendance at meetings of the board or of any committees to which he was named. It was this faithfulness to his duties, inbred in him, which caused his appointment as a member of the executive committee in 1928 and as chairman of the finance committee in the following year. Unassuming, sincere and dynamic with the highest ethical and religious principles, he kept his eye fixed unswervingly upon the goal for which the asylum was established—the creation in underprivileged children of worthy standards of character, the giving them a home in which they could come to maturity under normal and healthful influences.

It is difficult to express the board's sense of so heavy a loss. But we know the splendid service Mr. Ludlow performed throughout the years in which he was associated with us, and how much we shall miss him.

HOBART W. THOMPSON,
DAVID B. PLUM,
Committee.

The Times Record. Saturday, July 16, 1938.

Appendix O

Sample Intake Card

NAME: Morrow, William D.O.B. Dec. 6, 1900

PLACE OF BIRTH: Troy, N.Y.

MOTHER: Katherine Taylor D.O.B. Franklin Co

FATHER: Robert Morrow D.O.B. NYC

SIBLINGS:

May 27, 1907

DATE OF ADMISSION: Junell, 1915 REFERRED BY: Justice of Peace

REASON FOR ADMISSION: Mother died / Father died later Sand Lake NY

May 30, 1910--------------------Father

DATE OF DISCHARGE: March 27, 1916-----DISCHARGED TO: Mr D.B. Smith, Berlin NY

REASON FOR DISCHARGE:

SIGNIFICANT DOCUMENTS:

HOBART W. THOMPSON.

HOBART THOMPSON LONG CIVIC LEADER, DIES AT AGE OF 82

Served as Director on Many Boards; Funeral Services Monday

Hobart Warren Thompson, member of one of Troy's old families and active for years in the civic and social life of the city, died late yesterday at Samaritan Hospital after a long illness. He was 82 years old.

Mr. Thompson was of the ninth generation in America of Anthony Thompson who settled in Connecticut in 1637, eleventh in the Elder William Brewster line and of the tenth generation of the Sir Richard Saltonstall line.

He was born in this city April 2, 1862, son of the late John Isaac and Mary Mabbett Warren Thompson. He prepared for college at the Selleck School, Norwalk, Conn., and then entered Trinity College at Hartford, Conn., from which he was graduated in 1883 with the degree of bachelor of arts. He received his master's degree three

Student at R. P. I.

After post graduate work at Rensselaer Polytechnic Institute he entered the employ of John I. Thompson & Sons, remaining there two years. In 1885 the John I. Thompson Chemical Co. was incorporated with Mr Thompson as secretary-treasurer and manager. The company acquired a plant in Colonie for the manufacture of chemicals and continued operations for five years. In 1890 the business was sold to the Nichols Chemical Co. of New York, Mr Thompson continuing with the concern as manager until 1898 when the plant was absorbed by the General Chemical Co. For nine years, until 1907, he remained as manager until the General Chemical Co. suspended operations at its Troy plant.

He then became treasurer of the Sirocco Engineering Co. and for a year engaged in the manufacture of ventilating fans. The company sold the plant to the American Blower Co. in 1908. From then on Mr. Thompson engaged in various activities, principally relating to philanthropic and financial matters, as an officer, director or trustee.

Railroads Director.

He became a director of John I. Thompson Sons & Co., director and treasurer of the John I. Thompson Manufacturing Co., trustee of the Troy Savings Bank, director of the Union National Bank, director and vice president of the Troy & Greenbush Railroad, director of the Saratoga & Schenectady Railroad, Albany & Vermont Railroad, Rensselaer and Saratoga Railroad and Troy & Cohoes Railroad.

For 23 years he served as president of Troy Orphan Asylum, now Vanderheyden Hall. When he retired, he was made honorary president of the home. He had served the Troy Orphan Asylum for 41 years as a trustee. His term as president of the board was, with one exception, the longest in the history of the institution. He also had served as secretary of the board and member of the executive and finance committee.

He was a trustee of Samaritan Hospital, a governor of Marshall Sanitarium, and for many years a member of the board of the Y. M. C. A. Mr Thompson also served for about 25 years as a director and treasurer of the Troy Boys Club.

Although he had resigned many of the directorships because of ill health, he was still a member of the board of Troy Savings Bank, Marshall Sanitarium and the Samaritan Hospital.

Active in Church.

Always deeply interested in his church, he had been a lifelong member of St Paul's Episcopal Church and a vestryman since 1902. At the time of his death he was senior warden of St Paul's

The Times Record, Saturday September 23, 1944.

APPENDIX P.

Herbert Hunn Interview 1917

Farming for Profit

February 23, 1917

The Troy Times did an extensive interview with superintendent Herbert Hunn who had been recently hired to manage the Troy Orphan Asylum. Hunn made many improvements and the newspaper described the rise of the Asylum's farm community success. Following is the entire newspaper article.

Superintendent Troy Orphan Asylum Does Not Find Anything Gloomy About It - Has Realized Money for His Institution—By Applying Modern Methods-Stock Must Be More Than Ornamental-Making Everything Work.

Farming in Rensselaer County and anywhere else is profitable—If you know how and use modern methods, according to Herbert J. Hunn, Superintendent of the Troy Orphan Asylum. Herbert J. Hunn—"H. J." his friends call him—had no special farm-training; he is, however, a scientific worker. He prepared himself for Young Men's Christian Association work and was so successful at the Troy Young Men's Christian Association that he got into state charitable work, and then he was given the Superintendency of the Troy Orphan Asylum. The Directors who called Mr. Hunn to that position did a brilliant piece of business, because Mr. Hunn has made a great success of the whole thing. But that is a long story and this is an article on profitable farming.

A Prize Hog.

There was not very much comment about the farming feature of the Troy Orphan Asylum until one day it was announced that a hog had been killed there that weighed more than 900 pounds. That excited interest, and inquiry showed that Mr. Hunn and his efficient helpers had cleared from the Farm-work for the last two years $2,000 a year. Considering that the farm land at the disposal of the institution is ninety acres, allowing a cost price of $100 an acre (a fair price for land in this section) and it develops that the Troy Orphan Asylum is a gilt-edged investment, paying from ten to fifteen per cent. As Hunn expresses it, the institution sells all its product to itself and thereby eliminates a marketing charge, but financially, even including this item, the Troy Orphan Asylum farm is a good thing. More money could be made if more land could be secured.

How It Was Done.

Mr. Hunn says that scientific application and expert bookkeeping are responsible. "We charge to the farm everything we buy for it, and we credit to the farm everything we sell for it. Consequently we keep everything which pays and get rid of everything that doesn't. Very simple method, isn't it? When I went there I found that one of the cows was a great pet. She stood in the stable and looked pretty, and the children and, but we discovered that she was not furnishing anything but a beauty show, and she was eating her head off. So we made her pay by using her for meat. "Our first effort was to discover our needs and our available facilities. The Orphan asylum has children; children need milk, so it was necessary that we take up dairying. Your plant will produce certain things; it will not give everything. You cannot have a stock farm, a hay farm, a vegetable farm, a potato farm all in one; in short, your farm cannot be all things to all produce any more than a human being can be all things to all men. You must specialize. If we devoted our attention to raising potatoes exclusively at the orphan asylum we should have gone bankrupt. Our soil is not adapted to it, having too much clay and not enough sand. But you must have vegetables and hay if you are going into the dairy business, and there must be some potatoes, so we made the most of what we had.

Successful Hog Raising.

We found hog raising profitable. We had our own garbage, in addition to that of the Emma Willard School so feed for hogs cost us nothing. I found that the manure from the barns was allowed to run into

Smart's Pond, where our ice was harvested; so we built a first-class cement manure pit and save the valuable properties for use on the land. I found the ensilage was not being stored adequately so I had a new silo built, which is big enough for our cattle feed. I also found that the water from the roof of our barn was undermining the foundations, and I had eaves gutters put on. Our wagons and other machinery were kept out of doors, because of lack of storage room, and I had a shed built, thereby preventing a large depreciation charge. Considerable time had been wasted with errands, so we installed a telephone.

Increasing Milk Production.

Some cattle were eating up their value, so we started keeping records of their feed and the milk, and the unprofitable we got rid of. Our system of bookkeeping is so complete and informing that the state authorities complimented us upon it.

Believe in Pedigrees.

"I believe in pedigreed stock. I am convinced that animals are just the same as humans In this particular. We purchased a high-bred registered Holstein-Friesian bull, and the result has been that we secure about twice as much milk as formerly. By carefully watching the records we have increased the average milk from each of our cows from 6,000 to

8,000 pounds a year. One cow gave us 11,700 pounds in one year. "The pedigreed cattle effort worked so well that I tried the policy in regard to pigs. I bought a young boar for $16, as against $5, which we used to pay, and kept him for three years. He was the one that weighed 900 pounds, and when killed his overweight was enough over the average at market prices to more than pay for what he originally cost. We have in addition several of his sons and are able to sell our pigs to farmers, by showing them thc pedigree, at higher prices than we could otherwise secure.

Attention to Produce.

Some persons think that almost anything you put in the ground will grow; that all you have to do is to plant and reap. This is not so. We found we had to give our produce-raising as much careful attention as our stock, and we have obtained splendid results. They told us we could not make alfalfa grow but we did, and we utilized a piece of what had been a sidehill that produced only clay and gravel. We changed it into a field of alfalfa, from which we reap three crops a year. The reason alfalfa grows there is because of the great length of its roots, which extend into the soil from eight to ten feet. Thus the rains are not able to wash It out.

Sweetening The Soil.

We found it necessary to lime considerable land, due to the acidity of the soil. We discovered that by burying a piece of litmus paper we could ascertain whether or not the soil was acid. If the litmus turned red, the soil was acid and needed lime. The lime when properly used does not burn the soil, but sweetens it. Then we invested about $1 an acre in bacteria for our particular soil. We secured this bacteria from the state. It comes in the form of sand. We soaked our alfalfa seed In water, mixed it with the bacteria and sowed it, and the result was splendid.

Rotation of Crops

"Crops were not rotated at the farm, and we have been doing this. One field had been sown with the same crop for eleven years. Every year now we change the crop we sow."

Costly Eggs

Asked about poultry raising, Mr. Hunn laughed. No, the asylum did not find it profitable. "We kept records and found that it cost us $2 to produce one egg so we made up our minds that we did not know how to raise chickens and we purchased our eggs. Poultry-raising requires personal attention, and with all else we had to do we did not have the time." Mr.

Hunn's assistant on the farm is John H. Wisner, and his bookkeeping methods are aided by William H. Shields and William C. Geer, the committee from the Trustees, that has charge of the farm work. Mrs. George B. Cluett and Mrs. Stephen W. Barker allow the asylum the use of some land, but Superintendent Hunn thinks that an increased acreage would result in a larger income. If it could be advantageously done, Mr. Hunn would favor celling the present asylum farm and securing a larger one in the country."

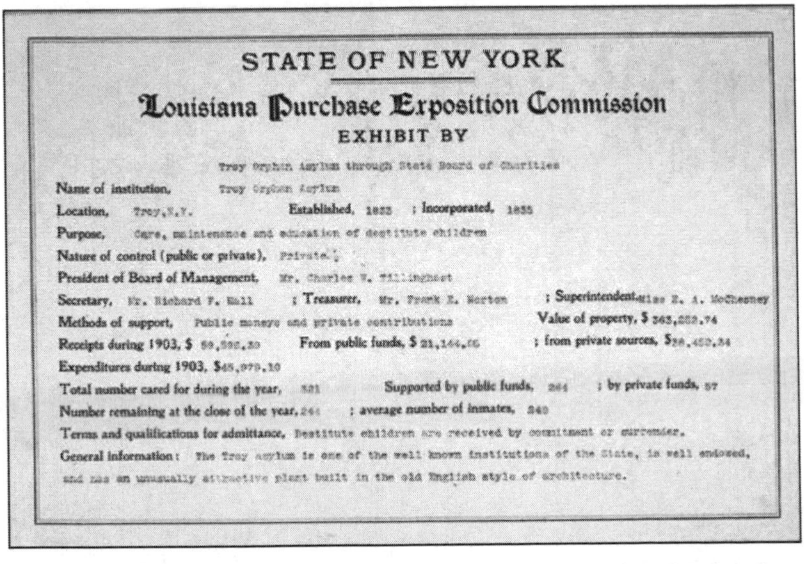

STATE OF NEW YORK

Louisiana Purchase Exposition Commission

EXHIBIT BY

Troy Orphan Asylum through State Board of Charities

Name of institution, Troy Orphan Asylum

Location, Troy, N.Y. Established, 1833 ; Incorporated, 1835

Purpose, Care, maintenance and education of destitute children

Nature of control (public or private), Private

President of Board of Management, Mr. Charles W. Tillinghast

Secretary, Mr. Richard F. Hall ; Treasurer, Mr. Frank E. Norton ; Superintendent, Miss E. A. McChesney

Methods of support, Public moneys and private contributions Value of property, $ [illegible]

Receipts during 1903, $ [illegible] From public funds, $ [illegible] ; from private sources, $ [illegible]

Expenditures during 1903, $45,979.10

Total number cared for during the year, 321 Supported by public funds, 264 ; by private funds, 57

Number remaining at the close of the year, 244 ; average number of inmates, 240

Terms and qualifications for admittance, Destitute children are received by commitment or surrender.

General information: The Troy asylum is one of the well known institutions of the State, is well endowed, and has an unusually attractive plant built in the old English style of architecture.

The St. Louis World's Fair in 1904 contained an exhibit by the Troy Orphan Asylum.

Yesterday morning, the children of the Orphan Asylum on Eighth street were provided with a treat that was hardly less pleasant than that of their more fortunate brothers and sisters who are blessed with parents and happy homes. The tree, presented by Thomas McManus, was an unusually fine one and was decorated and loaded with presents with a taste and generosity that speak well for the ladies who prepared it.

☞ ACKNOWLEDGMENT FROM THE TRUSTEES OF THE TROY ORPHAN ASYLUM.—The Trustees of the Troy Orphan Asylum acknowledge the following Christmas gifts: From Mr. F. A. Stow, one barrel apples, one barrel onions, one barrel beets, two barrels potatoes, three barrels turnips; Mrs. Stephen Warren, four turkeys; Mr. B. Starbuck, one turkey; Mayor Carroll, one turkey, one pig; Mrs. F. W. Farnham, a quantity of cakes; Mrs L. M. Tibbits, a quantity of cakes; Mrs. E. Westervelt, several mince pies; Keith & McGregor, a quantity of woolen stockings and mittens.

Troy Daily Whig. December 29, 1871.

rd y Orphan Asyl m Census 1900

Surname	First	Relation	Age	Born	Father	Mother	Yrs US	Occupation
Ackroyd	Sarah S	Attendant	56	NY	Eng	Eng		Seamstress
Alber	Freda	Inmate	2	NY	Ger	Ger		
Alber	Marguerite	Inmate	4	NY	Ger	Ger		
Albert	Harold	Inmate	8	NY	NJ	NY		In School
Albert	Paul	Inmate	3	NY	NJ	NY		
Allen	Harry	inmate	18	NE	unkn	unkn		in school
Bartlett	George	Inmate	10	NY	unknow n	unkno wn		In School
Bartlett	Nellie	Inmate	13	NY	UNK	UNK		in school
Bausch	Anna C	Attendant	22	NY	Ger	Ger		Seamstress
Becker	Albert	Inmate	9	NY	GER	NY		In School
Becker	Florance	Inmate	6	NY	Ger	NY		
Becker	John	Inmate	11	NY	Ger	NY		In School
Becker	Minetta	Inmate	9	NY	Ger	NY		in school
Beier	Carl	Inmate	6	NJ	GER	GER		
Beier	Johanna	Inmate	4	NY	Ger	Ger		
Blanchard	Elmer	Inmate	12	NY	NY	NY		In School
Bonacker	Fred	inmate	11	NY	Ger	NY		in school
Bonacker	Lilly	Inmate	5	NY	Ger	NY		
Bonesteel	Sidney	Inmate	14	NY	NY	NY		In School
Bonesteel	Willard	Inmate	11	NY	NY	NY		In School
Bounds	Warren J	Inmate	8	NY	NY	NY		In School
Branch	Frank	Inmate	12	NY	MA	CT		In School
Branch	George	Inmate	9	NY	MA	CT		In School

Bristol	Margaret	Inmate	4	NY	NY	NY		
Bristol	Nellie	Inmate	3	NY	NY	NY		
Brooks	Fred G	Inmate	14	NY	Unk	Unk		In School
Brown	:ouisa	Inmate	10	NY	NY	NY		In School
Bryant	Charles	Inmate	12	NY	Unk	NY		In School
Burke	Charles	Inmate	3	NY	unknow n	unkno wn		
Burke	George	Inmate	4	NY	unknow n	unkno wn		
Burke	Mary	Inmate	8	NY	Unk	Unk		In School
Campbell	Grace	Inmate	9	NY	NY	NY		In School
Campbell	Paul	Inmate	2	NY	NY	NY		
Chase	Wyatt C	Attendant	22	NY	NY	NY		Caretaker
Cilles	Cannio	Inmate	11	ITALY	ITALY	unkno wn	2	In School
Clark	Edward	Inmate	6	NY	PA	NY		
Cohen	Fannie	Inmate	7	NY	Russia	Russia		
Cohen	Ida	Inmate	8	NY	Russia	Russia		in school
Cohen	Samuel	Inmate	12	NY	RUSS	RUSS		In School
Cole	Irene	Inmate	7	NY	Unk	MA		
Cole	Lydia	Inmate	7	NY	NY	NY		
Cole	Mabel	Inmate	11	NY	NY	NY		in school
Copeland	John H	Inmate	15	NY	NY	NY		In School
Cullett	Andrew	Inmate	10	NY	NY	Can		In School
Cullett	Lizzie	inmate	13	NY	NY	Can		in school
Cumming	Edith	Inmate	16	NY	NY	NY		in school
Cumming	Gertrude	Inmate	11	NY	NY	NY		in school

[illegible] y Orphan Asyl m Census 1900

Cummings	Jessie M	Attendant	17	NY				Attendant
Daley	Mary J	Attendant	44	NY	Irel	Irel		Seamstress
DeHart	Emma	Inmate	7	NY	CA	NY		
DeLong	Arthur	Inmate	6	NY	NY	NY		
Dwyer	Arthur	Inmate	10	NY	NY	Irel		In School
Dwyer	Bessie	inmate	12	NY	NY	NY		in school
Edgscomb	Ida	Inmate	6	NY	NY	NY		
Edgscomb	Lula	Inmate	4	NY	NY	NY		
Edwards	Amelia	Attendant	36	NY	NY	Wale		Attendant
Felix	Ida	Inmate	8	NY	UNK	UNK		in school
Felix	John	Inmate	5	PA	unknown	unknown		
Felix	Lena	Inmate	9	NY	UNK	UNK		in school
Fuller	Ella	Inmate	13	NY	Ger	Ger		in school
Gary	Jennie	inmate	11	NY	NY	NY		in school
Geis	Bertha	Inmate	5	NY	Ger	NY		
Germond	Eva	Inmate	8	NY	NY	NY		in school
Germond	Ida	Inmate	13	NY	NY	NY		in school
Germond	Morriss	Inmate	10	NY	NY	NY		In School
Goeway	George	Inmate	5	unknown	unknown	unknown		
Goeway	William	Inmate	3	unknown	unknown	unknown		
Golden	Charles	Inmate	13	NY	NY	NY		In School
Golden	Edward	Attendant	19	NY	Unk	Unk		Laborer Farm
Granger	Mahlon	Inmate	13	NY	NY	NY		In School
Haines	Bertha	inmate	11	NY	Ger	NY		in school

Haines	Eva	inmate	8	NY	Ger	NY		in school
Haines	Maud	inmate	13	NY	Ger	NY		in school
Hammond	Joseph	Inmate	10	NY	NY	NY		In School
Hammond	Louise	inmate	7	NY	NY	NY		
Hammond	William	Inmate	8	NY	NY	NY		In School
Harltey	Lizzie	Inmate	10	UNK	UNK	UNK		in school
Harrison	Bertha	Inmate	5	NY	NY	NY		
Harrison	Henry	Inmate	4	NY	NY	NY		
Hart	Elisie	inmate	14	Eng	Eng	Eng		in school
Hart	Fred G	Inmate	12	Eng	Eng	Eng	5	In School
Hartley	Walter	Inmate	8	Unk	Unk	Unk		
Haulsapple	Alrengry	Inmate	8	NY	NY	NY		In School
Haulsapple	Warren	Inmate	2	NY	NY	NY		
Haywood	John	Inmate	13	NY	NY	NY		In School
Haywood	M Belle	inmate	14	NY	NY	NY		in school
Henners	Emma A	Attendant	24	NY	NY	NY		Domestic
Henry	Annie	Inmate	7	NY	NY	Ire		
Henry	Mary	Inmate	11	NY	Ire	Ire		in school
Higgins	Jennie	inmate	17	Irel	Irel	Irel		in school
Hofelich	Mary	Attendant	24	Ger	Ger	Ger	7	Cook
Horth	Ellis	Inmate	7	NY	NY	NY		
Horth	J Oliver	Inmate	12	NY	NY	NY		In School
Horth	William	Inmate	15	NY	NY	NY		In School
Houlsapple	Irene	Inmate	5	NY	NY	NY		

Jerry	Peter	Inmate	2	NY	NY	VT		
Johnson	Lilly	Inmate	3	NY	Unk	NY		
Kennedy	Jeannette	Inmate	7	NY	UNK	NY		in school
King	Emma	Inmate	11	NY	UNK	NH		in school
King	George	Inmate	7	NY	unknow n	NH		
Kinlock	Marguerite	inmate	11	NY	NY	Eng		in school
Kirkwood	May	Inmate	11	NY	Scot	Scot		in school
Knack	Mary	Inmate	8	NY	Ger	NY		In School
Knokf	Lillian	Inmate	12	NY	Ger	NY		in school
Knopf	Chester	Inmate	5	NY	GER	NY		
Knopf	Fred	Inmate	10	NY	GER	NY		In School
Kredenburgh	Bert	Inmate	9	NY	NY	NY		In School
Kredenburgh	Percy	Inmate	6	NY	NY	NY		
Lampman	Carrie	inmate	9	NY	NY	NY		in school
Lampman	Eddie	Inmate	7	NY	NY	NY		In School
Lane	Plina	inmate	11	NY	NY	unkn		in school
Lansing	E LeRoy	Inmate	12	NY	NY	Unk		In School
Larkins	Maud	inmate	14	NY	unkn	unkn		in school
Lauer	Howard	Inmate	8	NY	GER	NY		In School
Lavine	Abraham	inmate	6	NY	Ger	Ger		
Lavine	Freda	Inmate	1	NY	Ger	Ger		
Lavine	Harry	inmate	2	NY	Ger	Ger		
Lavine	Ida	Inmate	7	MA	Ger	Ger		
Lawson	Joseph	Inmate	15	NY	NY	NY		In School

Lepper	Annie	Inmate	3	NY	Can	Scot		
Lepper	Edith	Inmate	8	NY	Scot	Scot		in school
Lepper	Hattie	Inmate	15	NY	Scot	Scot		in school
Lepper	Ruby	Inmate	4	NY	Can	Scot		
Lepper	Susie	Inmate	13	NY	Scot	Scot		in school
Lewis	Adina	Attendant	22	Eng	Eng	Eng	20	Waitress
Matson	Celia	inmate	12	NY	NY	NY		in school
Matson	Grace	inmate	14	NY	NY	NY		in school
Matson	Ruth	inmate	7	NY	unkn	unkn		
McKee	Lillie	inmate	14	NY	Irel	Irel		in school
McKeever	Alice	Inmate	5	NY	Eng	Eng		
McKeever	Margaret	Inmate	9	NY	Eng	Eng		In School
McLaren	Lillie	inmate	15	NY	NY	Eng		in school
McLaren	Walter	Inmate	13	NY	NY	Eng		In School
Menten	William L	inmate	1	NY	NY	NY		
Mickel	Esther	inmate	14	NY	unkn	unkn		in school
Mickel	James	Inmate	15	NY	Unk	Unk		In School
Morris	Harriet	Attendant	69	NY	NY	NY		Teacher
Morris	James	Inmate	8	NY	Wale	Wale		In School
Morris	Lizzie	inmate	9	NY	Wales	Wales		in school
Morris	Mary	inmate	10	NY	Wales	Wales		in school
Morris	William	Inmate	13	NY	Wale	Wale		In School
Myers	Edwin	inmate	4	NY	NY	NY		
Myers	Hazel	Inmate	6	NY	NY	NY		

Myers	Willard	inmate	8	NY	NY	NY		in school
Nichols	Grace	Inmate	5	NY	MA	NY		
Nichols	Harold	Inmate	8	NY	MA	NY		In School
Niclols	Olive	Inmate	14	NY	MA	NY		
Nold	Charles F	Inmate	7	NY	GER	GER		
Nold	John P	Inmate	5	NY	GER	GER		
Nold	Joseph K	Inmate	4	NY	GER	GER		
Norton	Marguerite	Inmate	7	NY	NY	NY		
Norton	William	inmate	8	NY	NY	NY		in school
Nutt	Cora	Inmate	13	NY	NY	NY		In School
Nutt	Grace	Inmate	6	NY	NY	NY		
Nutt	Lucy	Inmate	12	NY	NY	NY		In School
Osborne	Bertha	Inmate	14	NY	NY	NY		in school
Osborne	George	Inmate	12	NY	NY	NY		In School
Page	Alfred	Inmate	10	NY	Ger	Ger		In School
Page	Elizabeth	Inmate	7	NY	Ger	Ger		
Perry	Mary	Inmate	4	VT		VT		
Peters	Eva May	Inmate	12	Can	NY	PA		in school
Phillips	Melissa L	Attendant	61	NY	MA	NY		Seamstress
Pierson	William	Inmate	10	NY	SWEDE N	IREL		In School
Pimlott?	Margaret	Attendant	42	Wale	Fran	Wale	30	Attendant
Powell	Floyd W	Inmate	15	NY	NY	NY		In School
Powell	Philo J	Inmate	16	NY	NY	NY		In School
Powell	Walter R	Inmate	10	NY	NY	NY		In School

Provanchy	Beatrice	inmate	11	NY	unkn	NY		in school
Provanchy	Frances	inmate	12	NY	unkn	NY		in school
Provanchy	Mabel	inmate	8	NY	unkn	NY		in school
Rennmerde	Joanna	Inmate	13	NY	Hol	Hol		In School
Rennmerde	Martina	Inmate	6	NY	Hol	Hol		
Rifenburgh	William	Inmate	8	NY	NY	NY		In School
Rogers	Josephine	inmate	13	NY	at sea	NY		in school
Romand	Raphael	Inmate	7	MO	ITALY	ITALY		
Romand	Samuel	Inmate	5	MO	ITALY	ITALY		
Romano	Anthony	Inmate	9	ME	Ital	Ital		In School
Romano	Vincent	Inmate	9	ME	Ital	Ital		In School
Rothermel	Eddie	Inmate	12	NY	Ger	Ger		In School
Rothermel	Marie	inmate	10	NY	Ger	Ger		in school
Rule	Harvey W	Inmate	12	NY	Scot	Eng		In School
Rule	William E	Inmate	11	NY	Scot	Eng		In School
Russell	George	Inmate	6	NY	OH	Ger		
Russell	Helen	Inmate	67	NY	NY	NY		
Saus	Gretchen	Attendant	33	Ger	Ger	Ger	1	Cook
Scrafford	William	Inmate	13	NY	NY	Scot		In School
Seibert	Walter	Inmate	9	NY	VT	NY		In School
Sharp	Margaret A	Attendant	54	NY	NY	NY		Nurse
Sherman	Alson	Inmate	6	NY	NY	NY		
Sherman	Alvin	Inmate	7	NY	VT	NY		
Shillinger	Rhoda	Inmate	10	NY	NY	Eng		in school

[illegible] y Orphan Asylum Census 1900

Shortsleeves	Henry	inmate	12	NY	NY	NY		in school
Shortsleeves	Isiah	inmate	11	NY	NY	NY		in school
Skaarup	Mary	Inmate	10	NY	Ger	Den		in school
Skaarup	Minnie	Inmate	6	NY	Ger	Den		
Smith	Clarence	Inmate	4	NY	WALES	IREL		
Smith	LLoyd	Inmate	15	NY	NY	unkno wn		In School
Smith	Thomas	Inmate	7	NY	WALES	IREL		
Snyder	Harvey	Inmate	9	NY	NY	NY		In School
Snyder	Jessie	inmate	11	NY	NY	NY		in school
Spencer	Nettie	Attendant	43	NY	NY	NY		House Keeper
Staples	John	inmate	11	NY	Eng	Eng		in school
Teator	Esther	Inmate	1	NY	Unk	NY		
Thayer	Leslie	Inmate	5	NY	MA	NY		
Thayer	William	Inmate	12	NY	MA	NY		In School
Thompson	Christine	inmate	13	Den	Den	Den		in school
Thompson	Hansine	inmate	15	Den	Den	Den		in school
Thompson	John	Inmate	8	NY	Den	Den		In School
Thompson	Martine	inmate	11	NY	Den	Den		in school
Tillison	Ella	Inmate	6	NY	Unk	NY		
VanEveren	Frank	Attendant	27	Unk	Unk	Unk		Farm Laborer
Wager	Viola	Attendant	38	NY	NY	NY		Caretaker
Wagner	Agnes	Attendant	19	Ger	Ger	Ger	3	Cook
Wagner	Caroline V	Attendant	22	Ger	Ger	Ger	4	Domestic
Wagner	Clarence	Inmate	7	NY	NY	NY		

Wagner	Hattie	Inmate	9	NY	NY	NY		in school
Waller	Sidney	Inmate	6	NY	NY	NY		
Warner	Albert L	Inmate	13	NY	NY	IL		In School
Warner	Gladys	Inmate	9	NY	NY	IL		in school
West	Frederick	Inmate	9	NY	NY	NY		In School
Wheeler	James H	Inmate	9	NY	Unk	Unk		In School
White	Lily	Inmate	7	NY	NY	NY		
White	A Carl	Inmate	4	NY	NY	NY		
White	H. Frank	Inmate	15	NY	NY	NY		In School
White	Harvey	Inmate	12	NY	NY	NY		In School
Wilkes	Hattie	Inmate	6	NY	Eng	Eng		
Wilkes	James	inmate	2	NY	Eng	Eng		
Witbeck	Mary B	Head	36	NY	NY	NY		Matron
Wood	Adelaide	Inmate	8	NY	Eng	NY		in school
Wood	Edwin A	Inmate	9	NY	Unk	NY		In School
Wood	Elizabeth	Inmate	10	NY	Eng	NY		in school
Wood	Lillian	Inmate	11	NY	Eng	NY		in school
Wood	Sarah	Inmate	7	MA	UNK	NY		

Appendix R

Indentured Orphans

Early in the operation of the Troy Orphan Asylum, the act of indenturing orphans was a common practice until the early 1900s. Indenture servitude was part of their bylaws when they incorporated in1833. As stated in earlier chapters, indenture servitude was used in the seventh century and later in North America by the Dutch and English and in other countries.1 It was used in Virginia as early as 1620 and the 1640s in New Netherland. In the Eastern part of the United States in the second part of the nineteenth century, many child protective organizations sent thousands of orphaned, half-orphaned, homeless and neglected children to

TO FARMERS AND MECHANICS.—The Troy Orphan Asylum has a number of Boys of suitable age to put out. Good places in the country would be preferred. Apply to *JOHN THOMAS*, *ELIAS LASELL*, or *JACOB MERRITT*. ap10

An advertisement in a Troy newspaper in 1838 announcing the availability of orphans as indentured workers.

---

1 Galenson, David W. The Rise and Fall of Indentured Servitude in the Americas: An Economic Analysis. The Journal of Economic History, Vol. 44, No. 1 (Mar., 1984), pp. 1-26.

foster family homes in the Midwest as well as local surrounding communities where they were often a source of cheap labor on farms, as domestics, and in retail, until they reached the age of independence.[2]

Here are a few examples of indentures found by Mar y Valek.

NAME: Miller, Peter D.O.B. March 1, 1847

PLACE OF BIRTH:

MOTHER: D.O.B.

FATHER: D.O.B.

SIBLINGS:

DATE OF ADMISSION: May 10, 1862 REFERRED BY: Rense. Co. Supt of poor

REASON FOR ADMISSION:

DATE OF DISCHARGE: May 16, 1862 DISCHARGED TO:

REASON FOR DISCHARGE:

SIGNIFICANT DOCUMENTS:

In formation from [illegible] indentures dated 1836-1872.

Peter Miller, a male child aged 16 yrs & 9 mos on Dec. 1, 1863, Indentured to Albert J. Hayward of the Town of Willsboro of the County of Essex to be employed as a farmer until he shall attain the full age of 21 yrs. Indenture dated December 3, 1863.

Peter has remained a farmer until lately in Essex County bearing an excellent character. One year ago went west to seek a better fortune. July 1878.

---

[2] Nelson, Kristine E. Child Placing in the Nineteenth Century: New York and Iowa. Social Service Review, Vol. 59, No. 1 (Mar., 1985), pp. 107-120.

Appendix R

NAME: Brennan, Michael D.O.B. ? 1847

PLACE OF BIRTH: Irish

MOTHER: D.O.B.

FATHER: D.O.B.

SIBLINGS: John

DATE OF ADMISSION: May 10, 1862 REFERRED BY: City Supt.

REASON FOR ADMISSION

DATE OF DISCHARGE: May22, 1865 DISCHARGED TO: James Lamphere Spencertown, N.Y.

REASON FOR DISCHARGE: Indentured

SIGNIFICENT DOCUMENTS:

Lamphere ran a farm known as the Wooley Farm and later a public house in Spencertown, N.Y. in April 1873. He also mended harnesses. Michael was also admitted the day of the Great Troy Fire of 1862.

NAME: Brennan, John D.O.B. Dec. 10, 1848

PLACE OF BIRTH: Irish

MOTHER: D.O.B.

FATHER: D.O.B.

SIBLINGS: Michael

DATE OF ADMISSION: May 10, 1862 REFERRED BY: City Supt.

REASON FOR ADMISSION

DATE OF DISCHARGE: May 16, 1862 DISCHARGED TO: Indentured - David Hayward Willsboro, N.Y.

REASON FOR DISCHARGE:

SIGNIFICENT DOCUMENTS:

John was also admitted the day of the Great Troy Fire of 1862. Michael's brother also survived the fire. In 1859, there was a David Hayward in Hillsboro who was one of the officers of the Essex County Agricultural Society and likely a farmer. Both Michael and John were separated by over 166 miles.

NAME: Farrell, Edward D.O.B.

PLACE OF BIRTH:

MOTHER: D.O.B.

FATHER: D.O.B.

SIBLINGS:

DATE OF ADMISSION: May 10, 1862 REFERRED BY:

REASON FOR ADMISSION:

DATE OF DISCHARGE: Feb. 2, 1965 DISCHARGED TO:

REASON FOR DISCHARGE:

SIGNIFICANT DOCUMENTS:

Information from Book of Indentures dated 1836-1872.

Edward Farrell, a male child aged 8 yrs. 5 mos. 12 days on Feb. 2, 1865, indentured to Reuben Shaw of the Town of Hebron in the County of Washington to be employed as a farmer until he shall attain the full age of 21 yrs. Indenture dated Feb. 2, 1865.

Incorrect discharge date of 1965. Should be 1865. Edward was also admitted the day of the Great Troy Fire of 1862.

NAME: Lovett, Oscar D.O.B. Nov 1848

PLACE OF BIRTH: USA

MOTHER: D.O.B.

FATHER: D.O.B.

SIBLINGS:

DATE OF ADMISSION: May 10, 1862 REFERRED BY:

REASON FOR ADMISSION:

DATE OF DISCHARGE: April 10, 1868 DISCHARGED TO:

REASON FOR DISCHARGE:

SIGNIFICANT DOCUMENTS:

He was also admitted the day of the Great Troy Fire of 1862.

Appendix R

NAME: Dullahanty, Julia Maria D.O.B. ____

PLACE OF BIRTH: ____

MOTHER: ____ D.O.B. ____

FATHER: ____ D.O.B. ____

SIBLINGS: ____

DATE OF ADMISSION: ____ REFERRED BY: ____

REASON FOR ADMISSION: ____

DATE OF DISCHARGE: ____ DISCHARGED TO: ____

REASON FOR DISCHARGE: ____

SIGNIFICANT DOCUMENTS:

Information from Book of Indentures date 1836-1872.

Julia Maria Dullahanty, a female child aged three years on Aug. 21, 1859 indentured to Cornelius W. Brush of the City of Troy County of Rensselaer to be employed as an apprentice until she shall attain the full age of 18 yrs. She to be instructed in the art of housewifery and plain sewing needle work. Indenture signed June 28, 1859.

Indentured at only three years old to be raised in the "art" of how to be a wife and sewing when she grows up. In 1861 Brush and his wife were sued by Augustus Lester and property on River Street confiscated and sold by the Supreme Court decision.

NAME: Conner, Mary E. D.O.B. June 17, 64

PLACE OF BIRTH: Indentured to George H. Losee, Clifton Park 3/31/75

MOTHER: ____ D.O.B. ____

FATHER: ____ D.O.B. ____

SIBLINGS: ____

DATE OF ADMISSION: ____ REFERRED BY: ____

REASON FOR ADMISSION: ____

DATE OF DISCHARGE: ____ DISCHARGED TO: ____

REASON FOR DISCHARGE: ____

SIGNIFICANT DOCUMENTS:

George Losee was a Town Supervisor of Clifton Park in 1889.

Appendix R

NAME: Hopkins, John D.O.B. ____

PLACE OF BIRTH: ____

MOTHER: ____ D.O.B. ____

FATHER: ____ D.O.B. ____

SIBLINGS: ____

DATE OF ADMISSION: ____ REFERRED BY: ____

REASON FOR ADMISSION: ____

DATE OF DISCHARGE: ____ DISCHARGED TO: ____

REASON FOR DISCHARGE: ____

SIGNIFICANT DOCUMENTS:

Information from Book of Indentures dated 1836-1872.

John Hopkins, born July 4, 1861indentured to Jeremiah V. Tifft residing in Hoags Corners, Rensselaer County, N. Y. to be instructed in the business of Farming until he shall arrive at 21 years of age. Indenture undated. Cancelled by the boy absconding unceremoniously.

Apparently John did not like farming and skipped. It is not sure if he was found and returned or his whereabouts. Tifft was married to Palmira Turner in 1838. Jeremiah died in 1888. He had four children. Hoags Corners is in the Town of Nassau, Rensselaer County.

NAME: Conkey, James D.O.B. ____

PLACE OF BIRTH: Indentured at 8 years 9 months on October 5, 1838

MOTHER: ____ D.O.B. ____

FATHER: ____ D.O.B. ____

SIBLINGS: ____

DATE OF ADMISSION: ____ REFERRED BY: ____

REASON FOR ADMISSION: ____

DATE OF DISCHARGE: ____ DISCHARGED TO: ____

RXXXXXXXXXXXXXXXXXX: Indenture cancelled 8/1/1840

SIGNIFICANT DOCUMENTS:

The indenture was cancelled in two years with no reason given.

Appendix R

NAME: Butchers, John D.O.B. November 25, 1828

PLACE OF BIRTH:

MOTHER: D.O.B.

FATHER: D.O.B.

SIBLINGS:

Indentured to Peter Stover, Pittstown, N.Y. March 30, 1839

DATE OF ADMISSION: REFERRED BY:

REASON FOR ADMISSION:

DATE OF DISCHARGE: DISCHARGED TO:

REASON FOR DISCHARGE:

SIGNIFICANT DOCUMENTS:

New York Daily Times, Feb., 10 1853: "Mr Peter Stover, a respected citizen of Pittstown, Rensselaer County, was killed instantly on Tuesday (2/1/1853) afternoon. He had been visiting in company with his wife and when returning home the horses took fright at the (railroad) cars, upset the sleigh and threw Mr. and Mrs. Stover out breaking the formers neck and slightly injuring the latter. He was a man of great respectability and was wealthy." They were crossing the track of the Troy and Boston Railroad, near Schaghticoke in a sleigh and came in collision with a freight train. He was instantly killed.

NAME: Campbell, Mary Ann D.O.B. October 1, 1843

PLACE OF BIRTH:

MOTHER: D.O.B.

FATHER: D.O.B.

SIBLINGS:

indentured to Wilson Snail - November 29, 1848

DATE OF ADMISSION: REFERRED BY:

REASON FOR ADMISSION:

DATE OF DISCHARGE: DISCHARGED TO:

REASON FOR DISCHARGE:

SIGNIFICANT DOCUMENTS:

Appendix R

NAME: DeLancey, Fanny D.O.B. March 6, 1873

PLACE OF BIRTH:

MOTHER: D.O.B.

FATHER: D.O.B.

SIBLINGS:

DATE OF ADMISSION: REFERRED BY:

REASON FOR ADMISSION:

DATE OF DISCHARGE: DISCHARGED TO:

REASON FOR DISCHARGE:

SIGNIFICANT DOCUMENTS:

Information from Book of Indentures dated 1836-1872.

Fanny Delancey, born March 6, 1873 indentured to Josiah G. Bean residing in Schuylerville, N. Y. to be instructed in the art of housekeeping untilshe shall attain the full age of 18 years. Indenture dated Nov. 28, 1882.

NAME: Dickens, John D.O.B. Aug. 1, 1863

PLACE OF BIRTH:

MOTHER: D.O.B.

FATHER: D.O.B.

SIBLINGS:

DATE OF ADMISSION: Aug. 3, 1868 REFERRED BY:

REASON FOR ADMISSION:

DATE OF DISCHARGE: Dec. 13, 1877 DISCHARGED TO:

REASON FOR DISCHARGE:

SIGNIFICANT DOCUMENTS:

Information from Book of Indentures dated 1836-1872.

John Dickens born August 1, 1863 indentured to Matthew E. Hyde residing in Wilton Saratoga County, N. Y. to be instructed in the art of farming until he shall arrive at 21 years. Indenture dated April 1, 1877.

NAME: Burke, George Frank D.O.B. July 12, 1860

PLACE OF BIRTH:

MOTHER: D.O.B.

FATHER: D.O.B.

SIBLINGS:

Information from book of Indentures dated 1836 - 1872

DATE OF ADMISSION: None Indentured to: G. W. Hitchcock XXXXXXXXXXX

XXXXXXXXXXXXXXXXXXXX West Hoosick until he shall arrive at the age of 21

DATE OF DISCHARGE: Sept. 18, 1872 DISCHARGED TO:

REASON FOR DISCHARGE: He is to be completely instructed in the business of farming.

SIGNIFICANT DOCUMENTS: cancelled by age 21 years 1881

NAME: Cruise, James D.O.B. March 1, 1830

PLACE OF BIRTH:

MOTHER: D.O.B.

FATHER: D.O.B.

SIBLINGS:

DATE OF ADMISSION: REFERRED BY:

REASON FOR ADMISSION:

DATE OF DISCHARGE: DISCHARGED TO:

REASON FOR DISCHARGE:

SIGNIFICANT DOCUMENTS:

Information from book of Indentures dated 1836-1872.

James Cruise a male child of the age of 10 years and 21 days on the 21st of March 1840. Indentured to Joseph Lockrow of the Town of Brunswick of the County of Rensselaer to be employed as a farmer until he shall attain the age of 21 years. Indenture dated March 21, 1840.

NAME: Kane, Harry D.O.B. May 17, 1906

PLACE OF BIRTH: New Rochelle NY

MOTHER: Hildegarde Busse D.O.B. NYC

FATHER: Harry P. Kane D.O.B. Port Jervis NY

SIBLINGS: Hildegard

DATE OF ADMISSION: Sept. 2, 1920 REFERRED BY: Police Justice - Rens Co Court

REASON FOR ADMISSION: Improper Guardianship

DATE OF DISCHARGE: April 19, 1922 DISCHARGED TO: Apollo Commandery Troy NY

REASON FOR DISCHARGE:

SIGNIFICANT DOCUMENTS:

"Improper guardianship." The Apollo Commandery, No 15 in Troy was part of the Freemasons. Kane probably learned how to drill. They were essentially a military order.

NAME: Hagarty, Julia Ann D.O.B.

PLACE OF BIRTH:

MOTHER: D.O.B.

FATHER: D.O.B.

SIBLINGS: George

DATE OF ADMISSION: REFERRED BY:

REASON FOR ADMISSION:

DATE OF DISCHARGE: DISCHARGED TO:

REASON FOR DISCHARGE:

SIGNIFICANT DOCUMENTS:

Information from book of Indentures dated 1836-1872.

Julia Ann Hagarty, a female child of 8 yrs. 2 mos. 21 days on Feb. 1, 1841, indentured to Andrew J. Waterman of the Town of Ballston of the County of Saratoga to be employed as a apprentice to be instructed in the art of house wifery and plain sewing needle work until she shall attain the full age of 18 years. Indenture dated February 5, 1841.

Waterman was a member of the Presbyterian Church in Ballston in 1834. Born in Ballston in 1816 died in Round Lake in 1877.

Appendix R

NAME: Dixon, William D.O.B. ____
PLACE OF BIRTH: ____
MOTHER: ____ D.O.B. ____
FATHER: ____ D.O.B. ____
SIBLINGS: ____
DATE OF ADMISSION: ____ REFERRED BY: ____
REASON FOR ADMISSION: ____
DATE OF DISCHARGE: ____ DISCHARGED TO: ____
REASON FOR DISCHARGE: ____
SIGNIFICANT DOCUMENTS:

Information from book of Indentures 1863-1872.

William Dixon, a male child aged eleven years and four months, indentured to Charles Hakes of the Town of Petersburgh in the County of Rensselaer to be employed as a farmer until he shall attain the age of twenty one. This indenture dated August 8, 1836.

NAME: Cummings, Joseph D.O.B. Feb. 4, 1840
PLACE OF BIRTH: ____
MOTHER: ____ D.O.B. ____
FATHER: ____ D.O.B. ____
SIBLINGS: ____
DATE OF ADMISSION: ____ REFERRED BY: ____
REASON FOR ADMISSION: ____
DATE OF DISCHARGE: ____ DISCHARGED TO: ____
REASON FOR DISCHARGE: ____
SIGNIFICANT DOCUMENTS:

Information from Book of Indenture dated 1836-1872.

Joseph Cummings a male child eleven years ten months and twenty six days on December 2, 1851, indentured to William A. Cullamer of the Town of Ballston of the county of Saratoga to be employed as a farmer to be instructed in the art of farming until he shall attain the full age of 21 years. Indenture dated December 2, 1851.

July 8, 1878.

Joseph Cummings at last advices was living and had been for a good many years in Brooklyn, N. Y. A very respectable business man and active man in the Chi. church, a good musician and much beloved.

Appendix R

NAME: Porter, Patrick D.O.B. ______

PLACE OF BIRTH: ______

MOTHER: ______ D.O.B. ______

FATHER: ______ D.O.B. ______

SIBLINGS: ______

DATE OF ADMISSION: ______ REFERRED BY: ______

REASON FOR ADMISSION: ______

DATE OF DISCHARGE: ______ DISCHARGED TO: ______

REASON FOR DISCHARGE: ______

SIGNIFICANT DOCUMENTS:

Information from book of Indentures 1836-1872.

Patrick Porter a male child aged thirteen years and three months indentured to James G. Payne of the Town of Sand Lake in the County of Rensselaer to be employed as an apprentice and to be well instructed in the art and mystery of a blacksmith until he shall attain the age of twenty one. This indenture dated June 15, 1838. This indenture was cancelled on June 13, 1844.

Patrick continued his residence in Sand Lake after leaving Mr. Payne with whom he lived six years until he was near 30 years of age was a consistent and active member of the Baptist Church there and took much interest in music, playing the melodian , leading the choir and sometime by way of amusement composing some simple harmonies. At one time after leaving Sand Lake was quite successful in business but by some bad mishap lost all. His mind became affected and at one time was in an Insane Asylum. He was kindly cared for in his latter years by a devoted sister and died in Troy in the summer of 1875 never regaining a healthy balance of mind.

A sad end to a promising life.

FAIRVIEW

NAME: McCracken, Jennie D.O.B. Dec 28, 1904

PLACE OF BIRTH: Watervliet NY

MOTHER: Mary D.O.B. Ireland

FATHER: James D.O.B. "

SIBLINGS: 2 brothers

2 sisters

DATE OF ADMISSION: Nov 2, 1908 REFERRED BY: C. Valentine- Justice of Peace

REASON FOR ADMISSION Father dead

DATE OF DISCHARGE: ______ DISCHARGED TO: Dr. Van Orken

REASON FOR DISCHARGE: 25th St. Watervliet NY

SIGNIFICENT DOCUMENTS:

There is no Van Orken in the city directory. Jennie was from Fairview.

Appendix R

FAIRVIEW

NAME: Miller, Henry W.A. D.O.B. March 18, 1897

PLACE OF BIRTH: Amsterdam NY

MOTHER: Agusta D.O.B. Germany

FATHER: Jacob J D.O.B. "

SIBLINGS:

1 brother

1 sister

DATE OF ADMISSION: Aug 19, 1910 REFERRED BY: H.P. Putnam - Recorder

REASON FOR ADMISSION: Petit Larceny

DATE OF DISCHARGE: March 27, 1911 DISCHARGED TO: Chief of Police - Amsterdam

REASON FOR DISCHARGE:

SIGNIFICANT DOCUMENTS:

Being discharged to the Police chief is probably not a good sign of his disposition. Henry was in the Fairview home.

NAME: Berger, Oscar D.O.B. 7 years old at admission

PLACE OF BIRTH: East New York State

MOTHER: Mary Berger D.O.B. Germany

FATHER: Alwin Berger D.O.B. Germany

SIBLINGS:

DATE OF ADMISSION: Sept. 5, 1892 REFERRED BY:

REASON FOR ADMISSION: Half orphan - Father dead

DATE OF DISCHARGE: Sept. 12, 1898 DISCHARGED TO: Oscar finished school and

REASON FOR DISCHARGE: took job as bell boy at 5th ave. Hotel

SIGNIFICANT DOCUMENTS:

The 5th Avenue Hotel was located at the Northwest corner of 5th Avenue and Fulton Street in Troy. It burned in the 1970s.

Appendix R

NAME: Overocker, Nettie D.O.B. 11years old at admission

PLACE OF BIRTH:

MOTHER: Mary D.O.B.

FATHER: Elmer D.O.B.

SIBLINGS: Jenette

2 brothers

DATE OF ADMISSION: May 12, 1905 REFERRED BY: Henry Farmer- Justice of peace

REASON FOR ADMISSION Disorderly child/Neglected/Mother dead

DATE OF DISCHARGE: April 27, 1908 DISCHARGED TO: Rev. L.A. Bard

REASON FOR DISCHARGE Green Island NY

SIGNIFICANT DOCUMENTS:

Bard was a well known minister for the Methodist Episcopal Church.

NAME: Miller, Sarah D.O.B. Dec. 26, 1828

PLACE OF BIRTH:

MOTHER: D.O.B.

FATHER: D.O.B.

SIBLINGS:

DATE OF ADMISSION: REFERRED BY:

REASON FOR ADMISSION:

DATE OF DISCHARGE: DISCHARGED TO:

REASON FOR DISCHARGE:

SIGNIFICANT DOCUMENTS:

Information from book of Indenture 1836-1872.

Sarah Miller - born December 26, 1828.

Sarah Miller a female child aged eight years seven months and five days indentured to Asa Bacon of the Town of Litchfield of the County of Litchfield in the State of Connecticut to be employed as an apprentice and to be well taught and instructed in the art of housewifery. This indenture dated August 3, 1837.

Not all indentures were local. This young woman was sent to Connecticut under the care of Asa Bacon, probably junior. Asa Bacon was the son of Asa Bacon, a captain in the Revolutionary War and a respected farmer in the state of Connecticut. Both father and son were well respected in the town.

NAME: Mullaly, Michael D.O.B. 12 years old

PLACE OF BIRTH:

MOTHER: D.O.B.

FATHER: D.O.B.

SIBLINGS:

DATE OF ADMISSION: REFERRED BY:

REASON FOR ADMISSION:

DATE OF DISCHARGE: DISCHARGED TO:

REASON FOR DISCHARGE:

SIGNIFICANT DOCUMENTS:

Information from Book of Indentures dated 1836-1872.

Michael Mullaly, a male child aged twelve years indentured to John M. Hall of the Town of Sand Lake, County of Rensselaer to be employed as an apprentice to be well instructed in the art and mystery of a blacksmith until he shall attain the full age of 21 years. Indenture datedDec. 30, 1845.

Not all indentures were for farming and wife duties. This twelve year old learned the art of blacksmithing.

FAIRVIEW

NAME: Lester, Leola D.O.B.

PLACE OF BIRTH:

MOTHER: D.O.B.

FATHER: D.O.B.

SIBLINGS:

DATE OF ADMISSION: May 12, 1896 / Oct. 26, 1900 / July 1, 1901 REFERRED BY: C. H. Armatage

REASON FOR ADMISSION:

DATE OF DISCHARGE: DISCHARGED TO: Dr. Battin, 510 Union St., Schenectady NY

REASON FOR DISCHARGE: Indentured

SIGNIFICANT DOCUMENTS:

Dr. H. E. Battin was a physician and surgeon at 510 Union where he lived and worked. It is now a parking lot.

Appendix R

NAME: Ostrander, Robert D.O.B. ______

PLACE OF BIRTH: ______

MOTHER: ______ D.O.B. ______

FATHER: ______ D.O.B. ______

SIBLINGS: ______

DATE OF ADMISSION: ______ REFERRED BY: ______

REASON FOR ADMISSION: ______

DATE OF DISCHARGE: ______ DISCHARGED TO: ______

REASON FOR DISCHARGE: ______

SIGNIFICANT DOCUMENTS:

Information ~~from~~ Indenture Book 1836-1872.

Robert Ostrander a male child aged ten years and six months indentured to Samuel I, McChesney of the Town of Brunswick of the County of Rensselaer, to be employed as a farmer until he shall attain the age of twenty one years. This indenture dated July 23, 1838.

Robert O. became a rover and at maturity bid fair to be no credit to himself or his friends.

NAME: Mahar, Mary D.O.B. June 1, 1846

PLACE OF BIRTH: ______

MOTHER: ______ D.O.B. ______

FATHER: ______ D.O.B. ______

SIBLINGS: ______

DATE OF ADMISSION: ______ REFERRED BY: ______

REASON FOR ADMISSION: ______

DATE OF DISCHARGE: ______ DISCHARGED TO: ______

REASON FOR DISCHARGE: ______

SIGNIFICANT DOCUMENTS:

Information from Book of Indentures dated 1836-1872.

Mary Maher aged eight years on the first day of June, 1852 was indentured to Walter Lawrence of the town of Macedon in the County of Wayne to be employed as an apprentice to be instructed in the art of housewifery and plain sewing needlework until she shall attain the full age of 18 years. Indenture dated June 1, 1852.

Mary Maher has visited the Asylum in later years appearing well in every respect.

Appendix R

NAME: Oakes, Minnie Mary D.O.B. July 26, 1866

PLACE OF BIRTH:

MOTHER: D.O.B.

FATHER: D.O.B.

SIBLINGS:

DATE OF ADMISSION: Aug. 23, 1875 / Dec 5, 1876 / May 4, 1877 REFERRED BY:

REASON FOR ADMISSION:

DATE OF DISCHARGE: Sept. 21, 1876 / Feb. 27, 1877 / July 7, 1877 DISCHARGED TO:

REASON FOR DISCHARGE:

SIGNIFICANT DOCUMENTS:

Information from Book of Indentures dated 1836-1872.

Minnie May Oakes born July 26, 1866 indentured to Aaron Wood residing in Clifton Park, N. Y. to be instructed in the business of housekeeping until she shall arrive at 21 years of age. Indenture dated April 3, 1878.

This indenture cancelled by the said Minnie Oakes leaving Mr. Wood without propwe dismissal in 1879.

Aaron Wood was Town Clerk in 1847 and Justice of the Peace in 1848.

NAME: Osborne, George D.O.B. March 2, 1888

PLACE OF BIRTH: Troy, N.Y.

MOTHER: Mary A. Carrigan D.O.B. Troy,N.Y.

FATHER: George W. Osborne D.O.B. Lansingburgh N.Y.

SIBLINGS: Bertha

DATE OF ADMISSION: Dec. 16, 1897 REFERRED BY: Guardian Mrs Richardson

REASON FOR ADMISSION: Orphan

DATE OF DISCHARGE: Oct. 31, 1903 DISCHARGED TO: Employment Mr. Spidels Grocery

REASON FOR DISCHARGE: Store - Troy,N.Y.

SIGNIFICANT DOCUMENTS:

Anna was indentured to a minister with no duties explained.

Appendix R

Information from
[illegible] of Indenture dated 1836-1872.

Napoleon B. Wilson a male child of Ten years two months and twenty seven days [illegible] the Twenty fourth of June 1839. Indentured to Silas Mosher of the Town of Morristown State of Vermont County of Lamaille, to be employed as a farmer until he shall attain the age of twenty one years. Indenture dated June 24, 1839

NAME: Wilson, Napoleon Bonaparte D.O.B. March 27, 1829

PLACE OF BIRTH:

MOTHER Louisa Wilson D.O.B.

FATHER: Samuel M. Wilson - Deceased D.O.B.

SIBLINGS:

DATE OF ADMISSION: REFERRED BY:

Orphan Napoleon Wilson was Indentured to Silas Mosher in Vermont as a farm hand in 1829.

NAME: Chatterton, Libbie D.O.B. 1880

PLACE OF BIRTH: Unknown

MOTHER: D.O.B.

FATHER: D.O.B.

SIBLINGS:

DATE OF ADMISSION: Sept. 30, 1885 REFERRED BY: County Poor

REASON FOR ADMISSION Orphan

DATE OF DISCHARGE: Sept. 30, 1896 DISCHARGED TO:

REASON FOR DISCHARGE: worked as a nursemaid @ $1.00 per week

SIGNIFICENT DOCUMENTS:

Appendix R

NAME: Bec ker, John D.O.B. July 20, 1888

PLACE OF BIRTH: Schenectady, N.Y.

MOTHER: D.O.B.

FATHER: D.O.B.

SIBLINGS: Minetta Becker

DATE OF ADMISSION: July 17, 1896 April 1, 1898 REFERRED BY: Supt. of poor Renss. Co.

REASON FOR ADMISSION: Mother dead

DATE OF DISCHARGE: March 26, 1897 - Father Feb. 2, 1903 DISCHARGED TO: Samaritan hospital

REASON FOR DISCHARGE: taken a position at $8.00 a month and board

SIGNIFICANT DOCUMENTS:

Worked at Samaritan Hospital for $8 a month with a room.

BINDING OUT CHILDREN.

SEC. 28. The said Commissioners of Emigration are, and each of them is, hereby vested with the same powers in regard to the administering oaths of office to employees, and to the binding out of children with consent of parents or next of kin, actually chargeable upon them, and also in regard to persons in the institution, or any of them, under the charge of said commissioners, for the prevention or punishment of an infraction or violation of the rules or orders and regulations of such commissioners, or their officers, in regard to such institutions, as are possessed by the governors of the almshouse in the city of New York, or any of them, for the same purposes; and the general agent or superintendent of the said commissioners, duly appointed and authorized by them shall have the same power to administer oaths that the said commissioners, or any of them, may have by any law of this State.

1 REVISED STATUTES, 1074, § 28, Laws 1869, Ch. 808, § 2.

NYS law allowing the binding out of children. Laws of the State of New York, and of the United States, Relating to Children. 1876.

Appendix R

It appears from the orphan asylum records that trustee John Payne arived at the idea of indenturing orphans early in the asylum's existence on November 17, 1835. In a later board meeting on the minutes that were approved contained the following:

"On motion of Mr. Paine, seconded by Mr. Landon [Gardner Landon, a carpenter and board member]. *Resolved that Judge Buel* [David Buell, Jr, vice- president of the board] *be appointed to report to this board a suitable form for blank indenturing for indenting children from the asylum."*

Later it was reported:

"Judge Buel by Mr. Paine also communicated a draft of Indentures to be used in indenting children from the asylum. — One motion of Mr. Paine, seconded by Mr. Hart,

Resolved that this draft be refereed to Misses Buel and Thomas with power to procure the printing of half a ream of Blanks, agreeably to said form or with such alterations as they shall deem expedient, four quires[3] of said blanks to be bound in a book for the use of the board."

Shortly after it was reported:

Judge Buel from the committee appointed to procure suitable blanks for indenting children from the Asylum, reported verbally that they had attended to that duty; he presented a book of blanks bound for the use of Trustees and stated that a quantity of loose blanks were provided agreeable to the resolution appointing them, on motion of Mr Kellogg,"

On Tuesday evening March 15, 1836, it was reported:

"The President communicated the Superintendent report showing that since her last report one boy and two girls have been admitted into the asylum; one boy discharged by being placed out [term for indenturing]*; and one girl and two boys removed by death, on motion ordered that said report be accepted and placed on file."*

---

3 * A quire is four sheets of paper folded to form eight leaves, as in medieval manuscripts.

Appendix R

John Paine was a Troy lawyer who served on a number of organizations including the Troy Gas Light Company, Troy Cemetery Association, Troy Savings Bank, as well as the Troy Orphan Asylum.

The original wording for induring orphans appeard in the 1835 corporate papers.

An Act
To Incorporate The Troy Orphan Asylum Passed April 10, 1835

"...the said trustees may, in their discretion, receive such child, and bind out such child, being of the full age of eight years, and not under, to some suitable employment, and in the same manner as overseers of the poor are by law authorized to bind out poor and indigent children; but proper provision shall in every case be made and inserted in the indentures by which such child shall be bound to service, for securing an education fitting and proper for the condition and circumstances in life of such child."

It does appear though that orphans younger than 8 were bound out.

Appendix S

The City of Troy and Its Vicinity
Arthur James Weise

The following is a description of the asylum in the Weise guidebook (1886, Page 10) of Troy in 1886.

TROY ORPHAN ASYLUM is on the east side of Eighth Street, between Hutton and Hoosick streets. A number of persons, desiring to ameliorate the condition of orphan and destitute children in the city, met in the mayor's court-room in the court house on October 22, 1833, and organized the Troy Association for the Relief of Destitute Children. The name of the association was changed on December 17,1834, to that of The Troy Orphan Asylum. The act incorporating the institution was passed, April 10, 1835. It gave the management of the estate and concerns of the asylum to a board of twenty-one trustees. The first were David Buel, jr., Thomas L. Ostrom, Gurdon Grant, Griffith P. Griffith, Thaddeus B. Bigelow, Asahel Gilbert, jr., William W. Whipple, Amos Allen, Richard P. Hart, John Thomas, Stephen Warren, P. H. Buckley, Elias Lasell, Jacob D. Lansing, Gardner Landon, Elias Pattison, George Vail, Jacob Merritt, John S. McCoun, Day O. Kellogg, and John Paine. In 1834, a building, then known as No. 52 Third Street, was rented for an asylum. In 1836, the institution was moved to a two-story, brick building, on a plot of ground running from Grand Division to Federal Street, between sixth and Eight Streets. On May 10, 1862, the building, No. 65 Grand Division Street, was

TROY ORPHAN ASYLUM.

burned in the great fire of that day. The asylum was then temporarily moved to Lansingburgh; 110 orphans being then in the intuition. Mrs Betsey A. Hart having given $10,000 and a number of citizens a similar amount, and the State of New York having appropriated $5,000, the three-story brick building, No, 294 Eight Street, was greeted and occupied in 1864. From 1850-1885, legacies and gifts amounting to $74,000 we're received.

In 1884, Apollo Commandery, Knights Templars, finished an unfitted part of the third story for a dormitory. In December, 1885, the asylum's permanent fund amounted to

$71,931.61, from which an income of $4,157.00 was derived. A large sum, however, is annually needed to meet the current expenses of the institution, which is till partly dependent upon the yearly contributions of its friends and payments made by the city. The present number of orphans in the asylum is about 100. The whole number of orphans registered since it organization, 1,743. The matron is Grace L. White. Present officers: Charles W. Tillinghast, president; Leis E. Gurley, vice president; William H. Hollister, Jr., secretary; Aaron Vail, treasurer; Otis G. Clark, John S. Perry, Harvey J. King, Joseph W. Fuller, George H. Starbuck, Dudley Tibbits, P.M. Converse, Francis N. Mann, Jr., Aaron Vail, John Wool Griswold, Charles W. Tillinghast, Uri Gilbert, Lewis E. Gurley, Charles N. Lockwood, William Kemp, William Howard Doughty, William H. Hollister, Jr., Liberty Gilbert, Walter P. Warren, Henry C. Ludlow, and George B. Cluett, trustees.

Source: The City Of Troy and Its Vicinity. Arthur James Weise. 376 pgs. Published by Edward Green, Troy, NY, 1886.

ORPHAN ASYLUM PUTS RIOTING PAIR ON STRAIGHT PATH

Fiery-Tempered Brothers Learn Lesson of Self-Discipline Through Training at City Institution.

("Doorstep babies" brought in market baskets, children from broken homes, boys and girls whose only living parent is unable to care for them, find a home at the Troy Orphan Asylum. A member of the Troy Community Chest which provides foster care for dependent and semi-dependent children from birth to 18 years of age. The following is another in a series based on case records of the twenty member agencies of the Community Chest, which open their joint campaign for $169,730 on Friday.)

By LIVINGSTON S. JONES

The flying brick would have killed him, had it not missed its mark. Brothers James and John were at it again. Hot tempered, they were always fighting with somebody. If uncontrolled as they grew older, they would undoubtedly end up in jail on a charge of assault or murder. Their tempers were as violent as the red of their hair.

James and John, the Sons of Thunder. Their mother was dead. Their father placed them at the Troy Orphan Asylum. For six years they lived there under the influence of a good home and school. Repeatedly they were counseled about leashing their tempers. You've got the pep to amount to something, they were told. Be impudent like that once in the Navy and you'll hit the deck.

James eventually was placed with an uncle. John got mad and ran away.

But Here We Are.

A few years later, two strapping fellows came to the home. "You told us we'd be in jail but here we are," was their greeting as they walked into the office. James was a motorman on a subway in New York. John had served a term in the Navy. Their hair was just as red as it ever had been, but they both had learned the lesson in self-discipline begun at the home.

Two girls, their mother dead and their father unable to provide for their care, were placed at the home. Not delinquent in any way, they were greatly in need of the home care which their father wanted them to have. The sisters went on through the grades and up through high school. One married and now has a home of her own. The other took a course at business college, obtained a confidential position in a state hospital, has married a doctor. She returns to her former home for a visit every summer.

Children of a not up-and-coming family in the country were placed at the home when their parents died. One, more ambitious than the rest, was found a home with a farmer in another county. He was graduated from high school and wanted college training in agriculture. His foster father was willing to help but could not finance the college course alone. The boy is a sophomore this year, his marks very high, at an agricultural college — his education made possible in part by help from the orphanage.

The "home," as alumni literally scattered all over the world affectionately refer to the Troy Orphan Asylum, allows the child's individuality to assert itself through an elastic program designed to meet the needs of each child. Don't be a leaner, be a lifter, he is taught.

Cared For 194 Last Year.

The Norman Gothic architecture of the buildings—the hallways, the dormitories, chapel, dining hall, study rooms, library, gymnasium and play grounds—provides a cultural setting for the educational training that is emphasized. Troy Orphan Asylum provided a home and schooling and guidance for 194 boys and girls last year.

When a child comes to the home, he is carefully tested, physically, mentally and temperamentally. A complete history of his background and family environment is studied. Right then a program for his possible future is begun. Then the Troy Orphan Asylum "sees him through" until he is satisfactorily adjusted in life.

Two thirds of the children at the home have both parents living and have been placed there because of homes broken through divorce, desertion or separation—a tragic indictment of modern life. Don't let anything break up your family when you have established your own home, is a final word of advice given "graduates" as they leave the home to take a job in the world.

Times Record. Monday, March 24, 1941.

Sources

Amenia Precinct Book for the Poor, 1768-1817 [names of poor supported by the town and expenses; indentures (binding out poor children as apprentices) 1768-1815. Dutchess County Genealogical Society. Volume 3, Issue #1 (September 1975).

Annual Report of the State Board of Charities for the Year 1904. 1904. Vol. 1. Albany Brandow Printing Company. Pg. 12.

Archives. Vanderheyden Hall Archives, Wyantskill, NY; New York State Archives, Albany, NY.

Baird, Charles W. (1974). Chronicle of a Border Town. History of Rye, Westchester County, New York, 1660-1870, Including Harrison and White Plains till 1788. Harbor Hill Books, Harrison, NY.

Care of children in New York City Almshouses, 1800. Rules for the Government of the Almshouse, Oct 6, 1800 in N.Y.C. Council Minutes, 1784-1831, II, Pg. 671.

Catterall, D and Campbell, J. 2012. Woman in Port. Gendering Communities, Economies, and Social Networks in Atlantic Port Cities, 1500-1800. Brill. Pg. 184.

Sources

De Tocqueville, Alexis. Democracy in America, 1862. Volume 2. Pg 129. Translated by Francis Bowen. Cambridge: Sever and Francis.

Coolidge, Charles A. Charles A. Coolidge *Proceedings of the American Academy of Arts and Sciences*, Vol. 68, No. 13 (Dec., 1933), pp. 689-691.

Documents of the Assembly of the State of New York. Ninety-Third Session. 1870. Vol 6, pg. 101-132.

Fernow, Berthold, 1902. The Minutes of the Orphanmasters of New Amsterdam, 1655-1663. New York. Francis P. Harper. Pg. 245.

Fick, Alexander C. History of the State of New York. (1935). Ten volumes. Columbia University Press.

Folks, Homer. The Care of Destitute, Neglected, and Delinquent Children. 1900. Monographs on American Social Economics. Department of Social Economy for the US Commission to the Paris Exposition of 1900. Pg. 7. The Charities Review.

Folks, H. (1921). Some historical aspects of relief in New York State. The Quarterly Journal of the New York State Historical Association 2(1): 33–46.

Sources

Galenson, David W. The Rise and Fall of Indentured Servitude in the Americas: An Economic Analysis. The Journal of Economic History, Vol. 44, No. 1 (Mar., 1984), pp. 1-26.

Gehring, C. T. (trans. and ed.). (1983). New York Historical Manuscripts: Dutch. Volume 5: Council Minutes, 1652–1654, Genealogical Publishing, Baltimore.

Gehring, C. T. (trans. and ed.). (1990). Fort Orange Court Minutes: 1652–1660, Syracuse University Press, Syracuse.

Gehring, C. T. (trans. and ed.). (1995). Council Minutes: 1655–1656, Syracuse University Press, Syracuse.

Gehring, C. T. (trans. and ed.). (1995). Council Minutes: 1638–1665, Syracuse University Press, Syracuse.

https://www.newnetherlandinstitute.org/research/online-publications/council-minutes-1638-1665/

Gehring, C. T. (trans. and ed.). (1995). Volumes Xi–Xv, Correspondence, 1646–1664, Syracuse University Press, Syracuse.

https://www.newnetherlandinstitute.org/research/online-publications/correspondence-1646-1664/

Journal of New York Assembly. 1691-1743, pg. 7. William Bradford Printer.

Lee, C. R. (1982). Public poor relief and the Massachusetts community, 1620–1715. The New England Quarterly 55(4): 564–585.

McEntegart, B. J. (1927). How seventeenth century New York cared for its poor: The Dutch period, 1609–1664. Thought: A Quarterly of the Sciences and Letters 1(4): 588–612.

Melder, Keith. "Ladies Bountiful: Organized Women's Benevolence In Early 19th-Century America." New York History, Vol. 48, No. 3 (July 1967), pp. 231-254.

Mencher, Samual. 1967. Poor Law to Poetry Program. Economic Security Policy in Britain and the United States. University of Pittsburgh Press, pg. 45.

Merwick, D. (1990). Possessing Albany, 1630–1710: The Dutch and English Experiences, Cambridge University Press, Cambridge.

Mohl, R. A. (1969). Poverty in early America, a reappraisal: the case of eighteenth-century New York. New York History 50(1): 5–27.

Muller, S. D. (1985). Charity in the Dutch Republic: Pictures of Rich and Poor for Charitable Institutions, UMI Research Press, Ann Arbor, MI.

Murray, John E. and Ruth Wallis Herndon. Markets for Children in Early America: A Political Economy of Pauper Apprenticeship. The Journal of Economic History, Vol. 62, No. 2 (Jun., 2002), pp. 356-382

Neill, Chas P. 1910. Report on condition of Woman and Child Wage-Earners in the United States. Vol. V. Wage Earning women in stores in factories. Washington Government Printing Office; Page 13. Doc. No. 645.

Nelson, Kristine E. Child Placing in the Nineteenth Century: New York and Iowa. Social Service Review, Vol. 59, No. 1 (Mar., 1985), pp. 107-120.

Sources

Newspaper Sources Consulted: The New York Times, New York Tribune, Albany Times Union, Knickerbocker News, Ballston Spa Daily Journal, Saratogian, Schenectady Cabinet, Schenectady Democrat, Schenectady Reflector, Daily Gazette, Troy Record, New York Mercury, Troy Budget. Troy Daily Times, Troy Daily Whig, and others.

New York City, Minutes of the Common Council, 1675-1776. New York: Dodd, Mead, 1905.

New York Colonial Manuscripts, 1664-1691. New York State Library.

O'Callaghan, E. B. (ed.). (1849). The Documentary History of the State of New-York, Vol. 2, Weed, Parsons & Co., Albany.

O'Callaghan, E. B. (ed.). (1855). Documents Relative to the Colonial History of the State of New-York, Vol. 5, Weed, Parsons & Co., Albany.

O'Callaghan, E. B. (ed.). (1856). Documents Relative to the Colonial History of the State of New-York,Vol. 1, Weed, Parsons & Co., Albany.

O'Callaghan, E. B. (ed.). (1858). Documents Relative to the Colonial History of the State of New-York, Vol. 2, Weed, Parsons & Co., Albany.

O'Callaghan, E. B. (ed.). (1865). Calendar of Historical Manuscripts in the Office of the Secretary of State, Albany, N. Y., Weed, Parsons & Co., Albany

Pascoe, C.F. (1901). Two hundred years of the S. P. G.: an historical account of the Society for the propagation of the gospel in foreign parts, 1701-1900 (Based on a digest of the Society's records.) Published by the Society's office.

Pearl, V. (1978). Puritans and poor relief: The London workhouse, 1649–1660. In Pennington, D., and Thomas, K. (eds.), Puritans and Revolutionarics: Essays in Seventeenth-Century History Presented to Christopher Hill, Clarendon Press, Oxford, pp. 206–232.

Records of the Town of Southhampton, V. 67 (1887). The Second Book of Records of The Town of Southampton , Long Island, NY. With Other Ancient Documents of Historical Value.

Register of the Provincial Secretary, Vol 1-3.

https://www.newnetherlandinstitute.org/research/online-publications/register-of-the-provincial-secretary-1638-1660/

Ross, S. J. (1988). "Objects of Charity: Poor relief, poverty, and the rise of the almshouse in early eighteenth-century New York City." In Pencak, W., and Wright, C. E. (eds.), Authority and Resistance in Early New York, The New-York Historical Society, New York, pp. 138–172.

Schneider, D. M. (1938). The History of Public Welfare in New York State: 1609–1866, University of Chicago Press, Chicago.

Scott, K. (1968). The church wardens and the poor in New York City. The New York Genealogical and Biographical Record 99(3): 157–164.

Scott, K. (1974). Orphan children sent to New Netherland. De Halve Maen 49(3): 5–6.

The Charities Review. Vol. IX- March-February, 1899-1900. New York. The Charities Review. 105 East 22nd Street.

Van der Donck, Adriaen. A Description of New Netherland. Syracuse University Press, 1968.

Van Laer, A. J. F. (trans. and ed.). (1908). Van Rensselaer Bowier Manuscripts, University of the State of New York, Albany.

Van Laer, A. J. F. (trans. and ed.). (1926). Minutes of the Court of Albany, Rensselaerswyck and Schenectady: 1668–1673, Vol. 1, University of the State of New York, Albany.

Van Laer, A. J. F. (trans. and ed.). (1923). Minutes of the Court of Albany, Rensselaerswyck and Schenectady: 1668–1673, Vol. 2, University of the State of New York, Albany.

Van Zwieten, Adriana E. The Orphan Chamber of New Amsterdam. The William and Mary Quarterly, Vol. 53, No. 2 (Apr., 1996), pp. 319-340.

Venema, J. (1990). "For the Benefit of the Poor: Poor relief in Albany/Beverwijck, 1652–1700." Master of Arts thesis, Department of History, State University of New York at Albany.

Venema, J. (1991). Poverty in seventeenth-century Albany. De Halve Maen 64(1): 1–8.

Venema, J. (1993) Beverwijck: A Dutch Village on the American Frontier, 1652-1664. State of New York University Press, Albany, NY.

Many songs were written about orphans. Composed and respectfully dedicated to Mrs. Elizabeth S. Park of Philadelphia by Charles Jar vis. Published by William Hall & Son, 239 Broadway, New York. 1855.

Index

A

C

D

L

N

O

P

T

U

V

W

29

(The Society for the Relief of Orphan and Destitute Children in the City of Troy.)

CORPORATE TITLE.

THE TROY ORPHAN ASYLUM.

January 9 1895

No. 29

FROM Troy, Rens. Co. N.Y.

NAME Jennie Gray

CHARGED TO

MEMORANDA IN REGARD TO THE CHILD.

Date of Admission, Jan. 9 1895
Date of birth, May 21, 1887
Color, white
Orphan or otherwise, Both parents living [father died since admission]
Sex, female
Permit by Mrs. L. E. Gurley
By whom brought, Mrs. A. L. Luther
Board charged to
Place of birth, Troy, N.Y.
Last place of residence, Troy
Has it been in other institutions? In this asylum for ... years
Date of surrender,
By whom given,
Physical condition,
Mental condition,
When vaccinated, 4 months - January 1891.
Contagious diseases—has had diphtheria, measles, scarlet fever, whooping cough
Cause of dependence, &c.

Has child any relatives in penal or charitable institutions? yes
If so, give names and addresses, Mother has been in Marshalls Infirmary

Has child near relatives who are mentally or physically defective?
If so, give name and addresses and nature of defect,

Date of discharge,
By whom taken,
Conditions,
Indenture terminates,
No. of indenture on files,
For history after indenture or adoption, see book No. , page

MEMORANDA IN REGARD TO THE RELATIVES.

Father's name, Levi B. Gray
Occupation, driver of ... Hooks S.F. Engine
Place of birth, Troy
If foreign born, how long in U. S.?
If foreign born, how long in county?
Address, if living, 2417 Sixth Ave. City
If dead, date and place of death, Troy, Jan. 20, 1895
If dead, cause of death, La grippe
Temperate or otherwise, Temperate
Religion, Protestant
Ever an inmate of any institution?
If so, what?

Mother's maiden name, Margarette Law
Place of birth, Troy
If foreign born, how long in U. S.?
If foreign born, how long in county?
Address, if living,
If dead, date and place of death,
If dead, cause of death,
Temperate or intemperate, intemperate
Religion,
Ever an inmate of any institution? Marshalls Infirmary
If so, what?
Names and addresses of relatives and friends:

RELATIONSHIP	NAME.	ADDRESS.
Father's father,		
Father's mother,		
Mother's father,		
Mother's mother,		
Father's brother,		
Father's brother,		
Father's brother,		
Father's sister,		
Father's sister,		
Father's sister,		
Mother's brother,		
Mother's brother,		
Mother's brother,		
Mother's sister,		
Mother's sister,		
Mother's sister,		
Child's brother,		
Child's brother,		
Child's brother,		
Child's sister,		
Child's sister,		
Child's sister,		

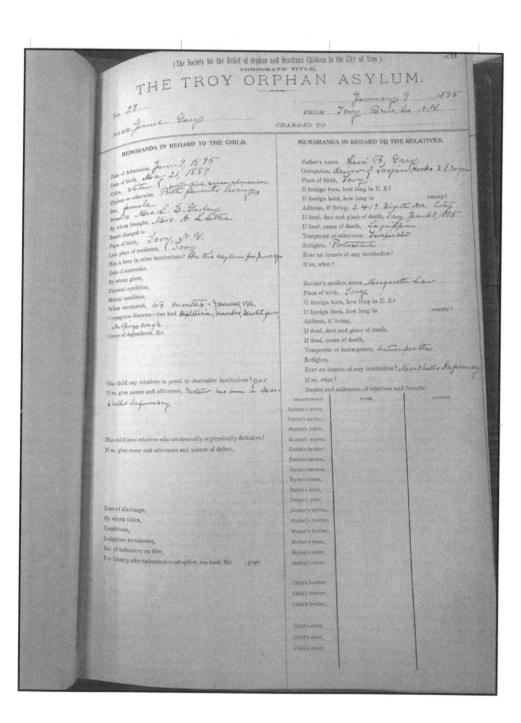

Orphan Deaths

Compiled by Mary Valek

The following is a list of orphan deaths that occurred at Troy Orphan Asylum/Vanderheyden, Fairfield Home, which later became part of Troy Orphan Asylum, and deaths from former residents living away from the orphanage.

Many deaths were caused by diseases that easily affected young people at the time though easily cured in modern times. There were several episodes of disease epidemics that affected children and adults in the city. The 1832, 1849, and 1853 Cholera Epidemic took its toll in Troy. There were also epidemics such as the American Influenza Epidemic of 1918-1919. Common diseases such as Typhoid Fever, Measles, Whooping Cough, Croup (laryngotracheobronchitis), Consumption (probably pulmonary tuberculosis), Mumps, Pneumonia, Bronchitis, Scarlet Fever (Scarlatina), and even the common cold were responsible for many of the deaths at the Troy Orphan Asylum.

This list of deaths can be useful for future scholarly research on orphan asylums and used as well for genealogical research.

Orphan Deaths

Unknown Female
Age: Unknown
Troy Orphan Asylum
Date of Death: February 1836
Cause of Death: Three deaths, two by whooping cough and one with "a disease contracted before it came to the Institution."
Burial: Unknown – Possible Burial Ground Cemeteries 2 or 3 (Mt. Ida) in Troy
Troy Orphan Asylum admission records lost in the May 10, 1862 fire in Troy.

Unknown Male
Age: Unknown
Troy Orphan Asylum
Date of Death: February 1836
Cause of Death: Three deaths, two by whooping cough and one with "a disease contracted before it came to the Institution."
Burial: Unknown – Possible Burial Ground Cemeteries 2 or 3 (Mt. Ida) in Troy
Troy Orphan Asylum admission records lost in the May 10, 1862 fire in Troy.

Unknown Male
Age: Unknown
Troy Orphan Asylum
Date of Death: March 1836
Cause of Death: Three deaths, two by whooping cough and one with "a disease contracted before it came to the Institution."
Burial: Unknown – Possible Burial Ground Cemeteries 2 or 3 (Mt. Ida) in Troy
Troy Orphan Asylum admission records lost in the May 10, 1862 fire in Troy.

Unknown Child
Age: Unknown
Troy Orphan Asylum
Date of Death: April 1838
Burial: Unknown – Possible Burial Ground Cemeteries 2 or 3 (Mt. Ida) in Troy
Troy Orphan Asylum admission records lost in the May 10, 1862 fire in Troy.

Unknown Child
Age: Unknown
Troy Orphan Asylum
Date of Death: March to December 1839
Burial: Unknown – Possible Burial Ground Cemeteries 2 or 3 (Mt. Ida) in Troy
Troy Orphan Asylum admission records lost in the May 10, 1862 fire in Troy.

Unknown Female
Age: 4 Years
Troy Orphan Asylum
Date of Death: August 1840
Burial: Unknown – Possible Old Mt Ida Cemetery in Troy
From June to September 1840, one death.
Troy Orphan Asylum admission records lost in the May 10, 1862 fire in Troy.

"A little girl 4 years of age, who was present at the last anniversary, has gone some months since, to appear in another assembly; bearing with her it is hoped, some tokens of the salutary influence of an Orphan Asylum; and leaving behind, to the patrons of this Institution, renewed incentives to unremitting exertion, in the reflection, that the seal of the grave may soon be set upon their labors."
"But though the Angel of Death seemed, for a time, to hover over the Asylum, through the good providence of God, only one of its inmates was permitted to be stricken down at his approach."

Lewis Rockwood/Rockwell
Age: Unknown
Troy Orphan Asylum
Birth Date/Location: April 4, 1846 in Troy, New York
Date of Death: Unknown 1846 – Possible Scarlet fever
Burial: Unknown – Possible Old Mt Ida Cemetery in Troy
Burial record at St. Paul's Episcopal Church, Troy
Troy Orphan Asylum admission records lost in the May 10, 1862 fire in Troy.

Alfred or James Croft
Age: 6 or 8 Years
Troy Orphan Asylum
Birth Date/Location: 1841
Date of Death: May 4, 1847
Cause of Death: Croup
Burial: Unknown – Possible Old Mt Ida Cemetery in Troy
"Died in 24 hours."
Troy Orphan Asylum admission records lost in the May 10, 1862 fire in Troy.

John Henry Cummings
Age: Unknown
Troy Orphan Asylum
Date of Death: 1847
Cause of Death: Affection of the brain
Burial: Unknown – Possible Old Mt Ida Cemetery in Troy
"After two weeks of suffering, his "spirit ascended to God who gave it."
Troy Orphan Asylum admission records lost in the May 10, 1862 fire in Troy.

Henry Porter
Age: 14 Years
Troy Orphan Asylum
Birth Date/Location: May 23, 1831
Date of Admission: 1838, then indentured out
Date of Death: June 21, 1847 at the Troy Orphan Asylum, Grand Division Street, Troy
Cause of Death: Consumption
Burial: Public Burial Grounds, Troy, New York
Indentured to Mr. Elizah Hyde of the Town of Pittstown, New York to be a farmer until he shall attain the full age of 21 years. Indenture date July 22, 1843. Returned to the TOA on

Grand Division Street in January 1847 "in a feeble state of health," and sick with consumption. He desired to remain at the Troy Orphan Asylum, and his request was granted. "He continued to decline until June, when death removed him, it is hoped to a happier state of existence." "He was often visited by several clergymen and managers, who faithfully conversed and prayed with him. He appeared intelligent, and gave good evidence that through the merits of our Lord Jesus Christ, he was made meet for the kingdom of heaven."
Troy Orphan Asylum admission records lost in the May 10, 1862 fire in Troy.

Mary Ann Farrell
Age: 3 or 4 Years
Troy Orphan Asylum
Date of Death: March 15, 1850
Cause of Death: Disease of the heart, general debility
Burial: Public Burial Grounds, Troy, New York
Funeral held at the Orphan Asylum. Rev. Edward Lounsbery officiated from St. John's Episcopal Church, Troy.
Troy Orphan Asylum admission records lost in the May 10, 1862 fire in Troy.

Margaret More or Purdy
Age: 6 Years
Troy Orphan Asylum
Date of Death: December 24, 1851
Cause of Death: Chronic diarrhea "child had when it came into the Asylum."
Burial: Unknown – Possible Old Mt Ida Cemetery in Troy
Troy Orphan Asylum admission records lost in the May 10, 1862 fire in Troy.

Marcellus Fox
Age: 5 Years
Troy Orphan Asylum
Date of Death: February 1, 1852
Cause of Death: Three 1852 deaths: One died of dropsy, one of scarlet fever and one "of disease unknown."
Burial: Unknown – Possible Old Mt Ida Cemetery in Troy
Funeral service record from St. Paul's Episcopal Church, Troy
Troy Orphan Asylum admission records lost in the May 10, 1862 fire in Troy.

Unknown Child
Age: Unknown
Troy Orphan Asylum
Date of Death: 1852
Cause of Death: Three 1852 deaths: One died of dropsy, one of scarlet fever and one "of disease unknown."
Burial: Unknown – Possible Old Mt Ida Cemetery in Troy
Troy Orphan Asylum admission records lost in the May 10, 1862 fire in Troy.

Orphan Deaths

Unknown Child
Age: Unknown
Troy Orphan Asylum
Date of Death: 1852
Cause of Death: Three 1852 deaths: One died of dropsy, one of scarlet fever and one "of disease unknown."
Burial: Unknown – Possible Old Mt Ida Cemetery in Troy
Troy Orphan Asylum admission records lost in the May 10, 1862 fire in Troy.

Michael Delany
Age: Unknown
Troy Orphan Asylum
Date of Death: Early September 1853
Cause of Death: Unknown "brief and painful illness"
Burial: Unknown – Possible Old Mt Ida Cemetery in Troy
Troy Orphan Asylum admission records lost in the May 10, 1862 fire in Troy.
"Two deaths, disease unknown." "Were both removed after a brief and painful illness, during which they were the objects of unremitting care and kindness and received the professional aid of several physicians of this city."

John Leonard
Age: Unknown
Troy Orphan Asylum
Date of Death: Early September 1853
Cause of Death: Unknown "brief and painful illness"
Burial: Unknown – Possible Old Mt Ida Cemetery in Troy
Troy Orphan Asylum admission records lost in the May 10, 1862 fire in Troy.
"Two deaths, disease unknown." "Were both removed after a brief and painful illness, during which they were the objects of unremitting care and kindness and received the professional aid of several physicians of this city."

***14 children died at the Troy Orphan Asylum in 1855 of various causes. Only three are identified.*

"The year had been signalized by an unusual prevalence of sickness, and by the death of 14 children of various diseases."

James Gain
Age: 11 Years
Troy Orphan Asylum
Birth Date/Location: 1844 in Troy, New York
Parents: Wm. C or G Gain
Date of Death: February 27, 1855 at Troy Orphan Asylum
Cause of Death: Urinary disease of organs
Burial: Catholic Ground at Mt. Ida Cemetery
Troy Orphan Asylum admission records lost in the May 10, 1862 fire in Troy.

Orphan Deaths

Hellen Sweetinan or Sweetman
Age: 4 Years
Troy Orphan Asylum
Birth Date/Location: 1851 in Troy, New York
Parents: Mr. and Mrs. Sweetinan
Date of Death: November 17, 1855 at the Troy Asylum, Troy
Cause of Death: Consumption
Burial: Catholic Ground, Old Mt Ida Cemetery
Troy Orphan Asylum admission records lost in the May 10, 1862 fire in Troy.

Hanora Donevan
Age: 2 Years
Troy Orphan Asylum
Birth Date/Location: 1853 in Troy
Parents: Mr and Mrs. Donevan
Date of Death: November 20, 1855 at Troy Asylum
Cause of Death: Cold
Burial: Catholic Ground (Mt. Ida)
Troy Orphan Asylum admission records lost in the May 10, 1862 fire in Troy.

Unknown Child
Age: Unknown
Troy Orphan Asylum
Date of Death: 1855
Burial: Unknown – Possible Old Mt Ida Cemetery in Troy
Troy Orphan Asylum admission records lost in the May 10, 1862 fire in Troy.

Unknown Child
Age: Unknown
Troy Orphan Asylum
Date of Death: 1855
Burial: Unknown – Possible Old Mt Ida Cemetery in Troy
Troy Orphan Asylum admission records lost in the May 10, 1862 fire in Troy.

Unknown Child
Age: Unknown
Troy Orphan Asylum
Date of Death: 1855
Burial: Unknown – Possible Old Mt Ida Cemetery in Troy
Troy Orphan Asylum admission records lost in the May 10, 1862 fire in Troy.

Unknown Child
Age: Unknown
Troy Orphan Asylum
Date of Death: 1855
Burial: Unknown – Possible Old Mt Ida Cemetery in Troy
Troy Orphan Asylum admission records lost in the May 10, 1862 fire in Troy.

Unknown Child
Age: Unknown
Troy Orphan Asylum
Date of Death: 1855
Burial: Unknown – Possible Old Mt Ida Cemetery in Troy
Troy Orphan Asylum admission records lost in the May 10, 1862 fire in Troy.

Unknown Child
Age: Unknown

Troy Orphan Asylum
Date of Death: 1855
Burial: Unknown – Possible Old Mt Ida Cemetery in Troy
Troy Orphan Asylum admission records lost in the May 10, 1862 fire in Troy.

Unknown Child
Age: Unknown
Troy Orphan Asylum
Date of Death: 1855
Burial: Unknown – Possible Old Mt Ida Cemetery in Troy
Troy Orphan Asylum admission records lost in the May 10, 1862 fire in Troy.

Unknown Child
Age: Unknown
Troy Orphan Asylum
Date of Death: 1855
Burial: Unknown – Possible Old Mt Ida Cemetery in Troy
Troy Orphan Asylum admission records lost in the May 10, 1862 fire in Troy.

Unknown Child
Age: Unknown
Troy Orphan Asylum
Date of Death: 1855
Burial: Unknown – Possible Old Mt Ida Cemetery in Troy
Troy Orphan Asylum admission records lost in the May 10, 1862 fire in Troy.

Unknown Child
Age: Unknown
Troy Orphan Asylum
Date of Death: 1855
Burial: Unknown – Possible Old Mt Ida Cemetery in Troy
Troy Orphan Asylum admission records lost in the May 10, 1862 fire in Troy.

Unknown Child
Age: Unknown
Troy Orphan Asylum
Date of Death: 1855
Burial: Unknown – Possible Old Mt Ida Cemetery in Troy
Troy Orphan Asylum admission records lost in the May 10, 1862 fire in Troy.

Julia Johnson
Age: 3 Years
Troy Orphan Asylum
Birth Date/Location: 1853 in Troy, New York
Parents: J or M and M Johnson
Date of Death: February 15, 1856 at the Troy Orphan Asylum, Troy
Cause of Death: Scarlatina "stricken down by the fever"
Burial: Mt. Ida Cemetery
"When all eyes watched her, and every lip smiled upon her, at the last Christmas festival, where she seemed radiant with light and gladness, none dreamed that little Julia Johnson was the chosen representative from that assembly, to appear presently amid the angst company of the guss made perfect."
Troy Orphan Asylum admission records lost in the May 10, 1862 fire in Troy.

Orphan Deaths

Unknown Child
Age: Unknown
Troy Orphan Asylum
Date of Death: 1857
Cause of Death: Unknown
Burial: Unknown – Possible Old Mt Ida Cemetery in Troy
Troy Orphan Asylum admission records lost in the May 10, 1862 fire in Troy.

Clarissa Douglas
Age: 9 Years
Troy Orphan Asylum
Birth Date/Location: 1848 in Pennsylvania
Parents: W. and P. Douglas
Date of Death: January 21, 1857 at Orphan Asylum, Troy
Cause of Death: Congestive lungs
Burial: Mt. Ida Cemetery

Nicholas Henrick
Age: 4 Years
Troy Orphan Asylum
Birth Date/Location: 1853 in Pittstown, New York
Parents/Siblings:
Date of Death: December 22, 1857 at the Troy Orphan Asylum, Troy
Cause of Death: Scarlatina
Burial: Mt. Ida Cemetery
Unnamed child on City of Troy log. Identity of child found in St. Paul's Episcopal Church log.
Troy Orphan Asylum admission records lost in the May 10, 1862 fire in Troy.

Unknown Child
Age: 2 years, 6 Months
Troy Orphan Asylum
Date of Death: 1858
Cause of Death: Whooping cough
Burial: Unknown
"An interesting child, two years and a half old, who was brought to the Asylum with whooping cough, and lived but three weeks."
Troy Orphan Asylum admission records lost in the May 10, 1862 fire in Troy.

Mary I. Stevenson
Age: 15 Years
Troy Orphan Asylum
Birth Date/Location: 1844 in Troy, New York
Parents: Mr. and Mrs. Stevenson
Date of Death: July 21, 1858 at the Troy Orphan Asylum, Troy
Cause of Death: Consumption
Burial: Mt Ida Cemetery
"The other a young girl of fifteen years, who died of consumption." "She exhibited throughout her sickness a gentle, patient spirit, and manifested entire resignation to the will of God. She often expressed much gratitude for the kind attention she received at the Asylum."
Troy Orphan Asylum admission records lost in the May 10, 1862 fire in Troy.

Unknown Female "Girl"
Age: Unknown
Troy Orphan Asylum
Birth Date/Location: Troy, New York
Date of Death: January 6, 1859
Cause of Death: Mumps, convulsions for 2 hours
Burial: New Mt. Ida Cemetery
"One little girl, who had just taken part in our anniversary exercises, and excited a great deal of interest by her modest and pleasing deportment, was suddenly removed by death."
Troy Orphan Asylum admission records lost in the May 10, 1862 fire in Troy.

Benjamin Ward
Age: Unknown
Troy Orphan Asylum
Date of Death: February 22, 1859 at Troy Asylum
Cause of Death: Pneumonia and convulsions
Burial: New Mt. Ida Cemetery
Troy Orphan Asylum admission records lost in the May 10, 1862 fire in Troy.

Catherine McCarty
Age: 8 Years
Troy Orphan Asylum
Birth Date/Location: 1851 in Troy, New York
Parents: J and M McCarty
Date of Death: March 6, 1859 at Troy Orphan Asylum at 65 Grand Division Street, Troy
Cause of Death: Convulsions
Burial: Mt. Ida Cemetery, Troy
Troy Orphan Asylum admission records lost in the May 10, 1862 fire in Troy.

John Folyard
Age: 4 Years
Troy Orphan Asylum
Birth Date/Location: 1855 in Troy
Parents: Jacob Folyard
Date of Death: March 22, 1859 at 65 Grand Division Street, Troy (TOA)
Cause of Death: Acute bronchitis
Burial: Old Ground, Troy
Troy Orphan Asylum admission records lost in the May 10, 1862 fire in Troy.

John Shields
Age: 22 Years
Troy Orphan Asylum
Birth Date/Location: 1837 in Ireland
Parents: A. and M. Shields
Date of Death: May 1, 1859
Cause of Death: Struck by Train, "killed by rail road cars"
Burial: Catholic Ground, Old Mt. Ida Cemetery
Resided at 65 Grand Division Street, Troy Orphan Asylum – possible worker
Troy Orphan Asylum admission records lost in the May 10, 1862 fire in Troy.

Unknown Male
Age: 8 Years
Troy Orphan Asylum
Date of Death: June 1859

Cause of Death: Unknown
Burial: Unknown
Troy Orphan Asylum admission records lost in the May 10, 1862 fire in Troy.
"Two little boys, one aged eight and the other ten, died during the month of June."

Unknown Male
Age: 10 Years
Troy Orphan Asylum
Date of Death: June 1859
Cause of Death: Unknown
Burial: Unknown
Troy Orphan Asylum admission records lost in the May 10, 1862 fire in Troy.
"Two little boys, one aged eight and the other ten, died during the month of June."

Jennie Warner
Age: 2 ½ Years
Troy Orphan Asylum
Date of Death: Summer 1861
Cause of Death: Small pox
Burial: Unknown
"In the month of September a severe case of small pox made its appearance in the Asylum. As soon as the character of the disease was fully established, the child, a little girl two years and a half old, was removed to the house prepared for the reception of this class of patients; Elizabeth Morrison taking it in her arms and Dr. Blatchford nobly assisting to remove her in his own carriage to the hospital."
Troy Orphan Asylum admission records lost in the May 10, 1862 fire in Troy.

Millard Kipp
Age: 7 Years
Troy Orphan Asylum
Birth Date/Location: Schaghticoke, New York
Parents/Siblings: L & R Kipp
Date of Death: September 19, 1861 at 65 Grand Division Street, Troy Orphan Asylum
Cause of Death: Suffered from inflammation of the lungs, died of consumption, some two months after he was first seized with whooping cough.
Burial: Schaghticoke Cemetery
Troy Orphan Asylum admission records lost in the May 10, 1862 fire in Troy.
"One little boy, seven years of age, having suffered much previously with inflammation of the lungs, died finally of consumption, some two months after he was first seized with whooping cough. The little sufferer passed peacefully from earth, as we trust, to a better inheritance above."

Unknown Female
Age: 5 Years
Troy Orphan Asylum
Date of Death: March 1863 at the Troy Orphan Asylum, Blatchford Mansion, Lansingburgh
Cause of Death: "Died after a severe illness of three weeks."

Burial: Unknown

Mary Miller
Age: 10 Years
Troy Orphan Asylum
Birth Date/Location: Albany, New York
Date of Death: October 11, 1865 at the Troy Orphan Asylum, Troy
Cause of Death: Typhoid fever
Burial: Mt. Ida Cemetery
"A little Germany girl, who died of inflammation of the lungs, in October last, and was buried from the asylum by the German minister in Troy."

John Demming or Downing
Age: 13 or 14 Years
Troy Orphan Asylum
Birth Date/Location: September 1, 1851
Parents: Francis Demming
Sibling: Charles Demming
Date of Death: May 26, 1866
Cause of Death: Consumption
Burial: Mt. Ida Cemetery
Was a resident before the fire of May 10, 1862
"One little boy, John Downing, was removed to another, and we trust a heavenly home, on the twenty-seventh day of May."

Jane Bentley
Age: 6 Years
Troy Orphan Asylum
Birth Date/Location: West Troy, New York
Date of Death: January 22, 1867
Cause of Death: Ravaged by measles, consumption, house pneumonia for two months
Burial: Mt. Ida Vault
"Who came to us sickly, and was so much prostrated by the disease, that after lingering several months, she died of consumption in January last."

Elizabeth "Betsy or Bessie" Remsen or Rennison
Age: 4 Years
Troy Orphan Asylum
Birth Date/Location: Unknown
Date of Death: July 29, 1867
Cause of Death: Typhoid fever, measles for 14 days, consumption for 6 months
Burial: Mt. Ida Cemetery
"Three children very ill with typhoid fever at the time when Remsen died."

Ann or Mary K. Quinn
Age: 4 Months
Troy Orphan Asylum
Birth Date/Location: Troy, New York
Parents/Siblings: E & M Quinn
Date of Death: July 10 or 26, 1868
Cause of Death: Cholera
Burial: St. Mary's Cemetery, Troy, New York

Oakwood Cemetery, Troy, New York

"From the annual report of 1868 we learn that: The Trustees of Oakwood Cemetery have presented the Asylum with a desirable lot, near the entrance to the Cemetery. In 1869, there is the note that a fine block of marble was presented to the Asylum by Mr. Charles Sheldon, Jr., of Rutland, Vermont, for their lot in Oakwood Cemetery. The monument is now completed, Mr. Peter Grant having given $20 towards the work upon it, and the Ladies paying the remainder. It bears the simple inscription, "Troy Orphan Asylum." – A History of the Troy Orphan Asylum, Irving E. Fancher, October 1933

Sophia B. Eastman
Second Matron and Superintendent of the Troy Orphan Asylum
Age: 67
Born: New Hampshire in 1803
Date of Death: February 5, 1870 at the Troy Orphan Asylum on 8th Street, Troy
Cause of Death: Apoplexy
Burial: Oakwood Cemetery, Troy, New York, at the base of the Troy Orphan Asylum obelisk
Started at the Troy Orphan Asylum as a teacher in 1834, and took over after the first Superintendent, Elizabeth Byers, died in 1835. Eastman and teacher Elizabeth Morrison rescued 110 children from fire in Troy of May 10, 1862.

Male Child with Leapole Surname
Age: 6 Years
Troy Orphan Asylum
Birth Date/Location: Troy, New York
Date of Death: August 20, 1870 in Troy
Cause of Death: Bowel complaint
Burial: Oakwood Cemetery (possibly unmarked at TOA obelisk)

Garibaldi or Garabaldi Petreena or Petreni
Age: 5 Years
Troy Orphan Asylum
Birth Date/Location: c. 1865 Italy or Troy, New York
Date of Death: September 26, 1870
Cause of Death: Dysentery, typhoid fever
Burial: Oakwood Cemetery (possibly unmarked at TOA obelisk)
"A little Italian boy" "He had no friends and was buried from the Asylum. Reverend Mr. George Van Deurs officiating at his funeral at the Oakwood Avenue Presbyterian Church, Troy."

John Montgomery
Age: 4 Years
Troy Orphan Asylum

Birth Date/Location:
Brooklyn, New York
Parents: James
Siblings: James and Laura (discharged from TOA August 25, 1872)
Date of Death: August 25, 1872 in Troy, New York
Cause of Death: Consumption, whooping cough
Burial: St. Peter's Cemetery

George Reibling
Age: 3 Years, 6 Months
Troy Orphan Asylum
Birth Date/Location: Troy, New York
Parents: Henry
Siblings: Charles Reibling (discharged May 3, 1875)
Date of Admission: March 17, 1872 and March 14, 1873
Date of Death: August 18, 1873
Cause of Death: Croup
Burial: New Mt. Ida Cemetery

Edward S. Archibald "Eddie" Hardy
Age: 3 Years
Troy Orphan Asylum
Birth Date/Location: 1871
Parents: Archibald Hardy and Mary Hardy
Siblings: Arthur Hardy
Date of Admission: December 4, 1873
Date of Death: January 9, 1874 at the Troy Orphan Asylum, Troy
Cause of Death: Typhoid fever
Burial: Unmarked grave at Troy Orphan Asylum plot in Section "S" at Oakwood Cemetery
"Last Winter there were several cases of typhoid fever, and one death from it."

Emma D. Hannah Hurd
Age: 7 Years
Troy Orphan Asylum
Birth Date/Location: 1867 in Troy, New York or State of New York
Date of Death: May 24, 1874 at the Troy Orphan Asylum, Troy
Cause of Death: Diphtheria
Burial: Unmarked grave at Troy Orphan Asylum plot in Section "S" at Oakwood Cemetery
"Last Winter there were several cases of typhoid fever, and one death from it, and another from diphtheria in the Spring."

Stephen Otis Thompson
Age: 4 Years
Troy Orphan Asylum (No #)
Birth Date/Location: 1873 in Troy, New York
Siblings: Two siblings, names unknown. Possibly Mary C. Thompson, 10 years, and George F. Thompson, 5 years, who were admitted to the Troy Orphan Asylum on November 28, 1876
Date of Admission: September 5, 1876

Date of Death: November 29, 1876
Cause of Death: Fits, epilepsy
Burial: Troy Orphan Asylum plot in Section "S" at Oakwood Cemetery, Grave #1
"One death, and only one has occurred, Stephen O. Thompson, aged four years, died on the 28th day of November last." "On the 29th of November, a little boy died very suddenly of epilepsy. He had been in the asylum but three weeks and was one of a family of three children who are all subject to the same attacks."

Albert J. Mayo
Age: 8 Years, 4 Months
Troy Orphan Asylum
Birth Date/Location: USA
Parents: Albert
Date of Death: October 13, 1878 at the Troy Orphan Asylum, 8th Street, Troy
Cause of Death: Scarlet fever
Burial: Mt. Ida Cemetery

John R. "Eddie" Halligan
Age: 5 Years
Troy Orphan Asylum
Birth Date/Location: Troy, New York
Parents: William (b. Troy, NY)
Date of Admission: June 28, 1879
Date of Death: December 25, 1879 at the Troy Orphan Asylum
Cause of Death: Congestion of the lungs
Burial: St. Mary's Cemetery
"And the only death was that of a little boy, who died suddenly last Christmas morning of congestion of the lungs."

Edward Treadwell
Age: 4 Years, 5 Months
Troy Orphan Asylum (No #)
Birth Date/Location: 1879 in England
Parents: Jas.
Date of Admission: December 8, 1881
Date of Death: June 2 or 10, 1883
Cause of Death: Abscess and lung disease
Burial: Troy Orphan Asylum plot in Section "S" at Oakwood Cemetery, Grave #2
"One of the little ones died from disease resulting from measles. This being the first death in three and a half years, in our institution, who average number is over a hundred."
Payments from the City of Troy to the TOA were cancelled on June 10, 1883 for his upkeep.

Charles Lutherman
Age: Unknown
Troy Orphan Asylum (No #)
Birth Date/Location: 1882 in Troy, New York
Siblings: Lizzie Lutherman
Date of Admission: December 31, 1884

Date of Death: July 17, 1887
Cause of Death: Meningitis
Burial: Troy Orphan Asylum plot in Section "S" at Oakwood Cemetery, Grave #3
"Who came to us in a delicate state." "Only one death occurring, and he a delicate little boy."

Maggie Ross
Age: 9 Years
Troy Orphan Asylum
Birth Date/Location: 1881 in Troy, New York
Siblings: John and Jennie
Date of Admission: May 19, 1887
Date of Death: March 12, 1888 at the Troy Orphan Asylum, Troy
Cause of Death: Phthisis
Burial: Troy Orphan Asylum plot in Section "S" at Oakwood Cemetery, Grave #4
"6 years old at admission"
"One child, a little girl, died in March, with consumption, a disease from which she was suffering when she came here."

Eugene Bryant
Age: 2 Months
Fairview Home for Friendless Children
Birth Date/Location: May 2, 1888
Date of Admission: July 2, 1888
Date of Death: July 20, 1888
Cause of Death: Unknown – City of Watervliet has records
Burial: Unknown – City of Watervliet has records

Abigal Jones
Age: Unknown
Fairview Home for Friendless Children
Birth Date/Location: Unknown
Siblings: Frederick, George and Myron
Date of Admission: July 20, 1888
Date of Death: August 23, 1888
Cause of Death: Unknown – City of Watervliet has records
Burial: Unknown – City of Watervliet has records

Charles Phillips
Age: Unknown
Fairview Home for Friendless Children
Birth Date/Location: Unknown
Parents: Sarah Phillips
Date of Admission: September 17, 1888
Date of Death: November 4, 1888
Cause of Death: Unknown – City of Watervliet has records
Burial: Unknown – City of Watervliet has records

Emma (Erma) V. Bennett
Age: 4 Years
Fairview Home for Friendless Children
Birth Date/Location: West Troy, New York
Parents: Sarah J and William A. Bennett

Siblings: Hazel Bennett
Date of Admission: November 27, 1888
Date of Death: Nov. 30, 1888 or Dec. 1, 1888
Cause of Death: Physisis pelmonitis
Burial: Family plot in Section 105, Lot 254 at Albany Rural Cemetery with no marker

Frank Wilsey
Age: 8 Years
Fairview Home for Friendless Children
Birth Date/Location: Mar. 8, 1880 in Coxsackie, NY
Date of Admission: Nov. 20, 1888
Parents: Laura Wilsey
Date of Death: Dec. 22, 1888
Cause of Death: Debility
City of Watervliet has records
Burial: Unknown – Not in City of Watervliet records

Hazel Bennett
Age: 3 Years
Fairview Home for Friendless Children
Birth Date/Location: West Troy, New York
Siblings: Emma (Erma) Bennett
Date of Admission: November 27, 1888
Date of Death: December 24, 1888
Parents: Sarah J and William A. Bennett
Cause of Death: Whooping Cough
Burial: Family plot in Section 105, Lot 254 at Albany Rural Cemetery with no marker

Jennie Warner
Age: Unknown
Troy Orphan Asylum
Date of Death: Summer 1890
Cause of Death: Consumption
Burial: Unknown
"One little girl, Jennie Warner, suffering with consumption was relieved by death in the summer."

Unknown Female
Age: Unknown
Troy Orphan Asylum
Date of Death: Summer 1891
Cause of Death: Unknown
Burial: Troy, New York
"One of our little girls who, on account of ill health, was kindly received into St. Christina Home, Saratoga, died there during the summer, after being most tenderly nursed and cared for. She was brought to Troy for burial."

Marion E. Leonard or Learned or Lennard
Age: 3 Years, 5 Months
Troy Orphan Asylum (No #)
Birth Date/Location: 1888 in West Troy, New York
Parents: Annie and William
Siblings: John Leonard
Date of Admission: July 24, 1891
Date of Death: November 30, 1891 at the Troy Orphan Asylum
Cause of Death: Cerebral spinal meningitis

Burial: Albany Rural Cemetery in Section 104, Lot 353. The plot of Maria Evans.

Corine Mathews
Age: 5 Years
Troy Orphan Asylum
Birth Date/Location: 1886 in Troy, New York
Parents: Mary E. and James G.
Siblings: Robbie #36 (discharged February 20, 1895)
Date of Admission: August 29, 1889
Date of Death: December 17, 1891 at the Troy Orphan Asylum, Troy
Cause of Death: Scarletina, scarlet fever
Burial: Troy Orphan Asylum plot in Section "S" at Oakwood Cemetery, Grave #5 with a gravestone

Rosa "Rosie" Kreiss or Kress
Age: 5 Years
Troy Orphan Asylum (No #)
Birth Date/Location: 1887 in Troy, New York
Parents: Henry and Sophia
Siblings: Henry and Willie
Date of Admission: March 17, 1890
Date of Death: January 8, 1892 at the Troy Orphan Asylum, Troy
Cause of Death: Pneumonia
Burial: New Mt Ida (FHK)

Isabel or Isabella Carson
Age: 2 Years, 10 Months
Fairview Home for Friendless Children
Birth Date/Location: August 6, 1889 in West Troy, New York
Parents: John Carson (b. West Troy, d. 1922) and Catherine Carson (b. Ireland, d. March 24, 1892 in childbirth)
Siblings: Catherine (d. March 24, 1892), Margaret and William
Date of Admission: March 28, 1892
Date of Death: June 18, 1892 in St. Margaret's Home in Albany
Cause of Death: Bronchitis
Burial: Section 104, Plot 354 with no stones at Albany Rural Cemetery, Family Plot

William John Carson
Age: 1 ½ Years
Fairview Home for Friendless Children
Birth Date/Location: January 6, 1891 in West Troy
Parents: John Carson (b. West Troy, d. 1922) and Catherine Carson (b. Ireland, d. March 24, 1892 in childbirth)
Siblings: Catherine (d. March 24, 1892), Isabel and Margaret
Date of Admission: March 28, 1892
Date of Death: July 5, 1892 in St. Margaret's Home in Albany
Cause of Death: Bronchitis
Burial: Section 104, Plot 354 with no stones at Albany Rural Cemetery, Family Plot

Lottie Wheland
Age: 8 Years
Troy Orphan Asylum (No #)
Birth Date/Location: Troy, New York
Parents: Charlotte Piggleman and Charles Wheland
Siblings: Freddie Wheland
Date of Admission: July 23, 1891 and discharged September 6, 1891; readmitted April 16, 1892
Date of Death: January 27, 1893 at the Troy Orphan Asylum, Troy
Cause of Death: Malignant diphtheria and blood poisoning
Burial: New Mt Ida Cemetery

***Siblings died a day apart.*

Henrietta "Etta" McKee
Age: 13 Years
Troy Orphan Asylum
Birth Date/Location: 1880 in Albany, New York
Parents: Jane Stinger and John McKee
Siblings: Stewart, Hugh, Robert J., Unnamed Male (d. 1884), John W. (d. 1879 scarlet fever) and David McKee
Date of Admission: February 2, 1889
Date of Death: February 3, 1893 at 284 4th Street, Troy
Cause of Death: Diphtheria
Burial: Albany Rural Cemetery Section 121, Lot 138, In lot of John McKee, his wife, and his mother Mary McKee (d. 1891). Buried the same day as her brother, David McKee.

David McKee
Age: 11 Years, 3 Months
Troy Orphan Asylum
Birth Date/Location: 1880 in Albany, New York
Parents: Jane Stinger and John McKee
Siblings: Stewart, Hugh, Robert J., Unnamed Male (d. 1884), John W. (d. 1879 scarlet fever) and Henrietta "Etta" McKee
Date of Admission: February 2, 1889
Date of Death: February 4, 1893 at 284 4th Street, Troy
Cause of Death: Diphtheria
Burial: Albany Rural Cemetery Section 121, Lot 138, In lot of John McKee, his wife, and his mother Mary McKee (d. 1891). Buried the same day as his sister, Henrietta "Etta" McKee.

Annie Elizabeth Paine
Age: 11 Years
Troy Orphan Asylum
Birth Date/Location: 1881 in England
Parents: Mary Sarah Charwood and John Sayer (b. England)
Siblings: Walter S. Paine #21
Date of Admission: June 15, 1887
Date of Death: February 14, 1893 at the Troy Orphan Asylum, Troy

Cause of Death: Diptheria and Exhaustion
Burial: Troy Orphan Asylum plot in Section "S" at Oakwood Cemetery, Grave #6
"6 years old in 1887"

Lillie Faulkner
Age: 7 Years, 5 Months
Fairview Home for Friendless Children
Birth Date/Location: 1886 in England or Germany
Parents: Josiah and Lydia Faulkner
Siblings: Charles, William and Isaiah
Date of Admission: April 2, 1891
Date of Death: May 26, 1893 at Fairview Home in Watervliet
Cause of Death: Tubercular Disease of the Spine, spine disease
Burial: Fairview Home plot in Section 104, Lot 453, Plot #1 at Albany Rural Cemetery
Lillie died in 1893, yet the Fairview Home did not purchase their burial plot until November 1894.

Unknown Female
Age: Unknown
Troy Orphan Asylum
Birth Date/Location: Unknown
Date of Death: 1894
Cause of Death: Unknown
Burial: Unknown

Emma Fritz
Age: 11 Years, 8 Months, 19 Days
Troy Orphan Asylum #20
Birth Date/Location: 1884 in New York State (c. December 10, 1884?)
Siblings: Lena Fritz and Truman Fritz (Discharged Sept 30, 1895 to a farm in Berlin, NY)
Date of Admission: April 23, 1887
Date of Death: August 29, 1895 at Troy Orphan Asylum, Troy
Cause of Death: Hodgkin's disease of throat
Burial: Troy Orphan Asylum plot in Section "S" at Oakwood Cemetery, Grave #7
Three years old at admission and ill for one year.
"During her illness she received many delicacies from kind friends, and the gift of a doll gave her the greatest pleasure. Indeed, she would not allow it to be taken out of her arms – and it never was – they sleep together in the little grave."
"Emma has been ill for one year."
"A little girl who had been in feeble health ever since she was admitted."

James E. Fonda
Age: 15 Years
Fairview Home for Friendless Children
Birth Date/Location: 1881

Date of Admission: January 4, 1890
Date of Death: July 27, 1896
Cause of Death: Unknown – Records at Town of Colonie
Burial: Unknown – Records at Town of Colonie

George Miner
Age: Unknown 15+ Years
Troy Orphan Asylum #72 #162 #157 #5
Birth Date/Location: 1881 in Greenbush, New York
Date of Admission: April 9, 1885 and October 10, 1895
Date of Death: Unknown
Cause of Death: Tuberculosis
Burial: Unknown
Indentured.
"Placed out September 24, 1895, and was returned to Asylum October 10, 1895."
"Was returned to Asylum because of disobedience. He was placed on a farm in Brunswick, NY September 12, 1896. Earned $1.00 per week."

Herman Doscher or Doche
Age: 11 Years
Fairview Home for Friendless Children
Birth Date/Location: June 6, 1886 in Buffalo, New York
Date of Admission: December 28, 1896
Date of Death: June 8, 1897 at the Fairview Home
Cause of Death: Acute rheumatism
Burial: Fairview Home plot in Section 104, Lot 453, at Plot #2 Albany Rural Cemetery

Frank M. Chase
Age: 14 Years
Troy Orphan Asylum #78
Birth Date/Location: January 1884 in Troy, New York
Parents: Theresa or Frances (b. Boston, MA) and Melvin A. Chase (b. Troy)
Siblings: Julia
Date of Admission: November 2, 1887, July 1, 1890 and September 1, 1893
Date of Death: July 14, 1897 in Smart's Pond, Troy
Cause of Death: Sudden drowning while swimming in Smart's Pond
Burial: Petersburgh Cemetery
Was also in the Fairview Home from May 2, 1890 to June 30, 1890

Clyde E. Hagin
Age: 4 Years
Troy Orphan Asylum #212
Birth Date/Location: 1893 in Schenectady, New York
Parents: Samuel M. Hagin (b. Schenectady, NY) Anna Roache (b. Schenectady, NY)
Date of Admission: January 14, 1897
Date of Death: February 11, 1898 at the Troy Orphan Asylum
Cause of Death: Diptheria, diphtheutic poisoning, sudden heart failure

Burial: Vale Cemetery, Schenectady, NY, Section D 48
Mother died in childbirth. A woman cared for Clyde until she died, and he was placed at TOA.
"Shortly after the holidays some of the nursery children were smitten with that dread disease, diphtheria, and soon 120 of the children soon recovered with the exception of one little boy."

Jennie Bartlett
Age: 16 Years
Troy Orphan Asylum #324
Birth Date/Location: c. December 1882 in North Nassau, New York
Parents: Martha Murphy Bartlett (b. North Nassau, NY) William Bartlett
Siblings: George and Nellie
Date of Admission: December 13, 1898
Date of Death: January 28, 1899 at the Troy Orphan Asylum
Cause of Death: Typhoid Fever
Burial: Mt Ida Cemetery
"16 years old – December 1898"
"Died of typhoid fever after five weeks of severe suffering."

Oscar Rudolf Peterson
Age: 9 Years
Troy Orphan Asylum #284
Birth Date/Location: October 4, 1889 in Troy, New York
Parents: Amanda Lundstrum (b. Sweden) John Peterson (b. Sweden)
Siblings: Gustof Adolph Peterson
Date of Admission: June 11, 1898
Date of Death: September 18, 1899 at the Troy Orphan Asylum, Troy
Cause of Death: Diphtheritic croup, membranous croup
Burial: New Mt Ida Cemetery

John E. Stickles
Age: 2 Years, 9 Months
Troy Orphan Asylum #327
Birth Date/Location: 1896 in North Nassau, New York
Parents: Emma Bartlett (b. North Nassau, NY) and John G. Stickles (b. Nassau, NY)
Date of Admission: December 13, 1898
Date of Death: October 6, 1899 at the Troy Orphan Asylum, Troy
Cause of Death: Catarrhal pneumonia and measles
Burial: East Chatham, New York
"Mother of John is sister to the Bartlett children – George, Jennie and Nellie."

Henry Claire Haley
Age: 1 Year, 7 Months
Troy Orphan Asylum #337
Birth Date/Location: June 28, 1897 in Boston, Massachusetts
Parents: Nellie Claire Haley (b. Troy, NY or Boston, MA)

Cortland Haley (b. Hoosick, NY)
Date of Admission: January 27, 1899
Date of Death: October 10, 1899 at the Troy Orphan Asylum
Cause of Death: Catarrhal pneumonia
Burial: Hoosick, New York

Frank "Frankie" Brooks
Age: 6 Years
Troy Orphan Asylum #278
Birth Date/Location: 1896? in Troy, New York
Parents: Nellie/Cornelia Maguire (b. Fort Edward, NY) and Jonathan Brooks (b. Millville, NY)
Siblings: Freddie Brooks #279 (Removed to Rochester Industrial School, April 30, 1902)
Date of Admission: April 28, 1898
Date of Death: October 18, 1899 at the Troy Orphan Asylum, Troy
Cause of Death: Acute Bright's Disease - acute nephritis and pneumonia
Burial: New Mt Ida Cemetery
**Confusion between brothers in TOA records. Clarified with Troy death certificate.

Mabel Goewey or Gowey
Age: 11 Months
Troy Orphan Asylum #371
Birth Date/Location: March 1899 in Troy, New York
Parents: John A Goewey (b. Rhinebeck, NY) Mattie Goewey (b. Albany, NY)
Siblings: George and William
Date of Admission: July 11, 1899
Date of Death: January 15, 1900 at the Troy Orphan Asylum
Cause of Death: Spinal meningitis, tubercular meningitis
Burial: Oakwood Cemetery Section "N" Lot 11, Grave 18 of John M and Jacob N. Goewey

William Frederick Horth
Age: 15 Years
Troy Orphan Asylum #254
Birth Date/Location: November 16, 1885 in Troy, New York
Parents: Susie E. Clendenning Horth (b. Troy, NY) Charles H. Horth (b. Troy, NY)
Siblings: Jesse Oliver Horth and Ellis Van Buren Horth
Date of Admission: October 11, 1897
Date of Death: August 1, 1900 in Samaritan Hospital
Cause of Death: Appendicitis and peritonitis
Burial: Oakwood Cemetery Section "T" Lot 22, Grave #15 of Clendinnen and Susan E. Horth
Occupation: Glassmaker

Chester W. S. Knopf
Age: 5 Years

Troy Orphan Asylum #344
Birth Date/Location: March 8, 1895 in Troy, New York
Parents: Minnie Wagner (b. Troy, NY or Germany) Henry Knopf (b. Germany)
Siblings: Freddie and Lillian
Date of Admission: April 5, 1899
Date of Death: December 18, 1900 at the Troy Orphan Asylum
Cause of Death: Typhoid fever and pneumonia
Burial: Oakwood Cemetery in Section "H" Sub 44, Lot 61, Grave #9 of Charles Wagner lot

Julian Cowan or Conan
Age: 6 Years
Fairview Home for Friendless Children
Birth Date/Location: March 4, 1895 in New York
Parents: Anna and Julian
Siblings: Elvina and Esther
Date of Admission: July 15, 1901
Date of Death: September 4, 1901 at Fairview Home in Colonie
Cause of Death: Diphtheria
Burial: Fairview Home plot at Albany Rural Cemetery, Section 104, Lot 453, Plot #3

Frederick Babb
Age: 2 Years
Troy Orphan Asylum #614
Birth Date/Location: April 3, 1900 in Lansingburgh, New York
Parents: Nancy Gray (b. Albany) and William George Babb (b. Krugers, NY)
Siblings: Florence E.
Date of Admission: August 7, 1902
Date of Death: January 6, 1903 at Troy Orphan Asylum
Cause of Death: Tuberculosis, hemorrhage from lungs
Burial: Oakwood Cemetery

Esther Ruth Davis
Age: 1 Year
Troy Orphan Asylum #706
Birth Date/Location: January 23, 1903 in Troy, New York
Parents: Nellie M. Taylor (b. Sandy Hill, NY) and Frederick Davis (b. Cambridge, NY)
Siblings: Frank, Burt and Earl
Date of Admission: August 29, 1903
Date of Death: January 25, 1904 at the Troy Orphan Asylum
Cause of Death: Pneumonia and exhaustion at the Troy Orphan Asylum
Burial: Oakwood Cemetery, Section "P North" Single interments Grave #457

Celia May Matson
Age: 16 Years
Troy Orphan Asylum #120
Birth Date/Location: August 4, 1887 in Albany, New York

Parents: Lorenda Wood (b. Unadilla, NY) and Robert Matson (b. Rensselaer or Greenbush, NY)
Siblings: Grace (worked at TOA), Ruth and Robert John
Date of Admission: March 27, 1895
Date of Death: May 29, 1904 at the Troy Orphan Asylum, Troy
Cause of Death: Valvular disease of heart
Burial: Troy Orphan Asylum plot in Section "S" at Oakwood Cemetery, Grave #8

William F. Rapport
Age: 11 Years
Fairview Home for Friendless Children
Birth Date/Location: May 14, 1891 in Yonkers, New York
Parents: Mary Rapport (b. Scotland) B.W. Rapport (b. Russia)
Siblings: George D. Rapport (b. July 2, 1895) and Margaret J. Rapport (b. August 14, 1893)
Date of Admission: November 19, 1902
Date of Death: June 8, 1904
Cause of Death: Unknown – Records at Town of Colonie
Burial: Unknown – Records at Town of Colonie

Loy F. or Leroy or Lloyd F. Johnson
Age: 8 Months
Troy Orphan Asylum #762
Birth Date/Location: October 21, 1903 in Troy, New York
Parents: Lena Beloy or Loy Johnson (b. Argyle, NY) and Frederick Johnson (b. Nassau or Argyle, NY)
Date of Admission: May 2, 1904
Date of Death: August 1, 1904 at the Troy Orphan Asylum
Cause of Death: Spinal trouble and acute gastro enteritis
Burial: Argyle, New York

Lula Pearl Lewis
Age: 3 Months
Troy Orphan Asylum #786
Birth Date/Location: April 20, 1904 in Easton or Greenwich, New York
Parents: Lulu Pearl Campbell (b. Greenwich, NY) Frank Lewis (b. Schuylerville, NY)
Date of Admission: July 7, 1904
Date of Death: August 29, 1904 at the Troy Orphan Asylum, Troy
Cause of Death: Marasmus
Burial: Greenwich, New York
Mother died in childbirth.

Clement Theodore Bowman
Age: 18 Months
Troy Orphan Asylum #771
Birth Date/Location: September 1, 1903 in Troy, New York
Parents: Margaret Carpenter (b. Poestenskill, NY) and Jacob Bowman (b. Switzerland)

Date of Admission: May 19, 1904
Date of Death: November 19, 1904 at Troy Orphan Asylum, Troy
Cause of Death: General marasmus
Burial: St. Mary's Cemetery, Troy, New York

Two death on December 3, 1904 at the Troy Orphan Asylum

Harold Gamble
Age: 1 Year, 8 Months
Troy Orphan Asylum #772
Birth Date/Location: March 27, 1903 in Middle Falls, New York
Parents: Ida Goodness (b. Glens Falls, NY) Charles Gamble (b. Danbury, CT)
Date of Admission: May 26, 1904
Date of Death: December 3, 1904 at Troy Orphan Asylum
Cause of Death: Broncho pneumonia, entero colitis and measles
Burial: Troy Orphan Asylum plot in Section "S" at Oakwood Cemetery, Grave #9

Helen M. Graham
Age: 15 Months
Troy Orphan Asylum #784
Birth Date/Location: August 11, 1903 in Cohoes or Waterford, New York
Parents: Bertha Surprise Graham (b. Hudson or Waterford, NY) Robert Graham (b. England or Scotland)
Date of Admission: June 30, 1904
Date of Death: December 3, 1904 at Troy Orphan Asylum, Troy
Cause of Death: Measles, broncho pneumonia, entero colitis
Burial: Waterford, New York

Charles Vanderhyden or Vanderheyden
Age: 7 Years
Troy Orphan Asylum #782
Birth Date/Location: July 15, 1903 in Troy, New York
Parents: Margaret English (b. Ireland or Albany, NY) and Garrett/Garet Vanderheyden or Vanderhyden (b. Troy, NY)
Date of Admission: June 20, 1904
Date of Death: December 5, 1904 at Troy Orphan Asylum, Troy
Cause of Death: Broncho pneumonia, enter colitis, measles
Burial: Albany, New York
Parents lived at 249 Congress Street, Troy
Father worked at Oakwood Cemetery, and mother worked in the laundry

Frank Viola
Age: 1 Year, 8 Months
Troy Orphan Asylum #753
Birth Date/Location: April 23, 1903 in North Adams,

Massachusetts or Troy, New York
Parents: Angelina Abando (b. Italy) and Joseph Viola (b. Italy)
Sibling: Charles Viola
Date of Admission: March 7, 1904
Date of Death: December 9, 1904 at the Troy Orphan Asylum, Troy
Cause of Death: Measles, broncho pneumonia, entero colitis
Burial: Rensselaer County House Alms House
Cemetery location is unknown off of Campbell Avenue in Troy

Cecelia or Celia Dailey or Daley or Daly
Age: 2 Years, 6 Months
Troy Orphan Asylum
Birth Date/Location: May 16, 1902
Parents: Sarah Kildren (b. New Jersey) Edward Dailey (b. Pittsfield, Massachusetts)
Siblings: Grace
Date of Admission: November 1, 1904
Date of Death: December 13, 1904 at the Troy Orphan Asylum
Cause of Death: Measles, Enter colitis
Burial: Rensselaer County House Cemetery
Location of cemetery is unknown off of Campbell Avenue in Troy

Two death on December 25, 1904 at the Troy Orphan Asylum

Irene Layton
Age: 2 Years, 6 Months
Troy Orphan Asylum #645
Birth Date/Location: June 20, 1902 in Rensselaer, New York
Parents: Clara Lawlar or Fowler (b. Mass.) and Frank Layton (b. New York)
Date of Admission: January 28, 1903
Date of Death: December 25, 1904 at the Troy Orphan Asylum, Troy
Cause of Death: Pneumonia and measles
Burial: Troy Orphan Asylum plot in Section "S" at Oakwood Cemetery, Grave #10

Lydia Bennett
Age: 2 Years, 7 Months
Troy Orphan Asylum #734
Birth Date/Location: May 5 or 15, 1902 in Greenwich, New York
Parents: Lois Harrington (Easton, NY) and Eugene Bennett (b. Greenwich, NY)
Siblings: Hattie Bennett #733 (b. August 19, 1899)
Date of Admission: December 23, 1903
Date of Death: December 25, 1904
Cause of Death: Pneumonia and measles
Burial: Troy Orphan Asylum plot in Section "S" at Oakwood Cemetery, Grave #11

Thirteen Deaths December 1904 – December 1905

December 1904 – Early 1905 Measles Victims

"We had in the early part of the year a severe epidemic of measles, and lost by death several of the youngest children. The disease was brought to the institution by the admittance of new children, who were placed in the infirmary, and after being there a few days they came down with the measles. We sent them at once to the hospital, but too late to prevent the spread of the disease. Soon all the babies came down with it as they were quartered in the upper room of the infirmary, and before the disease was exterminated we had one hundred and twenty (120) cases."

Unknown Child
Age: Unknown
Troy Orphan Asylum
Birth Date/Location:
Parents/Siblings:
Date of Death: Early 1905 at the Troy Orphan Asylum, Spring Avenue, Troy
Cause of Death: Measles
Burial: Unknown

Unknown Child
Age: Unknown
Troy Orphan Asylum
Birth Date/Location:
Parents/Siblings:
Date of Death: Early 1905 at the Troy Orphan Asylum, Spring Avenue, Troy
Cause of Death: Measles
Burial: Unknown

Unknown Child
Age: Unknown
Troy Orphan Asylum
Birth Date/Location:
Parents/Siblings:
Date of Death: Early 1905 at the Troy Orphan Asylum, Spring Avenue, Troy
Cause of Death:
Burial: Unknown

Unknown Child
Age: Unknown
Troy Orphan Asylum
Birth Date/Location:
Parents/Siblings:
Date of Death: Early 1905 at the Troy Orphan Asylum, Spring Avenue, Troy
Cause of Death: Measles
Burial: Unknown

Unknown Child
Age: Unknown
Troy Orphan Asylum
Birth Date/Location:
Parents/Siblings:
Date of Death: Early 1905 at the Troy Orphan Asylum, Spring Avenue, Troy
Cause of Death: Measles
Burial: Unknown

Gertrude E. Ruddell
Age: 14 Years

Fairview Home for Friendless Children
Birth Date/Location: August 8, 1890 in Troy, New York
Parents: Martha (b. NY) and William (b. NY)
Siblings: William T. and M. May
Date of Admission: April 28, 1900
Date of Death: January 17, 1905
Cause of Death: Pneumonia
Burial: Unknown – Records at Town of Colonie

Charles J. Sprosser
Age: 3 Years
Troy Orphan Asylum #656
Birth Date/Location: 1902 in Troy, New York
Parents: Mary Roleader (b. Germany) and Charles Sprosser (b. Germany)
Date of Admission: February 23, 1903
Date of Death: March 7, 1905 at the Troy Orphan Asylum, Troy
Cause of Death: Heart disease and pneumonia
Burial: New Mt Ida Cemetery

Freda Glazer or Glaser
Age: 6 Years
Fairview Home for Friendless Children
Birth Date/Location: April 16, 1891 in Albany or Amsterdam, New York
Parents: Anna and Gus
Date of Admission: April 2, 1904
Date of Death: May 7, 1905 in Colonie at the Fairview Home
Cause of Death: Coria
Burial: Fairview Home plot at Albany Rural Cemetery, Section 104, Lot 453, Plot #4

Florence M Daly or Daley
Age: 20 Years, 10 Months
Fairview Home for Friendless Children
Birth Date/Location: July 20, 1884 in Philadelphia, Pennsylvania/Camden, New Jersey
Parents: Emma and James Daley
Date of Admission: January 4, 1889, Discharged September 1, 1902, Employee of Fairview
Date of Death: May 9, 1905
Cause of Death: Tuberculosis in Colonie
Burial: Fairview Home plot in Section 104, Lot 453 at Albany Rural Cemetery, Plot #5

Glen LaFavere or LaDavere
Age: 10 Months
Troy Orphan Asylum #854
Birth Date/Location: July 29, 1904 in Saratoga Springs, New York
Parents: Mamie Strothers (b. Virginia) and Abraham (b. New Paltz, NY)
Sibling: Gladys
Date of Admission: April 22, 1905

Date of Death: May 18, 1905 at Troy Orphan Asylum in Troy
Cause of Death: Marasmus and malnutrition
Burial: Troy Orphan Asylum plot in Section "S" at Oakwood Cemetery, Grave #12

Ernest Smith
Age: 9 Years
Troy Orphan Asylum #763
Birth Date/Location: November 14, 1895 in Richmond, Virginia or Troy, New York
Parents: Helen Siles or Giles and George Smith
Date of Admission: May 2, 1904
Date of Death: June 4, 1905 at the Troy Orphan Asylum, Troy
Cause of Death: Acute pulmonary tuberculosis
Burial: Mt Ida Cemetery

Jaird Bowen
Age: 11 Months
Troy Orphan Asylum #847
Birth Date/Location: July 1904 in Troy, New York
Parents: Marie Hargraves or Carrie Schroot (b. Germany) and Jared Bowen (b. Vermont)
Siblings: Harold and Ivan
Date of Admission: March 20, 1905
Date of Death: July 9, 1905 at Troy Orphan Asylum
Cause of Death: Acute milliary of thymuses
Burial: Mt Ida Cemetery

Edward P.B. McBurney
Age: 1 Year
Troy Orphan Asylum #870
Birth Date/Location: July 29, 1904 in Brooklyn, New York
Parents: James G. McBurney (b. Ireland) and Margaret Armstrong (b. Ireland)
Siblings: Sarah and Robert A. McBurney
Date of Admission: June 28, 1905
Date of Death: August 4, 1905 at Troy Orphan Asylum, Troy
Cause of Death: Entero colitis and measles
Burial: Oakwood Cemetery in Angus Robertson Lot #242, Grave #2 in Section "T"

Benjamin "Benny" Kittaf or Geder
Age: 1 Year
Troy Orphan Asylum #971
Birth Date/Location: September 1, 1905 in Troy, New York
Parents: William Kittaf or Joseph Geder (b. Russia) and Sarah Wolfe (b. Russia)
Siblings: Nathan and Sadie
Date of Admission: May 31, 1906
Date of Death: July 14, 1906 at the Troy Orphan Asylum, Troy
Cause of Death: Pneumonia rickets
Burial: New Mt Ida Cemetery

William Hammond
Age: 14 Years
Troy Orphan Asylum

Birth Date/Location: August 13, 1891 in Saratoga, New York
Parents: Ella Alexander
Siblings: Joseph Hammond and Louise Hammond
Date of Admission: July 29, 1896
Date of Discharge: May 1, 1905 to work on a farm
Date of Death: June 23, 1906
Cause of Death: Instantly crushed to death due to a train and buggy accident in Saratoga County
Burial: Troy Orphan Asylum plot in Section "S" at Oakwood Cemetery, Grave #13
Discharged May 1, 1905 to work on the farm of Mr. Berchard. Died in a train/horse and buggy accident at Coon's crossing between Round Lake and Mechanicville, NY with soon-to-be adoptive mother Mrs. Charles Burchard. From Mechanicville Saturday Mercury newspaper article June 30, 1906.

Thomas Miller
Age: 12 Years
Fairview Home for Friendless Children
Birth Date/Location: February 23, 1894 in Watervliet, New York
Parents: Emma or Huldah (b. Germany) and Thomas (b. Watervliet, NY)
Date of Admission: August 13, 1899
Date of Death: December 12, 1906 at Troy Hospital
Cause of Death: Appendicitis, septic peritonitis perforated appendicitis
Burial: Albany Rural Cemetery, Section 106, Plot 36

Thomas Galbraith
Age: 4 Years
Troy Orphan Asylum #780
Birth Date/Location: April 5, 1903 in Rensselaer, New York
Parents: Libbie or Lillian Green (Ontario, Canada) and Frank Galbraith (Ontario, Canada)
Siblings: Frank and Richard
Date of Admission: June 11, 1904
Date of Death: May 26, 1907 at Troy Orphan Asylum, Troy
Cause of Death: Pertussis and pneumonia
Burial: Troy Orphan Asylum plot in Section "S" at Oakwood Cemetery, Grave #14

Matilda Dressler
Age: 10 Years
Fairview Home for Friendless Children
Birth Date/Location: March 22, 1897 in Albany, New York
Parents: Minnie (b. Lambertville, New Jersey) August Dressler (b. Troy, New York)
Siblings: Ida M, Marie, Elmer and Charles
Date of Admission: July 19, 1905

Date of Death: May 31, 1907
Cause of Death: Unknown – Records at Town of Colonie
Burial: Unknown – Records at Town of Colonie

John M. Bell
Age: 1 Year, 11 Months
Troy Orphan Asylum #1037
Birth Date/Location: September 30, 1905 in Watervliet, New York
Parents: Anna F. Sharp (b. Watervliet) and John/Nelson Bell (b. Cohoes)
Date of Admission: January 21, 1907
Date of Death: September 4, 1907 at the Troy Orphan Asylum, Troy
Cause of Death: Tubercular meningitis
Burial: Albany Rural Cemetery in Section 104 Lot 154 of Heirs J. W. Sharp

Ernest Osterhout
Age: 5 Months
Troy Orphan Asylum #1148
Birth Date/Location: October 12, 1907 in Johnsonville, New York
Parents: Lorraine Ridington Osterhout (b. Troy, NY) and Trebor Hemingway (b. NY)
Siblings: Edna Osterhout
Date of Admission: January 21, 1908
Date of Death: April 4, 1908 at the Troy Orphan Asylum, Troy
Cause of Death: Pneumonia, gastro enteritis, oritis oneida
Burial: Bloomingrove Cemetery, Town of North Greenbush

Floyd "Hawley" Hudson
Age: 4 Years
Fairview Home for Friendless Children
Birth Date/Location: 1904 in New York State
Parents: Etta Maud Hudson (b. New York) Willard Hudson (b. New York)
Siblings: Scott W. Hudson (b. 1902)
Date of Admission: April 9, 1908
Death: April 22, 1908 at Samaritan Hospital, Troy
Cause of Death: Scarlet fever
Burial: Fairview Home plot in Section 104, Lot 453 at Albany Rural Cemetery, Plot #6

St. John F. Smith
Age: 6 Years
Fairview Home for Friendless Children
Birth Date/Location: 1902 in Fort Edward, New York
Parents: Rose B. Smith (b. Washington County, NY) George W. Smith (b. Fort Edward, NY)
Siblings: Robert and Grant
Date of Admission: June 10, 1907
Date of Death: May 5, 1908 at Fairview Home, Colonie, New York

Cause of Death: Pneumonia
Burial: Albany Rural Cemetery. First buried at Fairview Home plot in Section 104, Lot 453, Plot #7, then moved to family plot on April 6, 1932 to Single Grave 1, Tier 3, Section 207. In same grave with his Mother. Rose Smith retrieved other children from Fairview Home shortly after St. John's death.

Walter Hartley
Age: 14 Years
Troy Orphan Asylum #233
Birth Date/Location: June 1893
Parents/Siblings: Elizabeth Hartley
Date of Death: May 31, 1908
Cause of Death: Unknown
Burial: Unknown

Evelyn Herrington or Harrington
Age: 3 Years, 4 Months
Troy Orphan Asylum #1108
Birth Date/Location: 1905 in Ireland or Salem, New York
Parents: Jennie Priest (b. Vermont) and Russell Harrington (b. Easton, NY)
Siblings: Esther
Date of Admission: October 7, 1907
Date of Death: June 6, 1908 at the Troy Orphan Asylum
Cause of Death: General tuberculosis at the Troy Orphan Asylum
Burial: Troy Orphan Asylum plot in Section "S" at Oakwood Cemetery, Grave #15

Drucilla or Drusilia Scofield/ Schofield
Age: 2 Months
Troy Orphan Asylum #1225
Birth Date/Location: July 8, 1908 in Pine Plains or Poughkeepsie, New York
Parents: Drusilla Stevens (b. England) Edward Scofield
Date of Admission: August 8, 1908
Date of Death: September 24, 1908 at Samaritan Hospital
Cause of Death: Marasmus
Burial: Troy Orphan Asylum plot in Section "S" at Oakwood Cemetery, Grave #16
Baptized at the Parish of Christ Church, Poughkeepsie, NY on August 4, 1908. Parish Records: Vol. IV, P. 186.

Charles Faulkner
Age: 16 Months
Troy Orphan Asylum #1213
Birth Date/Location: June 1, 1907 in Troy, New York
Parents: Irene Hanson (b. Denmark) Isaish Faulkner (b. England)
Date of Admission: July 3, 1908
Date of Death: October 24, 1908 at the Troy Orphan Asylum
Cause of Death: Tubercular meningitis

Burial: Oakwood Cemetery in Section "Q" Lot 236, Grave #2 of Isaiah Faulkner

Irene Cole
Age: 15 Years
Troy Orphan Asylum #415
Birth Date/Location: November 1, 1892 in Troy, New York
Parents: Rose Ingraham (b. Pittsfield, MA, d. Troy 1897) and Simon Cole
Date of Admission: February 24, 1900
Date of Death: February 21, 1909
Cause of Death: Tuberculosis meningitis of the lungs
Burial: Troy Orphan Asylum plot in Section "S" at Oakwood Cemetery, Grave #17

George F. Pike
Age: 11 Years
Troy Orphan Asylum #667
Birth Date/Location: April 24, 1888 in England or Albany, New York
Parents: Anna Allman/ Almond (b. England) and Ernest Pike (b. England)
Siblings: Albert, Ernest and Mary
Date of Admission: April 24, 1903
Date of Death: March 4, 1909 in Samaritan Hospital
Cause of Death: Acute peritonitis
Burial: Beverwyck Cemetery, Rensselaer, New York

Amy or Mary Amy Bardwell
Age: 8 Months
Troy Orphan Asylum #1342
Birth Date/Location: c. November 22, 1908 in Granville, New York
Date of Admission: July 22, 1909
Parents: Jennie and Lausen Bardwell
Date of Death: August 13, 1909 at the Troy Orphan Asylum
Cause of Death: Congenital hydrocephalus
Burial: Troy Orphan Asylum plot in Section "S" at Oakwood Cemetery, Grave #18

Helen M. or Ellen M. Pratt
Age: 16 Months
Troy Orphan Asylum #1343
Birth Date/Location: May 4, 1908 in Troy, New York
Parents: Jennie S. Higgins (b. Ireland) and Warren B. Pratt (b. Troy, NY)
Date of Admission: July 26, 1909
Date of Death: September 22, 1909 at the Troy Orphan Asylum, Troy
Cause of Death: General military tuberculosis
Burial: Oakwood Cemetery in Section "P" Lot 65, Grave #11 in lot of Joseph Higgins

Oban Classon
Age: 5 Months
Troy Orphan Asylum #1337

Birth Date/Location: May 10, 1909 in Troy, New York
Parents: Rosa Glasky (b. Russia) and Solomon Classen (b. Russia)
Date of Admission: June 19, 1909
Date of Death: December 8, 1909
Cause of Death: Unknown
Burial: Unknown

Kenneth Roberts
Age: 10 Months
Troy Orphan Asylum #1289
Birth Date/Location: February 5, 1909 in Troy, New York
Parents: Catherine Roberts (b. Vermont)
Date of Admission: February 22, 1909
Date of Death: December 20, 1909 at the Troy Orphan Asylum, Troy
Cause of Death: Acute suppression of urine, pulmonary tuberculosis
Burial: Troy Orphan Asylum plot in Section "S" at Oakwood Cemetery, Grave #19

William Henry Smith
Age: 5 Months
Troy Orphan Asylum #1382
Birth Date/Location: September 25, 1909 in Schenectady County, New York
Parents: Edith Lobb (b. Canada, America) Frederick Smith (b. NYS, America)
Date of Admission: November 19, 1909
Date of Death: January 4 or 13, 1910 at the Troy Orphan Asylum, Troy
Cause of Death: Marasmus
Burial: Schenectady, New York
"We have lost several young babies, but they came to us in an impoverished condition."

Rose B. Jakad
Age: 11 Months
Troy Orphan Asylum #1312
Birth Date/Location: January 25, 1909 in East Greenbush, New York
Parents: Mary Jakad (b. West Sand Lake, NY) Thomas Smith
Date of Admission: April 23, 1909
Date of Death: January 9, 1910 at the Troy Orphan Asylum
Cause of Death: Acute diptheritic septicemia, acute laryngeal stenosis, probably diphtheria, membranous croup
Burial: Troy Orphan Asylum plot in Section "S" at Oakwood Cemetery, Grave #20
"We have lost several young babies, but they came to us in an impoverished condition."

Ruth Frances or Frances Ruth Cline
Age: 20 Days
Troy Orphan Asylum #1276
Birth Date/Location: January 7, 1909 in Upper Troy, New York
Parents: Lulu Cline (b. Pittstown, NY)

Date of Admission: January 7, 1909
Date of Death: January 27, 1910 at Troy Orphan Asylum, Troy
Cause of Death: Pneumonia
Burial: Mt Ida Cemetery
"We have lost several young babies, but they came to us in an impoverished condition."

Louise Albina, Alline or Allmia Hill
Age: 3 Months
Troy Orphan Asylum (No #)
Birth Date/Location: November 2, 1909 in Mechanicville, New York
Parents: Albina Hill (b. Mechanicville, NY) Unknown father (b. Holyoke, MA)
Date of Admission: November 3, 1909 and discharged November 20, 1909; December 27, 1909 and discharged January 18, 1910; readmitted January 29, 1910
Date of Death: February 18, 1910 at the Troy Orphan Asylum, Troy
Cause of Death: Laryneal diphtheria
Burial: Troy Orphan Asylum plot in Section "S" at Oakwood Cemetery, Grave #21
Discharged twice for adoption, then died at TOA
"We have lost several young babies, but they came to us in an impoverished condition."

Walter Pike
Age: 10 Years
Fairview Home for Friendless Children
Birth Date/Location: 1900 in Fort Edward, New York
Parents: Mrs. John W. Harris
Date of Admission: February 26, 1910
Date of Death: April 25, 1910 at Fairview Home, Township of Colonie
Cause of Death: Ceptico pyemia
Burial: Fairview Home plot in Section 104, Lot 453 at Albany Rural Cemetery, Plot #8

Two death on July 24, 1910 at the Troy Orphan Asylum

Viola Fitzgerald
Age: 7 Weeks
Troy Orphan Asylum (No #)
Birth Date/Location: June 2, 1910 in Albany, New York
Parents: Ada Shutter (b. Albany, NY) Edward Fitzgerald (b. Albany, NY)
Date of Admission: July 1, 1910
Date of Death: July 24, 1910 at the Troy Orphan Asylum
Cause of Death: Acute gastro enteritis
Burial: St. Mary's Cemetery, Troy, New York
"We have lost several young babies, but they came to us in an impoverished condition."

Douglas Stillman
Age: 6 Months
Troy Orphan Asylum #1439
Birth Date/Location: February 24, 1910 in Berlin, New York
Date of Admission: May 1, 1910
Date of Death: July 24, 1910 at the Troy Orphan Asylum, Troy
Cause of Death: Acute gastro enteritis, marasmus
Burial: Troy Orphan Asylum plot in Section "S" at Oakwood Cemetery, Grave #22
"We have lost several young babies, but they came to us in an impoverished condition."

Elmer Boyce
Age: 14 Months
Troy Orphan Asylum
Birth Date/Location: October 24, 1909 in Schenectady, New York
Parents: Florence Boyce
Date of Admission: March 24, 1910
Date of Death: August 7, 1910
Cause of Death: Unknown
Burial: Unknown
"We have lost several young babies, but they came to us in an impoverished condition."

Beatrice Young
Age: 11 Days
Troy Orphan Asylum (No #)
Birth Date/Location: June 22, 1910 in Little Falls, New York
Parents: Unknown Young
Date of Admission: July 8, 1910
Date of Death: August 8, 1910 at the Troy Orphan Asylum, Troy
Cause of Death: Marasmus
Burial: Troy Orphan Asylum plot in Section "S" at Oakwood Cemetery, Grave #23
"We have lost several young babies, but they came to us in an impoverished condition."

Anna Koslankos/Keslouckos
Age: 4 Months
Troy Orphan Asylum #1494
Birth Date/Location: June 23, 1910 in Troy, New York
Parents: Anna Koslankes (b. Russia or Poland)
Date of Admission: September 8, 1910
Date of Death: November 16, 1910 at the Troy Orphan Asylum, Troy
Cause of Death: Broncho pneumonia
Burial: St. Mary's Cemetery, Troy, New York
"We have lost several young babies, but they came to us in an impoverished condition."

Joseph Lawson
Age: 25 Years
Troy Orphan Asylum #88
Birth Date/Location: April 10, 1885 in Troy, New York
Parents: Mary Nolan/Noonan (b. Ireland) and Christopher Lawson (b. Norway)
Date of Admission: November 20, 1893

Date of Death: December 12, 1910 at Lakeview Sanitarium, Troy
Cause of Death: Pulmonary Tuberculosis/Pulmonary Enteritis
Burial: Troy Orphan Asylum plot in Section "S" at Oakwood Cemetery, Grave #24
Admission: November 20, 1893. Lived at the TOA after discharge March 31, 1901. Employed as a machinist at the TOA. Had TB for 9 months before death.

Margaret/Marguerite Quackenbush
Age: 3 Months
Troy Orphan Asylum #1513
Birth Date/Location: November 7, 1910 at Leonard Hospital, Troy, New York
Parents: Grace Vibbard (b. Watervliet or Waterville, NY) Charles Quackenbush (b. NY)
Date of Admission: November 21, 1910
Date of Death: March 1, 1911 at the Troy Orphan Asylum, Troy
Cause of Death: Malnutrition and exhaustion
Burial: Elmwood Hill Cemetery, Troy

Henry Harrison
Age: 14 Years
Troy Orphan Asylum #290
Birth Date/Location: March 29, 1896 in Troy, New York
Parents: Annie Simpkins (b. Rensselaer County) Abraham Harrington (b. USA)
Siblings: Bertha
Date of Admission: June 23, 1898
Date of Death: March 22, 1911 at the Troy Orphan Asylum
Cause of Death: Tuberculosis of the spine
Burial: Mt Ida Cemetery

Henry Baucus
Age: 10 Months
Troy Orphan Asylum #1492
Birth Date/Location: August 23, 1910 in Troy
Parents: Bertha Doran (b. Troy) Henry Baucus (b. Syracuse, NY)
Date of Admission: September 1, 1910
Date of Death: July 6, 1911 at the Troy Orphan Asylum
Cause of Death: Heat Prostration and gastro enteritis
Burial: Troy Orphan Asylum plot in Section "S" at Oakwood Cemetery, Grave #25
"5-day heat wave, July 2-6, 1911 in the Capital Region."

John J. or Juason Jennings
Age: 2 Months
Troy Orphan Asylum #1640
Birth Date/Location: September 22, 1911 in St. Johnsville, New York or New York State
Date of Admission: October 1, 1911

Date of Death: December 13, 1911 at the Troy Orphan Asylum, Troy
Cause of Death: Malnutrition marasmus, artificial feeding, entero colitis
Burial: Troy Orphan Asylum plot in Section "S" at Oakwood Cemetery, Grave #26

Helen May Lincoln
Age: 5 Years
Troy Orphan Asylum #1686
Birth Date/Location: January 20, 1907 in Sayre, Pennsylvania
Parents: Lillian Coons (Alps, NY) Oscar J. Lincoln (b. Sayre, PA)
Date of Admission: January 17, 1912
Date of Death: January 27, 1912 at the Troy Orphan Asylum, Troy
Cause of Death: Diphtheria
Burial: Oakwood Cemetery, Page 452 and 372, Single interments Grave #252

Mary Jane or Mary Frances Crawmer
Age: 2 Months
Troy Orphan Asylum #1676
Birth Date/Location: December 4, 1911 in Troy, New York
Parents: Daniel Crawmer (b. Troy) Mary F. Jones (b. Petersburgh)
Siblings: John W., Arthur and Eva (TOA, also died at Samaritan Hospital in 1915)
Date of Admission: December 27, 1911
Date of Death: February 5, 1912 at Troy Orphan Asylum, Troy
Cause of Death: Marasmus
Burial: New Mt Ida Cemetery

Joseph Rosenbloom
Age: 5 Months
Troy Orphan Asylum #1712
Birth Date/Location: September 17, 1911 in Troy, New York
Parents: Anna Lewis (b. Germany) Louis Rosenbloom (b. Russia)
Date of Admission: March 9, 1912
Date of Death: March 11, 1912 at Troy Orphan Asylum, Troy
Cause of Death: Broncho pneumonia
Burial: Mt. Ida Cemetery

Edward Hickman
Age: 2 Months
Troy Orphan Asylum #1693
Birth Date/Location: January 23, 1912 in Pittsfield, Massachusetts
Parents: Ethel Hickman and Howard Bellview
Date of Admission: February 6, 1912
Date of Death: April 13, 1912 at the Troy Orphan Asylum in Troy
Cause of Death: Labor pneumonia and gastro enteritis

Burial: Troy Orphan Asylum plot in Section "S" at Oakwood Cemetery, Grave #27

Bernard Fleischer
Age: 13 Months
Troy Orphan Asylum #1670
Birth Date/Location: March 21, 1911 in Albany or Troy, New York
Parents: Fannie Freidman (b. Troy, NY) Abraham Fleischer (b. Austria or Russia)
Date of Admission: December 31, 1911
Date of Death: May 10, 1912 at Troy Orphan Asylum
Cause of Death: Acute labor pneumonia and congenital syphilis and rachitis
Burial: New Mt. Ida Cemetery

Ruth Virginia Crosby
Age: 6 Months
Troy Orphan Asylum #1741
Birth Date/Location: February 14, 1912 in Maternity Hospital, Troy, New York
Parents: Catherine/Katherine O'Connell (b. Vermont) and Thomas E. Crosby (b. New York)
Date of Admission: June 5, 1912
Date of Death: August 25, 1912 at 87 Hoosick Street, Troy
Cause of Death: Marasmus
Burial: St. John's Cemetery, Troy, New York

Richard Connors
Age: 3 Years
Troy Orphan Asylum #1753
Birth Date/Location: 1910 in Rensselaer, New York
Parents: Matilda Patterson (b. Rensselaer, NY) John F. Connors (b. Albany, NY)
Siblings: John #1752 (b. June 11, 1905)
Date of Admission: June 25, 1912
Date of Death: September 10, 1912 at Troy Orphan Asylum, Troy
Cause of Death: Broncho Pneumonia
Burial: St. John's Cemetery, Troy, New York

Iola Blanch Myers
Age: 3 Months
Troy Orphan Asylum #1746
Birth Date/Location: June 6, 1912 in Scotia, New York
Parents: Etta or Eva Myers (b. Schenectady, NY) Oscar Myers (b. Schenectady, NY)
Date of Admission: June 15, 1912
Date of Death: October 2, 1912 at the Troy Orphan Asylum, Troy
Cause of Death: Marasmus and malnutrition
Burial: New Mt. Ida Cemetery

Miles Gardner
Age: 5 Months
Troy Orphan Asylum #1762
Birth Date/Location: April 22, 1912 in Greenwich, New York

Parents: Jessie Perry (b. Greenwich, NY) and John Gardner
Date of Admission: July 9, 1912
Date of Death: October 4, 1912 at the Troy Orphan Asylum
Cause of Death: Thymus tod
Burial: New Mt. Ida Cemetery

Floyd Priest
Age: 5 Years
Fairview Home for Friendless Children
Birth Date/Location: August 6, 1907 in Salem, New York
Parents: Esther Licher (d. March 2, 1912) and Adelbert Priest
Siblings: Emory, Prescott, and an unnamed brother
Date of Admission: August 12, 1912
Date of Death: October 30, 1912
Cause of Death: Unknown – Records at Town of Colonie
Burial: Unknown – Records at Town of Colonie

Waldo E. Ducharme
Age: 5 Months
Troy Orphan Asylum #1764
Birth Date/Location: July 8, 1912 in Orwell, Vermont
Parents: Mary E. Ducharme (b. Orwell, VT) and Joseph Ducharme
Date of Admission: July 19, 1912
Date of Death: December 10, 1912 at Troy Orphan Asylum, Troy
Cause of Death: Broncho pneumonia
Burial: Troy Orphan Asylum plot in Section "S" at Oakwood Cemetery, Grave #28

Arthur Case
Age: 13 Years
Troy Orphan Asylum #1269
Birth Date/Location: 1900 in Saranac, New York
Parents: Ida and William Case
Siblings: Alice, Catherine, Susie and Clarence
Date of Admission: January 11, 1909
Date of Death: December 26, 1912 at Troy Orphan Asylum
Cause of Death: Acute articular rheumatism, acute endocarditis, infarct of lung
Burial: Troy Orphan Asylum plot in Section "S" at Oakwood Cemetery, Grave #29
Obituary in Daily Times, Troy, New York.
"Arthur Case, twelve years old, who for the last four years had been an inmate at the Troy Orphan Asylum, died there yesterday noon suddenly as the result of heart trouble. Young Case came from Saranac, Clinton County."

Erma Reynolds
Age: 7 Months
Troy Orphan Asylum #1796

Birth Date/Location: July 5, 1912 in Waterford, New York
Parents: Edna or Mary Abrams (b. Stillwater, NY) and William Reynolds (b. Waterford, NY)
Date of Admission: November 13, 1912
Date of Death: February 19, 1913 at the Troy Orphan Asylum
Cause of Death: Disease of intestinal tract, marasmus, non-assimilation of food
Burial: Waterford Rural Cemetery
William Reynolds is listed on the death certificate, but the child is Erma who died.

Ethel Wager
Age: 10 Months
Troy Orphan Asylum #1178
Birth Date/Location: September 15, 1906 in Troy, New York
Parents: Ella Calkins (b. Berlin, NY) and Elmer Wager (b. Grafton, NY)
Siblings: Jessie, Thelma and Eddie Wager aka Edward Calkins
Date of Admission: April 2, 1908
Date of Death: April 12, 1913 at the Troy Orphan Asylum, Troy
Cause of Death: Labor pneumonia and pulmonary tuberculosis
Burial: Eagle Mills Cemetery

Unknown Female called "Helen Troy"
Age: Approx. 2 Weeks
Troy Orphan Asylum #1914
Birth Date/Location: September 23, 1913 circa., found in Troy
Parents: Unknown, found in street
Date of Admission: September 30, 1913
Date of Death: October 8, 1913 at the Troy Orphan Asylum
Cause of Death: Hemorrhage from stomach, underdeveloped poorly nourished foundling
Burial: Troy Orphan Asylum plot in Section "S" at Oakwood Cemetery, Grave #30
Notes: "found in street living." Death certificate incorrectly states Mt Ida Cemetery for burial.

Anna Toretsky/Furzsky
Age: 2 Years
Troy Orphan Asylum #1882
Birth Date/Location: December 12, 1911 in Troy, New York
Parents: Rachel Bolonio Toretsky (b. Russia) or Sarah Silverstein (b. Russia) Israel Toretsky or Furzsky (b. Russia)
Siblings: Dorothy, Marmie and Fannie
Date of Admission: July 3, 1913
Date of Death: December 10, 1913

Cause of Death: Pneumonia, double apex pneumonia
Burial: Wynantskill Cemetery

Louis Mannix
Age: 2 Months
Troy Orphan Asylum #1937
Birth Date/Location: November 15, 1913 in Troy, New York
Parents: Jennie Mannix (b. Plattsburgh, NY) and Louis Perry
Date of Admission: December 2, 1913
Date of Death: January 18, 1914 at the Troy Orphan Asylum, Troy
Cause of Death: Gastric enteritis, acido anemia
Burial: Troy Orphan Asylum plot in Section "S" at Oakwood Cemetery, Grave #31

Marie Beaudoin
Age: 7 Months
Troy Orphan Asylum #1953
Birth Date/Location: January 28, 1914 in Castleton, New York
Parents: Agnes Buzzaska (b. Brooklyn, NY) Joseph Beaudoin (b. Pittsfield, MA)
Date of Admission: February 2, 1914
Date of Death: September 10, 1914 at the Troy Orphan Asylum
Cause of Death: Acute entero colitis
Burial: Oakwood Cemetery

Chester Snyder
Age: 5 Months
Troy Orphan Asylum #2004
Birth Date/Location: March 10, 1914 in Troy, New York
Parents: Estella Snyder (b. Grafton, NY) and Michael E. Kelly
Date of Admission: May 19, 1914
Date of Death: September 12, 1914 at the Troy Orphan Asylum, Troy
Cause of Death: Acute entero colitis
Burial: Oakwood Cemetery, Section "P" Single interments, Grave #658

Beatrice Long
Age: 6 Months
Troy Orphan Asylum #1983
Birth Date/Location: March 1, 1914
Parents: Bertha Long (b. NY) and Harry Weed (b. Troy, NY)
Date of Admission: March 25, 1914
Date of Death: September 14, 1914 at the Troy Orphan Asylum
Cause of Death: Acute entero colitis
Burial: New Mt. Ida Cemetery

Eva May Crawmer
Age: 15 Years
Troy Orphan Asylum #1684
Birth Date/Location: May 21, 1899 in Bloomingrove, New York (Rensselaer County)

Parents: Mary Frances Jones (b. Petersburgh) and Daniel Crawmer (b. Troy)
Siblings: John W., Arthur and Mary Jane or Mary Frances
Date of Admission: January 5, 1912
Date of Death: March 10, 1915 in Samaritan Hospital
Cause of Death: Acute pulmonary tuberculosis
Burial: Elmwood Hill Cemetery
Sister also died in 1912, TOA resident
Obituary in Daily Times, Troy, New York: Funeral at 1 Sheridan Avenue.
Officiated by Rev. W.W. Eaton of Levings Methodist Church

George P. Hazel
Age: 15 Years
Troy Orphan Asylum #1067
Birth Date/Location: December 24, 1900
Date of Admission: June 6, 1907
Date of Discharge: November 18, 1915 to Lakeview Sanitarium
Date of Death: Unknown
Cause of Death: Unknown
Burial: Unknown

Russell W. Sutton
Age: 8 Months
Troy Orphan Asylum #2195
Birth Date/Location: April 24, 1916 in Albany or Troy, New York
Parents: Mabel Lent Sutton (b. Valley Falls, NY) and William Wright (b. Troy, NY) or Frederick Sutton (b. England)
Date of Admission: June 3, 1916
Date of Death: December 28, 1916 at Samaritan Hospital
Cause of Death: Empyema of pleura
Burial: Elmwood Hill Cemetery, Schaghticoke, New York

Harold Thomas Helfand
Age: 7 Months
Troy Orphan Asylum #2250
Birth Date/Location: September 7, 1916 in Hudson, New York
Parents: Bertha Helfand (b. Russia)
Date of Admission: February 6, 1917
Date of Death: April 7, 1917 at the Troy Orphan Asylum, Troy
Cause of Death: Aprix pneumonia, cerebro spinal meningitis
Burial: Hudson, New York

Dorothy Harp
Age: 7 Years
Troy Orphan Asylum #1999
Birth Date/Location: September 3, 1909 in Troy, New York
Parents: Cora Smith Harp (b. Carolina) George Harps (b. Vermont)

Date of Admission: April 28, 1914
Date of Death: June 30, 1917 at Samaritan Hospital
Cause of Death: Bichloride of mercury poisoning. "Child too young to realize what she was taking."
Burial: Elmwood Hill Cemetery, Troy, New York

William Remsen
Age: 21 Months
Troy Orphan Asylum #2192
Birth Date/Location: November 6, 1915 in King County Hospital, Brooklyn, New York
Parents: Margaret Remsen (b. Brooklyn, NY)
Date of Admission: May 24, 1916
Date of Death: August 16, 1917 at the Troy Orphan Asylum, Troy
Cause of Death: Acute military tuberculosis and meningitis T.B.
Burial: Hudson, New York

Mary Margaret Mark
Age: 1 Month
Troy Orphan Asylum #2336
Birth Date/Location: November 7, 1917 in Samaritan Hospital, Troy, New York
Parents: Bertha M. Mark (b. Schenectady, NY) and Ida S. Kraus/Krause (b. Troy, NY)
Date of Admission: November 24, 1917
Date of Death: December 11, 1917 at the Troy Orphan Asylum, Troy
Cause of Death: Entero colitis
Burial: Mt. Ida Cemetery

Retia Ellen Davis
Age: 17 Months
Troy Orphan Asylum #2219
Birth Date/Location: June 7, 1916 in Warrensburg, New York
Parents: Anna L. Davis (b. Johnstown, NY) Lawrence Wallace (b. Warrensburg, NY)
Siblings: Twin sister Cretia Helen Davis #2218 (adopted October 7, 1916)
Date of Admission: September 15, 1916
Date of Death: January 3, 1918
Cause of Death: Unknown
Burial: Unknown
"To be placed for adoption."

Margaret Josephine Haywood
Age: 2 Years, 10 Months
Troy Orphan Asylum #2121
Birth Date/Location: March 11, 1915 in East Poestenskill, New York
Parents: Anna Franklin Haywood (b. White Plains, NY) George F. Haywood (b. Grafton, NY)
Siblings: Edith M., Nellie and William Henry
Date of Admission: August 25, 1915
Date of Death: January 25, 1918 at Samaritan Hospital

Cause of Death: Larynigeal diphtheria
Burial: New Mt. Ida Cemetery

Marion Lansing
Age: 13 Days
Troy Orphan Asylum #2367
Birth Date/Location: March 16, 1918 in Troy, New York
Parents: Marion Lansing and Wm. Joseph McMahon
Date of Admission: March 16, 1918
Date of Death: March 29, 1918
Cause of Death: Unknown
Burial: Unknown

Eva Elizabeth Morrow
Age: 3 Months
Troy Orphan Asylum
Birth Date/Location: January 11, 1918
Parents: Ida Morrow (b. Troy, NY) Henry Sturgeon (b. Canada)
Date of Death: April 10, 1918
Cause of Death: Unknown
Burial: Unknown
Mother Ida Morrow (b. July 1895) was a resident of TOA #1062. Admitted May 27, 1907, and discharged March 5, 1910. Ida Morrow's mother Katherine Taylor (b. Franklin County, NY) died May 16, 1907 at Samaritan Hospital. Ida's father is Robert (b. NYC) and her brothers are Alvia and William Morrow.

Thelma Elizabeth Bowlyer
Age: 6 Years, 5 Months
Troy Orphan Asylum #2302
Birth Date/Location: January 20, 1912 in Saranac Lake, New York
Parents: Hattie (Saranac Lake, NY) and Moses Bowlyer (Montreal, Canada)
Date of Admission: August 4, 1917
Date of Death: July 1, 1918 at Samaritan Hospital
Cause of Death: Lobar pneumonia and diphtheria
Burial: New Mt. Ida Cemetery

Gladys Evelyn LaVargne
Age: 1 Year
Troy Orphan Asylum #2325
Birth Date/Location: September 8, 1917 in Indian Lake, New York, Hamilton County
Parents: Ruby Benton (b. Indian Lake, NY) Charles Louis LaVargne (b. Indian Lake, NY)
Date of Admission: October 18, 1917
Date of Death: September 24, 1918
Cause of Death: Rickets, malnutrition
Burial: New Mt. Ida Cemetery

Andrew J. Putnam
Age: 2 Years, 11 Months
Troy Orphan Asylum #2398
Birth Date/Location: November 7, 1915 in Schenectady, New York

Parents: Florence Spencer (b. Troy, NY) Albert Putnam (b. Gregg, Lewis County, NY)
Date of Admission: August 1, 1918
Date of Death: October 22, 1918 at Troy Hospital
Cause of Death: Broncho pneumonia and influenza
Burial: Graceland Cemetery, Albany, New York

Vera Olga Shoemaker
Age: 7 Months
Troy Orphan Asylum #2427
Birth Date/Location: March 18, 1918 in Schenectady, New York
Parents: Florence Jones (b. at sea on British Ship) Earl H. Shoemaker (b. Scotia, NY)
Date of Admission: October 5, 1918
Date of Death: November 9, 1918 at the Troy Orphan Asylum, Troy
Cause of Death: Acute congestion of lungs and cardius syncope
Burial: Oakwood Cemetery, Section "P" Grave #770

Harold Jackson
Age: 22 Months
Troy Orphan Asylum #2247
Birth Date/Location: January 1, 1917 in Saratoga Springs, New York
Parents: Annie Smith Jackson (b. USA) John Jackson (b. USA)
Date of Admission: January 25, 1917
Date of Death: November 13, 1918 at the Troy Orphan Asylum, Troy
Cause of Death: Influenza and bronchial pneumonia
Burial: New Mt. Ida Cemetery

Forrest Merithen/Merithew
Age: 11 Years
Troy Orphan Asylum #2129
Birth Date/Location: December 12, 1906 in South Shaftsbury, Vermont
Parents: Martha E. Whipple Merithen (b. Berlin, NY) George A. Merithen (b. S. Petersburgh, NY)
Siblings: Harvey
Date of Admission: September 25, 1915
Date of Death: November 20, 1918 at the Troy Orphan Asylum, Troy
Cause of Death: Broncho pneumonia and influenza
Burial: Hoosick Falls, New York

Leona Gardner
Age: 19 Years
Troy Orphan Asylum #1990
Birth Date/Location: December 14, 1898 in Troy, New York
Parents: Annette Harrington (b. Syracuse, NY) Lester A. Gardner (b. Averill Park, NY)
Siblings: Lester, Marcia and Isabelle

Date of Admission: April 9, 1914
Date of Discharge: December 31, 1914
Date of Death: December 24, 1918
Became employee of the Troy Orphan Asylum

Earl Carson
Age: 2 Years, 7 Months
Troy Orphan Asylum #2385
Birth Date/Location: December 6, 1916 in Clifton Park, New York
Parents: Jennie De Graff or De Groff (b. New York) and John W. Carson (b. New York)
Siblings: Carl
Date of Admission: May 27, 1918
Date of Death: January 17, 1919 at Samaritan Hospital
Cause of Death: T.B. Meningitis, Influenza
Burial: Clifton Park, New York

***Twin Sisters Died on January 7, 1919*

Beatrice Hayner
Age: 17 Days
Troy Orphan Asylum #2465
Birth Date/Location: January 7, 1919 in Troy, New York
Parents: Lulu Maud Bresee/Brazee (b. Cooperstown, NY) and Arthur Albert Hayner (b. West Sand Lake)
Siblings: Bernice (twin sister)
Date of Admission: January 22, 1919
Date of Death: January 24, 1919 at the Troy Orphan Asylum, Troy
Cause of Death: Prematurity and inanition
Burial: West Sand Lake, New York

Bernice Hayner
Age: 17 Days
Troy Orphan Asylum #2464
Birth Date/Location: January 7, 1919 in Troy, New York
Parents: Lulu Maud Bresee/Brazee (b. Cooperstown, NY) and Arthur Albert Hayner (b. West Sand Lake)
Siblings: Beatrice (twin sister)
Date of Admission: January 22, 1919
Date of Death: January 24, 1919 at the Troy Orphan Asylum, Troy
Cause of Death: Prematurity and inanition
Burial: West Sand Lake, New York

Karl (Carl) Weckmuller
Age: 11 Months
Troy Orphan Asylum #2452
Birth Date/Location: March 4, 1917? in Troy, New York
Parents: Margaret Molbeck (b. Denmark) and Arthur Weckmuller (b. Germany)
Date of Admission: December 6, 1918
Date of Death: February 6, 1919 at the Troy Orphan Asylum

Cause of Death: Lobar pneumonia and cardiac syncope
Burial: Mt. Ida Cemetery

Dorothy Littlejohn
Age: 1 Year
Troy Orphan Asylum #2370
Birth Date/Location: March 2, 1918 in Brunswick or Troy, New York
Parents: Hattie Wyckoff (b. New Jersey) Lewis Littlejohn (b. England)
Siblings: Louis, Leona, Robert and Harold Littlejohn
Date of Admission: March 21, 1918
Date of Death: February 28, 1919 at the Troy Orphan Asylum
Cause of Death: Broncho pneumonia and measles
Burial: Elmwood Hill Cemetery

Clarence DeKalb
Age: 10 Years, 3 Months
Troy Orphan Asylum #2491
Birth Date/Location: December 6, 1908 in Granville, New York
Parents: Molly Duel (b. New York) and Frank DeKalb (b. New York)
Date of Admission: February 26, 1919
Date of Death: March 11, 1919 at Samaritan Hospital
Cause of Death: Broncho pneumonia following operation for appendicitis at Samaritan Hospital
Burial: Granville, New York

Etta May or Mary Wilson
Age: 7 Years
Troy Orphan Asylum #2477
Birth Date/Location: November 24, 1911 in Wooster, New York
Parents: William Wilson (b. Hydeburg, NY) and Pearl Frayer (b. NY)
Siblings: Howard Wilson
Date of Admission: February 6, 1919
Date of Death: April 9, 1919 in Samaritan Hospital
Cause of Death: Diphtheria
Burial: New Mt. Ida Cemetery

Vera Ross
Age: 14 Years
Troy Orphan Asylum #2479
Birth Date/Location: February 25, 1905 in Griffin, New York
Parents: Blanche Richards Ross (b. Johnsbury, NY) George Ross (b. Bay Center, NY)
Siblings: Ida and Edna
Date of Admission: February 6, 1919 and February 27, 1919
Date of Death: April 27, 1919 at Samaritan Hospital
Cause of Death: Diptheria, acute nephritis
Burial: New Mt. Ida Cemetery

Sylvester Brown
Age: 3 Years
Troy Orphan Asylum #2380
Birth Date/Location: May 2, 1916 in New York State

Parents: Frances Brown and Ira Brown
Date of Admission: May 17, 1918
Date of Death: May 4, 1919 at Samaritan Hospital
Cause of Death: Diptheria
Burial: New Mt. Ida Cemetery

Edward Moll
Age: 8 Years
Fairview Home for Friendless Children
Birth Date/Location: April 25, 1911 in Stillwater, New York
Parents: Fannie Quackenbush (b. Schaghticoke, NY) Lewis Moll (b. Stillwater, NY)
Date of Admission: December 1, 1918
Date of Death: May 4, 1919
Cause of Death: Unknown – Records at Town of Colonie
Burial: Unknown – Records at Town of Colonie

Bernard/Bertram Page
Age: 6 Years
Troy Orphan Asylum #2586
Birth Date/Location: September 19, 1913 in Corinth or Glens Falls, New York
Parents: Lydia Hurd (b. Corinth, NY) William Page (b. Lake Pleasant, NY)
Siblings: Charles, Anna and Russell
Date of Admission: April 15, 1920
Date of Death: July 12, 1920 at Samaritan Hospital
Cause of Death: General septicemia and scarlet fever
Burial: New Mt. Ida Cemetery

Henry Eggleston
Age: 2 Months
Troy Orphan Asylum #2626
Birth Date/Location: August 15, 1920 in Poestenkill, New York
Parents: Ruth Eggleston (b. Corinth, New York)
Date of Admission: August 15, 1920
Date of Death: October 26, 1920 at the Troy Orphan Asylum
Cause of Death: Marasmus, congenital weakness of constitution depending on heredity
Burial: New Mt. Ida Cemetery

Harry C.S. Maguire
Age: 5 Months
Troy Orphan Asylum #2754
Birth Date/Location: June 9, 1921 in Troy, New York
Parents: Lucia Letitia Maguire (b. Troy, NY) Harry C. Shaughnessy (b. Troy, NY)
Siblings: Half siblings listed on Find A Grave
Date of Admission: June 25, 1921
Date of Death: November 7, 1921 at the Troy Orphan Asylum, Troy
Cause of Death: Chronic gastro enteritis and broncho pneumonia

Burial: Forest Hills Cemetery, Brunswick, New York unmarked at his family plot.

Margaret Anne Dearstyne
Age: 8 Months
Troy Orphan Asylum #2763
Birth Date/Location: July 24, 1921 in Watervliet, New York
Parents: Edith F. Dearstyne (b. Schaghticoke, NY) Walter C. Jensen (b. North Troy, NY)
Date of Admission: July 24, 1921
Date of Death: March 5, 1922 at the Troy Orphan Asylum
Cause of Death: Broncho pneumonia and marasmus
Burial: Mt. Ida Cemetery

Hilda Anne or Ann Klock
Age: 3 Months
Troy Orphan Asylum #2873
Birth Date/Location: July 14, 1922 in Hudson Falls, New York
Parents: Dorothy Klock (b. Ann Arbor, Michigan)
Date of Admission: August 2, 1922
Date of Death: October 21, 1922 at the Troy Orphan Asylum, Troy
Cause of Death: Acute entero colites and marasmus
Burial: Mt. Ida Cemetery

Jennie McDowell
Age: 4 Years
Troy Orphan Asylum #2883
Birth Date/Location: May 28, 1918 in Mooers, New York
Parents: Emma Duffina (b. Mooers, NY) and Wallace H. McDowell (b. Mooers, NY)
Date of Admission: September 22, 1922
Date of Death: December 11, 1922 at the Troy Orphan Asylum, Troy
Cause of Death: Vincent's angina
Burial: Moores, Clinton County, New York

Jennie Chaplin
Age: 7 Months
Troy Orphan Asylum #2865
Birth Date/Location: April 23, 1922 in Whitehall, New York
Parents: Elsie Chaplin Johnson
Date of Admission: June 29, 1922
Date of Discharge: October 3, 1922 to St. Margaret's Hospital in Albany
Date of Death: December 12, 1922 in St. Margaret's Hospital in Albany
Cause of Death: Syphilis
Burial: Albany Rural Cemetery, Section 121, Plot 313

James Edward Blackburn II
Age: 22 Days
Troy Orphan Asylum #2933
Birth Date/Location: December 3, 1922 in Bennington, Vermont
Parents: Frances Carver (b. Bennington, VT) James Edward Blackburn, Jr. (b. Troy, NY)

Date of Admission: December 4, 1922
Date of Death: December 25, 1922 at the Troy Orphan Asylum
Cause of Death: Debility congenital
Burial: New Mt. Ida Cemetery

Harry Taylor
Age: 13 Years
Troy Orphan Asylum #2521 and #2844
Birth Date/Location: August 25, 1909 in Westport, New York
Parents: Jennie or Annie Amos Taylor (b. NY) and William Taylor (b. NY)
Date of Death: January 13, 1923 at Samaritan Hospital
Cause of Death: Broncho pneumonia and acute dialation of heart
Burial: New Mt. Ida Cemetery

Frederick Thomas Holmes
Age: 3 Months
Troy Orphan Asylum #2963
Birth Date/Location: January 27, 1923 in Troy, New York
Parents: Theresa Madden (b. Plattsburgh, NY) Frederick C. Holmes (b. London, England)
Date of Admission: February 15, 1923
Date of Death: May 6, 1923
Cause of Death: Gastro enteritis
Burial: St. John's Cemetery, Schenectady, New York in a single grave.
Was baptized at St. Peter's Catholic Church, Troy, and a St. Peter's priest officiated at burial.

Donald Kornetzky
Age: 4 Months
Troy Orphan Asylum #2989
Birth Date/Location: March 10, 1923 in Troy, New York
Parents: Mae Elizabeth Kornetzky (b. Troy, NY)
Date of Admission: April 2, 1923
Date of Death: July 8, 1923 at Samaritan Hospital
Cause of Death: Malnutrition
Burial: Oakwood Cemetery in Section "A" Lot 368, Grave #1 of Martha Kornetzki

William Francis Vandercook
Age: 6 Months
Troy Orphan Asylum #2939
Birth Date/Location: December 27, 1922 in Cohoes, New York
Parents: Esther Vandercook (b. Cohoes, NY)
Date of Admission: December 29, 1922
Date of Death: July 21, 1923 at the Troy Orphan Asylum
Cause of Death: Broncho pneumonia and malnutrition
Burial: Mt. Ida Cemetery

Leola E. Hoffay
Age: 1 Month, 22 Days
Troy Orphan Asylum #3074
Birth Date/Location: October 7, 1923 in Troy, New York

Parents: Elsie May Burns (b. Troy, NY) David E. Hoffay (b. Brunswick, NY)
Siblings: Liona
Date of Admission: October 28, 1923
Date of Death: November 29, 1923 at the Troy Orphan Asylum, Troy
Cause of Death: Acute intero colitis, congenital debility weak heart
Burial: Sand Lake, New York

John Solomon Fry
Age: 6 Months
Troy Orphan Asylum #3011
Birth Date/Location: May 22, 1923 in Utica, New York
Parents: William E. Fry (b. Johnstown, NY) and Mary Sponalle (Ephrata, NY)
Date of Admission: June 3, 1923
Date of Death: December 2, 1923 at the Troy Orphan Asylum
Cause of Death: Acute entero colitis
Burial: Mt. Ida Cemetery

Elizabeth May Capell
Age: 6 Months
Troy Orphan Asylum #3020
Birth Date/Location: June 12, 1923 in Cohoes
Parents: Elizabeth Capell and James
Date of Admission: June 26, 1923
Date of Death: December 28, 1923 in Whitehall, NY
Cause of Death: Unknown
Burial: Unknown
Discharged to Mr & Mrs Lohnas Van Wagner, RFD 3, Ballston Spa, NY. Was to be adopted.

Margaret Wager
Age: 1 Year, 8 Months
Troy Orphan Asylum #2889 #3063
Birth Date/Location: July 11, 1922 in Troy, New York
Parents: Henry E. Wagar (b. Troy, NY) Celia E. Hunsinger (b. Grafton, NY)
Siblings: Elizabeth, Stanley, Grace, Celia and Harold
Date of Admission: September 22, 1922 and October 10, 1923
Date of Death: April 6, 1924 at Samaritan Hospital
Cause of Death: Marasmus, rickets, broncho pneumonia
Burial: Old Mt. Ida Cemetery

Unknown Child
Age: 2 Months, 1 Day
Troy Orphan Asylum
Birth Date/Location: 1925
Date of Death: 1925
Cause of Death: Unknown
Burial: Unknown
"Length of stay, one month and 18 days."

Richard Cullett
Age: 2 Months, 6 Days
Troy Orphan Asylum #3217
Birth Date/Location: January 29, 1925 at St. Joseph's Maternity Hospital, Troy

Parents: Margaret Cullett (b. Troy)
Date of Admission: February 18, 1925
Date of Death: April 4, 1925 at Samaritan Hospital
Cause of Death: Marasmus and chronic intestinal indigestion
Burial: Oakwood Cemetery, Section "P" Single interments, Grave #147

Geraldine Elizabeth White
Age: 3 Months, 12 Days
Troy Orphan Asylum #3219
Birth Date/Location: February 22, 1925 in North Adams, Massachusetts
Parents: Anna G. White (b. North Adams, MA) and John Walton (b. Thomasonne, CT)
Date of Admission: February 28, 1925
Date of Death: June 4, 1925 at the Troy Orphan Asylum, Troy
Cause of Death: Excessive heat, no other factors known
Burial: Troy Orphan Asylum plot in Section "S" at Oakwood Cemetery, Grave #32
"6-day heat wave, June 3-8, 1925 in the Capital Region."

Lois Van Vleck
Age: 4 Months, 29 Days
Troy Orphan Asylum #3242
Birth Date/Location: April 16, 1925 in North Troy, New York
Parents: Mildred Van Vleck (b. Troy, NY) Clayton McRay (b. Schenectady, NY)
Date of Admission: May 1, 1925
Date of Death: September 14, 1925 at Samaritan Hospital
Cause of Death: Marasmus (from birth) intestional edema (terminal) (no other diagnosis possible) congenital debility
Burial: Mt. Ida Cemetery

Robert Andrew Wilt
Age: 7 Years
Troy Orphan Asylum #3174
Birth Date/Location: September 1, 1918 in New York City
Parents: Martha A. Useted (b. NY) Harold Roy Wilt (b. Brooklyn, NY)
Siblings: Harold Roy, Jr, Andrew, Stuart and Bernard
Date of Admission: September 15, 1924
Date of Death: November 2, 1925 at the Troy Orphan Asylum, Troy
Cause of Death: Bronchial pneumonia
Burial: East Greenbush, New York

Harold Bouplon
Age: 2 Months
Troy Orphan Asylum #3326
Birth Date/Location: December 28, 1925 in Hoosick Falls, New York
Parents: Helen E. Bouplon (b. North Bennington, VT)
Date of Admission: December 29, 1925

Date of Death: March 9, 1926 at Samaritan Hospital
Cause of Death: Marasmus due to improper nourishment of food, congenital debility
Burial: Hoosac, New York

Elizabeth Keefe Williams
Age: 2 Months
Troy Orphan Asylum
Birth Date/Location: September 3, 1926 in Troy, New York
Parents: Elizabeth Keefe (b. Troy, NY) and Clarence Williams (b. Troy, NY)
Date of Admission: September 11, 1926
Date of Death: November 7, 1926 at Samaritan Hospital
Cause of Death: Broncho pneumonia and marassmus
Burial: Waterford Rural Cemetery

John Berry
Age: 2 Months
Troy Orphan Asylum #3506
Birth Date/Location: August 12, 1927 at St. Joseph's Hospital, Troy
Parents: Margaret Berry (b. Watervliet, NY) John Berry
Date of Admission: August 30, 1927
Date of Death: November 9, 1927 at Troy Orphan Asylum
Cause of Death: Congenital debility and pyloric stenosis, hemarilgia diabetes
Burial: Albany Rural Cemetery in Lot 126, Section 100a, Single Grave 8, Tier 13

Robert "Bobby" Quillan
Age: 5 Months
Troy Orphan Asylum #3723
Birth Date/Location: June 5, 1929 in Amsterdam, New York
Parents: Catherine Quillan (b. Benson, NY, USA) Fred Fredericks (b. Johnstown, NY, USA)
Date of Admission: September 21, 1929
Date of Death: November 15, 1929 at the Troy Orphan Asylum
Cause of Death: Thymus death and very large at autopsy, and nothing else pathological found.
Burial: New Mt. Ida Cemetery

Henry Brazee
Age: 8 Years
Troy Orphan Asylum #3711
Birth Date/Location: November 1, 1921 in Sharon, New York (Schoharie County)
Parents: Lena M. Crippen (b. Seward, NY) and Martin Brazee
Siblings: William
Date of Admission: September 11, 1929
Date of Death: March 16, 1930 at Samaritan Hospital
Cause of Death: Diphtheria meningitis, pharyngeal diphthsis, diphtherpis mastoditis
Burial: New Mt. Ida Cemetery

Had a mastoid right ear operation at Samaritan Hospital on March 9, 1930

James G. Sherman/Keenan
Age: 26 Days
Troy Orphan Asylum #3966
Birth Date/Location: November 16, 1931 in Troy, New York
Parents: Elsie Brenenstuhl (b. Rensselaer County, NY or USA) Joseph Keenan (b. USA)
Date of Admission: November 16, 1931
Date of Death: December 12, 1931 at Samaritan Hospital, Troy
Cause of Death: Inanition by order of State Department of Health
Burial: Troy Orphan Asylum plot in Section "S" at Oakwood Cemetery, Grave #33

Francis Stanley Armstrong
Age: 7 Years, 10 Months
Troy Orphan Asylum #4521
Birth Date/Location: January 23, 1933 in Hoosick Falls, New York
Parents: Ruth Crosier (b. Jackson, NY) and Herbert Armstrong (b. Hoosick Falls, NY)
Siblings: Edward John, Carson Leroy, Albert, Inez, James Gordon, Shirley, Polly Ann and Ernest Joseph
Date of Admission: September 7, 1940
Date of Death: November 30, 1940
Cause of Death: Suffocation. Drowned in Smart's Pond, Troy, New York
Burial: Maple Grove Cemetery, Hoosick Falls, New York

Dolores Irene Boone
Age: 11 Months
Vanderheyden Hall/Troy Orphan Asylum #4685
Birth Date/Location: February 23, 1942 in Watervliet, New York
Parents: Doris Horne (b. Virginia) and Henry Boone (b. Oneonta, New York)
Siblings: Lora Mae and George Thomas
Date of Admission: September 13, 1942
Date of Death: January 26, 1943 at Samaritan Hospital, Troy
Cause of Death: Acute pneumonia
Burial: Albany Rural Cemetery, Lot 126, Section 100A, Grave 2, Tier 1

Richard Hill Moore (Wilkinson)
Age: 8 Months
Vanderheyden Hall/Troy Orphan Asylum #5027
Birth Date/Location: February 20, 1946 in Glens Falls, New York
Parents: Lois Wilkinson (b. Albany, NY)

Date of Admission: March 7, 1946
Date of Death: November 12, 1946 at Vanderheyden Hall
Cause of Death: Possible respiratory infection. Autopsy was inconclusive. Natural causes undetermined until further pathological bacteriological studies are completed.
Burial: Troy Orphan Asylum plot in Section "S" at Oakwood Cemetery, Grave #34

Carolyn/Caroline Ruth Poffahl
Age: 15 Years
Fairview Home for Friendless Children
Birth Date/Location: October 18, 1933 in Albany, New York
Parents: Jean Newkirk (b. 1901 USA) Edward Poffahl (b. 1900 USA)
Siblings: Edward, Jr, Ernest, Mary, Gene, Anthony and Charles
Date of Admission: June 29, 1944
Date of Death: June 20, 1949 at Samaritan Hospital
Cause of Death: Intestinal obstruction and gangerine of bowel due to volirillus. Congenital anomaly, mobile cerium and ascending colon
Burial: East Greenbush Cemetery, East Greenbush, New York

Theresa Ann Turner
Age: 1 Year
Vanderheyden Hall/Troy Orphan Asylum #5975
Birth Date/Location: May 18, 1953 in Troy, New York
Parents: Doris Doyle (b. 1924) and Joseph Turner (b. 1923)
Date of Admission: May 13, 1954
Date of Death: May 27, 1954 at Samaritan Hospital
Cause of Death: Respiratory illness, bronchopneumonia diffuse bilateral
Burial: Troy Orphan Asylum plot in Section "S" at Oakwood Cemetery, Grave

Thomas E. "Jake" Collins
Age: 16 Years
Vanderheyden Hall #7295
Birth Date/Location: September 3, 1958 in Glens Falls, New York
Date of Admission: July 3, 1974
Date of Death: Discovered February 8, 1975 in a vacant home on Catherine Street in Glens Falls
Cause of Death: Asphyxiated from carbon monoxide fumes from a charcoal fire
Burial: St. Mary's Cemetery, Section R, South Glens Falls, New York
"While AWOL from Vanderheyden Hall since January 11, 1975."

"Thomas was a really top individual, a dependable, hard working kid."

Cathy Corcoran
Age: 16 Years
Vanderheyden Hall #7308
Birth Date/Location: January 20, 1959 in Glens Falls, New York
Date of Admission: October 7, 1974
Date of Discharge: January 24, 1975 to Saratoga County Department of Social Services
Date of Death: Discovered February 8, 1975 in a vacant home on Catherine Street in Glens Falls
Cause of Death: Asphyxiated from carbon monoxide fumes from a charcoal fire
Burial: St. Mary's Cemetery, Section U, South Glens Falls, New York
"While AWOL from Vanderheyden Hall since January 10, 1975."

Antoinette Marie "Toni" Strope
Age: 15 Years
Vanderheyden Hall #9246
Birth Date/Location: June 1, 1977 in Samaritan Hospital, Troy, New York
Parents: Albert and Annina Dennison Strope
Siblings: Helen, Debra, Annina, Albert III, and Christopher
Date of Admission: July 9, 1991
Date of Death: February 15, 1993
Cause of Death: Toni and her unborn daughter Danielle were victims of murder.
Burial: St. Peter's Cemetery, Troy
From her sister, Helen Strope Baker: Toni was a very big part of Vanderheyden at the time of her death and very well loved by everyone there, including her classmates. She loved everyone there and they loved her as much as we her family did. Toni loved her family, her three nieces her new two-month-old nephew, and was pregnant with her own first little girl that she planned on naming after the baby's dad. She loved life and was changing for the better. Toni and her daughter now have a name sake, my first granddaughter, that Toni came to me in a dream and named."
From the 1993 Vanderheyden Hall yearbook: "Toni, a good friend and student, was a pleasure to know. Though, her life was brief, it was filled with love. She will be missed by her family, friends and teachers. We were all grateful to have known her and to have shared in her kindness."
"Because of Toni's guidance from above, Vanderheyden was able to commemorate the over 200 children who died at the

Troy Orphan Asylum, the Fairview Home for Friendless Children and Vanderheyden Hall. This listing of deceased children is dedicated in her memory."

This listing is still a "work in progress." More information about the unknown individuals who died and more deaths are possible. The following list is our children who died after being transferred to other agencies/facilities/hospitals, indentured service, reunited with their families or after adoptions:

Frank Everingham
Age: Unknown
Troy Orphan Asylum No #
Sibling: Roy A. Everingham (discharge: January 23, 1873)
Date of Admission: March 2, 1871
Date of Discharge: July 8, 1871 – Possibly indentured.
Date of Death: 1874
Cause of Death: Unknown
Burial: Unknown

Andrew Schreiner
Age: Unknown
Troy Orphan Asylum No #
Date of Admission: September 15, 1868
Date of Discharge: April 28, 1874
Date of Admission: April 18, 1876, and discharged again on May 6, 1876
Date of Death: July 1878 – Possibly indentured.
Cause of Death: Unknown
Burial: Unknown

John Wright.
Age: 7 Years
Fairview Home for Friendless Children
Birth Date/Location: July 1897
Date of Admission: November 6, 1899
Date of Discharge: April 11, 1903 to Children's Aid Society NYC to be placed with a family.
Date of Death: December 15, 1904 at Manhattan Eye & Ear Hospital, New York
Cause of Death: Unknown
Burial: Unknown

Elizabeth Hartley
Age: 17 Years
Troy Orphan Asylum #232
Birth Date/Location: May 1890
Siblings: Walter Hartley
Date of Admission: June 8, 1897
Date of Death: July 31, 1907
Cause of Death: Unknown
Burial: Unknown

Edward "Eddie" Wager (Calkins)
Age: 16+ Years
Troy Orphan Asylum #1175
Birth Date/Location: December 19, 1900 in Grafton, New York
Parents: Parents: Ella Calkins (b. Berlin, NY) and Elmer Wager (b. Grafton, NY)

Siblings: Jessie, Ethel and Thelma
Date of Admission: April 2, 1908
Date of Discharge: December 6, 1916 to his Mother
Date of Death: Unknown
Cause of Death: Unknown
Burial: Possible Eagle Mills Cemetery
His sister Ethel Wager died April 12, 1913 at the Troy Orphan Asylum, Troy

Gordon Springer
Age: 9 Years
Troy Orphan Asylum #2153
Birth Date/Location: March 10, 1909 in Corinth, New York
Parents: Lydia Hurd and Mervin Springer
Siblings: Walter, Helen, Edna and Mildred
Date of Admission: February 3, 1916, April 18, 1917 and September 11, 1918
Date of Discharge: November 17, 1916, November 3, 1917 and October 11, 1918 to Rome State School
Date of Death: October 24, 1918
Cause of Death: Unknown
Burial: Unknown

Marion Baker
Age: 16 Years
Troy Orphan Asylum #2142
Birth Date/Location: February 9, 1902 in Cobleskill, New York
Parents: Cora Baker and Charles Baker
Siblings: Helen Baker
Date of Admission: February 26, 1916
Date of Discharge: August 31, 1917
Date of Death: December 25, 1918 at Lakeview Sanitarium
Cause of Death: Tubercular
Burial: Unknown

Elva Carlon
Age: Unknown
Troy Orphan Asylum #1878
Date of Admission: June 23, 1913
Date of Discharge: December 11, 1917
Date of Death: December 28, 1918 in Schenectady, New York
Cause of Death: Unknown
Burial: Unknown

Peter Risoley
Age: 8 Years
Troy Orphan Asylum #2702
Birth Date/Location: November 25, 1914 in Troy, New York
Parents: Rachel Powers (b. NY State) Nicholas Risoley (b. Italy)
Siblings: Catherine, Fred, Lillian, Joseph, Thomas and Nicholas
Date of Admission: February 14, 1921 and November 14, 1922
Date of Discharge: September 4, 1922 and April 7, 1923 to Father
Date of Death: June 4, 1923
Cause of Death: Drowning
Burial: Unknown

Minnie Shook
Age: 20 Years
Troy Orphan Asylum #1452
Birth Date/Location: December 23, 1904 in Rhinebeck, New York
Parents: Mary Briggs (b. NY) and William Shook (b. NY)
Siblings: Emma, Mary, Maggie, William, Edward and half-brother John Shufelt
Date of Admission: May 17, 1910
Date of Discharge: August 18, 1910 to Dutchess Agent for transfer to Craig Colony for Epileptics
Date of Death: 1924
Cause of Death: Pulmonary tuberculosis
Burial: Unknown

Joseph Russell Bishop
Age: 18 Years
Troy Orphan Asylum
Birth Date/Location: March 14, 1907 in Watervliet, New York
Parents: Joseph Bishop (b. Watervliet, NY) Unknown Mother (b. Albany, NY)
Date of Admission: February 6, 1916
Date of Discharge: March 6, 1916 to Childs Hospital, Albany, New York
Date of Death: April 22, 1925
Cause of Death: Unknown
Burial: Albany Rural Cemetery, Section 202, Plot 203
Was transferred to Craig Colony in Sonyea, New York

Helen May Mitchell
Age: 6 Years
Troy Orphan Asylum #3134
Birth Date/Location: May 10, 1922 at the Salvation Army Home, Buffalo, New York
Parents: Edith Tucker (b. Carbondale City, PA) and Victor F. Mitchell (b. Lowell, MA)
Date of Admission: April 16, 1924 and July 11, 1924
Date of Discharge: July 5, 1924
Date of Death: October 27, 1928
Cause of Death: Unknown
Burial: Unknown

George Alfred Houle
Age: 11+ Years
Troy Orphan Asylum #2946
Birth Date/Location: February 18, 1918 in Burke, New York
Parents: Bertha Hazen Houle (b. Burke, NY) William Houle (b. Canada)
Siblings: Frank, Nellie Mary and Raymond
Date of Admission: January 23, 1923
Date of Discharge: July 15, 1929
Date of Death: Unknown
Sister deceased after discharged from TOA.
Cause of Death: Unknown
Burial: Unknown

Ella Evelyn Hartman
Age: 9 Years
Troy Orphan Asylum #3594

Birth Date/Location: February 3, 1920 in Troy, New York
Parents: Ida E. Shutt (b. Danville, PA) and Charles N. Hartman (b. Baltimore, MD)
Siblings: Ralph, Charles and Violet
Date of Admission: April 30, 1928
Date of Discharge: September 13, 1928 to parents
Date of Death: August 19, 1929 in Albany, NY
Cause of Death: Unknown
Burial: Albany Rural Cemetery, Lot 93, Section 56, in lot purchased by her parents.

Laura Bellville
Age: Unknown
Troy Orphan Asylum #3477
Birth Date/Location: Lebanon, New Hampshire
Parents: Mary Bellville and George Bellville
Date of Admission: June 6, 1927
Date of Discharge: August 6, 1927 to Rome State School
Date of Death: January 29, 1932
Cause of Death: Unknown
Burial: Unknown

Clifford Howe
Age: 3 Years
Troy Orphan Asylum #3715
Birth Date/Location: March 11, 1929 in Troy, New York
Parents: Minnie Schultz (b. Brooklyn, NY) Eben H. Howe (b. Troy, NY)
Siblings: Arthur, Dorothy, Phyllis, Lorraine, Walter and Warren
Date of Admission: September 17, 1929
Date of Discharge: September 18, 1932 to Rome State School
Date of Death: January 26, 1933
Cause of Death: Unknown
Burial: Unknown

Barbara Jane Cottrell
Age: 3 Years
Troy Orphan Asylum #3841
Birth Date/Location: September 1, 1930 in Oneonta, New York
Parents: Ruth Charlotte Cottrell and William Dewan
Date of Admission: November 13, 1930
Date of Discharge: September 5, 1931
Date of Death: September 12, 1933 at home of adoptive parents in Kingston, New York
Cause of Death: Meningitis
Burial: Unknown

Nellie Mary Houle
Age: 18 Years
Troy Orphan Asylum #2945
Birth Date/Location: November 17, 1915 in Burke, New York
Parents: Bertha Hazen Houle (b. Burke, NY) William Houle (b. Canada)

Siblings: Frank Joseph, George and Raymond Arthur
Date of Admission: January 6, 1923
Date of Discharge: September 24, 1932 to mother
Date of Death: June 15, 1934
Cause of Death: Unknown
Burial: Unknown

Helen Allen
Age: 13 years
Troy Orphan Asylum #3392
Birth Date/Location: January 31, 1922 in Rupert, Vermont
Parents: Olive Waters and Arthur Allen
Siblings: Frank, Mae, Richard and Eleanor
Date of Admission: October 1, 1926
Date of Discharge: April 18, 1929 to Rome State School
Date of Death: October 26, 1935
Cause of Death: Unknown
Burial: Unknown

Joseph Bombard
Age: 13 Years
Troy Orphan Asylum #3434 #3344
Birth Date/Location: May 4, 1923 in Black Brook New York
Parents: Julia Bombard
Date of Admission: April 15, 1926 and February 9, 1927
Date of Discharge: October 19, 1926 and April 3, 1930 to Rome State School
Date of Death: November 24, 1936
Cause of Death: Unknown
Burial: Craig Colony Cemetery, Livingston County, New York
"Died at Craig Colony for Epileptics"

Gladys R. Alexander
Age: 26 Years
Troy Orphan Asylum #2975
Birth Date/Location: October 1, 1912 in Troy, New York
Parents: Victoria Michigian (b. Turkey) and Jacob Alexander (b. Turkey)
Date of Admission: March 3, 1923
Date of Discharge: September 4, 1926 to sister Rose Alexander, Hudson, New York
Date of Death: July 18, 1938
Cause of Death: Unknown
Burial: Unknown

Mary Butt
Age: 33 Years
Troy Orphan Asylum #1836
Birth Date/Location: August 10, 1911 in Albany, New York
Parents: Jennie Chism (b. Campbell) and Frank Butt
Siblings: Anna, Frank and Bernice
Date of Admission: March 30, 1913 and August 7, 1913
Date of Discharge: July 25, 1913 to Samaritan Hospital, December 4, 1915 to Father, and December 2, 1927 to the Hospital for Ruptured and Crippled Children
Date of Death: 1945
Cause of Death: Unknown

Burial: Unknown

James H. Raymond
Age: 15 Years
Troy Orphan Asylum #6019
Birth Date/Location: March 19, 1939 in Troy, New York
Parents: Vivian L. Raymond (b. USA in 1899)
Date of Admission: September 11, 1939 and September 10, 1954
Date of Discharge: January 14, 1955 to La Salle School in Albany, New York
Date of Death: September 10, 1955 in White Horse Canyon, east of Rawlins, Wyoming
Cause of Death: Pushed off a moving freight train. Found between the tracks. Murder victim.
Burial: Rawlins Cemetery, Carbon County, Wyoming
The Casper Tribute Herald newspaper articles. Perpetrators received 40 to 50 years in prison.
"Just one of those unfortunate kids who's been knocked around from pillar to post."

Walter Hacker
Age: 16 Years
Troy Orphan Asylum
Birth Date/Location: January 7, 1965 in Albany, New York
Date of Admission: June 16, 1980 and September 5, 1980
Date of Discharge: August 14, 1981 to Hospitality House
Date of Death: November 1981
Cause of Death: Unknown
Burial: Unknown

City of Troy Superintendent Records Indicate "Orphan Asylum" as place of death for the following children.

The children may be from the Troy Orphan Asylum, Troy Catholic Male Asylum, St. Vincent's Male Catholic Asylum or St. Mary's Catholic Female Asylum.

James Conly
Age: 10 Years
Birth Date/Location: 1844 in Troy, New York
Parents: Mr. and Mrs. Conly
Date of Death: April 20, 1854
Cause of Death: Typhoid fever
Burial: Mt. Ida Cemetery

Richard Harding
Age: 8 Years
Birth Date/Location: 1846 in Troy, New York
Parents/Siblings: Harding
Date of Death: April 11, 1854 at Asylum, Troy
Cause of Death: Measles
Burial: Mt. Ida Cemetery

Mary Ward
Age: 3 Months
Birth Date/Location: 1856 in Troy, New York
Parents: Mr. and Mrs. Ward
Date of Death: March 4, 1856
Cause of Death: Cold

Burial: Catholic Ground at Mt. Ida Cemetery

Elizabeth Gleason
Age: 1 Years, 3 Months
Birth Date/Location: 1857 in Troy, New York
Parents: J and C Gleason
Date of Death: September 1, 1858
Cause of Death: Teething
Burial: Catholic Ground

James Elder
Age: 18 Months
Birth Date/Location: Troy, New York
Date of Death: August 2,, 1869
Cause of Death: Teething
Burial: Mt. Ida Cemetery

William Walsh
Age: 8 Years
Birth Date/Location: Troy, New York
Date of Death: March 27, 1870
Cause of Death: Bronchitis
Burial: St. Mary's Cemetery

Rosanna Casey
Age: 3 Years
Born: Ireland
Died: March 28, 1874
Cause of Death: Fever
Buried: St. Mary's Cemetery

Willie Mooney
Age: 29 Years
Born: Troy
Died: June 3, 1876
Cause of Death: Consumption
Buried: St. Mary's Cemetery

John Mangass
Age: 6 Years
Born: Troy
Died: May 26, 1879
Cause of Death: Consumption
Buried: St. Peter's Cemetery

Emma Banker
Age: 8 Years
Born: Troy
Died: September 1, 1879
Cause of Death: Brian Disease
Buried: St. Mary's Cemetery

Chester A. Muller
Age: 5 Years
Died: May 30, 1886
Cause of Death: Pneumonia
Buried: Mt. Ida

Lizzie King
Age: 5 Years
Born: Troy
Died: June 6, 1886
Cause of Death: Chol. Infantine
Buried: St Mary's Cemetery

Pat Donohue
Age: 4 Years
Died: June 7, 1886
Cause of Death: Pneumonia
Buried: St. Mary's Cemetery

May Perkins
Age: 12 Years
Born: Troy
Died: June 8, 1886
Cause of Death: Pneumonia

Buried: St. Mary's Cemetery

Annie Kennedy
Age: 9 Months
Born: Troy
Died: June 13, 1886
Cause of Death: Chol. Infantum
Buried: St. Joseph's Cemetery

Nellie Williams
Age: 2 years
Fair view Home for Friendless Children
Birth Date/Location: Troy, NY
Parents: Mary Williams
Date of Death: Dec. 12, 1888
Cause of Death: Marasmus
Burial: Mt Ida Cemetery, Troy, NY

Index to Orphan Deaths

FINIS
W.H.A.

1833 Society

Thank you to the following people and organizations that contributed $1,833 to become an 1833 Society Member in honor of the date that the Troy Orphan Asylum started.

Alissa Cahill-Henderson, Duncan & Cahill, Inc.
Andrea Crisafulli, Crisafulli Brothers
Carla Chiaro
Daniel Van Plew, Regeneron Pharmaceutical, Inc.
David & Florence Hunn, "In Memory of Herbert J. Hunn, Superintendent 1913-1941"
David and Diane Fazioli
Dawn Abbuhl, Repeat Business Systems
Deb Pollard, Fenimore Asset Management, Inc.
Deirdre Brodie
E. Stewart Jones and Kimberly Sanger
Elaine Phelan Dale and Craig Raisig
George, Ann and Ben McAvoy
Georgia Kelly
Guy and Joanne Alonge
James Faranda
James Lozano, CFO for Hire, Inc.
James Stone
Jane Brennan
Joella Viscusi, Ambient Environmental, Inc.
John Morley, M.D. David Nocenti
John Panichi, Benetech
Karen Capenter Palumbo
Kirk Huang, "In Honor of Kevin Huang"
Laura Dillon
Lisa Smith, BST & Co. CPAs, LLP
Massry Charitable Foundation, Inc. Endowment

Melissa and Brian Clement
Michael Barrett, Barrett Associates
Michael Ginsberg,
Neil and Jane Golub, Neil Jane William Estelle
Golub Family Foundation, Inc.
Patrick Hughes, Hugh Johnson Advisors
Pattison, Sampson, Ginsberg & Griffin, PLLC
Paul and Karen Macielak
Polly Mason
Robert Hunn, "In Memory of Herbert J. Hunn,
Superintendent 1913-1941" Martha and Donald
Wilmot, "In Memor y of Herbert J. Hunn,
Superintendent 1913-1941"
Sandra Mardigian
Stewart's Shops Corporation
Susan Dake, Stewart's Shops Foundation
Thomas Amell, Pioneer Bank
Todd Slingerland, Capital Financial Planning LLC
Tracy Metzger, TL Metzger & Associates LLC
Virginia Touhey and Kathleen Simmonds
William and Audrey Koester
William Fagan, Wm J. Fagan & Sons, Inc.

Made in the USA
Columbia, SC
19 December 2020

28817644R00376